S0-DFB-037

WITHDRAWN
UTSA LIBRARIES

U.S. NATIONAL SECURITY POLICY AND STRATEGY, 1987–1994

Greenwood Reference Volumes on American Public Policy Formation

These reference books deal with the development of U.S. policy in various "single-issue" areas. Most policy areas are to be represented by three types of sourcebooks: (1) Institutional Profiles of Leading Organizations, (2) Collections of Documents and Policy Proposals, and (3) Bibliography.

Public Interest Law Groups: Institutional Profiles
Karen O'Connor and Lee Epstein

U.S. National Security Policy and Strategy, 1947–1986: Documents and Policy Proposals
Sam C. Sarkesian with Robert A. Vitas

U.S. National Security Policy Groups: Institutional Profiles
Cynthia Watson

U.S. Agricultural Groups: Institutional Profiles
William P. Browne and Allan J. Cigler, editors

Military and Strategic Policy: An Annotated Bibliography
Benjamin R. Beede, compiler

U.S. Energy and Environmental Interest Groups: Institutional Profiles
Lettie McSpadden Wenner

Contemporary U.S. Foreign Policy: Documents and Commentary
Elmer Plischke

U.S. Aging Policy Interest Groups: Institutional Profiles
David D. Van Tassel and Jimmy Meyer, editors

U.S. NATIONAL SECURITY POLICY AND STRATEGY, 1987–1994

Documents and Policy Proposals

Edited by
Robert A. Vitas
John Allen Williams

Foreword by Sam C. Sarkesian

Greenwood Reference Volumes on American Public Policy Formation

Greenwood Press
Westport, Connecticut • London

Library of Congress Cataloging-in-Publication Data

U.S. national security policy and strategy, 1987–1994 : documents and policy proposals / [edited by] Robert A. Vitas and John Allen Williams, foreword by Sam C. Sarkesian.
p. cm.
Includes bibliographical references (p.) and index.
ISBN 0–313–29635–9 (alk. paper)
1. United States—Foreign relations—1981–1989—Sources.
2. United States—Foreign relations—1989–1993—Sources. 3. United States—Foreign relations—1993– —Sources. 4. National security—United States—History—20th century—Sources. I. Vitas, Robert A. II. Williams, John Allen.
E876.U845 1996
355′.033′073′09048—dc20 95–47147

British Library Cataloguing in Publication Data is available.

Library of Congress Catalog Card Number: 95–47147
ISBN: 0–313–29635–9

First published in 1996

Greenwood Press, 88 Post Road West, Westport, CT 06881
An imprint of Greenwood Publishing Group, Inc.

Printed in the United States of America

The paper used in this book complies with the Permanent Paper Standard issued by the National Information Standards Organization (Z39.48–1984).

10 9 8 7 6 5 4 3 2 1

Contents

Foreword

This is the third of three books related to the topic, U.S. National Security Policy and Strategy. The first book provided extracts of important documents and publications in the field for the period 1947 through 1986. This one covers the period 1987 through 1994. In addition, the editors offer their interpretations and chapter summaries of the various documents.

The editors of this volume stress the importance of defining terminology, clarifying issues, and providing historical reference points in coming to grips with U.S. national security. This is particularly important in the period covering the latter part of the 1980s through the first part of the 1990s— a decade of change and transition, and a particularly confusing and uncertain national security landscape. As a result, it is even more important to focus on original sources and documents to grasp the transitional themes and issues of uncertainty that evolve from the national security establishment. This is a first step in defining the issues of national security and in attempting to design a relevant national security strategy and policy.

To repeat the caution expressed in the first book, these books do not claim to be all-encompassing in surveying and analyzing groups, documents, and publications in national security strategy and policy. But they do provide a real sense of history and a necessary background for studying the subject.

Sam C. Sarkesian

Preface

This book hopes to establish a sense of history and perspective in the study and teaching of contemporary national security. It will also try to bring a sense of balance to current debates on national security policy. This is done by providing the reader with a series of selected official U.S. documents covering the past decade. A careful reading should bring insights into the policy process along with the meaning of American values, interests and national strategy — at least from the perspective of U.S. government officials. In this respect, the primary source documents speak for themselves.

This is not a substitute for secondary studies of foreign and national security policy, and specific security issues, but a companion to them. Some of these are noted in the Select Bibliography at the end of this volume. A serious study of U.S. national security will require critical reading of such works. Yet there is a valuable place for the study of materials emanating directly from the U.S. government that are often cited but too seldom seen, particularly those that articulate intentions, perceptions, and policy goals. There is no substitute for examining these primary sources. At the very least, they can establish the necessary background for understanding U.S. national security policy and for critical analyses of serious studies of the subject.

This is a companion to an earlier book by Sam C. Sarkesian and Robert A. Vitas, *U.S. National Security Policy and Strategy: Documents and Policy Proposals 1947-1986* (Greenwood, 1988). Greenwood subsequently published another related book, Cynthia Watson's, *U.S. National Security Policy Groups: Institutional Profiles* (1990), with annotated listings. The present book picks up with 1987 and takes the reader through the end of 1994 with the U.S. invasion of Haiti. This period saw profound changes in the U.S. and international security landscape.

No attempt was made to be comprehensive; this cannot be done in one volume. The purpose of this volume is not to provide all the documents relevant to U.S. national security policy. Selections attempt to provide the critical reference points with an eye towards identifying and reflecting the attitudes and mindsets at the time. To be sure, the selection of the documents reflects the discretion of the editors and a certain view of U.S. national security. To minimize this problem, an attempt is made to follow a systematic and balanced approach in framing chapters and selecting documents appropriate to them.

With the above in mind, the editors present a landscape of U.S. national security policy over the past decade that can serve as a road map for its study and teaching. Students and serious readers should have access to selected documents to establish a sense of contemporary history and to provide a research framework for the study of U.S. national security policy. A selected collection of documents touching on events over the past decade may assist in establishing a more balanced and accurate view for critically analyzing public debates and policy decisions on national security. Perhaps even policymakers will receive perspective for assessing current policy and developing future direction.

Most of the material contained herein is excerpted from the original documents. Shorter documents are reproduced in their entirety, but this is the exception rather than the rule. Only those documents that are available through public sources are included. The public character of these documents allows extensive quotation without prior permission.

The first book contained speeches mainly by the presidents. Other officials' addresses were included, but to a limited extent. This volume contains presidential statements, as well, but also includes more addresses and analyses by other U.S. government officials. The editors hope these will better frame the other documents.

The source is placed at the end of each document. In certain cases, one citation is given for a group of related documents at the end of the first document in that group. Though some documents come from other sources, cited as such, the bulk of the documents come from the sources noted here. Complete citations are not provided, but are abbreviated as follows:

PPP	*Public Papers of the Presidents*, published by the Office of the Federal Register;
WCPD	*Weekly Compilation of Presidential Documents*, published by the Office of the Federal Register;
DSB	*Department of State Bulletin*, published by the U.S. State Department, Bureau of Public Affairs, through December 1989;
DSD	*Department of State Dispatch*, published by the U.S. State Department, Bureau of Public Affairs, beginning January 1990;
USS	*United States Statutes at Large*, published by the Office of the Federal Register;
CD	*Cumulative Digest of United States Practice in International Law*, published by the U.S. State Department, Office of the Legal Adviser.

The use of these and other sources is more fully discussed in Chapter 9. They are put in perspective in Chapter 1 and the introduction to each thematic chapter, 2 through 8. A Select Bibliography of secondary sources follows Chapter 9.

The utility of this volume is found in its attempt to identify documents that provide signposts and reference points to U.S. national security from 1987 through 1994, as well as in providing critical substantive dimensions to them. Also, by categorizing U.S. national security thematically, rather than chronologically, a clearer pattern emerges: continuity, a balanced perspective, and a sense of history — now and in the future.

Chicago, Illinois *R.A.V.*
April, 1996 *J.A.W.*

Acknowledgements

We are grateful to a number of people for making this volume possible. We note with special appreciation the continuing influence of Sam C. Sarkesian in our lives. He facilitated our entry into the scholarly profession in ways too numerous to recount and remains a strong professional influence on us as well as for generations of scholars. We appreciate his willingness to contribute a Foreword to this book.

The detailed duplication and scanning of documents selected was done by James Wilson, who also did much of the correction of the resulting text files. Significant contributions to the latter effort were also made by Dean Schloyer, Scott Weyandt, and Judy Calix. The extensive research collections of the libraries of Loyola University Chicago were the primary sources for the documents.

Typefaces were chosen and page layouts were done by Kazys Motekaitis, whose sense of style added much to the appearance of the book. The Lithuanian Research and Studies Center in Chicago provided the technical support and facilities in the preparation of the final text.

We are particularly grateful to our editors at Greenwood Press. Mildred Vasan has a clear vision of what books are useful to the scholarly community, and the ability to organize academics (a process we have heard described as like herding cats) and focus their energies on a practical result. Cynthia Harris assumed responsibility for our book in midstream and carried the project through to its successful completion. Liz Leiba and Jane Lerner provided valuable direction to assure that the presentation of the material was as effective as possible. Catherine Lee oversaw the management of releases and other legal work.

The co-editors worked on different parts of the book, but have reviewed the work in its entirety and jointly accept the credit or blame for the result. In our work, as in our lives, we have been helped more than they may realize by our wives, Gaile Antanaitis Vitas and Karen Lauterbach Williams. Their love and understanding makes everything worthwhile.

1

The Study of U.S. National Security

John Allen Williams

As the world becomes more complex, the national security landscape becomes more difficult to manage and to interpret. No individual threat to the United States approaches the danger of a global thermonuclear war with the Soviet Union. Yet collectively there are a number of threats in the national security environment that have a strong potential for harm to U.S. interests and that pose difficult challenges to policy makers.

Current national security problems are markedly different from those of the past. The primary difference is one of ambiguity. It is not always clear where U.S. interests lie, and it is increasingly difficult to determine what the "right" policy should be. Americans are not comfortable with moral ambiguity; they prefer clear-cut alternatives that permit them to choose the policy that is consistent with their values and, of course, their interests. The U.S. desire to be on the correct side morally is particularly challenged by crises such as the current situation in Bosnia, a slow-motion catastrophe where American interests are unclear and all choices seem difficult and unpalatable. The policy environment is complicated by fact that the earlier U.S. intervention in Somalia, undertaken for purely humanitarian grounds, ended badly and soured both the public and policy makers on altruism as a primary motivation for military intervention.

The period covered by the documents, 1987-1994, was one of unexpected, even unparalleled, change in the world security environment. Commentators practicing "prognostication by extrapolation," that is, making predictions based on the continuation of current trends, were greatly surprised by the collapse of the Soviet empire in 1989 (Central Europe) and the Russian empire in 1991 (the Soviet Union). They would be even more surprised to see the current strains on the empire of the Moscow Rus (Russia itself), and there is strong reason to believe that Chechnya, whose misery continues as these words are written, is only one of many parts of the Russian Federation with strong separatist sentiments.

Other developments were more predictable, such as increased strains in the Third World and a greater ability of those countries to threaten the interests of the great powers as sophisticated military weaponry proliferated. The rise of militant forces in many areas made the use of these weapons more likely, and the United States is entering a period in which there are significant threats to its homeland from countries that could hardly be described as great powers.

So many groups have vested interests in particular interpretations that one must be careful in accepting the views of even the most knowledgeable observers. In the above case, for example, many members of the ethnic groups encompassed in the Soviet Union spoke of the strains in that system and their hope or expectation that it would eventually decompose, but these views were easily dismissable as wishful thinking on their part. Soviet historian Andrei Amalrik predicted a breakup in *Will the Soviet Union Survive Until 1984?* (New York: Harper and Row, 1970). While the date was surely chosen to suggest George Orwell's famous novel, the analysis itself deserves a rereading. A revised and expanded edition was published in 1981. In this case, however, they were correct.

In studying the national security policies of any era, neither facts nor documents speak for themselves; they require a theoretical context in which to be understood. The problem for those wishing to understand great changes or, which is more difficult, predict such changes before they occur, is developing an appropriate theory which will tie the facts together in a meaningful way. This volume is not intended to meet this need, but it is also true that theory alone is an inadequate guide to policy makers. Theoretical constructs unconnected to facts are misleading at best and dangerous at worst, particularly in the area of national security policy.

As noted in the Preface, our purpose is to gather together original materials to help students, scholars, and policy makers understand the momentous events in American national security policy over the last decade. It picks up where the previous volume, edited by Sam C. Sarkesian and Robert A. Vitas, left off. As in the earlier work, the selections were chosen not to advance any particular interpretation, but to provide as representative a record as possible in this relatively brief space of "official" governmental positions on the issues in question. Given the wide range of documents from which to choose, no claim is made that these selections are in any sense exhaustive. Other scholars might have made different choices, of course, but we hope these will be worthwhile.

The degree to which official documents reveal what really takes place in complex institutions is a subject of continuing discussion among historians and social scientists. Nevertheless, such writings are certainly part of the equation, and a careful reading can often provide insights into the inner workings of government. It would, of course, be naive to accept them uncritically, and readers will have to provide their own theoretical understandings to make sense of them. Although we have our opinions on these matters, as may be evident in the chapter introductions, the advancement of our views is not our purpose. We will be gratified if this collection helps others to form their own judgments, whatever they may be.

2

The National Security Establishment

INTRODUCTION

The Reagan administration's legacy in the area of national defense was largely, but not entirely, one of greatly increased resources. The defense buildup was actually begun in 1980, at the end of the Carter administration, in response to the seizing of hostages at the U.S. embassy in Teheran and the Soviet invasion of Afghanistan. It is doubtful if a reelected Carter would have maintained a high level of defense expenditures, but it is not too much to say that what the Reagan administration initially did was to fund fully the Carter defense budget. See John Allen Williams, "Defense Policy: The Carter-Reagan Record," *The Washington Quarterly* 6, no. 4 (Autumn 1993): 77-92. It also marked a more militant approach to security issues, a direction largely continued by the Bush administration. The Clinton administration, faced with similar challenges, evolved in its approach from reliance on international institutions to the need for unilateral actions — preferably undertaken with the blessing of the international community.

The period of these documents saw dramatic changes in the military establishment itself, both institutionally and socially. Based on the earlier Goldwater-Nichols Act of 1986, there was a watershed in inter-service relations and the way in which wars would be fought. Services were expected to cooperate fully in the planning and execution of military operations, and no service could expect to operate with complete independence.

The primary impetus for these changes was operational. Operations in Grenada in 1983 showed several problems in joint operations (those involving more than one military service), primarily involving communication. This is a special problem when, for example, one service is conducting close air support operations for another.

Another impetus was fiscal. The Reagan defense buildup was phenomenally expensive and, combined with a large cut in taxes, resulted in a greatly increased national debt. As it became clear that the supply of funds was not inexhaustible, more choices had to be made. Among them was to abandon the building of a Navy of 600 battle force capable ships, centered around 15 deployable aircraft carriers. Since one carrier was always in extended overhaul as part of the service life extension program (SLEP), this required 16 carriers to accomplish. The resignation of Navy Secretary James Webb was a result of this decision. Budgetary decisions are a continuing feature of defense policy, and they will reflect strategic choices and the orientation to risk of the people making them.

Another item of continuing discussion is the roles and missions of the four services: Army, Navy, Air Force, and Marines. The issue is not yet resolved, but a major shift in responsibilities, for example, of shifting the responsibility for land-based sea surveillance aircraft to the Air Force from the Navy, is not likely. Additionally, much effort was expended on a Unified Command Plan (UCP), designed to reorient the warfighting command structure.

Many consider special operations forces the equivalent of a fifth service in view of their independence from their parent services. The motivation for this emphasis on special operations was a dramatic increase in U.S. concern for terrorist incidents, perhaps best exemplified by the terrorist bomb that destroyed a Pan American jetliner over Lockerbie, Scotland in 1988. Americans felt increasingly vulnerable to such events, and leaders took the security steps they felt necessary in an increasingly chaotic world.

The military remains one of the more conservative institutions in American society, but it is not immune from social forces in the country. One of these is the increased role of women in society, and as a result the military has largely opened up all activities except ground combat itself and service in submarines to women. Even more contentious is the role of homosexuals in the military. Although many lesbians and gay men have served honorably in the military, military leaders felt that such servicemembers had a deleterious effect on unit cohesion and morale once their sexual orientation became known. They were, therefore, expelled from the service if discovered. Under the Reagan administration, even a homosexual inclination, whether acted on or not, was a bar to recruitment or to continued service.

The Clinton administration entered office with a promise to lift the ban on homosexuals serving in the armed forces. The resulting policy of "don't ask, don't tell" was a severe disappointment to gay activists. It prevented some harassment of lesbian and gay servicemembers, but homosexual activity, on or off base, remained a punishable offense under the Uniform Code of Military Justice (UCMJ). Even the announcement of a homosexual inclination, while not in itself illegal, is regarded as *prima facie* evidence that the speaker intends to act on his or her inclination. Such an assumption is rebuttable, but a claim of celibacy among young servicemembers is difficult to sustain, and the "don't ask, don't tell" policy may not long survive court scrutiny.

THE INSTITUTIONS OF NATIONAL SECURITY

President Reagan's Radio Address to the Nation on the Defense Budget
January 17, 1987

...Think back just 6 years: our Navy had dwindled from more than 1,000 ships to less than 500. Many of our planes couldn't fly for lack of spare parts. And our men and women in uniform were seeing their pay in real terms shrink while pay in the private sector rose. Well, I believed on first taking office, as I do today, that the defense of this Republic is not just one of the duties of the Federal Government, it is the first duty. So, with bipartisan congressional support, we took action at once on the rebuilding of our nation's defenses. Since 1980 we've increased the number of Army divisions from 16 to 18. We've reactivated 4 battleships and purchased 124 new ships for the Navy, including 2 new aircraft carriers and 21 high-technology Aegis-class cruisers and destroyers. We've purchased over 2,500 new tactical fighter aircraft. And just as important, we've more than doubled our vital stocks of spare parts and munitions, stocks that were dangerously low in 1981. Pay and benefits for our Armed Forces has increased substantially. And perhaps most heartening, the proportion of recruits holding high school diplomas has risen from less than 70 percent in 1980 to more than 90 percent today.

At the same time we've been spending the needed funds, we've found important new ways to spend that money better. The Defense Department, for example, has greatly expanded competitive bidding and is this year submitting to Congress the first-ever 2-year defense budget to replace the old, inefficient, year-by-year process. Add to these the changes contained in last year's Goldwater-Nichols legislation, and those set in place at the recommendation of the Packard Commission, and you have perhaps the most dramatic defense reforms since the formation of the Department of Defense itself. All of this is having a profound effect. Morale in our Armed Forces has soared. All the world has taken note that the United States has reasserted its role on behalf of freedom. And in the past 6 years, not 1 inch of territory has fallen to Communist aggression; while one nation, Grenada, has been set free.

Now Congress and our administration have the opportunity to continue the vital work of rebuilding our defenses, already so well begun. But I must tell you that we cannot take continued progress for granted. In 1985 and '86 Congress cut the defense budget sharply.... I appeal to Congress. In the days ahead, let's work together to provide 2-year defense funding that is both adequate and steady....
(PPP Reagan 1987 I: 29-30)

President Reagan's Message to the Congress on United States Military Combatant Commands
April 23, 1987

...In accordance with Section 161(b) of Title 10, United States Code, this is to inform you of changes to the unified and specified combatant structure which I have recently approved.

1) Establishment of the unified U.S. Special Operations Command (USSOC).
2) Establishment of the specified Forces Command (FORSCOM).
3) Establishment of the unified U.S. Transportation Command (USTRANSCOM).
4) Disestablishment of the specified Military Airlift Command (MAC), to be accomplished upon the certification of CINCTRANS to the Secretary of Defense and the Chairman, Joint Chiefs of Staff, that TRANSCOM is fully operational.
5) Disestablishment of the unified U.S. Readiness Command (USREDCOM) with transfer of designated functions to U.S. Central Command, U.S. European Command. U.S. Southern Command, U.S. Transportation Command, and Forces Command....

(PPP Reagan 1987 I: 409)

President Reagan's Letter to the Speaker of the House of Representatives and the President of the Senate on Low Intensity Conflict Policy
December 16, 1987

...Conflict in the Third World can pose serious threats to our security interests. Low intensity conflicts, which take place at levels below conventional war, but above routine peaceful competition among states, can be particularly troublesome....

In June of this year, I approved a new national policy and strategy for low intensity conflict and established a Board for Low Intensity Conflict that is chaired by my National Security Adviser....

We have also activated the new Unified Command for Special Operations, improved our special operations capabilities, and established the office of the new Assistant Secretary of Defense for Special Operations and Low Intensity Conflict.

More work lies ahead. The United States must continue to respond to challenges arising from low intensity conflict — to defend our interests and support those who put their lives on the line in the common cause of freedom. For the United States to be effective in this most important

undertaking, there must be public understanding and strong congressional support....
(PPP Reagan 1987 II: 1526)

Review by Secretary of Defense Dick Cheney
July 1989

The overall framework adopted for decisionmaking within DoD must reflect sound management principles if the President and Secretary of Defense are to be well served. The management framework that follows has been guided by several fundamental principles:

- The individual responsibilities of senior managers must be well understood.
- Managers must be given a range of authority commensurate with their responsibility.
- Subject to final decision by the President, the Secretary, or the Deputy Secretary, managers' participation in the process of establishing central policies should be encouraged.
- Approved policy, including longer-term priorities and objectives for the defense program, must be widely and clearly communicated within DoD.
- Within this context, managers must expect to be held strictly accountable for the overall results of their efforts, for adhering to approved policy, and for executing decisions.
- The full talents, dedication, experience and judgment of all DoD employees must be brought to bear in the execution of their diverse missions. Policy must be implemented in a wide variety of settings, and the process by which this is done must be carefully monitored in order to take full advantage of opportunities for cost savings and quality improvement. Innovation will come most naturally from the military and civilian professionals entrusted to do the job. They must be encouraged to examine and improve continuously the processes in which they are engaged — and to raise, at all levels, new ideas and approaches that will contribute to a sound, affordable program to maintain adequate U.S. military strength....

The terms of reference provided by the President for the Defense Management Review focused principally on the defense acquisition system. Major challenges remain to be addressed if DoD is to implement fully the Packard Commission's recommendations in this area, including the various organizational arrangements, personnel improvements, and revised practices and procedures projected by the Commission to reduce the cost and improve the performance of new weapon systems. Efforts to date have not produced the tangible results envisioned by the Commission. This is indicative of the dimension of the problems the Commission identified, the far-reaching solutions it offered, and the persistence required if DoD's management of major acquisition programs is to emulate the characteristics of the most successful commercial and government projects. Among these characteristics, described in the Commission's reports, were:

- Clear Command Channels — the clear alignment of responsibility and authority, preserved and promoted through short, unambiguous chains of command to the most senior decision makers;
- Program Stability — a stable environment of funding and management, predicated on an agreed baseline for cost, schedule, and performance;
- Limited Reporting Requirements — adherence to the principle of "management by exception," and methods of ensuring accountability that focus on deviations from the agreed baseline;
- Small, High Quality Staffs — reliance on small staffs of specially trained and highly motivated personnel;
- Communications with Users — sound understanding of user needs achieved early-on and reflecting a proper balance among cost, schedule, and performance considerations;
- Better System Development — including aggressive use of prototyping and testing to identify and remedy problems well before production, investment in a strong technology base that emphasizes lower-cost approaches to building capable weapon systems, greater reliance on commercial products, and increased use of commercial-style competition.

When considered in this framework, it is apparent that the Packard Commission's recommendations intended to make more fundamental changes in the defense acquisition system than have yet been accomplished. Additional actions are required — including steps that substantially depart from or go well beyond DoD's and Congress' efforts to date.

Any effort to improve the relationship between government and defense industry must be rooted in this proposition: DoD will not tolerate illegal or unethical behavior on the part of anyone in the acquisition system. As a matter of fundamental policy, DoD, with the Department of Justice (DoJ), will devote its full energies and resources to enforcement of applicable laws.

All too obscured by the glare of recent investigations and prosecutions, however, is a corollary proposition emphasized by the Packard Commission: bringing law-breakers to book for past deeds is not by itself enough; more affirmative efforts are necessary if DoD is to acquire, and industry to supply, equipment and materiel in a manner that meets the highest standards of accountability and performance. Among the specific approaches recommended by the Commission were the following:

- Better administration of existing ethical standards for civilian and military acquisition personnel in DoD;
- greatly improved contractor self-governance, entailing the voluntary assumption by industry management of demanding new responsibilities for oversight of their contract operations;
- and more effective use of DoD auditing and other oversight resources.

The Defense Management Review took stock of progress in implementing these and other recommendations of the Packard Commission, as well as a variety of related initiatives to encourage improved industry performance and promote the health of the U.S. defense industrial base....
(Department of Defense, July 1989)

Public Law 102-88: Intelligence Authorization Act for Fiscal Year 1991
August 14, 1991
SEC. 601. REPEAL OF HUGHES-RYAN AMENDMENT

Section 662 of the Foreign Assistance Act of 1961 (22 U.S.C. 2422) is repealed.

SEC. 602. OVERSIGHT OF INTELLIGENCE ACTIVITIES

(a) IN GENERAL. — Title V of the National Security Act of 1947 is amended —

(1) by redesignating sections 502 and 503 as sections 504 and 505, respectively; and

(2) by striking out section 501 (50 U.S.C. 413) and inserting in lieu thereof the following new sections:

"GENERAL CONGRESSIONAL OVERSIGHT PROVISIONS"

"SEC. 501. (a)(1) The President shall ensure that the intelligence committees are kept fully and currently informed of the intelligence activities of the United States, including any significant anticipated intelligence activity as required by this title.

"(2) As used in this title, the term 'intelligence committees' means the Select Committee on Intelligence of the Senate and the Permanent Select Committee on Intelligence of the House of Representatives.

"(3) Nothing in this title shall be construed as requiring the approval of the intelligence committees as a condition precedent to the initiation of any significant anticipated intelligence activity.

"(b) The President shall ensure that any illegal intelligence activity is reported promptly to the intelligence committees, as well as any corrective action that has been taken or is planned in connection with such illegal activity.

"(c) The President and the intelligence committees shall each establish such procedures as may be necessary to carry out the provisions of this title.

"(d) The House of Representatives and the Senate shall each establish, by rule or resolution of such House, procedures to protect from unauthorized disclosure all classified information, and all information relating to intelligence sources and methods, that is furnished to the intelligence committees or to Members of Congress under this title. Such procedures shall be established in consultation with the Director of Central Intelligence. In accordance with such procedures, each of the intelligence committees shall promptly call to the attention of its respective House, or to any appropriate committee or committees of its respective House, any matter relating to intelligence activities requiring the attention of such House or such committee or committees.

"(e) Nothing in this Act shall be construed as authority to withhold information from the intelligence committees on the grounds that providing the information to the intelligence committees would constitute the unauthorized disclosure of classified information or information relating to intelligence sources and methods.

"(f) As used in this section, the term 'intelligence activities' includes covert actions as defined in section 503(e).

"REPORTING OF INTELLIGENCE ACTIVITIES OTHER THAN COVERT ACTIONS"

"SEC. 502. To the extent consistent with due regard for the protection from unauthorized disclosure of classified information relating to sensitive intelligence sources and methods or other exceptionally sensitive matters, the Director of Central Intelligence and the heads of all departments, agencies, and other entities of the United States Government involved in intelligence activities shall —

"(1) keep the intelligence committees fully and currently informed of all intelligence activities, other than a covert action (as defined in section 503(e)), which are the responsibility of, are engaged in by, or are carried out for or on behalf of, any department, agency, or entity of the United States Government, including any significant anticipated intelligence activity and any significant intelligence failure; and

"(2) furnish the intelligence committees any information or material concerning intelligence activities, other than covert actions, which is within their custody or control, and which is requested by either of the intelligence committees in order to carry out its authorized responsibilities.

"PRESIDENTIAL APPROVAL AND REPORTING OF COVERT ACTIONS"

"SEC. 503. (a) The President may not authorize the conduct of a covert action by departments, agencies, or entities of the United States Government unless the President determines such an action is necessary to support identifiable foreign policy objectives of the United States and is important to the national security of the United States, which determination shall be set forth in a finding that shall meet each of the following conditions:

"(1) Each finding shall be in writing, unless immediate action by the United States is required and time does not permit the preparation of a written finding, in which case a written record of the President's decision shall be contemporaneously made and shall be reduced to a written finding as soon as possible but in no event more than 48 hours after the decision is made.

"(2) Except as permitted by paragraph (1), a finding may not authorize or sanction a covert action, or any aspect of any such action, which already has occurred.

"(3) Each finding shall specify each department, agency, or entity of the United States Government authorized to fund or otherwise participate in any significant way in such action. Any employee, contractor, or contract agent of a department, agency, or entity of the United States Government other than the Central Intelligence Agency directed to participate in any way in a covert action shall be subject either to the policies and regulations of the Central Intelligence Agency, or to written policies or regulations adopted by such department, agency, or entity, to govern such participation.

"(4) Each finding shall specify whether it is contemplated that any third party which is not an element of, or a contractor or contract agent of, the United States Government, or is not otherwise subject to United States Government policies and regulations, will be used to fund or otherwise participate in any significant way in the covert action concerned, or be used to undertake the covert action concerned on behalf of the United States.

"(5) A finding may not authorize any action that would violate the Constitution or any statute of the United States.

"(b) To the extent consistent with due regard for the protection from unauthorized disclosure of classified information relating to sensitive intelligence sources and methods or other exceptionally sensitive matters, the Director of Central Intelligence and the heads of all departments, agencies, and entities of the United States Government involved in a covert action —

"(1) shall keep the intelligence committees fully and currently informed of all covert actions which are the responsibility of, are engaged in by, or are carried out for or on behalf of, any department, agency, or entity of the United States Government, including significant failures; and

"(2) shall furnish to the intelligence committees any information or material concerning covert actions which is in the possession, custody, or control of any department, agency, or entity of the United States Government and which is requested by either of the intelligence committees in order to carry out its authorized responsibilities.

"(c)(1) The President shall ensure that any finding approved pursuant to subsection (a) shall be reported to the intelligence committees as soon as possible after such approval and before the initiation of the covert action authorized by the finding, except as otherwise provided in paragraph (2) and paragraph (3).

"(2) If the President determines that it is essential to limit access to the finding to meet extraordinary circumstances affecting vital interests of the United States, the finding may be reported to the chairmen and ranking minority members of the intelligence committees, the Speaker and minority leader of the House of Representatives, the majority and minority leaders of the Senate, and such other member or members of the congressional leadership as may be included by the President.

"(3) Whenever a finding is not reported pursuant to paragraph (l) or (2) of this section, the President shall fully inform the intelligence committees in a timely fashion and shall provide a statement of the reasons for not giving prior notice.

"(4) In a case under paragraph (1), (2), or (3), a copy of the finding, signed by the President, shall be provided to the chairman of each intelligence committee. When access to a finding is limited to the Members of Congress specified in paragraph (2), a Statement of the reasons for limiting such access shall also be provided.

"(d) The President shall ensure that the intelligence committees, or, if applicable, the Members of Congress specified in subsection (c)(2), are notified of any significant change in a previously approved covert action, or any significant undertaking pursuant to a previously approved finding, in the same manner as findings are reported pursuant to subsection (c).

"(e) As used in this title, the term 'covert action' means an activity or activities of the United States Government to influence political, economic, or military conditions abroad, where it is intended that the role of the United States Government will not be apparent or acknowledged publicly, but does not include—

"(1) activities the primary purpose of which is to acquire intelligence, traditional counterintelligence activities, traditional activities to improve or maintain the operational security of United States Government programs, or administrative activities;

"(2) traditional diplomatic or military activities or routine support to such activities;

"(3) traditional law enforcement activities conducted by United States Government law enforcement agencies or routine support to such activities; or

"(4) activities to provide routine support to the overt activities (other than activities described in paragraph (1), (2), or (3)) of other United States Government agencies abroad.

"(f) No covert action may be conducted which is intended to influence United States political processes, public opinion, policies, or media."...
(USS, 1991)

Public Law 102-496: Intelligence Authorization Act for Fiscal Year 1993
October 24, 1992
...SEC. 303. SENSE OF CONGRESS REGARDING DISCLOSURE OF ANNUAL INTELLIGENCE BUDGET

It is the sense of Congress that, beginning in 1993, and in each year thereafter, the aggregate amount requested and authorized for, and spent on, intelligence and intelligence-related activities should be disclosed to the public in an appropriate manner....

SEC. 709. PARTICIPATION OF THE DIRECTOR OF CENTRAL INTELLIGENCE IN THE NATIONAL SECURITY COUNCIL

Section 101 of the National Security Act of 1947 (50 U.S.C. 402) is amended by adding at the end thereof the following new subsection:

"(h) The Director of Central Intelligence (or, in the Director's absence, the Deputy Director of Central Intelligence) may, in the performance of the Director's duties under this Act and subject to the direction of the President, attend and participate in meetings of the National Security Council."

SEC. 704. APPOINTMENT OF THE DIRECTOR AND DEPUTY DIRECTOR OF CENTRAL INTELLIGENCE

Section 102 of the National Security Act of 1947 (50 U.S.C. 403(a)) is amended —

..."(2)There shall be a Director of Central Intelligence who shall be appointed by the President, by and with the advice and consent of the Senate. The Director shall —

"(A) serve as head of the United States intelligence community;

"(B) act as the principal adviser to the President for intelligence matters related to the national security; and

"(C) serve as head of the Central Intelligence Agency.

"(b) To assist the Director of Central Intelligence in carrying out the Director's responsibilities under this Act, there shall be a Deputy Director of Central Intelligence, who shall be appointed by the President, by and with the advice and consent of the Senate, who shall act for, and exercise the powers of, the Director during the Director's absence or disability.

"(c)(l) The Director or Deputy Director of Central Intelligence may be appointed from among the commissioned officers of the Armed Forces, or from civilian life, but at no time shall both positions be simultaneously occupied by commissioned officers of the Armed Forces, whether in an active or retired status.

"(2) It is the sense of the Congress that under ordinary circumstances, it is desirable that either the Director or the Deputy Director be a commissioned officer of the Armed Forces or that either such appointee otherwise have, by training or experience, an appreciation of military intelligence activities and requirements.

"(3)(A) A commissioned officer of the Armed Forces appointed pursuant to paragraph (2) or (3), while serving in such position —

"(i) shall not be subject to supervision or control by the Secretary of Defense or by any officer or employee of the Department of Defense;

"(ii) shall not exercise, by reason of the officer's status as a commissioned officer, any supervision or control with respect to any of the military or civilian personnel of the Department of Defense except as otherwise authorized by law; and

"(iii) shall not be counted against the numbers and percentages of commissioned officers of the rank and grade of such officer authorized for the military department of which such officer is a member.

"(B) Except as provided in clause (i) or (ii) of paragraph (A), the appointment of a commissioned officer of the Armed Forces pursuant to paragraph (2) or (3) shall in no way affect the state, position, rank, or grade of such officer in the Armed Forces, or any emolument, perquisite, right, privilege, or benefit incident to or arising out of any such status, position, rank, or grade.

"(C) A commissioned officer of the Armed Forces appointed pursuant to subsection (a) or (b), while serving in such position, shall continue to receive military pay and allowances (including retired pay) payable to a commissioned officer of the officer's grade and length of service for which the appropriate military department shall be reimbursed from funds available to the Director of Central Intelligence.

"(d) The Office of the Director of Central Intelligence shall, for administrative purposes, be within the Central Intelligence Agency."

SEC. 705. RESPONSIBILITIES AND AUTHORITIES OF THE DIRECTOR OF CENTRAL INTELLIGENCE

..."SEC. 103. (a) PROVISION OF INTELLIGENCE. — 1) Under the direction of the National Security Council, the Director of Central Intelligence shall be responsible for providing national intelligence —

"(A) to the President;

"(B) to the heads of departments and agencies of the executive branch;

"(C) to the Chairman of the Joint Chiefs of Staff and senior military commanders; and

"(D) where appropriate, to the Senate and House of Representatives and the committees thereof.

"(2) Such national intelligence should be timely, objective, independent of political considerations, and based upon all sources available to the intelligence community.

"(b) NATIONAL INTELLIGENCE COUNCIL. — (l)(A) There is established within the office of the Director of Central Intelligence the National Intelligence Council (hereafter in this section referred to as the 'Council'). The Council shall be composed of senior analysts within the intelligence community and substantive experts from the public and private sector, who shall be appointed by, report to, and serve at the pleasure of, the Director of Central Intelligence.

"(B) The Director shall prescribe appropriate security requirements for personnel appointed from the private sector as a condition of service on the Council to ensure the protection of intelligence sources and methods while avoiding, wherever possible, unduly intrusive requirements which the Director considers to be unnecessary for this purpose.

"(2) The Council shall —

"(A) produce national intelligence estimates for the Government, including, whenever the Council considers appropriate, alternative views held by elements of the intelligence community; and

"(B) otherwise assist the Director in carrying out the responsibilities described in subsection (a).

"(3) Within their respective areas of expertise and under the direction of the Director, the members of the Council shall constitute the senior intelligence advisers of the intelligence community for purposes of representing the views of the intelligence community within the Government.

"(4) The Director shall make available to the Council such staff as may be necessary to permit the Council to carry out its responsibilities under this subsection and shall take appropriate measures to ensure that the Council and its staff satisfy the needs of policymaking officials and other consumers of intelligence.

"(6) The heads of elements within the intelligence community shall, as appropriate, furnish such support to the Council, including the preparation of intelligence analyses, as may be required by the Director....
(USS, 1992)

President Clinton's Radio Address to the Nation on Defense Conversion
March 13, 1993

...All around us, we see changes transforming our economy. Global competition, new technologies, and the reductions in military spending after we won the cold war. We can't stop the world from changing, but there is one decision we can and must make. Will we leave our people and our Nation unprepared for changes that are remaking our world, or will we invest in our people's jobs, our education, our training, our technology to build a high-skilled, high-wage future for ourselves and for our children....

We must never forget that the world is still a dangerous place. Our military is continuing to change, not to downsize for its own sake but so that we can meet the challenges of the 21st century. In the post-cold-war era, our military can be cut even while we maintain the forces necessary to protect our interests and our people.

The preliminary announcements of base closings in this morning's paper are part of that process. What we need to decide is whether we will invest in the economic security of the people who defend our national security. For the past 4 years our Government has done essentially nothing. Since 1989, 300,000 soldiers, sailors, and flyers have been mustered out of the service. One hundred thousand civilian employees of the Defense Department have also lost their jobs. And 440,000 workers from defense industries have been laid off.

As the business magazine *Fortune* has reported, these cuts cost 840,000 jobs over the past 4 years. That's more than the combined total layoffs at GM, IBM, AT&T, and Sears. Too many of the men and women affected by defense cuts are still looking for full-time jobs or working at jobs that pay much lower wages and use fewer of their skills.

These Americans won the cold war. We must not leave them out in the cold. That's why I propose a new national strategy to make these Americans have the training, the skills, and the support they need to compete and win in the post-cold-war economy.

Last year the Congress appropriated $1.4 billion for defense conversion activities. But the previous administration did not put any of that money to work. Our administration's plan gets those funds moving immediately and calls for an additional $300 million in resources, for a total of $1.7 billion this year alone, and for nearly $20 billion over the next 5 years.

Our plan invests in job training and employment services for military personnel and defense workers who have been displaced by declining military spending. And we'll make sure that every community affected by a base closing will have the help they need right away to plan for new businesses and new jobs. It takes 3 to 5 years for a base to close. We need to use that time to be ready.

That's why I'm proposing a national strategy to make sure that all these communities and all these workers can use this valuable time to plan and to acquire the tools to build a new future.

Our plan also invests in dual use technologies, that is, those that have both civilian and military applications and in advanced civilian technologies

as well. With these technologies defense companies can create new products and new jobs....
(WCPD Clinton 1993: 412-413)

TERRORISM AND COUNTERTERRORISM

Terrorism and the Rule of Law
Address by L. Paul Bremer, III, Ambassador at Large for Counter-Terrorism, before the Commonwealth Club in San Francisco
April 23, 1987

...Terrorism has continued to plague governments and peoples all over the world. Last year, there were almost 800 incidents of international terrorism, affecting citizens and property of over 80 countries. In 1986, terrorists caused almost 2,000 casualties.

America's Counterterrorism Strategy

In the face of these grim statistics, though let me stress that we are not sitting still. We have an active strategy to combat terrorism and one which we believe is beginning to show results. Our strategy rests on three pillars.

- The first is that we will not make concessions to terrorists.
- The second is to bring pressure on states supporting terrorism.
- The third is developing practical measures designed to identify, track, apprehend, prosecute, and punish terrorists.

Our government believes that a policy of no concessions is the best way to discourage terrorist acts. For if terrorists can gain their objectives through terror one time, they will be encouraged to repeat terror in the future. President Reagan has stated that sending arms to Iran was a mistake and will not be done again. It is clear that a policy of firmness has the overwhelming support of the American people.

It has been longstanding U.S. Government policy that we will talk to anyone who might be able to effect the safe release of Americans held hostage. That remains true. Speaking with hostage holders does not mean, however, that we will make concessions which would only further encourage terrorists to undertake such acts in the future.

The second aspect of our counter terrorism strategy is to put pressure on states which support terrorism. State support of terrorism represents a special danger. In accordance with the law, the Secretary of State has identified five countries as states which support terrorism — Syria, Libya, Iran, Cuba, and South Yemen. Our aim is to raise the economic, diplomatic, and — if necessary — the military costs to such states to a level which they are unwilling to pay.

Over the past year, there has been important progress in developing these pressures — not only by America but also by our allies. In April, after our attack on Libyan terrorist sites, the Europeans took strong steps against Libya, including dramatically reducing the size of Libyan diplomatic establishments. And, in the fall, we and the Europeans invoked limited sanctions on Syria after British and German courts proved Syrian complicity in terrorist attacks.

The third pillar, seeking practical measures to combat terrorism, is one of the most effective elements of our strategy. In attempting to identify terrorists, we work with a number of governments to facilitate intelligence sharing and the circulation of "lookout" lists. As terrorists are identified, we can begin to track them, especially as they attempt to cross international borders. Even the most democratic states can require detailed identification and conduct very thorough searches at border points. This is a terrorist vulnerability we are trying to exploit. For example, a Lebanese terrorist and principal suspect in the TWA 847 hijacking, Mohammed Hamadei, was arrested as he attempted to smuggle explosives into Germany in January.

Finally, we work with friendly governments to assure that once apprehended, terrorists are brought to justice through prosecution and punishment.

Over the past year, the role of the rule of law in combatting terrorism has expanded. It is this particular element of our policy that I would like to address today.

Terrorists are Criminals

Perhaps the most important development in the fight against terrorism in the past year has been the renewed determination on the part of the world's democracies to get tough with terrorists and to apply the rule of law to terrorism.

Time and again over the past months, terrorists have been arrested, brought to trial, and received long sentences for the crimes they have committed. In October, a British court sentenced Nizar Hindawi to 45 years in jail for his attempt to blow up an El Al flight. In November, West Germany found Ahmad Hasi and Farouk Salameh guilty of bombing the German-Arab Friendship Society, which injured 9 people. They were sentenced to 14 and 13 years imprisonment, respectively. And just 2 months ago, French courts convicted Georges Ibrahim Abdallah, a leader of the Lebanese Armed Revolutionary Faction, to life imprisonment for his role in the assassinations of U.S. and Israeli diplomats.

For Western democracies, the firm hand of the law is the best defense against terrorism. Democratic nations must treat terrorists as criminals, for to do otherwise legitimizes terrorists not only in their own eyes but in the eyes of others.

Let me deal briefly with the problem of defining terrorism. There are as many definitions around as there are definers. Some people argue that no matter how heinous the crime, if the cause is justified the act cannot be terrorism. This attitude, though, only serves to confound the fight against terrorism. As Brian Jenkins of the Rand Corporation puts it: "If cause is the criterion, only to the extent that everyone in the world can agree on the justice of a particular cause is there likely to be agreement that an action does or does not constitute terrorism."

Instead of focusing on the cause, therefore, our government focuses on the terrorist act itself, for it is the act which ultimately distinguishes the criminal. Our government believes that terrorist acts have certain characteristics. They are premeditated and politically motivated. They are conducted against noncombatant targets and usually have as their goal trying to intimidate or influence a government's policy. It is by their acts that terrorists indict themselves as criminals. All nations have criminal statutes to deal with criminals, and it only makes sense that all states should apply their existing statutes to terrorists.

Terrorist Threats to the Rule of Law

Terrorists despise democracy because democracy cherishes that which terrorists seek to destroy: the sanctity of the individual and the rule of law.

There are two main categories of terrorist threat to our legal systems.

First, there are indigenous, or domestic, terrorists who seek to provoke governments into extralegal excesses and hence, to undermine political support for democratically elected regimes. Precisely because the rule of law is so fundamental to safeguarding a free citizen's basic rights, terrorists frequently attack the rule of law in general and legal institutions specifically. There are many cases of this kind of threat.

- In November 1985, guerrillas belonging to the M-19 movement seized the Palace of Justice in Bogota, Colombia, and held it for more than 27 hours. The targets of this attack were the judges who were rendering verdicts for extradition of drug traffickers. By the time the incident was over, 90 people were dead, including 12 Supreme Court judges.
- Last September, when jurors in France were threatened with terrorist retaliation and refused to show up at criminal hearings, a jury of magistrates had to be established in order that terrorist prosecutions would not be thwarted.
- In Spain, ETA [Basque Fatherland and Freedom] terrorists have attacked Spanish magistrates. And in Portugal, terrorists have made threats against jurors in the trial of Portuguese terrorists. In Italy, judges have been a favorite target of the Red Brigades.

The second major category of threat comes from transnational terrorists, those who travel from one country to another to commit terrorist acts. Often their objective is to coerce foreign governments into compromising their legal ethics.

The events surrounding the Abdallah arrest and trial in France are a good example of this phenomenon. Shortly after French security services imprisoned Abdallah in Paris, his colleagues initiated a bloody series of bombings in downtown Paris. Bombs exploded in crowded stores, at cafes, on the sidewalks during rush hour traffic. Many innocent people died or were wounded as a result. The intent was to force the French Government into releasing Abdallah, thereby thwarting French efforts to bring this terrorist to justice. Fortunately, the tactic did not work. It was a victory for the French legal system and the rule of law.

Today the German Government is facing a similar attempt at blackmail at the hands of other Middle East terrorists. In January, the Germans arrested the terrorist Hamadei, accused of being one of the hijackers of TWA 847 and the brutal murderer of U.S. Navy diver Robert Stethem. Shortly after his arrest in Germany, two Germans were snatched off the streets of Beirut, apparently by associates of Hamadei. They are holding them hostage there, demanding the release of Hamadei. We have formally requested the Federal Republic of Germany to extradite Hamadei to the United States for trial on murder and hijacking charges. We hope the German legal system will prove as invulnerable to terrorist blackmail as France's was last fall.

We must preserve the integrity of our judiciaries in dealing with terrorism. We must treat terrorists as we would other criminals. We acknowledge that it may be difficult not to capitulate to terrorists' demands. But to give in only encourages additional terrorist acts — once terrorists see that they can get away with their crimes, they will commit more.

Strengthening Domestic Legislation Against Terrorism

In the face of rising terrorism over the past two decades, democratic nations have not stood still. The United States and our allies abroad have strengthened our legal systems to deal with terrorism both through improved domestic procedures and through international agreements.

In the United States, we have strengthened statutes covering crimes most typically committed by terrorists. The anticrime bill of 1984 makes certain acts of overseas terrorism, such as hostage taking and aircraft sabotage committed anywhere in the world, crimes punishable in U.S. Federal courts. The Omnibus Diplomatic Security and Anti-Terrorism Act of 1986 provides the U.S. Government with several important legal tools for combatting terrorism.

- It provided U.S. jurisdiction over terrorist crimes committed against Americans overseas. This landmark provision gives us the legal right to prosecute in the United States terrorists who murder or violently attack Americans abroad.
- The act also established a counter terrorism witness protection fund, so that the United States may reimburse other governments for costs related to security for those who come forward to provide testimony or evidence in terrorist cases.
- It increased funding for the protection of our diplomats and embassies overseas from terrorist attack.
- The act further enhanced support for the State Department's rewards program, initially created in 1984, whereby the Department offers substantial cash awards to anyone who provides information leading to the arrest and prosecution of terrorists. To date, we have established rewards totalling $1.1 million for five major terrorist incidents.

Other countries have also strengthened their domestic judicial systems against terrorism. Almost all our allies have adopted laws which improve their ability to prosecute terrorists for crimes related to aircraft hijacking and sabotage, attacks on diplomats, hostage taking, and theft of nuclear materials. The French, in addition, recently passed a new set of laws that change the procedures for terrorist trials: such trials are now heard by professional magistrates to lessen the chance of intimidation of jurors. The new French laws also double the period of time a terrorist can be held for interrogation and provide expanded police powers to deal with terrorists.

Strengthening International Conventions on Terrorism

Improving the domestic legal framework for combatting terrorism is an important step in bringing the law to bear on this problem. Just as important are efforts of the international community to expand the international legal regime for combatting terrorism.

The United States and many of our allies are parties to a number of international conventions covering terrorist acts, including the Hague Convention on the unlawful seizure of aircraft, the Montreal Convention on civil aviation safety, the Convention Against the Taking of Hostages, the convention on crimes against internationally protected persons, and the convention on the protection of nuclear materials.

These conventions and the laws implementing them provide important legal authority to prosecute international terrorists. They form the basis of our charges pending against Mohammad Hamadei. And the Hague Convention obligates the Germans either to extradite or prosecute him.

There has been encouraging progress in specialized international organizations to combat terrorism. The International Maritime Organization

(IMO) has undertaken a number of measures in the wake of the *Achille Lauro* hijacking and the murder of Leon Klinghoffer. In September 1986, the IMO adopted new security guidelines to prevent unlawful acts against passengers and crews on board ships. In November, the IMO Council began consideration of a joint Austrian-Egyptian-Italian draft of an international convention to outlaw various acts like hijacking a ship and to obligate states to prosecute or extradite offenders.

In the air security area, the International Civil Aviation Organization (ICAO) is working on a Canadian proposal to expand the language of existing international conventions to include broader protection for airports. Furthermore, the ICAO meets regularly to consider improvements to its security regulations for aviation and airports.

In another legal arena, the United States is renegotiating our bilateral extradition treaties to strengthen our ability to seek the extradition of terrorists. Many of these existing treaties contain so-called political exception clauses which could protect terrorists and other criminals from extradition if the host government determines that the crime was of a political nature. We have been working hard to limit this clause by revising our extradition treaties. Our supplementary extradition treaty with Great Britain was ratified last year. We have since concluded agreements with Germany and Belgium.

All of this work is beginning to pay off. Democratic nations are exercising the rule of law, and with encouraging frequency. For example:

- Early this year, a Canadian court sentenced to life imprisonment two Sikh terrorists who conspired to blow up a New York-to-London Air India flight in 1986.
- Last month in Italy, a Lebanese terrorist, Bashir al-Khodr was sentenced to 13 years in prison following his arrest at a Milan airport for carrying explosives and detonators hidden in Easter eggs and picture frames.
- In March, the Japanese Supreme Court upheld the death penalty for two terrorists convicted in a 1971-75 series of bombings that killed eight and injured 187. The court also upheld earlier rulings for two others convicted in the bombings: one received life imprisonment and the other an 8-year prison term.

More terrorists will be brought to justice in 1987, as important trials are scheduled to take place in Austria, Italy, Malta, Pakistan, Spain, and Turkey.

The recent steps taken by the world community to improve the legal framework to fight terrorism are having a measurable effect. Some previous efforts became bogged down in some of the near-metaphysical discussions which terrorism provokes. For example, I am not surprised that the 1972 UN document entitled "Measures To Prevent International Terrorism Which Endangers or Takes Innocent Human Lives or Jeopardizes Fundamental

Freedoms, and Study of the Underlying Causes of Those Forms of Terrorism, and Acts of Violence Which Lie in Misery, Frustration, Grievances and Despair and Which Cause Some People to Sacrifice Human Lives, Including Their Own, in an Attempt To Effect Radical Changes" seemed to have little effect in stemming the rise of terrorism.

Are Terrorists Warriors?

So the rule of law, which treats terrorist acts as criminal acts and terrorists as criminals, is beginning to work. But precisely because they fear the rule of law, terrorists have often tried to slip away from being called criminals by claiming to be warriors instead. Terrorists, and often their sympathizers invoke the banal phrase that "terrorism is the poor man's war." By this argument, terrorists are presented as merely soldiers, forced by circumstances into an unconventional mode of conventional war but, nonetheless, entitled to the same privileges extended to "lawful combatants."

But even the internationally accepted rules of war provide no hiding place for terrorists. The Geneva conventions on rules of war outlaw nearly every act of terrorism. For example:

- The rules of war define combatants and grant civilians who do not take a part in hostilities immunity from deliberate attack. A terrorist who attacks innocent civilians at an airport clearly violates this rule.
- The rules of war prohibit taking hostages. Terrorists in Lebanon holding Americans and others hostage clearly violate this rule of war.
- The rules of war prohibit violence against those held captive. Freed American hostages have told of repeated beatings by their captors.
- The rules of war require combatants to wear uniforms or insignia identifying their status. Terrorists identify themselves only after they have committed their crimes and, in fact, almost always conceal their true identities during their criminal acts.

Do terrorists adhere to the rules of war? Consider their actions during the attempted hijacking of a Pan American plane in Karachi last fall. The terrorists stormed the airplane full of civilians. They killed two of them at the outset in cold blood. They held the rest hostage. They beat some passengers. At the end of the incident, the terrorists tried to conceal their identity and escape by mixing in with their victims. In short, this incident, typical of other terrorist incidents, shows that terrorists do not act like warriors; they behave like criminals.

In the chaos of war, soldiers may violate laws. Our own forces have been guilty of crimes, and we have punished them for it. The key point is that there are legal norms applicable even in war. So even if we were to dignify terrorists with the term "warriors," it would not excuse in any way their criminal acts.

Indeed, one possible definition of a terrorist act is an act committed in peacetime which, if committed in wartime, would be considered a violation of the rules of war.

Using the Law Against States Supporting Terrorism

One of the more dangerous developments in terrorism in the past few years has been the emergence of state support. Several states — notably Libya, Syria, and Iran — have funded, trained, and provided logistical support for terrorists to further their foreign policy goals. This kind of support greatly complicates the job of fighting terrorism. States can provide easy money, weapons, and explosives to terrorists. We have found that some states have used their embassies, diplomats, and official airlines to pass money, weapons, instructions, maps, and official passports to terrorists.

When the United States has identified a particular state engaged in supporting terrorism, we have tried to impose a series of measures to make the leaders of that country realize that their support for terrorism carries a high cost.

Take the case of Libya. We decided years ago that Colonel Qadhafi was engaged in supporting terrorists. We suspended diplomatic relations. We impose economic sanctions by reducing the amount of oil and other products that we imported from that country. Ultimately, after years of economic and political sanctions and in the face of clear evidence of Libyan involvement in terrorist acts, we had to resort to military action. Many people, including some of our allies, questioned the legality of our action. But the law amply justified our action.

Under customary international law, a state is responsible for acts of force, whether they are carried out by the state's own armed forces or other agents. That state is also responsible if the act of force is conducted from its own territory by terrorists or others whose activities the host state should have prevented. In other words, every state has a duty to every other state to take appropriate steps to ensure that its territory is not used for such purposes.

But if a state like Libya does not exercise this fundamental international obligation, then the state which has been injured has the right to use a reasonable and proportionate amount of force in times of peace to eliminate the breach. This right is established by Article 51 of the UN Charter....
(DSB August 1987: 83-86)

Statement by Deputy Press Secretary Arsht on the Crash of an American Jetliner in Lockerbie, Scotland

December 28, 1988

This morning the President was informed by national security adviser Colin Powell that the British Department of Transport has determined that the crash of Pan Am Flight 103 was caused by a high explosive device. We have closely cooperated with the British investigation. We agree with the results of their investigation.

The investigation will continue to determine how the explosives were introduced into the plane. The FBI and the FAA are working closely with the British and Scottish authorities on the investigation. We are determined to find out who did it, using all available resources.
(PPP Reagan 1988-1989 II: 1663)

Statement by Press Secretary Fitzwater on the Execution of Lieutenant Colonel William R. Higgins
August 7, 1989

The Federal Bureau of Investigation today released the results of forensic examinations of the videotape purported to be of Lieutenant Colonel Higgins. Mrs. Higgins was informed of the results by the Commandant of the Marine Corps, General Al Gray. President Bush called Mrs. Higgins at about 2 p.m. to offer his support and encouragement. The President said the U.S. Government will continue to do all it can to obtain a full accounting of what happened to her husband.

Note: Lt. Col. William R. Higgins, USMC, chief of the U.N. peacekeeping force in southern Lebanon, was kidnapped on February 17, 1988, and executed by pro-Iranian terrorists on July 31, 1989. After examining a videotape released by the terrorists, FBI forensic experts and pathologists concluded that, although a positive identification could not be made, the person depicted in the videotape probably was Lieutenant Colonel Higgins and that he was "within a reasonable degree of medical certainty" dead.
(PPP Bush 1989 II: 1068)

President Bush's Statement on United States Emergency Antidrug Assistance for Colombia
August 25, 1989

At the request of President Barco and in order to support the Government of Colombia in its battle against narcotics traffickers, I have today decided to authorize a $65 million emergency antidrug support package for the Colombian police and military. The package will include equipment for police and military personnel, with initial shipments to arrive as early as next week. In addition, it will include aircraft and helicopters to improve the mobility of Colombian forces engaged in the antidrug effort. The package was developed over the last few days, during which there was close consultation between President Barco and myself and among our key advisers.

No United States troops have been requested by the Colombian Government. We will provide only materiel support and training. The United States has complete confidence in the capability of the Colombian police and military to deal with this situation. The support package will be made available under the provisions of the 1986 Foreign Assistance Act, which enables the President to direct the Department of Defense to provide military equipment and services to a foreign country in the event of an emergency.

In addition to this emergency assistance and the funds being provided under the Justice Department's judicial protection program, I will authorize an expanded police and military assistance program for FY '90 which will provide an increased level of support for the Colombian Government's ongoing antidrug efforts.

The recent wave of assassinations and threats by the drug cartel against all Colombians who cooperate in President Barco's antidrug crackdown makes it clear that it is time for the United States and other countries of the world to stand with President Barco during his courageous challenge to these insidious forces that threaten the very fabric of Colombian society.

We intend to work closely with the Colombian Government to bring to justice those responsible for the scourge of drug trafficking and will continue in our efforts to assist the Colombian effort to provide protection for judges and other Colombian officials who are on the front line of the war against drugs. The Departments of State and Justice are working closely with their Colombian counterparts on extradition matters.
(PPP Bush 1989 II: 1109)

President Bush's Statement Announcing Joint Declarations on the Libyan Indictments
November 27, 1991
Statement of the Government of the United States Regarding the Bombing of Pan Am 103

After the indictments were handed down on November 14 we conveyed them to the Libyan regime. We have also consulted closely with the governments of France and the United Kingdom and in concert with those two governments we have the following two declarations to present publicly today.

Joint Declaration of the United States and United Kingdom

The British and American governments today declare that the Government of Libya must:

- surrender for trial all those charged with the crime; and accept responsibility for the actions of Libyan officials;

- disclose all it knows of this crime, including the names of all those responsible, and allow full access to all witnesses, documents and other material evidence, including all the remaining timers;
- pay appropriate compensation.

We expect Libya to comply promptly and in full.

Declaration of the United States, France, and the United Kingdom on Terrorism

The three states reaffirm their complete condemnation of terrorism in all its forms and denounce any complicity of states in terrorist acts. The three states reaffirm their commitment to put an end to terrorism.

They consider that the responsibility of states begins whenever they take part directly in terrorist actions or indirectly through harboring, training, providing facilities, arming, or providing financial support or any form of protection, and that they are responsible for their actions before individual states and the United Nations.

In this connection, following the investigations carried out into the bombings of Pan Am 103 and UTA 772 the three states have presented specific demands to Libyan authorities related to the judicial procedures that are underway. They require that Libya comply with all these demands, and, in addition, that Libya commit itself concretely and definitively to cease all forms of terrorist action and all assistance to terrorist groups. Libya must promptly, by concrete actions, prove its renunciation of terrorism.
(PPP Bush 1991 II: 1527-1528)

Public Law 101-222: Anti-Terrorism and Arms Export Amendments Act of 1989

...SEC. 2. PROHIBITION OF ARMS TRANSACTIONS WITH COUNTRIES SUPPORTING TERRORISM

(a) PROHIBITION. — Section 40 of the Arms Export Control Act (22 U.S.C. 2780) is amended to read as follows:

"SEC. 40. TRANSACTIONS WITH COUNTRIES SUPPORTING ACTS OF INTERNATIONAL TERRORISM.

(a) PROHIBITED TRANSACTIONS BY THE UNITED STATES GOVERNMENT. — The following transactions by the United States Government are prohibited:

"(1) Exporting or otherwise providing (by sale, lease or loan, grant, or other means), directly or indirectly, any munitions item to a country described in subsection (d) under the authority of this Act, the Foreign Assistance Act of 1961, or any other law (except as provided in subsection (h)). In implementing this paragraph, the United States Government —

"(A) shall suspend delivery to such country of any such item pursuant to any such transaction which has not been completed at the time the Secretary of State makes the determination described in subsection (d), and

"(B) shall terminate any lease or loan to such country of any such item which is in effect at the time the Secretary of State makes that determination.

"(2) Providing credits, guarantees, or other financial assistance under the authority of this Act, the Foreign Assistance Act of 1961, or any other law (except as provided in subsection (h)), with respect to the acquisition of any munitions item by country described in subsection (d). In implementing this paragraph, the United States Government shall suspend expenditures pursuant to any such assistance obligated before the Secretary of State makes the determination described in subsection (d). The President may authorize expenditures otherwise required to be suspended pursuant to the preceding sentence if the President has determined, and reported to the Congress that suspension of those expenditures causes undue financial hardship to a supplier, shipper, or similar person and allowing the expenditure will not result in any munitions item being made available for use by such country.

"(3) Consenting under section 3(a) of this Act, under section 505(a) of the Foreign Assistance Act of 1961, under the regulations issued to carry out section 38 of this Act, or under any other law (except as provided in subsection (h)), to any transfer of any munitions item to a country described in subsection (d). In implementing this paragraph, the United States Government shall withdraw any such consent which is in effect at the time the Secretary of State makes the determination described in subsection (d), except that this sentence does not apply with respect to any item that has already been transferred to such country.

"(4) Providing any license or other approval under section 38 of this Act for any export or other transfer (including by means of a technical assistance agreement, manufacturing licensing agreement, or coproduction agreement) of any munitions item to a country described in subsection (d). In implementing this paragraph, the United States Government shall suspend any such license or other approval which is in effect at the time the Secretary of State makes the determination described in subsection (d), except that this sentence does not apply with respect to any item that has already been exported or otherwise transferred to such country.

"(5) Otherwise facilitating the acquisition of any munitions item by a country described in subsection (d). This paragraph applies with respect to activities undertaken —

"(A) by any department, agency, or other instrumentality of the Government,

"(B) by any officer or employee of the Government (including members of the United States Armed Forces), or

"(C) by any other person at the request or on behalf of the Government.

The Secretary of State may waive the requirements of the second sentence of paragraph (1), the second sentence of paragraph (3), and the second sentence of paragraph (4) to the extent that the Secretary determines, after consultation with the Congress, that unusual and compelling circumstances require that the United States Government not take the actions specified in that sentence.

(b) PROHIBITED TRANSACTIONS BY UNITED STATES PERSONS

"(1) IN GENERAL. — A United States person may not take any of the following actions:

"(A) Exporting any munitions item to any country described in subsection (d).

"(B) Selling, leasing, loaning, granting, or otherwise providing any munitions item to any country described in subsection (d).

"(C) Selling, leasing, loaning, granting, or otherwise providing any munitions item to any recipient which is not the government of or a person in a country described in subsection (d) if the United States person has reason to know that the munitions item will be made available to any country described in subsection (d).

"(D) Taking any other action which would facilitate the acquisition, directly or indirectly, of any munitions item by the government of any country described in subsection (d), or any person acting on behalf of that government, if the United States person has reason to know that that action will facilitate the acquisition of that item by such a government or person....

"(f) RESCISSION. — A determination made by the Secretary of State under subsection (d) may not be rescinded unless the President submits to the Speaker of the House of Representatives and the chairman of the Committee on Foreign Relations of the Senate —

"(1) before the proposed rescission would take effect, a report certifying that —

"(A) there has been a fundamental change in the leadership and policies of the government of the country concerned.

"(B) that government is not supporting acts of international terrorism; and

"(C) that government has provided assurances that it will not support acts of international terrorism in the future; or

"(2) at least 45 days before the proposed rescission would take effect, a report justifying the rescission and certifying that —

"(A) the government concerned has not provided any support for international terrorism during the preceding 6-month period; and

"(B) the government concerned has provided assurances that it will not support acts of international terrorism in the future.

"(g) WAIVER. — The President may waive the prohibitions contained in this section with respect to a specific transaction if —

"(1) the President determines that the transaction is essential to the national security interests of the United States; and

"(2) not less than 15 days prior to the proposed transaction, the President —

"(A) consults with the Committee on Foreign Affairs of the House of Representatives and the Committee on Foreign Relations of the Senate, and

"(B) submits to the Speaker of the House of Representatives and the chairman of the Committee on Foreign Relations of the Senate a report containing —

"(i) the name of any country involved in the proposed transaction, the identity of any recipient of the items to be provided pursuant to the proposed transaction, and the anticipated use of those items;

"(ii) a description of the munitions items involved in the proposed transaction (including their market value) and the actual sale price at each step in the transaction (or if the items are transferred by other than sale, the manner in which they will be provided).

"(iii) the reasons why the proposed transaction is essential to the national security interests of the United States and the justification for such proposed transaction;

"(iv) the date on which the proposed transaction is expected to occur; and

"(v) the name of every United States Government department, agency, or other entity involved in the proposed transaction, every foreign government involved in the proposed transaction, and every private party with significant participation in the proposed transaction.

To the extent possible, the information specified in subparagraph (B) of paragraph (2) shall be provided in unclassified form, with any classified information provided in an addendum to the report....

(j) CRIMINAL PENALTY. — Any person who willfully violates this section shall be fined for each violation not more than $1,000,000, imprisoned not more than 10 years, or both....

SEC. 4. EXPORTS TO COUNTRIES SUPPORTING TERRORISM

Section 6(j) of the Export Administration Act of 1979 (50 U.S.C. App 2405(j)) is amended to read as follows:

(j) COUNTRIES SUPPORTING INTERNATIONAL TERRORISM. — (1) A validated license shall be required for the export of goods or technology to a country if the Secretary of State has made the following determinations:

"(A) The government of such country has repeatedly provided support for acts of international terrorism.

"(B) The export of such goods or technology could make a significant contribution to the military potential of such country, including its military logistics capability, or could enhance the ability of such country to support acts of international terrorism....

"(4) A determination made by the Secretary of State under paragraph (1)(A) may not be rescinded unless the President submits to the Speaker of the House of Representatives and the chairman of the Committee on Banking, Housing, and Urban Affairs and the chairman of the Committee on Foreign Relations of the Senate —

"(A) before the proposed rescission would take effect, a report certifying that —

"(i) there has been a fundamental change in the leadership and policies of the government of the country concerned;

"(ii) that government is not supporting acts of international terrorism; and

"(iii) that government has provided assurances that it will not support acts of international terrorism in the future; or

"(B) at least 45 days before the proposed rescission would take effect, a report justifying the rescission and certifying that —

"(i) the government concerned has not provided any support for international terrorism during the preceding 6-month period; and

"(ii) the government concerned has provided assurances that it will not support acts of international terrorism in the future."...

(USS, 1989, Volume 103, Part 2)

SOCIAL CHANGES IN THE MILITARY

Statement by the Director of Communications on President Clinton's Meeting With the Joint Chiefs of Staff

January 25, 1993

The President and the Joint Chiefs of Staff had a cordial, honest, and respectful meeting. They covered a range of issues but focused primarily on gays in the military.

The President reiterated his commitment to ending discrimination against homosexuals in the military solely on the basis of status and to maintaining morale and cohesion in the military.

The Joint Chiefs of Staff expressed their concerns and difficulties with the President's commitment but also expressed their respect for his decision-making power as Commander in Chief.

(WCPD Clinton 1993: 98)

President Clinton's News Conference: Gays in the Military
January 29, 1993

...I believe that American citizens who want to serve their country should be able to do so unless their conduct disqualifies them from doing so. Military life is fundamentally different from civilian society; it necessarily has a different and stricter code of conduct, even a different code of justice. Nonetheless, individuals who are prepared to accept all necessary restrictions on their behavior, many of which would be intolerable in civilian society, should be able to serve their country honorably and well.

I have asked the Secretary of Defense to submit by July the 15th a draft Executive order after full consultation with military and congressional leaders and concerned individuals outside of the Government, which would end the present policy of the exclusion from military service solely on the basis of sexual orientation and at the same time establish rigorous standards regarding sexual conduct to be applied to all military personnel.

This draft order will be accompanied by a study conducted during the next 6 months on the real, practical problems that would be involved in this revision of policy, so that we will have a practical, realistic approach consistent with the high standards of combat effectiveness and unit cohesion that our armed services must maintain.

I agree with the Joint Chiefs that the highest standards of conduct must be required. The change cannot and should not be accomplished overnight. It does require extensive consultation with the Joint Chiefs, experts in the Congress and in the legal community, joined by my administration and others. We've consulted closely to date and will do so in the future. During that process, interim measures will be placed into effect which, I hope, again, sharpen the focus of this debate. The Joint Chiefs of Staff have agreed to remove the question regarding one's sexual orientation from future versions of the enlistment application, and it will not be asked in the interim.

We also all agree that a very high standard of conduct can and must be applied. So the single area of disagreement is this: Should someone be able to serve their country in uniform if they say they are homosexuals, but they do nothing which violates the code of conduct or undermines unit cohesion or morale, apart from that statement? That is what all the furor of the last few days has been about. And the practical and not insignificant issues raised by that issue are what will be studied in the next 6 months.

Through this period ending July 15th, the Department of Justice will seek continuances in pending court cases involving reinstatement. And administrative separation under current Department of Defense policies based on status alone will be stayed pending completion of this review. The final discharge in cases based only on status will be suspended until the President has an opportunity to review and act upon the final recommendations of the Secretary of Defense with respect to the current policy. In the meantime, a member whose discharge has been suspended by the Attorney General will be separated from active duty and placed in standby reserve until the final report of the Secretary of Defense and the final action of the President. This is the agreement that I have reached with Senator Nunn and Senator Mitchell.... *(WCPD Clinton 1993: 108-109)*

President Clinton's Remarks Announcing the New Policy on Gays and Lesbians in the Military

July 19, 1993

...The policy I am announcing today is, in my judgment, the right thing to do and the best way to do it. It is right because it provides greater protection to those who happen to be homosexual and want to serve their country honorably in uniform, obeying all the military's rules against sexual misconduct. It is the best way to proceed because it provides a sensible balance between the rights of the individual and the needs of our military to remain the world's number one fighting force. As President of all the American people, I am pledged to protect and to promote individual rights. As Commander in Chief, I am pledged to protect and advance our security. In this policy, I believe we have come close to meeting both objectives....

Let me review the events which bring us here today. Before I ran for President, this issue was already upon us. Some of the members of the military returning from the Gulf War announced their homosexuality in order to protest the ban. The military's policy has been questioned in college ROTC programs. Legal challenges have been filed in court, including one that has since succeeded. In 1991, the Secretary of Defense, Dick Cheney, was asked about reports that the Defense Department spent an alleged $500 million to separate and replace about 17,000 homosexuals from the military service during the 1980's, in spite of the findings of a Government report saying there was no reason to believe that they could not serve effectively and with distinction. Shortly thereafter, while giving a speech at the Kennedy School of Government at Harvard, I was asked by one of the students what I thought of this report and what I thought of lifting the ban. This question had never before been presented to me, and I had never had the opportunity to discuss it with anyone. I stated then what I still believe, that I thought there ought to be a presumption that people who wish to do so should be able to serve their country if they are willing to conform to the high standards of the military and that the emphasis should be always on people's conduct, not their status....

The central facts of this issue are not much in dispute. First, notwithstanding the ban, there have been and are homosexuals in the military service who serve with distinction. I have had the privilege of meeting some of these men and women, and I have been deeply impressed by their devotion to duty and to country.

Second, there is no study showing them to be less capable or more prone to misconduct than heterosexual soldiers. Indeed, all the information we have indicates that they are not less capable or more prone to misbehavior.

Third, misconduct is already covered by the laws and rules which also cover activities that are improper by heterosexual members of the military.

Fourth, the ban has been lifted in other nations and in police and fire departments in our country with no discernible negative impact on unit cohesion or capacity to do the job, though there is, admittedly, no absolute analogy to the situation we face and no study bearing on this specific issue.

Fifth, even if the ban were lifted entirely, the experience of other nations and police and fire departments in the United States indicates that most homosexuals would probably not declare their sexual orientation openly thereby making an already hard life even more difficult in some circumstances.

But as the sociologist Charles Moskos noted after spending many years studying the American military, the issue may be tougher to resolve here in the United States than in Canada, Australia, and in some other nations because of the presence in our country of both vocal gay rights groups and equally vocal antigay rights groups, including some religious groups who believe that lifting the ban amounts to endorsing a lifestyle they strongly disapprove of....

These past few days I have been in contact with the Secretary of Defense as he has worked through the final stages of this policy with the Joint Chiefs. We now have a policy that is a substantial advance over the one in place when I took office. I have ordered Secretary Aspin to issue a directive consisting of these essential elements: One, service men and women will be judged based on their conduct, not their sexual orientation. Two, therefore the practice, now 6 months old, of not asking about sexual orientation in the enlistment procedure will continue. Three, an open statement by a service member that he or she is a homosexual will create a rebuttable presumption that he or she intends to engage in prohibited conduct, but the service member will be given an opportunity to refute that presumption; in other words, to demonstrate that he or she intends to live by the rules of conduct that apply in the military service. And four, all provisions of the Uniform Code of Military Justice will be enforced in an even-handed manner as regards both heterosexuals and homosexuals. And thanks to the policy provisions agreed to by the Joint Chiefs, there will be a decent regard to the legitimate privacy and associational rights of all service members.

Just as is the case under current policy, unacceptable conduct, either heterosexual or homosexual, will be unacceptable 24 hours a day, 7 days a week from the time a recruit joins the service until the day he or she is discharged. Now, as in the past, every member of our military will be required to comply with the Uniform Code of Military Justice, which is Federal law, and military regulations at all times and in all places....

Our military is a conservative institution, and I say that in the very best sense, for its purpose is to conserve the fighting spirit of our troops, to conserve the resources and the capacity of our troops, to conserve the military lessons acquired during our Nation's existence, to conserve our very security, and yes, to conserve the liberties of the American people. Because it is a conservative institution, it is right for the military to be wary of sudden changes. Because it is an institution that embodies the best of America and must reflect the society in which it operates it is also right for the military to make changes when the time for change is at hand....
(WCPD Clinton 1993: 1369-1373)

3

Changing Visions of the World

INTRODUCTION

The optimistic reaction of American presidents to the rapid changes in the Soviet Union, culminating in its dissolution, is reflected in the documents in this chapter. President Reagan spoke of the evolving U.S.-Soviet relationship at a time when the Soviet challenge was still intense. As the historical changes unfolded, U.S. presidents spoke of the importance of demoracy and free market institutions in the world that was evolving.

The tone of President Reagan's speech to the Cadets at West Point is noteworthy, as he referred back consciously to the "duty, honor, country" speech given there in 1962 by General of the Army Douglas MacArthur. Reagan's oratorical style was more appropriate for the old world order than the new, with its wide-ranging and ambiguous challenges to U.S. interests. The remarks of President Bush reflect not only his own less grandiloquent style, but also the nature of the confusing national security landscape that was developing.

In retrospect, the United States response to the breakup of the Soviet Union was handled better than the construction of the order that was to follow. Historians will debate for some time whether a clearer vision on the part of U.S. leaders would have produced a better result and sustained the will of the American people to support democratic institutions abroad.

DOCUMENTS

President Reagan's Address to the 42nd Session of the United Nations General Assembly

September 21, 1987

...All over the world today, the yearnings of the human heart are redirecting the course of international affairs, putting the lie to the myth of materialism and historical determinism. We have only to open our eyes to see the simple aspirations of ordinary people writ large on the record of our times.

Last year in the Philippines, ordinary people rekindled the spirit of democracy and restored the electoral process. Some said they had performed a miracle, and if so, a similar miracle — a transition to democracy — is taking place in the Republic of Korea. Haiti, too, is making a transition. Some despair when these new, young democracies face conflicts or challenges, but growing pains are normal in democracies. The United States had them, as has every other democracy on Earth.

In Latin America, too, one can hear the voices of freedom echo from the peaks and across the plains. It is the song of ordinary people marching, not in uniforms and not in military file but, rather, one by one, in simple, everyday working clothes, marching to the polls. Ten years ago only a third of the people of Latin America and the Caribbean lived in democracies or in countries that were turning to democracy; today over 90 percent do.

But this worldwide movement to democracy is not the only way in which simple, ordinary people are leading us in this room — we who are said to be the makers of history — leading us into the future. Around the world, new businesses, new economic growth, new technologies are emerging from the workshops of ordinary people with extraordinary dreams.

Here in the United States, entrepreneurial energy — reinvigorated when we cut taxes and regulations — has fueled the current economic expansion. According to scholars at the Massachusetts Institute of Technology, three-quarters of the more than 13 ½ million new jobs that we have created in this country since the beginning of our expansion came from businesses with fewer than 100 employees, businesses started by ordinary people who dared to take a chance. And many of our new high technologies were first developed in the garages of fledgling entrepreneurs. Yet America is not the only, or perhaps even the best, example of the dynamism and dreams that the freeing of markets set free.

In India and China, freer markets for farmers have led to an explosion in production. In Africa, governments are rethinking their policies, and where they are allowing greater economic freedom to farmers, crop production has improved. Meanwhile, in the newly industrialized countries of the Pacific rim, free markets in services and manufacturing as well as agriculture have led to a soaring of growth and standards of living. The ASEAN nations, Japan, Korea, and Taiwan have created the true economic miracle of the last two decades, and in each of them, much of the magic came from ordinary people who succeeded as entrepreneurs.

In Latin America, this same lesson of free markets, greater opportunity, and growth is being studied and acted on. President Sarney of Brazil spoke for many others when he said that "private initiative is the engine of economic development. In Brazil we have learned that every time the state's penetration in the economy increases, our liberty decreases." Yes, policies that release to flight ordinary people's dreams are spreading around the world. From Colombia to Turkey to Indonesia, governments are cutting taxes, reviewing their regulations, and opening opportunities for initiative.

There has been much talk in the halls of this building about the right to development. But more and more the evidence is clear that development is not itself a right. It is the product of rights: the right to own property; the right to buy and sell freely; the right to contract; the right to be free of excessive taxation and regulation, of burdensome government. There have been studies that determined that countries with low tax rates have greater growth than those with high rates....

For 40 years the United States has made it clear, its vital interest in the security of the Persian Gulf and the countries that border it. The oil reserves there are of strategic importance to the economies of the free world. We're committed to maintaining the free flow of this oil and to preventing the domination of the region by any hostile power. We do not seek confrontation or trouble with Iran or anyone else. Our object is — or, objective is now, and has been at every stage, finding a means to end the war with no victor and no vanquished. The increase in our naval presence in the Gulf does not favor one side or the other. It is a response to heightened tensions and followed consultations with our friends in the region. When the tension diminishes, so will our presence.

The United States is gratified by many recent diplomatic developments: the unanimous adoption of Resolution 598, the Arab League's statement at its recent meeting in Tunis, and the Secretary-General's visit. Yet problems remain.

The Soviet Union helped in drafting and reaching an agreement on Resolution 598, but outside the Security Council, the Soviets have acted differently. They called for removal of our Navy from the Gulf, where it has been for 40 years. They made the false accusation that somehow the United States, rather than the war itself, is the source of tension in the Gulf. Well, such statements are not helpful. They divert attention from the challenge facing us all: a just end to the war. The United States hopes the Soviets will join the other members of the Security Council in vigorously seeking an end to a conflict that never should have begun, should have ended long ago, and has become one of the great tragedies of the postwar era.

Elsewhere in the region, we see the continuing Soviet occupation of Afghanistan. After nearly 8 years, a million casualties, nearly 4 million others driven into exile, and more intense fighting than ever, it's time for the Soviet Union to leave. The Afghan people must have the right to determine their own future free of foreign coercion. There is no excuse for prolonging a brutal war or propping up a regime whose days are clearly numbered. That regime offers political proposals that pretend compromise, but really would ensure the perpetuation of the regime's power. Those proposals have failed the only significant test: They have been rejected by the Afghan people. Every day the resistance grows in strength. It is an indispensable party in the quest for a negotiated solution. The world community must continue to insist on genuine self-determination, prompt and full Soviet withdrawal, and the return of the refugees to their homes in safety and honor. The attempt may be made to pressure a few countries to change their vote this year but this body, I know, will vote overwhelmingly, as every year before, for Afghan independence and freedom. We have noted General Secretary Gorbachev's statement of readiness to withdraw. In April I asked the Soviet Union to set a date this year when this withdrawal would begin. I repeat that request now in this forum for peace. I pledge that, once the Soviet Union shows convincingly that it's ready for a genuine political settlement, the United States is ready to be helpful.

Let me add one final note on this matter. Pakistan, in the face of enormous pressure and intimidation, has given sanctuary to Afghan refugees. We salute the courage of Pakistan and the Pakistani people. They deserve strong support from all of us.

Another regional conflict, we all know, is taking place in Central America, in Nicaragua. To the Sandinista delegation here today I say: Your people know the true nature of your regime. They have seen their liberties suppressed. They have seen the promises of 1979 go unfulfilled. They have seen their real wages and personal income fall by half — yes, half — since 1979, while your party elite live lives of privilege and luxury. This is why, despite a billion dollars in Soviet-bloc aid last year alone, despite the largest and best equipped army in Central America, you face a popular revolution at home. It is why the democratic resistance is able to operate freely deep in your heartland. But this revolution should come as no surprise to you; it is only the revolution you promised the people and that you then betrayed.

The goal of United States policy toward Nicaragua is simple. It is the goal of the Nicaraguan people and the freedom fighters, as well. It is democracy — real, free, pluralistic, constitutional democracy. Understand this: We will not, and the world community will not, accept phony democratization designed to mask the perpetuation of dictatorship. In this 200th year of our own Constitution, we know that real democracy depends on the safeguards of an institutional structure that prevents a concentration of power. It is that which makes rights secure. The temporary relaxation of controls, which can later be tightened, is not democratization.

And, again, to the Sandinistas, I say: We continue to hope that Nicaragua will become part of the genuine democratic transformation that we have seen throughout Central America in this decade. We applaud the principles embodied in the Guatemala agreement, which links the security of the Central

American democracies to democratic reform in Nicaragua. Now is the time for you to shut down the military machine that threatens your neighbors and assaults your own people. You must end your stranglehold on internal political activity. You must hold free and fair national elections. The media must be truly free, not censored or intimidated or crippled by indirect measures, like the denial of newsprint or threats against journalists or their families. Exiles must be allowed to return to minister, to live, to work, and to organize politically. Then, when persecution of religion has ended and the jails no longer contain political prisoners, national reconciliation and democracy will be possible. Unless this happens, democratization will be a fraud. And until it happens, we will press for true democracy by supporting those fighting for it....

We're heartened by new prospects for improvement in East-West and particularly U.S.-Soviet relations. Last week Soviet Foreign Minister Shevardnadze visited Washington for talks with me and with the Secretary of State, Shultz. We discussed the full range of issues, including my longstanding efforts to achieve, for the first time, deep reductions in U.S. and Soviet nuclear arms. It was 6 years ago, for example, that I proposed the zero-option for U.S. and Soviet longer range, intermediate-range nuclear missiles. I'm pleased that we have now agreed in principle to a truly historic treaty that will eliminate an entire class of U.S. and Soviet nuclear weapons. We also agreed to intensify our diplomatic efforts in all areas of mutual interest. Toward that end, Secretary Shultz and the Foreign Minister will meet again a month from now in Moscow, and I will meet again with General Secretary Gorbachev later this fall.

We continue to have our differences and probably always will. But that puts a special responsibility on us to find ways — realistic ways — to bring greater stability to our competition and to show the world a constructive example of the value of communication and of the possibility of peaceful solutions to political problems. And here let me add that we seek, through our Strategic Defense Initiative, to find a way to keep peace through relying on defense, not offense, for deterrence and for eventually rendering ballistic missiles obsolete. SDI has greatly enhanced the prospects for real arms reduction. It is a crucial part of our efforts to ensure a safer world and a more stable strategic balance.

We will continue to pursue the goal of arms reduction, particularly the goal that the General Secretary and I agreed upon: a 50-percent reduction in our respective strategic nuclear arms. We will continue to press the Soviets for more constructive conduct in the settling of regional conflicts. We look to the Soviets to honor the Helsinki accords. We look for greater freedom for the Soviet peoples within their country, more people-to-people exchanges with our country, and Soviet recognition in practice of the right of freedom of movement....

We hear much about changes in the Soviet Union. We're intensely interested in these changes. We hear the word *glasnost*, which is translated as "openness" in English. "Openness" is a broad term. It means the free, unfettered flow of information, ideas, and people. It means political and intellectual liberty in all its dimensions. We hope, for the sake of the peoples of the U.S.S.R., that such changes will come. And we hope, for the sake of peace, that it will include a foreign policy that respects the freedom and independence of other peoples....
(PPP Reagan 1987 II: 1058-1063)

President Reagan's Remarks at the United States Military Academy in West Point

October 28, 1987

...From the beginning, our administration has insisted that this country base its relations with the Soviet Union upon realism, not illusion. Now, this may sound obvious, but when we took office, the historical record needed restatement. So, restate it we did. We told the truth about the massive Soviet buildup. We told the truth about Afghanistan and Poland. We told the truth about economic growth and standards of living — that it is not the democracies that have backward economies, that it is not the Western World in which life expectancy is actually on the decline. We told the truth about the moral distinction between their system and ours.

When our administration took office, we found America's military forces in a state of disrepair. Today the situation is very different. Pay and training for our Armed Forces are up. The Navy has been expanded. Weapons systems of all kinds have been modernized, making full use of the technological revolution. As a result of our efforts, you in the Army will see the fielding of more than 400 new systems. And we've begun work upon a dramatic, new departure, both in military strategy and technology; our Strategic Defense Initiative, which offers the hope of rendering ballistic missiles obsolete and of ensuring deterrence by protecting lives, not threatening them. In brief: We have replaced weakness with strength.

To turn now from background to specific substance, the agenda of our relations with the Soviet Union has focused upon four critical areas: first, human rights, because freedom is what we stand for as Americans; second, negotiated settlements to regional conflicts; third, expanded exchanges between our peoples; and fourth, arms reduction.

In some areas of this four-part agenda, we have seen progress. Cultural, scientific, and other bilateral exchanges have shown a dramatic increase since my 1985 meeting with Mr. Gorbachev in Geneva. In human rights, too, we've seen some positive developments. Some political prisoners have been released. Emigration figures are up somewhat. And of course, there's talk of reform in the Soviet Union, of some liberalizing changes in Soviet laws, and of economic reforms that could give greater scope to individual initiative.

We harbor no illusions: While changes have taken place in the Soviet system, the one-party system unchecked by democratic institutions remains unchanged. And yet we welcome such changes as have taken place, and we call upon them to make still more. It is in regional conflicts where Soviet performance has been most disturbing. Anyone searching for evidence that the Soviets remain expansionist, indeed imperialist, need look no farther than Nicaragua or Afghanistan.

Our policy in these regional conflicts is straightforward. We will continue to engage the Soviets, seeking to find political solutions to regional conflicts, solutions that eliminate foreign troops and return the fate of nations to their own people. In Nicaragua, we support the peace plan agreed upon by the Central American Presidents last August, insisting upon the establishment of full and genuine democracy in Nicaragua. Moreover, Soviet-bloc and Cuban forces must leave that nation; this is essential to protect our own security.

As for the democratic resistance in Nicaragua, year upon year, for 7 years now, they have fought and sacrificed and endured. It is the resistance — the brave members of the resistance, many of them no more than teenagers — who have kept the Communist Sandinistas from consolidating their power and forced them into the current peace plan. It is the resistance, in short, that has given Nicaragua at least a chance for true freedom. And my friends, I know you agree: We must not abandon these courageous men and women, these soldiers. So, let me promise: Nicaragua will have its freedom. And we will help the resistance carry on its brave fight until freedom is secure.

And this brings me to the final area on our agenda for U.S.-Soviet relations: arms reductions. For here our realism and commitment are close to producing historic results. It was in 1977 that the Soviet Union first deployed the SS-20. The SS-20 was, as you know, a qualitatively new and unprovoked threat against our friends and allies, a triple-warhead nuclear missile capable of striking anywhere in Western Europe and much of Asia mere minutes after being launched. You must remember that NATO had no comparable weapon in its arsenal with which to counter this new force.

By 1979 the Soviets had deployed some 130 INF missiles, with 390 warheads. General Secretary Brezhnev declared that "a balance now exists." In March 1982 they declared a moratorium on the deployment of new INF missiles in Europe. But this was only a cover, and by August of 1982, the number of Soviet INF missiles had climbed to over 300, with more than 900 warheads.

How did the West respond? In 1977 Chancellor Helmut Schmidt of West Germany led the call for the deployment of NATO's own INF missiles to counter this new Soviet threat. And in December 1979 NATO made a two-track decision. First, the United States would negotiate with the Soviets, attempting to persuade them to withdraw the SS-20's. And second, as long as the Soviets refused to do so, the United States would indeed deploy a limited number of its own INF missiles — Pershing II and ground-launched cruise missiles — in Europe....

I'm pleased to say that the agreement we're nearing is based upon the proposal that the United States, in consultation with our allies, first put forward in 1981: the zero-option. The zero-option calls very simply for the elimination of this entire class of U.S. and Soviet INF missiles. According to this agreement, the Soviets will be required to remove four times as many nuclear warheads as will the United States. Moreover, the Soviets will be required to destroy not only their entire force of SS-20's and SS-4's but also their shorter range ballistic missiles, the SS-12's and SS-23's. As I said, all these missiles will be eliminated....

Now, some have argued that when the INF missiles have been removed, our commitment to Europe will have been weakened. Yet this is simply untrue. We maintain our firm commitment to the NATO strategy of flexible response, ensuring that the alliance is capable of blocking aggression at any level. In Europe itself, we will retain a large force of many types, including ground-based systems and aircraft and submarines capable of delivering nuclear weapons. And in consultation with our NATO allies, we've agreed that further nuclear reductions can take place only in the context of a substantial improvement in the balance of chemical and conventional forces.... *(PPP Reagan 1987 II: 1238-1242)*

White House Fact Sheet on the National Security Strategy Report
March 20, 1990

The President today transmitted to Congress his report on the national security strategy of the United States as required by the 1986 amendment to the National Security Act. The 32-page report reflects the recent dramatic changes in the international environment and outlines U.S. policies to both shape and respond to these changes. It observes that we have reached a moment of historic opportunity, one created by the success of our postwar strategy. Highlights of the report include:

- A policy that moves beyond containment and supports the integration of the Soviet Union into the international system.
- The goal of a new Europe, whole and free, as Eastern European States rejoin the European cultural and political tradition that is their heritage.
- A commitment to a strengthened Europe ... in an Atlantic alliance that remains rooted in shared values and that will continue to sustain the overall structure of stability in Europe.

- Support for German unification coming about through peaceful means, on the basis of democracy, and in the framework of Western relationships that have nurtured freedom for four decades, including full German membership in NATO.
- Continued commitment to advance the march of democracy and freedom in the Western hemisphere.
- Recognition of the continuing importance of East Asia and the Pacific, the vital role our security ties play there, and the need to sustain a dialog with China.
- Renewed commitment to an arms control agenda broader than ever before with a goal of agreements this year in START, CFE, chemical weapons, and Open Skies.
- Recognition that our economic well-being is the foundation of America's long-term strength and that, in a new era, we must assess which risks can be ameliorated by means other than military capabilities— means like negotiations, burden sharing, economic and security assistance, economic leverage, and political leadership.
- A commitment to adapting U.S. military power to a strategy that looks beyond containment and provides us capabilities appropriate to new opportunities and challenges.
- A movement to a smaller military, one more global in its orientation, responsive to changes in warning time, and well-suited to the demands of likely contingencies. This includes improved capabilities for the unique requirements posed by potential Third World battlefields, themselves growing in complexity and lethality.
- Changing patterns of U.S. forward deployments as adjustments are made based on new perceptions of the threat the improved reach of our forces and the growing capabilities of our allies.
- Burden sharing marked by growing national specialization in defense activities. For the United States this would include nuclear and space forces, advanced technologies, strategic mobility, a worldwide presence, power projection, and a secure mobilization base.
- Identification of drug interdiction as a high-priority national security requirement.
- A restatement that deterrence of nuclear attack remains the cornerstone of U.S. strategy and meeting the requirements of strategic deterrence will remain our first priority.

The report outlines the historical roots of U.S. security strategy: our fundamental values as a people, our tradition of joining in common cause with those who share our values, our commitment to an open international economic system, and the strategic demands placed on us by geography.

The report also points out that America's basic goals are enduring:

- The survival of the United States as a free and independent nation, with its fundamental values intact and its institutions secure.
- A healthy and growing U.S. economy to ensure opportunity for individual prosperity and a resource base for national endeavors at home and abroad.
- A stable and secure world, fostering political freedom, human rights, and democratic institutions.
- Healthy, cooperative, and politically vigorous relations with allies and friendly nations.

The report explains that the fundamental challenge is to relate the means available to these enduring goals in a world marked by change that is breathtaking in its character, scope, and pace. It is clearly a time of great hope accompanied by the recognition that the future world will not automatically be a safer one for American interests or values. Elements of change that deserve special attention are:

- The democratic restructuring of Eastern Europe and the potential that exists for instability as these states enter uncharted territory.
- A shifting balance of global economic power and the danger that trade disputes could strain political and security ties.
- The proliferation of advanced weaponry, especially weapons of mass destruction and associated delivery systems, to Third World states.
- The growth of threats like illicit drug trafficking, subversion, and terrorism, which are often fed by poverty, injustice, and ethnic or religious strife.

The report also emphasizes that even with great change there will be substantial continuity. The United States will remain fully engaged in the larger world and will continue to pursue its objectives in concert with those who share its values and concerns. Our approach to security will continue to be shaped by the fact that we are a nation separated by large oceans from many of our most important friends and interests. As a global power the United States will continue to bear primary responsibility for deterring global war and will defend the interests it has in common with its allies as far forward as possible. And this will still require the presence of American forces overseas backed up by an ability to project power from the United States.... *(PPP Bush 1990 I: 389-390)*

President Bush's Address to the 46th Session of the United Nations General Assembly

September 23, 1991

...Communism held history captive for years. It suspended ancient disputes, and it suppressed ethnic rivalries, nationalist aspirations, and old prejudices. As it has dissolved, suspended hatreds have sprung to life. People who for years have been denied their pasts have begun searching for their own identities, often through peaceful and constructive means, occasionally through factionalism and bloodshed.

This revival of history ushers in a new era teeming with opportunities and perils. And let's begin by discussing the opportunities. First, history's renewal enables people to pursue their natural instincts for enterprise. Communism froze that progress until its failures became too much for even its defenders to bear. And now citizens throughout the world have chosen enterprise over envy, personal responsibility over the enticements of the state, prosperity over the poverty of central planning.

The U.N. Charter encourages this adventure by pledging "to employ international machinery for the promotion of the economic and social advancement of all peoples." And I can think of no better way to fulfill this mission than to promote the free flow of goods and ideas. Frankly, ideas and goods will travel around the globe with or without our help. The information revolution has destroyed the weapons of enforced isolation and ignorance. In many parts of the world technology has overwhelmed tyranny, proving that the age of information can become the age of liberation if we limit state power wisely and free our People to make the best use of new ideas, inventions, and insights.

By the same token, the world has learned that free markets provide levels of prosperity, growth, and happiness that centrally planned economies can never offer. Even the most charitable estimates indicate that in recent years the free world's economies have grown at twice the rate of the former Communist world.

Growth does more than fill shelves. It permits every person to gain, not at the expense of others but to the benefit of others. Prosperity encourages people to live as neighbors, not as predators. Economic growth can aid international relations in exactly the same way. Many nations represented here are parties to the General Agreement on Tariffs and Trade. The Uruguay round, the latest in the postwar series of trade negotiations, offers hope to developing nations, many of which have been cruelly deceived by the false promises of totalitarianism.

Here in this chamber we hear about North-South problems. But free and open trade, including unfettered access to markets and credit, offer developing countries means of self-sufficiency and economic dignity. If the Uruguay round should fail, a new wave of protectionism could destroy our hopes for a better future. History shows all too clearly that protectionism can destroy wealth within countries and poison relations between them. And therefore, I call upon all members of GATT to redouble their efforts to reach a successful conclusion for the Uruguay round. I pledge that the United States will do its part.

I cannot stress this enough: Economic progress will play a vital role in the new world. It supplies the soil in which democracy grows best. People everywhere seek government of and by the people. And they want to enjoy their inalienable rights to freedom and property and person.

Challenges to democracy have failed. Just last month coup plotters in the Soviet Union tried to derail the forces of liberty and reform, but Soviet citizens refused to follow. Most of the nations in this Chamber stood with the forces of reform, led by Mikhail Gorbachev and Boris Yeltsin, and against the coup plotters.

The challenge facing the Soviet peoples now, that of building political systems based upon individual liberty, minority rights, democracy, and free markets, mirrors every nation's responsibility for encouraging peaceful, democratic reform. But it also testifies to the extraordinary power of the democratic ideal.

As democracy flourishes, so does the opportunity for a third historical breakthrough, international cooperation. A year ago, the Soviet Union joined the United States and a host of other nations in defending a tiny country against aggression and opposing Saddam Hussein. For the very first time on a matter of major importance, superpower competition was replaced with international cooperation. The United Nations, in one of its finest moments, constructed a measured, principled, deliberate, and courageous response to Saddam Hussein. It stood up to an outlaw who invaded Kuwait, who threatened many states within the region, who sought to set a menacing precedent for the post-cold-war world. The coalition effort established a model for the collective settlement of disputes. Members set the goal, the liberation of Kuwait, and devised a courageous, unified means of achieving that goal....

In Europe and Asia, nationalist passions have flared anew, challenging borders, straining the fabric of international society. At the same time, around the world, many age-old conflicts still fester. You see signs of this tumult right here. The United Nations has mounted more peacekeeping missions in the last 36 months than during its first 43 years. And although we now seem mercifully liberated from the fear of nuclear holocaust, these smaller, virulent conflicts should trouble us all. We must face this challenge squarely: First, by pursuing the peaceful resolution of disputes now in progress; second and more importantly, by trying to prevent others from erupting.

No one here can promise that today's borders will remain fixed for all time. But we must strive to ensure the peaceful, negotiated settlement of border disputes. We also must promote the cause of international harmony by addressing old feuds. We should take seriously the charter's pledge "to practice tolerance and live together in peace with one another as good neighbors."...

The renewal of history also imposes an obligation to remain vigilant about new threats and old. We must expand our efforts to control nuclear proliferation. We must work to prevent the spread of chemical and biological weapons and the missiles to deliver them. It is for this reason that I put forward my Middle East arms initiative, a comprehensive approach to stop and, where possible, reverse the accumulation of arms in that part of the world most prone to violence....

In a world defined by change, we must be as firm in principle as we are flexible in our response to changing international conditions. That's especially true today of Iraq. Six months after the passage of U.N. Security Council Resolutions 687 and 688, Saddam continues to rebuild his weapons of mass destruction and subject the Iraqi people to brutal repression. Saddam's contempt for U.N. resolutions was first demonstrated back in August of 1990. And it continues even as I am speaking. His government refuses to permit unconditional helicopter inspections and right now is refusing to allow U.N. inspectors to leave inspected premises with documents relating to an Iraqi nuclear weapons program.

And it is the United States view that we must keep the United Nations sanctions in place as long as he remains in power. And this also shows that we cannot compromise for a moment in seeing that Iraq destroys all of its weapons of mass destruction and the means to deliver them. And we will not compromise.

This is not to say, and let me be clear on this one, that we should punish the Iraqi people. Let me repeat, our argument has never been with the people of Iraq. It was and is with a brutal dictator whose arrogance dishonors the Iraqi people. Security Council Resolution 706 created a responsible mechanism for sending humanitarian relief to innocent Iraqi citizens. We must put that mechanism to work.

We must not abandon our principled stand against Saddam's aggression. This cooperative effort has liberated Kuwait, and now it can lead to a just government in Iraq. And when it does, when it does, the Iraqi people can look forward to better lives, free at home, free to engage in a world beyond their borders....

(PPP Bush 1991 II: 1199-1203)

4

From Cold War to an Uncertain Alliance

INTRODUCTION

The centerpiece of the changes from 1987 to 1994 remains the breakup of the Soviet Union and the resulting security implications of that momentous change. Despite all the problems unleashed by the breakup, including the eruption of instability in Southeastern Europe and in the Caucasus, it is well to pause and reflect on the problem that has passed: war between the United States and the Soviet Union and their respective allies. This does not mean that conflict between the United States and Russia, the major residual component of the Soviet Union, could never resume, but it should be avoidable and there is much for which to be grateful.

As noted in Chapter One, the period saw the collapse of the Soviet empire in 1989 (Central Europe) and the Russian empire in 1991 (the Soviet Union). There are also significant strains on the empire of the Moscow Rus (Russia itself), calling into question the territorial integrity of the Russian Federation. American policy evolved, as well. Initial disbelief was replaced with an outpouring of optimism about the future of Russia and Russian-American relations. This optimism was at least partly misplaced, since Russia remains a country with no democratic tradition and over seventy years of mismanagement by an inefficient economic system and a corrupt political administration. That such a country should have difficulties in its transition to democracy and a market economy should surprise no one.

The Soviet breakup and subsequent power vacuum in Eastern Europe (actually Central Europe) posed two serious strategic questions for the West: how should the former "satellite" states of the Soviet Union (Poland, the former Czechoslovakia, Hungary, Rumania, and Bulgaria) be integrated as quickly as possible into Western economic, political, and perhaps military structures, and what should be the mission and membership of the North

Atlantic Treaty Organization (NATO)? Economic integration, while not directly threatning to Russia, was stymied by the vastly differing levels of economic development and quality of manufactured products between East and West. Economic integration of Central Europe with the West was a more serious concern for the Soviet Union in 1947 and 1948, and was a main reason for the Soviet decision not to participate in the Marshall Plan for the reconstruction of Europe. The Soviets wanted the Central European states tied to them, not to the capitalist West.

NATO has not yet determined its future role. Now that the number of United States forces in Europe has declined significantly, the influence of the U.S. on NATO decisions is also declining. American leadership of the alliance was not preordained or based on superior strategic judgments, but was supported by American military power and the contribution this made to NATO credibility. NATO's relationship to the former Warsaw Pact states and to the states of the former Soviet Union is also evolving, with many of the states wishing to be under the NATO umbrella. But NATO, understandably, is reluctant to extend its security degrees to the border of Russia. Such commitments would be difficult to fulfill, and the effect on Russian domestic politics of such an expansion is likely to be negative with respect to Western interests.

U.S.-SOVIET RELATIONS

U.S. Inspects Soviet Military Exercise

September 22, 1987

On August 30, 1987, the United States successfully completed the first-ever on site inspection of a Soviet military exercise. We are today releasing a public report on the inspection. This inspection was under the terms of the document of the Stockholm Conference on Confidence- and Security-Building Measures and Disarmament in Europe (CDE), which was signed a year ago this month.

The U.S. request to inspect the exercise, which took place northeast of the city of Minsk, was submitted to the Soviet Union through normal diplomatic channels on August 26. The Soviet Union responded positively to the U.S. request on August 27, several hours before the deadline established by the Stockholm document and permitted the U.S. team to enter the Soviet Union within the 36-hour time period specified in the document. Our inspectors conducted their inspection for 48 hours.

A U.S. inspection report — which is confidential — has been forwarded to all CSCE participating states in accordance with the document. The United States has concluded on the basis of this inspection that the Soviet activity in question conformed to the provisions of the document. The United States is satisfied with the Soviet Union's positive approach to this first-ever on-site inspection under CDE auspices.

We consider the successful conclusion of this inspection a step in the process of improving openness and enhancing confidence and security-building in Europe....

On August 26, 1987, the United States elected to exercise its right under paragraphs 65 and 66 of the Stockholm Document to conduct an inspection of a Soviet military activity taking place in the Belorussian Military District, northeast of Minsk in the U.S.S.R. The activity to be inspected had been notified by the Soviet Union on July 13 as a military exercise of ground forces involving elements of one tank and one motorized rifle division, 16,000 troops and 425 tanks. A request for inspection was submitted simultaneously to the Soviet Foreign Ministry in Moscow and the Soviet Embassy in Washington at 1800 hours Greenwich Mean Time (GMT) on August 26. The Soviet reply. to the inspection request was received in Moscow at 1500 hours GMT on August 27 and was also provided in Washington approximately 45 minutes later. The Soviet response granted the request and indicated that the U.S. inspection team would be permitted to enter the Soviet Union within 36 hours of the time the request was made as required by the document....

In the inspection request the United States had indicated that the inspection team planned to travel to the U.S.S.R. via U.S. Government aircraft and land at a military airfield southeast of Minsk. The Soviet response permitted that inspection team to fly to Minsk but indicated that the flight should land at the Minsk civilian airfield. The United States did not object to this change. A Soviet escort crew, consisting of a navigator and an interpreter, accompanied the U.S. aircraft from Stuttgart to Minsk....

In the request, the United States sought two helicopters for the duration of the inspection. The official Soviet reply had indicated that only one would be provided. However, when the inspection team renewed its request for two helicopters upon arrival in Minsk, two Soviet MI-8/HIP helicopters were provided and made available throughout the inspection. Two ground vehicles also were provided....

The inspection team made extensive use of the ground vehicles throughout the course of inspection. Drivers followed inspectors' instructions without difficulty. However, the Soviets, citing safety concerns, required permanent observation points in the Borisov training area. At all times, inspectors were accompanied by Soviet military officers.

Whether in helicopters or ground vehicles, constant communication between the subgroups was provided and was generally of excellent quality. The inspectors utilized both air-to-air and ground-to-ground communications. For ground-to-ground, a Soviet communication van accompanied each land inspection vehicle at all times. Due to the limited use of the helicopters, no opportunity was presented to use air-to-ground communications.

The inspection team experienced no interference with the full use of the equipment they were permitted under the terms of the document (i.e., maps, photo-cameras, binoculars, dicta phones, and aeronautical charts). For their own part, the Soviets also made a photographic record of the inspection.

The inspectors were not permitted, in accordance with the document, to enter or overfly certain points designated by the Soviets as sensitive points — specific installations surrounded by fences or walls. However, in general, the concept of sensitive points and/or restricted areas did not appear to be used to obstruct the conduct of the inspection....

The inspection team's initial overflights of the specified area made it clear that the phase of the exercise being conducted during the inspection was largely confined to the Borisov training area.

Upon arrival at the Borisov training area, the team was met by the exercise director, Commander of the Belorussian Military District. He told the inspectors that the exercise consisted of a tank division attacking from the south against a motorized rifle division from the north. The concept of the training, he said, was the conduct of the defense by the motorized rifle division and the attack by the tank division with a forced river crossing. He stated that the preparatory phase of the exercise would end August 28 and that the practical phase of the exercise would be conducted on August 29-30. He also indicated that the defending motorized rifle division has three motorized rifle regiments and one tank regiment, while the tank division consisted of two tank regiments and one motorized rifle regiment.

Following the briefing, the team undertook a systematic inspection of the Borisov training area, once again dividing into two subteams — one to inspect the northern force, the other to inspect the southern force. The team walked tank lines, visited units, and photographed equipment and personnel without interference. Observation of the attack, counterattack, and meeting engagement was only from prepared observation points, but the team moved freely among the participating forces between events. Inspectors observed prepared defensive positions and spoke to unit commanders about the size of their forces. The inspection team was not prevented from speaking directly with the troops participating in the exercise. During the 48-hour inspection period, the team also inspected the Minsk training area, which was also in the specified area. No significant military activity was found there....

Based on the inspection team's findings, the United States also concludes that the purpose of the activity was in conformity with the purpose stated in the notification.

While some questions of procedures and interpretation were raised during the course of the inspection which will require further consideration, the United States is satisfied by the positive approach demonstrated by the Soviet Union in its treatment of the inspection request and of the inspection team.

The United States welcomes the spirit of cooperation shown by many Soviet officers and enlisted men toward the inspectors and hopes that this spirit will extend to others as participating states gain more experience in security-building measures (CSBMs).

This inspection has demonstrated the significant and essential contribution which inspection can make to the confidence-building process. As a means of resolving uncertainties about military activities in Europe, it reinforces all the other measures and is an integral component of the CSBMs regime.

The United States believes that one of the significant achievements of the Stockholm document is its contribution to the process of increasing openness and transparency in the military-security sphere in Europe. The implementation of the inspection provisions is a vital and positive step in that process and an encouraging development for East-West relations.
(DSB, November 1987: 44-46)

Joint Statement on the Soviet-United States Summit Meeting
December 10, 1987

Ronald W. Reagan, President of the United States of America, and Mikhail S. Gorbachev, General Secretary of the Central Committee of the Communist Party of the Soviet Union, met in Washington on December 7-10, 1987....

I. Arms Control
The INF Treaty

The two leaders signed the Treaty between the United States of America and the Union of Soviet Socialist Republics on the Elimination of Their Intermediate-Range and Shorter-Range Missiles. This treaty is historic both for its objective — the complete elimination of an entire class of U.S. and Soviet nuclear arms — and for the innovative character and scope of its verification provisions. This mutual accomplishment makes a vital contribution to greater stability.

Nuclear and Space Talks

The President and the General Secretary discussed the negotiations on reductions in strategic offensive arms. They noted the considerable progress which has been made toward conclusion of a treaty implementing the principle of 50-percent reductions. They agreed to instruct their negotiators in Geneva to work toward the completion of the Treaty on the Reduction and Limitation of Strategic Offensive Arms and all integral documents at the earliest possible date, preferably in time for signature of the treaty during the next meeting of leaders of state in the first half of 1988. Recognizing that areas of agreement and disagreement are recorded in detail in the Joint Draft Treaty Text, they agreed to instruct their negotiators to accelerate resolution of issues within the Joint Draft Treaty Text including early agreement on provisions for effective verification.

In so doing, the negotiators should build upon the agreements on 50-percent reductions achieved at Reykjavik as subsequently developed and now reflected in the agreed portions of the Joint Draft START Treaty Text being developed in Geneva, including agreement on ceilings of no more than 1600 strategic offensive delivery systems, 6000 warheads, 1540 warheads on 154 heavy missiles; the agreed rule of account for heavy bombers and their nuclear armament; and an agreement that as a result of the reductions the aggregate throw-weight of the Soviet Union's ICBMs and SLBMs will be reduced to a level approximately 50-percent below the existing level, and this level will not be exceeded by either side. Such an agreement will be recorded in a mutually satisfactory manner.

As priority tasks, they should focus on the following issues:

(a) The additional steps necessary to ensure that the reductions enhance strategic stability. This will include a ceiling of 4900 on the aggregate number of ICBM plus SLBM warheads within the 6000 total.

(b) The counting rules governing the number of long-range, nuclear-armed air-launched cruise missiles (ALCMs) to be attributed to each type of heavy bomber. The Delegations shall define concrete rules in this area.

(c) The counting rules with respect to existing ballistic missiles. The sides proceed from the assumption that existing types of ballistic missiles are deployed with the following numbers of warheads. In the United States: PEACE KEEPER (MX): 10, MINUTEMAN III: 3, MINUTEMAN II: 1, TRIDENT I: 8, TRIDENT II: 8, POSEIDON: 10. In the Soviet Union: SS-17: 4, SS-19: 6, SS-18: 10, SS-24: 10, SS-25: 1, SS-11: 1, SS-13: 1, SS-N-6: 1, SS-N-8: 1, SS-N-17: 1, SS-N-18: 7, SS-N-20: 10 and SS-N-23: 4. Procedures will be developed that enable Verification of the number of warheads on deployed ballistic missiles of each specific type. In the event either side changes the number of warheads declared for a type of deployed ballistic missile, the sides shall notify each other in advance. There shall also be agreement on how to account for warheads on future types of ballistic missiles covered by the Treaty on the Reduction and Limitation of Strategic Offensive Arms.

(d) The sides shall find a mutually acceptable solution to the question of limiting the deployment of long-range, nuclear armed SLCMs. Such limitations will not involve counting long-range, nuclear armed SLCMs within the 6000 warhead and 1600 strategic offensive delivery systems limits. The sides committed themselves to establish ceilings on such missiles, and to seek mutually acceptable and effective methods of verification of such limitations, which could include the employment of National Technical Means, cooperative measures and on-site inspection.

(e) Building upon the provisions of the Treaty on the Elimination of Intermediate-Range and Shorter-Range Missiles, the measures by which the provisions of the Treaty on the Reduction and Limitation of Strategic Offensive Arms can be verified will, at a minimum, include:

1. Data exchanges, to include declarations by each side of the number and location of weapon systems limited by the Treaty and of facilities at which such systems are located and appropriate notifications. These facilities will include locations and facilities for production and final assembly, storage, testing, and deployment of systems covered by this Treaty. Such declarations will be exchanged between the sides before the Treaty is signed and updated periodically after entry into force.
2. Baseline inspection to verify the accuracy of these declarations promptly after entry into force of the Treaty.
3. On-site observation of the elimination of strategic systems necessary to achieve the agreed limits.
4. Continuous on-site monitoring of the perimeter and portals of critical production and support facilities to confirm the output of these facilities.
5. Short-notice on-site inspection of:
   (i) declared locations during the process of reducing to agreed limits;
   (ii) locations where systems covered by this Treaty remain after achieving the agreed limits; and
   (iii) locations where such systems have been located (formerly declared facilities).
6. The right to implement, in accordance with agreed-upon procedures, short-notice inspections at locations where either side considers covert deployment, production, storage or repair of strategic offensive arms could be occurring.
7. Provisions prohibiting the use of concealment or other activities which impede verification by national technical means. Such provisions would include a ban on telemetry encryption and would allow for full access to all telemetric information broadcast during missile flight.
8. Measures designed to enhance observation of activities related to reduction and limitation of strategic offensive arms by National Technical Means. These would include open displays of treaty-

limited items at missile bases, bomber bases, and submarine ports at locations and times chosen by the inspecting party.

Taking into account the preparation of the Treaty on Strategic Offensive Arms, the leaders of the two countries also instructed their delegations in Geneva to work out an agreement that would commit the sides to observe the ABM Treaty, as signed in 1972, while conducting their research, development, and testing as required, which are permitted by the ABM Treaty, and not to withdraw from the ABM Treaty, for a specified period of time. Intensive discussions of strategic stability shall begin not later than three years before the end of the specified period, after which, in the event the sides have not agreed otherwise, each side will be free to decide its course of action. Such an agreement must have the same legal status as the Treaty on Strategic Offensive Arms, the ABM Treaty, and other similar, legally binding agreements. This agreement will be recorded in a mutually satisfactory manner. Therefore, they direct their delegations to address these issues on a priority basis.

The sides shall discuss ways to ensure predictability in the development of the U.S.-Soviet strategic relationship under conditions of strategic stability, to reduce the risk of nuclear war.

Other Arms Control Issues

The President and the General Secretary reviewed a broad range of other issues concerning arms limitation and reduction. The sides emphasized the importance of productive negotiations on security matters and advancing in the main areas of arms limitation and reduction through equitable, verifiable agreements that enhance security and stability.

Nuclear Testing

The two leaders welcomed the opening on November 9, 1987, of full-scale, step-by-step negotiations, in accordance with the joint Statement adopted in Washington on September 17, 1987, by the Secretary of State of the United States and the Minister of Foreign Affairs of the USSR.

The U.S. and Soviet sides have agreed to begin before December 1, 1987, full-scale stage-by-stage negotiations which will be conducted in a single forum. In these negotiations the sides as the first step will agree upon effective verification measures which will make it possible to ratify the U.S.-USSR Threshold Test Ban Treaty of 1974 and Peaceful Nuclear Explosions Treaty of 1976, and proceed to negotiating further intermediate limitations on nuclear testing leading to the ultimate objective of the complete cessation of nuclear testing as part of an effective disarmament process. This process, among other things, would pursue, as the first priority, the goal of the reduction of nuclear weapons and, ultimately, their elimination. For the purpose of the elaboration of improved verification measures for the U.S.-USSR Treaties of 1974 and 1976 the sides intend to design and conduct joint verification experiments at each other's test sites.

These verification measures will, to the extent appropriate, be used in further nuclear test limitation agreements which may subsequently be reached.

The leaders also welcomed the prompt agreement by the sides to exchange experts' visits to each other's nuclear testing sites in January 1988 and to design and subsequently to conduct a Joint Verification Experiment at each other's test site. The terms of reference for the Experiment are set forth in the Statement issued on December 9, 1987, by the Foreign Ministers of the United States and the Soviet Union. The leaders noted the value of these agreements for developing more effective measures to verify compliance with the provisions of the 1974 Threshold Test Ban Treaty and the 1976 Peaceful Nuclear Explosions Treaty.

Nuclear Non-Proliferation

The President and the General Secretary reaffirmed the continued commitment of the United States and the Soviet Union to the non-proliferation of nuclear weapons, and in particular to strengthening the Treaty on the Non-Proliferation of Nuclear Weapons. The two leaders expressed satisfaction at the adherence since their last meeting of additional parties to the Treaty, and confirmed their intent to make, together with other states, additional efforts to achieve universal adherence to the Treaty.

The President and the General Secretary expressed support for international cooperation in nuclear safety and for efforts to promote the peaceful uses of nuclear energy, under further strengthened IAEA safeguards and appropriate export controls for nuclear materials, equipment and technology. The leaders agreed that bilateral consultations on non-proliferation were constructive and useful, and should continue.

Nuclear Risk Reduction Centers

The leaders welcomed the signing on September 15, 1987, in Washington of the agreement to establish Nuclear Risk Reduction Centers in their capitals. The agreement will be implemented promptly.

Chemical Weapons

The leaders expressed their commitment to negotiation of a verifiable, comprehensive and effective international convention on the prohibition and destruction of chemical weapons. They welcomed progress to date and reaffirmed the need for intensified negotiations toward conclusion of a truly global and verifiable convention encompassing all chemical weapons-capable states. The United States and Soviet Union are in favor of greater openness and intensified confidence-building with respect to chemical weapons both on a bilateral and a multilateral basis. They agreed to continue periodic discussions by experts on the growing problem of chemical weapons proliferation and use.

Conventional Forces

The President and the General Secretary discussed the importance of the task of reducing the level of military confrontation in Europe in the area of armed forces and conventional armaments. The two leaders spoke in favor of early completion of the work in Vienna on the mandate for negotiations on this issue, so that substantive negotiations may be started at the earliest time with a view to elaborating concrete measures. They also noted that the implementation of the provisions of the Stockholm Conference on Confidence- and Security-Building Measures and Disarmament in Europe is an important factor in strengthening mutual understanding and enhancing stability, and spoke in favor of continuing and consolidating this process. The President and the General Secretary agreed to instruct their appropriate representatives to intensify efforts to achieve solutions to outstanding issues.

They also discussed the Vienna (Mutual and Balanced Force Reduction) negotiations.

Follow-Up Meeting of the Conference on Security and Cooperation in Europe

They expressed their determination, together with the other 33 participants in the Conference on Security and Cooperation in Europe, to bring the Vienna CSCE Follow Up Conference to a successful conclusion, based on balanced progress in all principal areas of the Helsinki Final Act and Madrid Concluding Document.

II. Human Rights and Humanitarian Concerns

The leaders held a thorough and candid discussion of human rights and humanitarian questions and their place in the U.S.-Soviet dialogue.

III. Regional Issues

The President and the General Secretary engaged in a wide-ranging, frank and businesslike discussion of regional questions, including Afghanistan, the Iran-Iraq War, the Middle East, Cambodia, southern Africa, Central America and other issues. They acknowledged serious differences but agreed on the importance of their regular exchange of views. The two leaders noted the increasing importance of settling regional conflicts to reduce international tensions and to improve East-West relations. They agreed that the goal of the dialogue between the United States and the Soviet Union on these issues should be to help the parties to regional conflicts find peaceful solutions that advance their independence, freedom and security. Both leaders emphasized the importance of enhancing the capacity of the United Nations and other international institutions to contribute to the resolution of regional conflicts.

IV. Bilateral Affairs

The President and the General Secretary reviewed in detail the state of U.S.-Soviet bilateral relations. They recognized the utility of further expanding and strengthening bilateral contacts, exchanges and cooperation.

Bilateral Negotiations

Having reviewed the state of ongoing U.S.-Soviet negotiations on a number of specific bilateral issues, the two leaders called for intensified efforts by their representatives, aimed at reaching mutually advantageous agreements on: commercial maritime issues; fishing; marine search and rescue; radio navigational systems; the U.S.-USSR maritime boundary; and cooperation in the field of transportation and other areas.

They noted with satisfaction agreement on the expansion, within the framework of the U.S.-Soviet Air Transport Agreement, of direct air passenger service, including joint operation of the New York-Moscow route by Pan American Airways and Aeroflot, and on the renewal of the U.S.-Soviet World Ocean Agreement.

People-to-People Contacts and Exchanges

The two leaders took note of progress in implementing the U.S.-Soviet General Exchanges Agreement in the areas of education, science, culture and sports, signed at their November 1985 Geneva meeting and agreed to continue efforts to eliminate obstacles to further progress in these areas. They expressed satisfaction with plans to celebrate jointly the 30th anniversary of the first Exchanges Agreement in January 1988.

The two leaders reaffirmed the importance of contacts and exchanges in broadening understanding between their peoples. They noted with particular satisfaction the progress made in the development of people-to-people contacts under the initiative they launched at their 1985 meeting in Geneva — a process which has involved tens of thousands of U.S. and Soviet citizens over the past two years. The leaders reaffirmed their strong commitment further to expand such contacts, including among the young.

Global Climate and Environmental Change Initiative

With reference to their November 1985 agreement in Geneva to cooperate in the preservation of the environment, the two leaders approved a bilateral initiative to pursue joint studies in global climate and environmental change through cooperation in areas of mutual concern, such as protection and conservation of stratospheric ozone, and through increased data exchanges pursuant to the U.S.-Soviet Environmental Protection Agreement and the Agreement Between the United States of America and the Union of Soviet Socialist Republics Concerning Cooperation in the Exploration and Use of Outer Space for Peaceful Purposes. In this context, there will be a detailed study on the climate of the future. The two sides will continue to promote broad international and bilateral cooperation in the increasingly important area of global climate and environmental change.

Cooperative Activities

The President and the General Secretary supported further cooperation among scientists of the United States, the Soviet Union and other countries in utilizing controlled thermonuclear fusion for peaceful purposes. They affirmed the intention of the U.S. and the USSR to cooperate with the European Atomic Energy Community (EURATOM) and Japan, under the auspices of the International Atomic Energy Agency, in the quadripartite conceptual design of a fusion test reactor.

The two leaders noted with satisfaction progress under the bilateral Agreement on Peaceful Uses of Atomic Energy towards establishing a permanent working group in the field of nuclear reactor safety, and expressed their readiness to develop further cooperation in this area.

The President and the General Secretary agreed to develop bilateral cooperation in combatting international narcotics trafficking. They agreed that appropriate initial consultations would be held for these purposes in early 1988.

They also agreed to build on recent contacts to develop more effective cooperation in ensuring the security of air and maritime transportation.

The two leaders exchanged views on means of encouraging expanded contacts and cooperation on issues relating to the Arctic. They expressed support for the development of bilateral and regional cooperation among the Arctic countries on these matters, including coordination of scientific research and protection of the region's environment.

The two leaders welcomed the conclusion of negotiations to institutionalize the COSPAS/SARSAT space-based global search and rescue system, operated jointly by the United States, the Soviet Union, France and Canada.

Trade

The two sides stated their strong support for the expansion of mutually beneficial trade and economic relations. They instructed their trade ministers to convene the U.S.-USSR Joint Commercial Commission in order to develop concrete proposals to achieve that objective, including within the framework of the Long-Term Agreement between the United States of America and the Union of Soviet Socialist Republics to Facilitate Economic, Industrial, and Technical Cooperation. They agreed that commercially viable joint ventures complying with the laws and regulations of both countries could play a role in the further development of commercial relations.

Diplomatic Missions

Both sides agreed on the importance of adequate, secure facilities for their respective diplomatic and consular establishments, and emphasized the need to approach problems relating to the functioning of Embassies and Consulates General constructively and on the basis of reciprocity....
(PPP Reagan 1987 II: 1491-1497)

President Reagan's Remarks Announcing the Signing of the Afghanistan Accords
April 11, 1988

...I've just received a briefing from my national security advisers on the contents of the proposed Geneva agreements on Afghanistan that would provide for the complete withdrawal of Soviet occupation forces from that country. I believe the U.S. can now join the Soviet Union as a guarantor of the Geneva instruments. I've therefore asked Secretary [of State] Shultz to represent us at a signing ceremony for the historic accords as scheduled to take place in Geneva later this week.

This development would not have been possible had it not been for the valiant struggle of the Afghan people to rid their country of foreign occupation. We take great pride in having assisted the Afghan people in this triumph, and they can count on our continued support. We also pledge our continued friendship and support to the Government and people of Pakistan, who have so generously hosted millions of Afghan refugees during this period of Soviet domination of Afghanistan.
(PPP Reagan 1988 I: 437)

President Reagan's Statement on the Soviet Withdrawal from Afghanistan
February 16, 1989

Today marks the start of a new chapter in the history of Afghanistan. For the first time in over 9 years, Soviet forces no longer occupy that country. This development marks an extraordinary triumph of spirit and will by the Afghan people, and we salute them for it.

Much remains to be done, however. For the Afghan people, the struggle for self-determination goes on. We support Afghan efforts to fashion a stable, broadly based government, responsive to the needs of the Afghan people. We call upon Afghan resistance leaders to work together towards this end. As long as the resistance struggle for self-determination continues, so too will America's support.

Throughout the long, dark years of Afghanistan's occupation, the international community has been steadfast in its support of the Afghan cause. This is also true for the United States. U.S. support for the Afghan people and the subsequent Soviet military withdrawal from Afghanistan constitute a powerful example of what we Americans can accomplish when Executive and Congress, Republican and Democrat, stand together. The Government and people of Pakistan also can take particular satisfaction from this event; their courage and solidarity contributed significantly to the Afghan struggle.

Now, more than ever, the Afghan people deserve the continuing help of the international community as they begin the difficult process of reclaiming their country, resettling their people, and restoring their livelihood. The commitment of the United States to the Afghan people will remain firm, both through our bilateral humanitarian aid program and through United Nations efforts to remove mines, resettle refugees, and reconstruct Afghanistan's war-torn economy. We call upon other nations to contribute all they can and hope that the United Nations and the resistance can come to mutually acceptable arrangements for the nation-wide distribution of needed food supplies.

The Soviet Union has now fulfilled its obligation to withdraw from Afghanistan. We welcome that decision. We call upon the Soviet Union to refrain from other forms of interference in Afghan affairs. The Soviet Union has nothing to fear from the establishment of an independent, nonaligned Afghanistan. At the same time, the U.S.S.R. bears special responsibility for healing the wounds of this war, and we call upon it to support generously international efforts to rebuild Afghanistan.

(PPP Bush 1989 I: 106)

White House Fact Sheet on the Meeting with Soviet Chairman Mikhail Gorbachev in Malta

December 4, 1989

The President and Chairman Gorbachev exchanged views on a variety of issues during their meetings in Malta, including the remarkable events leading to peaceful and democratic change in Eastern and Central Europe.

The President noted his strong support for *perestroika* and suggested that the two leaders work to give major new impetus to the U.S.-Soviet relationship. The President conveyed his strong personal commitment to this goal.

In this spirit, the President put forward the following ideas:

Next Steps

1. Holding the summit in the United States during the last 2 weeks in June.
2. Having the next meeting of Foreign Ministers next month in the Soviet Union to prepare for the summit.

Economic and Commercial Relations

1. Targeting the 1990 summit for completion of a trade agreement granting most-favored-nation status to the Soviet Union so that the President can grant a Jackson-Vanik waiver at that time. To reach that goal, the President proposed beginning negotiations on a trade agreement now and urged the Supreme Soviet to complete action on its emigration legislation early next year.
2. Supporting observer status for the Soviet Union in GATT after the Uruguay round is completed next year. The President urged the Soviet Union to use the intervening time to move toward market prices at the wholesale level so its economy will become more compatible with the GATT system.
3. Expanding U.S.-Soviet technical economic cooperation. The President presented a paper proposing specific economic projects covering topics such as finance, agriculture, statistics, small business development, budgetary and tax policy, a stock exchange, and antimonopoly policy.
4. Exploring with Congress the lifting of statutory restrictions on export credits and guarantees after a Jackson-Vanik waiver.
5. Beginning discussions of a bilateral investment treaty that would provide protections for American business people who want to invest in the Soviet Union.
6. Improving ties between the Soviets and the OECD, and East-West economic cooperation through the economic basket of the CSCE process.

Human Rights

Resolving all divided family issues by the time of the 1990 summit. In this regard, the President handed over a list of people wishing to emigrate.

Regional Issues

Expressed disappointment with Soviet policy on Central America, noting it was out of step with the new Soviet direction domestically in Eastern Europe and in arms control. Nicaragua/Cuba remains the single most disruptive factor in the relationship.

Arms Control

1. Speeding achievement of a chemical weapons ban by offering to end U.S. production of binary weapons when the multilateral convention on chemical weapons enters into force in return for Soviet acceptance of the terms of our U.N. proposal to ban chemical weapons.
2. Proposing to sign an agreement at the 1990 summit to destroy U.S. and Soviet chemical weapons down to 20 percent of the current U.S. level.
3. Suggesting joint U.S.-Soviet support for a CFE summit to sign a CFE treaty in 1990.

4. Accelerating the START process in order to resolve all substantive issues and to conclude a treaty, if possible, by the 1990 summit. To this end, the President suggested that Secretary Baker and Foreign Minister Shevardnadze concentrate on resolving at their January meeting three of the outstanding START issues: ALCM's [air launched cruise missiles], non deployed missiles and telemetry encryption.
5. Completing work on the Threshold Test Ban Treaty (TTBT) and the Peaceful Nuclear Explosions Treaty (PNET) for signature at the 1990 summit.
6. Proposing that the Soviet Union join efforts to constrain missile proliferation more effectively by observing the limits developed by the U.S. and its allies in the Missile Technology Control Regime.

Military Openness

Making public more information on military programs. The President suggested that the Soviet Union make public the details of its military budget, force posture, and weapons production figures, just as the United States now does.

Olympics

Suggesting joint U.S.-Soviet support for Berlin as the site of the 2004 Olympic Games.

Environment

1. Hosting a conference next fall to negotiate a framework treaty on global climate change, after the working groups of the U.N.-sponsored Intergovernmental Panel on Climate Change submit their final report.
2. Convening an international meeting at the White House next spring for top-level scientific, environmental, and economic officials to discuss global climate change issues. The President expressed hope that the Soviets will join us by sending their top officials in the field.

Student Exchanges

Increasing significantly university exchanges so that an additional 1,000 American and 1,000 Soviet college students are studying in each other's country by the beginning of the 1991 school year.
(PPP Bush 1989 II: 1642-1643)

FROM SOVIET UNION TO RUSSIA: CHANGING THE GUARD AT THE KREMLIN

President Bush's Statement on the Attempted Coup in the Soviet Union
August 19, 1991

We are deeply disturbed by the events of the last hours in the Soviet Union and condemn the unconstitutional resort to force. While the situation continues to evolve and information remains incomplete, the apparent unconstitutional removal of President Gorbachev, the declaration of a state of emergency, and the deployment of Soviet military forces in Moscow and other cities raise the most serious questions about the future course of the Soviet Union. This misguided and illegitimate effort bypasses both Soviet law and the will of the Soviet peoples.

Accordingly, we support President Yeltsin's call for "restoration of the legally elected organs of power and the reaffirmation of the post of USSR President M.S. Gorbachev."

Greater democracy and openness in Soviet society, including steps toward implementation of Soviet obligations under the Helsinki Final Act and the Charter of Paris, have made a crucial contribution to the welcome improvement in East-West relations during the past few years. In these circumstances, U.S. policy will be based on the following guidelines:

- We believe the policies of reform in the Soviet Union must continue, including democratization, the process of peaceful reconciliation between the center and the Republics, and economic transformation;
- We support all constitutionally elected leaders and oppose the use of force or intimidation to suppress them or restrict their right to free speech;
- We oppose the use of force in the Baltic States or against any Republics to suppress or replace democratically elected governments;
- We call upon the Soviet Union to abide by its international treaties and commitments, including its commitments to respect basic human rights and democratic practices under the Helsinki Accords, and the Charter of Paris;
- We will avoid in every possible way actions that would lend legitimacy or support to this coup effort;
- We have no interest in a new cold war or in the exacerbation of East-West tensions.
- At the same time, we will not support economic aid programs if adherence to extra-constitutional means continues.

(PPP Bush 1991 II: 1063)

President Bush's Statement on the Resignation of Mikhail Gorbachev as President of the Soviet Union

December 25, 1991

Mikhail Gorbachev's resignation as President of the Soviet Union culminates a remarkable era in the history of his country and in its long and often difficult relationship with the United States. As he leaves office, I would like to express publicly and on behalf of the American people my gratitude to him for years of sustained commitment to world peace and my personal respect for his intellect, vision, and courage.

President Gorbachev is responsible for one of the most important developments of this century, the revolutionary transformation of a totalitarian dictatorship and the liberation of his people from its smothering embrace. His personal commitment to democratic and economic reform through *perestroika* and *glasnost*, a commitment which demanded the highest degree of political and personal ingenuity and courage, permitted the peoples of Russia and other Republics to cast aside decades of dark oppression and put in place the foundations of freedom. Working with President Reagan, myself, and other allied leaders, President Gorbachev acted boldly and decisively to end the bitter divisions of the cold war and contributed to the remaking of a Europe whole and free. His and Foreign Minister Eduard Shevardnadze's "New Thinking" in foreign affairs permitted the United States and the Soviet Union to move from confrontation to partnership in the search for peace across the globe. Together we negotiated historic reductions in chemical, nuclear, and conventional forces and reduced the risk of a nuclear conflict.

Working together, we helped the people of Eastern Europe win their liberty and the German people their goal of unity in peace and freedom. Our partnership led to unprecedented cooperation in repelling Iraqi aggression in Kuwait, in bringing peace to Nicaragua and Cambodia, and independence to Namibia. And our work continues as we seek a lasting and just peace between Israelis and Arabs in the Middle East and an end to the conflict in Afghanistan.

President Gorbachev's participation in these historic events is his legacy to his country and to the world. This record assures him an honored place in history and, most importantly for the future, establishes a solid basis from which the United States and the West can work in equally constructive ways with his successors.

(PPP Bush 1991 II: 1653-1655)

Address to the Nation on the Commonwealth of Independent States
December 25, 1991

The United States applauds and supports the historic choice for freedom by the new States of the Commonwealth. We congratulate them on the peaceful and democratic path they have chosen, and for their careful attention to nuclear control and safety during this transition. Despite a potential for instability and chaos, these events clearly serve our national interest.

We stand tonight before a new world of hope and possibilities for our children, a world we could not have contemplated a few years ago. The challenge for us now is to engage these new States in sustaining the peace and building a more prosperous future.

And so today, based on commitments and assurances given to us by some of these States concerning nuclear safety, democracy, and free markets, I am announcing some important steps designed to begin this process.

First, the United States recognizes and welcomes the emergence of a free, independent, and democratic Russia, led by its courageous President, Boris Yeltsin. Our Embassy in Moscow will remain there as our Embassy to Russia. We will support Russia's assumption of the U.S.S.R.'s seat as a permanent member of the United Nations Security Council. I look forward to working closely with President Yeltsin in support of his efforts to bring democratic and market reform to Russia.

Second, the United States also recognizes the independence of Ukraine, Armenia, Kazakhstan, Byelarus, and Kyrgyzstan, all States that have made specific commitments to us. We will move quickly to establish diplomatic relations with these States and build new ties to them. We will sponsor membership in the United Nations for those not already members.

Third, the United States also recognizes today as independent States the remaining six former Soviet Republics: Moldova, Turkmenistan, Azerbaijan, Tadjikistan, Georgia, and Uzbekistan. We will establish diplomatic relations with them when we are satisfied that they have made commitments to responsible security policies and democratic principles, as have the other States we recognize today....
(PPP Bush 1991 II: 1653-1655)

Vancouver Declaration: Joint Statement of the Presidents of the United States and the Russian Federation
April 4, 1993

Having met in Vancouver, Canada on April 3-4, President Bill Clinton of the United States of America and President Boris Yeltsin of the Russian Federation declared their firm commitment to a dynamic and effective U.S.-Russian partnership that strengthens international stability. The two presidents approved a comprehensive strategy of cooperation to promote democracy, security, and peace. President Yeltsin stressed his firm commitment to fostering democratization, the rule of law, and a market economy. As the United States moves to reinvigorate its own economy, President Clinton assured President Yeltsin of active American support for the Russian people as they pursue their own chosen course of political and economic reform.

The Presidents agreed on a new package of bilateral economic programs and measures to address Russia's immediate human needs and contribute to the building of necessary structures for successful transition to a market economy. They recognized the critical importance of creating favorable external conditions in which the Russian economy can the realize its maximum potential. In this connection, the Presidents expressed their determination to promote access to each other's markets, cooperation in defense conversion, removal of impediments to trade and investment, and resumption of U.S. food exports to Russia on a stable long-term basis.

President Yeltsin informed President Clinton about the Russian program of economic reforms. In particular, President Yeltsin stressed such key questions of the Russian reform as the necessity of combatting inflation and achieving financial stabilization by improvement of the banking system. He also emphasized the importance of privatization, encouragement of entrepreneurship, structural policy and social support. In this context, the Presidents discussed the role of the international community in supporting specific elements of the reform program.

The Presidents agreed that Russia's harmonious integration into the community of democratic nations and the world economy is essential. They therefore called for accelerated G-7 development of substantial and effective new economic initiatives to support political and economic reform in Russia. In this connection, the Presidents welcomed the extraordinary meeting of the foreign and finance ministers of the G-7 countries and the Russian Federation scheduled for April 14-15 in Tokyo. Presidents Clinton and Yeltsin also expressed their satisfaction with the successful conclusion of negotiations in Paris on the rescheduling of the international debt of the former USSR. The United States announced its support for Russia's intention to become a full member of GATT and to begin, in the near future, official talks on the conditions of Russia's accession to GATT.

The Presidents agreed to give fresh impetus to development of the U.S.-Russian relationship in all its dimensions. To coordinate and direct this effort and to activate a comprehensive and intensive dialogue, they agreed on measures to improve the mechanism for mutual consultations. In particular, working groups will be set up involving high level officials of both governments with broad authority in the areas of economic and scientific and technological cooperation. The Presidents agreed to establish a United States-Russian Commission on technological cooperation in the fields of energy and space. They intend to designate Prime Minister Chernomyrdin and Vice President Gore to head this commission.

The leaders of the United States and Russia attached great importance to the prevention of the proliferation of weapons of mass destruction and their delivery systems. They reaffirmed their determination to strengthen the Nuclear Non-Proliferation Treaty (NPT), make it universal, and give it an unlimited duration. The Presidents stressed their expectation that all countries of the former USSR which are not already NPT members will promptly confirm their adherence to the treaty as non-nuclear weapon states. They urged the Democratic Peoples Republic of Korea to comply fully with its IAEA safeguards obligations, which remain in force, and to retract its announcement of withdrawal from the NPT.

The Presidents agreed that efforts of the United States and Russia will be directed toward the entry into force of the START I Treaty and the ratification of the START II Treaty as soon as possible. They affirmed that the United States and Russia intend to cooperate, on the basis of their mutual interest, in environmentally safe elimination of nuclear forces pursuant to relevant arms control agreements, in construction of a storage facility for nuclear materials and in the controlling, accounting, and physical protection of nuclear materials. The United States reiterated its readiness to provide assistance to Russia for these purposes. The Presidents called for prompt conclusion, on mutually acceptable terms, of the negotiations on an agreement on the conversion and sale for peaceful purposes of nuclear materials removed from nuclear weapons.

The Presidents underscored their determination to broaden interaction and consultations between Russia and the United States in the areas of defense and security. They instructed their Ministers of Defense to explore further possibilities in that direction.

The Presidents noted the progress achieved at the recent United States-Russian talks on chemical weapons in Geneva. They welcomed the progress made in preparing the protocols necessary to submit the "Agreement on Destruction and Non-Production of Chemical Weapons" of June 1, 1990 for approval by the legislative bodies of the Russian Federation and the United States. They also welcomed progress achieved in developing agreement on the preparation and implementation of the second phase of the Wyoming Memorandum of Understanding of September 23, 1989 regarding a bilateral verification experiment and data exchange related to prohibition of chemical weapons.

The Presidents agreed that it is necessary to achieve the earliest possible resolution of questions about cooperation in non-proliferation of missiles and missile technology in all its aspects, in accordance with the principles of existing international agreements. They also decided to work together to remove obstacles impeding Russia's access to the global market in high technology and related services. The Presidents agreed that negotiations on a multilateral nuclear test ban should commence at an early date, and that their governments would consult with each other accordingly.

Mindful of their countries' responsibilities as permanent members of the UN Security Council, the Presidents affirmed that U.S.-Russian cooperation is essential to the peaceful resolution of international conflicts and the promotion of democratic values, the protection of human rights, and the solution of global problems, such as environmental pollution, terrorism, and narcotics trafficking. The United States and Russia stressed their determination to improve the effectiveness of peacemaking and peacekeeping capabilities of the United Nations, the CSCE, and other appropriate regional organizations.

Recognizing that the problem of mistreatment of minorities and ethnic communities is increasingly a source of international instability, the Presidents stressed the critical importance of full protection for individual human rights, including those of ethnic Russian and all other minorities on the territory of the former Soviet Union. They affirmed their commitment to the peaceful resolution of conflicts in that region on the basis of respect for the independence, territorial integrity, and security of all member states of the UN and the CSCE.

The Presidents announced their intention to expand and improve their joint work in the area of environmental protection. They agreed to coordinate on joint ecological measures to be taken and research to be done, and on support for financing agreed programs. The Presidents agreed that the level of mutual openness achieved makes it possible to proceed with new forms of cooperation in science and technology, including programs in the field of outer space. The two countries will further develop bilateral cooperation in fisheries in the Bering Sea, the North Pacific, and the Sea of Okhotsk, including for the purpose of preservation and reproduction of living marine resources and of monitoring the ecosystem in the Northern Pacific. The Presidents further agreed to expand significantly their contacts, exchanges, and cooperation in the areas of culture, education, the humanities, and the mass media.

The joint efforts of both countries have succeeded in establishing a new character for Russian-American relations. The Presidents reaffirmed the principles and provisions of the Camp David Declaration of February 1, 1992, and the Charter of U.S.-Russian Partnership and Friendship of June 11, 1992, as a basis for relations between the two countries.
(WCPD Clinton 1993: 545-547)

THE INTEGRATION OF THE EAST

President Bush's Statement on Signing the Support for East European Democracy (SEED) Act of 1989 [Public Law 101-179]
November 28, 1989

...This legislation authorizes $938 million in assistance to promote democratization in Poland and Hungary. It authorizes various programs to help promote reform in these countries including economic stabilization, trade liberalization, Enterprise Funds to nurture private sector development, labor market reform, and enhanced environmental protection.

We are nearing the end of a year that future generations will remember as a watershed year when the human spirit was lifted and spurred on by the bold and courageous actions of two great peoples — the people of Poland and Hungary.

The year began with the first session of the Roundtable discussions in Poland. In April the Polish Communist Party reached an agreement with Solidarity that led to elections in June. Although not all of the seats of the Parliament were open to free elections, the Polish people succeeded in voicing their opinion — and in remaking the political map of Poland. The end result was the first non-communist-led government in Eastern Europe since 1948. This government has continued to transform Polish society. A new economic program which holds the promise of converting Poland into a market economy has been put forward.

Events in Hungary have also stirred imagination of the world. In May, Hungary decided to tear down the barbed-wire fence that separated it from the West. In September, Hungary gained the support of the entire world with its decision to honor its international commitments and allow East Germans to pass through its borders on their way to the West. More recently, Hungary has dropped virtually all of the trappings of a Stalinist state — a new constitution based on democratic principles was adopted, the name of the country was changed from the "People's Republic" to simply the "Republic of Hungary," and the ruling Communist Party dissolved itself to create a vastly different and much smaller Socialist Party, which must compete with all the other parties for the votes of the Hungarian people. On November 26, Hungary held a referendum to determine the timing of free presidential elections. Contested parliamentary elections will be held no later than next summer. These elections hold the promise of transforming Hungary politically as the elections in Poland transformed that country....

This legislation contains one other measure I requested in October — the authorization for a contribution to a Stabilization Fund in response to a request from the Polish Government. I applaud the Congress for responding to this request in such an expeditious fashion. We are now working with our major allies and the G-24 — the group established by the Paris Summit to coordinate aid for Poland and Hungary — to obtain the additional financing needed for this Fund.

The passage of this legislation marks a major and positive step in bipartisan foreign policy. The national consensus for support for Poland and Hungary has been strong. The Congress has crafted a bill responsive to my requests, as well as providing a number of additional programs, all designed to support our national goals; to help further the cause of political and economic freedom in Poland and Hungary....
(PPP Bush 1989 II: 1596-1597)

Public Law 101-179: Support for East European Democracy (SEED) Act of 1989
November 28, 1989
...SEC. 2. SUPPORT FOR EAST EUROPEAN DEMOCRACY (SEED) PROGRAM

(a) SEED PROGRAM. — The United States shall implement, beginning in fiscal year 1990, a concerted Program of Support for East European Democracy (which may also be referred to as the "SEED Program"). The SEED Program shall be comprised of diverse undertakings designed to provide cost-effective assistance to those countries of Eastern Europe that have taken substantive steps toward institutionalizing political democracy and economic pluralism.

(b) Objectives of SEED Assistance. — The President should ensure that the assistance provided to East European countries pursuant to this Act is designed —

(1) to contribute to the development of democratic institutions and political pluralism characterized by —

(A) the establishment of fully democratic and representative political systems based on free and fair elections,

(B) effective recognition of fundamental liberties and individual freedoms, including freedom of speech, religion, and association,

(C) termination of all laws and regulations which impede the operation of a free press and the formation of political parties,

(D) creation of an independent judiciary, and

(E) establishment of non-partisan military, security, and police forces;

(2) to promote the development of a free market economic system characterized by —

(A) privatization of economic entities,

(B) establishment of full rights to acquire and hold private property, including land and the benefits of contractual relations,

(C) simplification of regulatory controls regarding the establishment and operation of businesses,

(D) dismantlement of all wage and price controls,

(E) removal of trade restrictions, including on both imports and exports,

(F) liberalization of investment and capital, including the repatriation of profits by foreign investors,

(G) tax policies which provide incentives for economic activity and investment,

(H) establishment of rights to own and operate private banks and other financial service firms, as well as unrestricted access to private sources of credit, and

(I) access to a market for stocks, bonds, and other instruments through which individual may invest in the private sector; and

(3) not to contribute any substantial benefit —

(A) to Communist or other political parties or organizations which are not committed to respect for the democratic process, or

(B) to the defense or security forces of any member country of the Warsaw Pact.

(c) SEED ACTIONS. — Assistance and other activities under the SEED Program (which may be referred to as "SEED Actions") shall include activities such as the following:

(1) LEADERSHIP IN THE WORLD BANK AND INTERNATIONAL MONETARY FUND. — United States leadership in supporting —

(A) loans by the International Bank for Reconstruction and Development and its affiliated institutions in the World Bank group that are designed to modernize industry, agriculture, and infrastructure, and

(B) International Monetary Fund programs designed to stimulate sound economic growth.

(2) CURRENCY STABILIZATION LOANS. — United States leadership in supporting multilateral agreement to provide government-to-government loans for currency stabilization where such loans can reduce inflation and thereby foster conditions necessary for the effective implementation of economic reforms.

(3) DEBT REDUCTION AND RESCHEDULING. — Participation in multilateral activities aimed at reducing and rescheduling a country's international debt, when reduction and deferral of debt payments can assist the process of political and economic transition.

(4) AGRICULTURAL ASSISTANCE. — Assistance through the grant and concession sale of food and other agricultural commodities and products when such assistance can ease critical shortages but not inhibit agricultural production and marketing in the recipient country.

(5) ENTERPRISE FUNDS. — Grants to support private, nonprofit "Enterprise Funds", designated by the President pursuant to law and governed by a Board of Directors, which undertake loans, grants, equity investments, feasibility studies, technical assistance, training, and other forms of assistance

to private enterprise activities in the Eastern European country for which the Enterprise Fund so is designated.

(6) LABOR MARKET-ORIENTED TECHNICAL Assistance. — Technical assistance programs directed at promoting labor market reforms and facilitating economic adjustment.

(7) TECHNICAL TRAINING. — Programs to provide technical skills to assist in the development of a market economy.

(8) PEACE CORPS. — Establishment of Peace Corps programs.

(9) SUPPORT FOR INDIGENOUS CREDIT UNIONS. — Support for the establishment of indigenous credit unions.

(10) GENERALIZED SYSTEM OF PREFERENCES. — Eligibility for trade benefits under the Generalized System of Preferences.

(11) MOST FAVORED NATION TRADE STATUS. — The granting of temporary or permanent nondiscriminatory treatment (commonly referred to as "most favored nation status") to the products of an East European country through the application of the criteria and procedures established by section 402 of the Trade Act of 1974 (19 U.S.C. 2432; commonly referred to as the "Jackson-Vanik amendment").

(12) OVERSEAS PRIVATE INVESTMENT CORPORATION. — Programs of the Overseas Private Investment Corporation.

(13) EXPORT-IMPORT BANK PROGRAMS. — Programs of the Export-Import Bank of the United States.

(14) TRADE AND DEVELOPMENT PROGRAM ACTIVITIES. — Trade and Development Program activities under the Foreign Assistance Act of 1961.

(15) INVESTMENT TREATIES. — Negotiation of bilateral investment treaties.

(16) SPECIAL TAX TREATMENT OF BELOW-MARKET LOANS. — Exempting bonds from Internal Revenue Code rules relating to below-market loans.

(17) EXCHANGE ACTIVITIES. — Expanded exchange activities under the Fulbright, International Visitors, and other programs conducted by the United States Information Agency.

(18) CULTURAL CENTERS. — Contributions toward the establishment of reciprocal cultural centers that can facilitate educational and cultural exchange and expanded understanding of Western social democracy.

(19) SISTER INSTITUTIONS. — Establishment of sister institution programs between American and East European schools and universities, towns and cities, and other organizations in such fields as medicine and health care, business management, environmental protection, and agriculture.

(20) SCHOLARSHIPS. — Scholarships to enable students to study in the United States.

(21) SCIENCE AND TECHNOLOGY EXCHANGES. — Grants for the implementation of bilateral agreements providing for cooperation in science and technology exchange.

(22) ASSISTANCE FOR DEMOCRATIC INSTITUTIONS. — Assistance designed to support the development of legal, legislative, electoral, journalistic, and other institutions of free, pluralist societies.

(23) ENVIRONMENTAL ASSISTANCE. — Environmental assistance directed at overcoming crucial deficiencies in air and water quality and other determinants of a healthful society.

(24) MEDICAL ASSISTANCE. — Medical assistance specifically targeted to overcome severe deficiencies in pharmaceuticals and other basic health supplies.

(25) ENCOURAGEMENT FOR PRIVATE INVESTMENT AND VOLUNTARY ASSISTANCE. — Encouraging private investment and voluntary private assistance, using a variety of means including a SEED Information Center System and the provision by the Department of Defense of transportation for private nonfinancial contributions....
(USS, 1989, Volume 103, Part 2)

President Bush's Statement on Signing the FREEDOM Support Act [Public Law 102-511]
October 24, 1992

...This historic legislation authorizes a range of programs to support free market and democratic reforms being undertaken in Russia, Ukraine, Armenia, and the other states of the former Soviet Union. In particular, the bill endorses the $12 billion increase in the U.S. share of the International Monetary Fund (IMF) and authorizes $410 million in U.S. bilateral assistance. In addition, the bill removes a number of outdated Cold War legislative restrictions on U.S. relations with the new independent states....

I am pleased that the bill draws our private sector, as never before, into the delivery of technical assistance to Russia and the other new states. Various provisions of this bill will call upon the specialized skills and expertise of the U.S. private sector. S. 2532 will provide support for the trade and investment activities of U.S. companies to help lay the economic and commercial foundations upon which the new democracies will rest. This is an investment in our future as well as theirs.

The IMF quota increase will ensure that the IMF has adequate resources to promote free markets in the former Soviet Union and elsewhere throughout the world. By contributing to a more prosperous world economy, the IMF will expand markets for U.S. exporters and increase jobs for American workers.

This bill will allow us to provide humanitarian assistance during the upcoming winter; to support democratic reforms and free market systems; to encourage trade and investment; to support the development of food distribution systems; to assist in health and human services programs; to help overcome problems in energy, civilian nuclear reactor safety, transportation, and telecommunications; to assist in dealing with dire environmental problems in the region; and to establish a broad range of people-to-people exchanges designed to bury forever the distrust and misunderstanding that characterized our previous relations with the former Soviet Union.

The bill also provides additional resources and authorities to support efforts to destroy nuclear and other weapons, and to convert to peaceful purposes the facilities that produce these weapons.

We undertake these programs of assistance out of a commitment to increased security for ourselves, our allies, and the peoples of the new independent states. These programs will enhance our security through demilitarization and humanitarian and technical assistance....
(PPP Bush 1992-1993 II: 1973-1974)

Statement by the Presidents of the United States, Russia, and Ukraine
January 14, 1994

Presidents Clinton, Yeltsin and Kravchuk met in Moscow on January 14. The three Presidents reiterated that they will deal with one another as full and equal partners and that relations among their countries must be conducted on the basis of respect for the independence, sovereignty and territorial integrity of each nation.

The three Presidents agreed on the importance of developing mutually beneficial, comprehensive and cooperative economic relations. In this connection, they welcomed the intention of the United States to provide assistance to Ukraine and Russia to support the creation of effective market economies.

The three Presidents reviewed the progress that has been made in reducing nuclear forces. Deactivation of strategic forces is already well underway in the United States, Russia and Ukraine. The Presidents welcomed the ongoing deactivation of RS-18s (SS-19s) and RS-22s (SS-24s) on Ukrainian territory by having their warheads removed.

The Presidents look forward to the entry into force of the START I Treaty, including the Lisbon Protocol and associated documents, and President Kravchuk reiterated his commitment that Ukraine accede to the Nuclear Non-Proliferation Treaty as a non-nuclear-weapon state in the shortest possible time. Presidents Clinton and Yeltsin noted that entry into force of START I will allow them to seek early ratification of START II. The

Presidents discussed, in this regard, steps their countries would take to resolve certain nuclear weapons questions.

The Presidents emphasized the importance of ensuring the safety and security of nuclear weapons pending their dismantlement.

The Presidents recognize the importance of compensation to Ukraine, Kazakhstan and Belarus for the value of the highly-enriched uranium in nuclear warheads located on their territories. Arrangements have been worked out to provide fair and timely compensation to Ukraine, Kazakhstan and Belarus as the nuclear warheads on their territory are transferred to Russia for dismantling.

Presidents Clinton and Yeltsin expressed satisfaction with the completion of the highly-enriched uranium contract, which was signed by appropriate authorities of the United States and Russia. By converting weapons grade uranium into uranium which can only be used for peaceful purposes, the highly enriched uranium agreement is a major step forward in fulfilling the countries' mutual non-proliferation objectives.

The three Presidents decided on simultaneous actions on transfer of nuclear warheads from Ukraine and delivery of compensation to Ukraine in the form of fuel assemblies for nuclear power stations.

Presidents Clinton and Yeltsin informed President Kravchuk that the United States and Russia are prepared to provide security assurances to Ukraine. In particular, once the START I Treaty enters into force and Ukraine becomes a non-nuclear-weapon state party to the Nuclear Non-Proliferation Treaty (NPT), the United States and Russia will:

- Reaffirm their commitment to Ukraine, in accordance with the principles of the CSCE Final Act, to respect the independence and sovereignty and the existing borders of the CSCE member states and recognize that border changes can be made only by peaceful and consensual means; and reaffirm their obligation to refrain from the threat or use of force against the territorial integrity or political independence of any state, and that none of their weapons will ever be used except in self-defense or otherwise in accordance with the Charter of the United Nations;
- Reaffirm their commitment to Ukraine, in accordance with the principles of the CSCE Final Act, to refrain from economic coercion designed to subordinate to their own interest the exercise by another CSCE participating state of the rights inherent in its sovereignty and thus to secure advantages of any kind;
- Reaffirm their commitment to seek immediate UN Security Council action to provide assistance to Ukraine, as a non nuclear weapon state party to the NPT if Ukraine should become a victim of an act of aggression or an object of a threat of aggression in which nuclear weapons are used; and

- Reaffirm, in the case of Ukraine, their commitment not to use nuclear weapons against any non-nuclear-weapon state party to the NPT, except in the case of an attack on themselves, their territories or dependent territories, their armed forces, or their allies, by such a state in association or alliance with a nuclear weapon state.

Presidents Clinton and Yeltsin informed President Kravchuk that consultations have been held with the United Kingdom, the third depositary state of the NPT, and the United Kingdom is prepared to offer the same security assurances to Ukraine once it becomes a non nuclear weapon state party to the NPT.

President Clinton reaffirmed the United States commitment to provide technical and financial assistance for the safe and secure dismantling of nuclear forces and storage of fissile materials. The United States has agreed under the Nunn-Lugar program to provide Russia, Ukraine, Kazakhstan and Belarus with nearly USD 800 million in such assistance, including a minimum of USD 175 million to Ukraine. The United States Congress has authorized additional Nunn-Lugar funds for this program, and the United States will work intensively with Russia, Ukraine, Kazakhstan and Belarus to expand assistance for this important purpose. The United States will also work to promote rapid implementation of the assistance agreements that are already in place.
(WCPD Clinton 1994: 79-80)

Statement on Withdrawal of Russian Forces from Eastern Europe
August 31, 1994

Today marks the completion of the withdrawal of Russian military forces from the Republic of Estonia and the Latvian Republic, under terms of bilateral agreements concluded between Russia and each of these sovereign states. Russian military forces are also completing their withdrawal today from the Federal Republic of Germany, in accordance with the agreements reached between Germany and the Soviet Union in October 1990. These withdrawals constitute the final departure of Russian troops that have been present in Eastern Europe since 1945. This effectively brings to an end a chapter in post-World War II European history, opening the door to a new era of regional stability and cooperation. I congratulate the people of Estonia, Germany, Latvia, and Russia on this historic occasion and salute their leaders for the vision and statesmanship they have demonstrated on behalf of European integration. The United States will continue its active support for this process with the goal of a brighter and more peaceful future for all of our people in the next century.
(WCPD Clinton 1994: 1728-1729)

THE REORIENTATION OF NATO

Improving the Balance of Conventional Forces in Europe
Deputy Assistant Secretary for Politico-Military Affairs John H. Hawes' Address before a National Defense University (NDU) symposium entitled "The Future of Conventional Defense Improvements in NATO"
March 27, 1987

...Opportunities and Pitfalls

This is a potentially promising moment. The Soviet logjam in Geneva may be breaking. Arms agreements which NATO has long sought may now be reached. We may see major changes in Eastern and Western forces. At the same time, the new Soviet leadership poses a new and more dynamic challenge. Patterns of competition are shifting. There are opportunities for the West, but also pitfalls.

NATO needs to exploit the opportunities to enhance stability and security. NATO must also avoid the pitfalls. To do both requires understanding. We cannot rely on partial or simplistic images.

This is easier said than done. There was a cartoon last week which typified the problem. In the first scene, a U.S. arms control delegation proposes the removal of medium-range missiles from Europe. In the next scene, the Soviets accept. The last scene shows the U.S. delegates in consultation, supposedly shocked and at a loss for what to do next.

That cartoon echoes a lot of superficial commentary. It does not, however, reflect the facts. In the real world, the President immediately tabled a treaty. Far from being embarrassed, we moved to nail down an LRINF [longer range intermediate-range nuclear forces] agreement at zero in Europe and 100 globally.

In the cartoon world, NATO minus LRINF is pictured as naked or "denuclearized" opposite heavily armored Soviet conventional forces. In the real world, we know better. We are constantly concerned with the Soviet conventional threat and the need to improve NATO forces— this conference testifies to that. But we know that decades of effort have not been without result. We know that the alliance deterrent triad, flexible response, and the U.S. commitment to Europe would remain unshaken.

That's more complicated and less funny than the cartoons. But it is just such complications that are the basis for understanding NATO's conventional defense problems. There are four factors we must weigh in considering the future of conventional defense improvements:

First, the nuclear/conventional interaction in doctrine, programs, and public perceptions;

Second, the implications of the conventional debate for trans-Atlantic and intra-European relations;

Third, the resources available; and
Fourth, the actual improvement programs.

The Nuclear/Conventional Interaction

Historically, weaknesses in NATO's conventional posture have — perhaps paradoxically — helped feed a vicious circle of public fixation on our nuclear forces. While alliance military experts have devoted time to conventional problems, publics have been bored with conventional force complexity, or convinced it is politically or economically hopeless, or diverted (and not a little frightened) by nuclear issues, which are far sexier for the media and the layman.

The upshot of this paradox is that conventional weaknesses, rather than stimulating public pressure for their remedy, may actually lead publics away from the hard issues.

Not all members of the public make this mistake. Many are aware of conventional issues and concerned with doing something about them. But often one finds that their concern is less motivated by the conventional balance itself than by a desire to diminish nuclear risks. This is a noble goal which no one would question. It is shared by policy makers on both sides of the Atlantic. But it sometimes leads proponents to favor shoddy "quick fixes." And it has never proven adequate to generate the impetus for serious conventional force improvements.

It may never be possible to free the conventional debate from the nuclear issue. But we should seek a treatment of conventional issues that is as objective as possible under the circumstances. A debate that depends on images of nuclear escalation to generate monies for conventional defense is not likely to be productive and has not been. Nor is a debate that regards the conventional problem as a derivative issue likely to attract long-term commitment.

Last November in Chicago, Secretary of State Shultz addressed conventional forces and nuclear weapons cuts, such as had been projected at the Reykjavik summit. His remarks, however, were not tied to a particular scheme but to the overall challenges of a less nuclear world. He noted the prospect of such a world had provoked anxiety — ironically, given the arguments nuclear weapons provoke. He said he was not signalling the end of the nuclear era, which will be with us for the foreseeable future. But he specifically urged new thinking on defense including, specifically, conventional defense improvement. Reviewing NATO thinking over several decades, he concluded:

...our reliance for so long on nuclear weapons has led some to forget that these arms are not an inexpensive substitute — mostly paid for by the United States — for fully facing up to the challenges of conventional defense and deterrence.

The Trans-Atlantic Political Context

A second element of NATO conventional defense improvements is the political context between Europe and North America. The trans-Atlantic tie is both competitive and cooperative.

There are two subthemes of this trans-Atlantic context. One is the issue of burden sharing, with its corollary, the level of U.S. forces in Europe. The other is the nature of intra-European cooperation. Both themes go back to the beginning of the alliance.

The postwar withdrawal, and reintroduction, of U.S. forces reflected an enduring debate in the United States. We have seen it flare up again this winter, with renewed calls for U.S. troop withdrawals. As [U.S. Ambassador to the Federal Republic of Germany] Rick Burt noted recently, such calls make no more sense from the right than from the left. We can and will rebut these suggestions. But we cannot eliminate the source of the tension. A recent poll found that a majority of Americans would go to war to help defend Europe. That is an encouraging sign of international responsibility. But it does not resolve budget problems or remove the burden sharing question from the agenda.

Similarly, the issue of intra-European cooperation has affected European/North American relationships, from initial EDC [European Defense Community] debates, to arms cooperation, to the variety of national participation in NATO activities.

In the best of worlds, the interaction of trans-Atlantic and intra-European politics should multiply Western forces. That happened at the founding of NATO and in the fight over INF. At times, however, interactions have been centrifugal. To some people, the most effective argument for European security cooperation is the alleged difficulty of working with Washington. Perhaps we should not quibble if NATO gets more defense, even for the wrong reason. However, a negative political spin has its own costs.

The U.S. view of European collaboration has been ambivalent and, at times, counterproductive. That is not the intent of the present Administration. We support all efforts to enhance defense collaboration. We support WEU [Western European Union] revitalization. We are concerned only that intra-European collaboration not become stuck at the lowest common denominator; that it lead to more, not less, defense; and that it produce more, not less, clarity on security issues.

The Need for Adequate Resources

The third area to discuss is resources. In his November speech, Secretary of State Shultz underscored the West's advantages.

In any competition ultimately depending upon economic and political dynamism and innovation, the United States, Japan, and Western Europe have tremendous inherent advantages. Our three-to-one superiority in GNP [gross national product] over the Warsaw Pact, our far greater population, and the Western lead in modern technologies — these are only partial measures of our advantages. The West's true strength lies in the fact that we are not an ideological or military bloc like the Warsaw Pact — we are an alliance of free nations, able to draw upon the best of the diverse and creative energies of our peoples.

Commentators immediately said that is all well and good, but it is politically naive to expect democracies to allocate enough of that advantage to security. And an advantage which is only theoretical does not build tanks. They noted that defense budgets may shrink in real terms. They noted demographic changes and political constraints which make it difficult to sustain large standing armies. They noted the history of the burden sharing debate as an antidote to misplaced optimism.

None of these objections is false. But in their pessimism, they themselves constrict our options. It is often said we get the kind of defense we choose. And a preemptive narrowing of options leads to anomalies. People lament the conventional forces gap but wish to fill it only with nuclear weapons, then lament the dangers in nuclear weapons, agonize over imbalances in those weapons, and expect the Soviets to solve our problems in negotiations. That chain would be funny if it were not real. Breaking it requires a serious policy on conventional forces.

Improvement Programs

Which brings us to the fourth area: programs. There has been remarkable continuity in prescriptions. Despite fads, NATO concerns have been consistent.

- AD-70 looked at aircraft shelters, antiarmor capabilities, war reserve stocks, and air defense.
- The long-term defense program looked at readiness; rapid reinforcement; reserve forces and mobilization; air defenses; maritime forces; command, control, and communications; rationalization and standardization; electronic warfare; and tactical nuclear forces, as well as NATO's long-term planning mechanisms.
- The emerging technology program looked at systems for defense against first-echelon Warsaw Pact forces and Soviet operational maneuver groups; defense against follow-on forces; counterair operations; attacks on command, control, communications, and intelligence capabilities; and strengthened long-term planning.
- The conventional defense improvement program has looked at redressing deficiencies in munitions supplies and ammunition stocks; improved long-term planning; armaments cooperation and planning; infrastructure planning; better coordination in the areas of medium- and long-term

force requirements, strategies, and doctrines, and the weapons acquisition and infrastructure programs.

These initiatives have brought NATO a long way. Programmatically, NATO has adapted to a dynamic threat. Politically, it has moved beyond debate over whether conventional forces need strengthening. Conventional forces are a central part of the agenda.

One of the reasons for continuity in prescriptions is the continuity of the Soviet challenge. Talk of the Soviet challenge produces sharp reactions. Some people brush aside analysis as mere "bean counting" and tend to downplay the military threat. On the other side, some people overdraw the analysis and attribute superhuman capabilities to the Soviets. Both views inhibit clear thinking about what needs to be done.

The task is to soberly evaluate the facts and the trends. On the negative side, the Warsaw Pact has kept and expanded its numerical advantage in almost every major weapons system. More ominously, the pact has reduced NATO's qualitative edge.

- The reorganization of Soviet air forces and the creation of theaters of military operations have significantly improved Soviet ability to conduct combined operations.
- The prepositioning of fuel, ammunition, and other logistics support with forward-deployed Soviet divisions has given the pact an edge in sustainability.
- The introduction of operational maneuver groups and Spetznaz forces enhances capability for deep operations.
- The upgrading of equipment — for example, deployment of the T-80, the MiG 29/31, and the Mi-24 combat helicopter — augment combat firepower.

At the same time, the Soviets have a number of weaknesses.

- Despite trends, NATO still holds a qualitative edge in several weapons systems and in training and intelligence. Moreover, Western leads in underlying technologies — e.g., computers, sensors, and optics — suggest we should be able to keep that edge.
- Second, Eastern Europe is a problem. Pact equipment is falling behind Soviet equipment. The reliability of East European forces would be uncertain. And the overall political situation is delicate.
- Third, the Soviets face resource constraints. A command economy can allocate resources, but it cannot abolish need for tradeoffs, as, for example, between defense and industrial modernization. Demographic trends may also affect the armed forces and defense industries.

Looking at these strengths and weaknesses must give the Soviets pause. For example, they appear to believe new technologies have ushered in a revolution in warfare. From what Marshal Ogarkov — the former Soviet Chief of the General Staff and apparent current Commander of the Western Theater of Military Operations — and others are saying, the Soviets seem uncertain whether NATO's achievements in high technology have undermined the pact's ability to win conventionally. The object of NATO conventional defense improvement is to sustain and increase that Soviet uncertainty.

A viable force improvement program must meet several tests: political consensus, resource feasibility, cost effectiveness, and military utility. Many proposals to improve NATO's conventional forces are unrealistic or impractical. There is no quick fix to NATO's problems; if there were, NATO would have adopted it long ago.

NATO, for example, is not going to replace forward defense with heavily offensive or dispersed defensive strategies. Nor is NATO going to radically change force structure or make unprecedented defense spending increases. Nor are members likely to subordinate commercial interests sufficiently to achieve major defense procurement savings.

NATO can, however, improve its conventional forces without drastic changes in strategy or force structure and with a reasonable application of resources. The alliance is headed in the right general direction: it needs to do what it is doing, only better and faster. This does not mean we relax. As in many fields, the real profits are at the margin....
(DSB July 1987: 18-21)

London Declaration on a Transformed North Atlantic Alliance
July 6, 1990

Issued by the Heads of State and Government participating in the Meeting of the North Atlantic Council in London on 5th-6th July 1990

1. Europe has entered a new, promising era. Central and Eastern Europe is liberating itself. The Soviet Union has embarked on the long journey toward a free society. The walls that once confined people and ideas are collapsing. Europeans are determining their own destiny. They are choosing freedom. They are choosing economic liberty. They are choosing peace. They are choosing a Europe whole and free. As a consequence, this Alliance must and will adapt.

2. The North Atlantic Alliance has been the most successful defensive alliance in history. As our Alliance enters its fifth decade and looks ahead to a new century, it must continue to provide for the common defence. This Alliance has done much to bring about the new Europe. No-one, however,

can be certain of the future. We need to keep standing together, to extend the long peace we have enjoyed these past four decades. Yet our Alliance must be even more an agent of change. It can help build the structures of a more united continent, supporting security and stability with the strength of our shared faith in democracy, the rights of the individual, and the peaceful resolution of disputes. We reaffirm that security and stability do not lie solely in the military dimension, and we intend to enhance the political component of our Alliance as provided for by Article 2 of our Treaty.

3. The unification of Germany means that the division of Europe is also being overcome. A united Germany in the Atlantic Alliance of free democracies and part of the growing political and economic integration of the European Community will be an indispensable factor of stability, which is needed in the heart of Europe. The move within the European Community towards political union, including the development of a European identity in the domain of security, will also contribute to Atlantic solidarity and to the establishment of a just and lasting order of peace throughout the whole of Europe.

4. We recognize that, in the new Europe, the security of every state is inseparably linked to the security of its neighbors. NATO must become an institution where Europeans, Canadians and Americans work together not only for the common defence, but to build new partnerships with all the nations of Europe. The Atlantic Community must reach out to the countries of the East which were our adversaries in the Cold War, and extend to them the hand of friendship.

5. We will remain a defensive alliance and will continue to defend all the territory of all of our members. We have no aggressive intentions and we commit ourselves to the peaceful resolution of all disputes. We will never in any circumstance be the first to use force.

6. The member states of the North Atlantic Alliance propose to the member states of the Warsaw Treaty organization a joint declaration in which we solemnly state that we are no longer adversaries and reaffirm our intention to refrain from the threat or use of force against the territorial integrity or political independence of any state, or from acting in any other manner inconsistent with the purposes and principles of the United Nations Charter and with the CSCE Final Act. We invite all other CSCE member states to join us in this commitment to non-aggression.

7. In that spirit, and to reflect the changing political role of the Alliance, we today invite President Gorbachev on behalf of the Soviet Union, and representatives of the other Central and Eastern European countries to come to Brussels and address the North Atlantic Council. We today also invite the governments of the Union of Soviet Socialist Republics, the Czech and Slovak Federal Republic, the Hungarian Republic, the Republic of Poland, the People's Republic of Bulgaria and Romania to come to NATO, not just to

visit, but to establish regular diplomatic liaison with NATO. This will make it possible for us to share with them our thinking and deliberations in this historic period of change.

8. Our Alliance will do its share to overcome the legacy of decades of suspicion. We are ready to intensify military contacts, including those of NATO Military Commanders, with Moscow and other Central and Eastern European capitals.

9. We welcome the invitation to NATO Secretary General Manfred Wörner to visit Moscow and meet with Soviet leaders.

10. Military leaders from throughout Europe gathered earlier this year in Vienna to talk about their forces and doctrine. NATO proposes another such meeting this Autumn to promote common understanding. We intend to establish an entirely different quality of openness in Europe, including an agreement on "Open Skies".

11. The significant presence of North American conventional and US nuclear forces in Europe demonstrates the underlying political compact that binds North America's fate to Europe's democracies. But, as Europe changes, we must profoundly alter the way we think about defence.

12. To reduce our military requirements, sound arms control agreements are essential. That is why we put the highest priority on completing this year the first treaty to reduce and limit conventional armed forces in Europe (CFE) along with the completion of a meaningful CSBM package. These talks should remain in continuous session until the work is done. Yet we hope to go further. We propose that, once a CFE Treaty is signed, follow-on talks should begin with the same membership and mandate, with the goal of building on the current agreement with additional measures, including measures to limit manpower in Europe. With this goal in mind, a commitment will be given at the time of signature of the CFE Treaty concerning the manpower levels of a unified Germany.

13. Our objective will be to conclude the negotiations on the follow-on to CFE and CSBMs as soon as possible and looking to the follow-up meeting of the CSCE to be held in Helsinki in 1992. We will seek through new conventional arms control negotiations, within the CSCE framework, further far-reaching measures in the 1990s to limit the offensive capability of conventional armed forces in Europe, so as to prevent any nation from maintaining disproportionate military power on the continent. NATO's High Level Task Force will formulate a detailed position for these follow-on conventional arms control talks. We will make provisions as needed for different regions to redress disparities and to ensure that no one's security is harmed at any stage.

Furthermore, we will continue to explore broader arms control and confidence building opportunities. This is an ambitious agenda, but it matches our goal: enduring peace in Europe.

14. As Soviet troops leave Eastern Europe and a treaty limiting conventional armed forces is implemented, the Alliance's integrated force structure and its strategy will change fundamentally to include the following elements:

- NATO will field smaller and restructured active forces. These forces will be highly mobile and versatile so that Allied leaders will have maximum flexibility in deciding how to respond to a crisis. It will rely increasingly on multinational corps made up of national units.
- NATO will scale back the readiness of its active units, reducing training requirements and the number of exercises.
- NATO will rely more heavily on the ability to build up larger forces if and when they might be needed.

15. To keep the peace, the Alliance must maintain for the foreseeable future an appropriate mix of nuclear and conventional forces, based in Europe, and kept up to date where necessary. But, as a defensive Alliance, NATO has always stressed that none of its weapons will ever be used except in self-defence and that we seek the lowest and most stable level of nuclear forces needed to secure the prevention of war.

16. The political and military changes in Europe, and the prospects of further changes, now allow the Allies concerned to go further. They will thus modify the size and adapt the tasks of their nuclear deterrent forces. They have concluded that, as a result of the new political and military conditions in Europe, there will be a significantly reduced role for sub-strategic nuclear systems of the shortest range. They have decided specifically that, once negotiations begin on short-range nuclear forces, the Alliance will propose, in return for reciprocal action by the Soviet Union, the elimination of all its nuclear artillery shells from Europe.

17. New negotiations between the United States and the Soviet Union on the reduction of short-range nuclear forces should begin shortly after a CFE agreement is signed. The Allies concerned will develop an arms control framework for these negotiations which takes into account our requirements for far fewer nuclear weapons, and the diminished need for sub-strategic nuclear systems of the shortest range.

18. Finally, with the total withdrawal of Soviet stationed forces and the implementation of a CFE agreement the Allies concerned can reduce their reliance on nuclear weapons. These will continue to fulfil an essential role in the overall strategy of the Alliance to prevent war by ensuring that there are no circumstances in which nuclear retaliation in response to military action might be discounted. However, in the transformed Europe, they will be able to adopt a new NATO strategy making nuclear force truly weapons of last resort.

19. We approve the mandate given in Turnberry to the North Atlantic Council in Permanent Session to oversee the ongoing work on the adaptation of the Alliance to the new circumstances. It should report its conclusions as soon as possible.

20. In the context of these revised plans for defense and arms control, and with the advice of NATO Military Authorities and all member states concerned, NATO will prepare a new Allied military strategy moving away from "forward defense", where appropriate, towards a reduced forward presence and modifying "flexible response" to reflect a reduced reliance on nuclear weapons. In that connection, NATO will elaborate new force plans consistent with the revolutionary changes in Europe. NATO will also provide a forum for Allied consultation on the upcoming negotiations on short-range nuclear forces.

21. The Conference on Security and Cooperation in Europe (CSCE) should become more prominent in Europe's future, bringing together the countries of Europe and North America. We support a CSCE Summit later this year in Paris which would include the signature of a CFE agreement and would set new standards for the establishment, and preservation, of free societies. It should endorse, inter alia:

- CSCE principles on the right to free and fair elections;
- CSCE commitments to respect and uphold the rule of law.
- CSCE guidelines for enhancing economic cooperation, based on the development of free and competitive market economies; and
- CSCE cooperation on environmental protection.

22. We further propose that the CSCE Summit in Paris decide how the CSCE can be institutionalized to provide a forum for wider political dialogue in a more united Europe. We recommend that CSCE governments establish:

- a programme for regular consultations among member governments at the Heads of State and Government or Ministerial level, at least once each year, with other periodic meetings of officials to prepare for and follow up on these consultations.
- a schedule of CSCE review conferences once every two years to assess progress toward a Europe whole and free;
- a small CSCE secretariat to coordinate these meetings and conferences;
- a CSCE mechanism to monitor elections in all the CSCE countries, on the basis of the Copenhagen Document;
- a CSCE Center for the Prevention of Conflict that might serve as a forum for exchanges of military information, discussion of unusual

military activities, and the conciliation of disputes involving CSCE member states; and

- a CSCE parliamentary body, the Assembly of Europe, to be based on the existing parliamentary assembly of the Council of Europe, in Strasbourg, and include representatives of all CSCE member states.

The sites of these new institutions should reflect the fact that the newly democratic countries of Central and Eastern Europe form part of the political structures of the new Europe.

23. Today, our Alliance begins a major transformation. Working with all the countries of Europe, we are determined to create enduring peace on this continent.

(PPP Bush 1990 II: 964-967)

President Bush's Statement on German Membership in the North Atlantic Treaty Organization

July 16, 1990

I welcome President Gorbachev's statement, at his press conference with Chancellor Kohl, accepting a united Germany's right to choose to remain a member of NATO. This comment demonstrates statesmanship and strengthens efforts to build enduring relationships based on cooperation. It can be seen as a response, perhaps in part, to the outcome of the NATO summit in London, where the alliance displayed its readiness to adapt to the new realities in Europe and reach out to former adversaries in the East.

Five months ago, in February, Chancellor Kohl and I agreed that a united Germany should remain a full member of the North Atlantic alliance, including its military structures. East German Prime Minister de Maiziere joins us in supporting continued German membership in NATO. The Helsinki Final Act guarantees Germany's right to make this choice. And we think this solution is in the best interests of all the countries of Europe, including the Soviet Union.

(PPP Bush 1990 II: 1013)

Treaty on the Final Settlement with Respect to Germany

September 12, 1990

The Federal Republic of Germany, the German Democratic Republic, the French Republic, the Union of Soviet Socialist Republics, the United Kingdom of Great Britain and Northern Ireland, and the United States of America, ... have agreed as follows:

Article 1

(1) The united Germany shall comprise the territory of the Federal Republic of Germany, the German Democratic Republic, and the whole of Berlin. Its external borders shall be the borders of the Federal Republic of Germany and the German Democratic Republic and shall be definitive from the date on which the present Treaty comes into force. The confirmation of the definitive nature of the borders of the united Germany is an essential element of the peaceful order in Europe.

(2) The united Germany and the Republic of Poland shall confirm the existing border between them in a treaty that is binding under international law.

(3) The united Germany has no territorial claims whatsoever against other states and shall not assert any in the future.

(4) The Governments of the Federal Republic of Germany and the German Democratic Republic shall ensure that the constitution of the united Germany does not contain any provision incompatible with these principles. This applies accordingly to the provisions laid down in the preamble, the second sentence of Article 23, and Article 146 of the Basic Law for the Federal Republic of Germany....

Article 2

The Governments of the Federal Republic of Germany and the German Democratic Republic reaffirm their declarations that only peace will emanate from German soil. According to the constitution of the united Germany, acts tending to and undertaken with the intent to disturb the peaceful relations between nations, especially to prepare for aggressive war, are unconstitutional and a punishable offense. The Governments of the Federal Republic of Germany and the German Democratic Republic declare that the united Germany will never employ any of its weapons except in accordance with its constitution and the Charter of the United Nations.

Article 3

(1) The Governments of the Federal Republic of Germany and the German Democratic Republic reaffirm their renunciation of the manufacture and possession of and control over nuclear, biological and chemical weapons. They declare that the united Germany, too, will abide by these commitments. In particular, rights and obligations arising from the Treaty on the Non-Proliferation of Nuclear Weapons of July 1, 1968, will continue to apply to the united Germany.

(2) The Government of the Federal Republic of Germany, acting in full agreement with the Government of the German Democratic Republic, made the following statement on August 30, 1990 in Vienna at the Negotiations on Conventional Armed Forces in Europe:

> "The Government of the Federal Republic of Germany undertakes to reduce the personnel strength of the armed forces of the united Germany to 370,000 (ground, air, and naval forces) within three to four years. This reduction will commence on the entry into force of the first CFE agreement. Within the scope of this overall ceiling no more than 345,000 will belong to the ground and air forces which, pursuant to the agreed mandate, alone are the subject of the Negotiations on Conventional Armed Forces in Europe. The federal government regards its commitment to reduce ground and air forces as a significant German contribution to the reduction of conventional armed forces in Europe. It assumes that in follow-on negotiations the other participants in the negotiations, too, will render their contribution to enhancing security and stability in Europe, including measures to limit personnel strengths."

The Government of the German Democratic Republic has expressly associated itself with this statement....

Article 4

(1) The Governments of the Federal Republic of Germany, the German Democratic Republic, and the Union of Soviet Socialist Republics state that the united Germany and the Union of Soviet Socialist Republics will settle by treaty the conditions for and the duration of the presence of Soviet armed forces on the territory of the present German Democratic Republic and of Berlin, as well as the conduct of the withdrawal of these armed forces which will be completed by the end of 1994, in connection with the implementation of the undertaking of the Federal Republic of Germany and the German Democratic Republic referred to in paragraph 2 of Article 3 of the present treaty....

Article 5

(1) Until the completion of the withdrawal of the Soviet armed forces from the territory of the present German Democratic Republic and of Berlin in accordance with Article 4 of the present treaty, only German territorial defense units which are not integrated into the alliance structures to which German armed forces in the rest of German territory are assigned will be stationed in that territory as armed forces of the united Germany. During that period and subject to the provisions of paragraph 2 of this Article, armed forces of other states will not be stationed in that territory or carry out any other military activity there.

(2) For the duration of the presence of Soviet armed forces in the territory of the present German Democratic Republic and of Berlin, armed forces of the French Republic, the United Kingdom of Great Britain and Northern Ireland, and the United States of America will, upon German re-

quest, remain stationed in Berlin by agreement to this effect between the government of the united Germany and the governments of the states concerned. The number of troops and the amount of equipment of all non-German armed forces stationed in Berlin will not be greater than at the time of signature of the present treaty. New categories of weapons will not be introduced there by non-German armed forces. The government of the united Germany will conclude with the governments of those states which have armed forces stationed in Berlin treaties with conditions which are fair taking account of the relations existing with the states concerned.

(3) Following the completion of the withdrawal of the Soviet armed forces from the territory of the present German Democratic Republic and of Berlin, units of German armed forces assigned to military alliance structures in the same way as those in the rest of German territory may also be stationed in that part of Germany, but without nuclear weapon carriers. This does not apply to conventional weapon systems which may have other capabilities in addition to conventional ones but which in that part of Germany are equipped for a conventional role and designated only for such. Foreign armed forces and nuclear weapons or their carriers will not be stationed in that part of Germany or deployed there.

Article 6

The right of the united Germany to belong to alliances, with all the rights and responsibilities arising therefrom, shall not be affected by the present treaty.

Article 7

(1) The French Republic, the Union of Soviet Socialist Republics, the United Kingdom of Great Britain and Northern Ireland, and the United States of America hereby terminate their rights and responsibilities relating to Berlin and to Germany as a whole. As a result, the corresponding related quadripartite agreements, decisions and practices are terminated and all related Four Power institutions are dissolved.

(2) The united Germany shall have accordingly full sovereignty over its internal and external affairs....

(DSD 8 October 1990: 165-167)

Treaty on Conventional Armed Forces in Europe

November 19, 1990

...White House Fact Sheet

Today the 22 members of NATO and the Warsaw Pact signed a landmark agreement limiting conventional armed forces in Europe (CFE). The CFE treaty will establish parity in major conventional armaments between East and

West in Europe from the Atlantic to the Urals. The treaty will limit the size of Soviet forces to about one third of the total armaments permitted to all the countries in Europe. The treaty includes an unprecedented monitoring regime, including detailed information exchange, on-site inspection, challenge inspection, and monitoring of destruction.

East-West Limits

The treaty sets equal ceilings from the Atlantic to the Urals on key armaments essential for conducting surprise attack and initiating large-scale offensive operations. Neither side may have more than:

20,000 tanks
20,000 artillery pieces
30,000 armored combat vehicles (ACV's)
6,800 combat aircraft
2,000 attack helicopters.

To further limit the readiness of armed forces, the treaty sets equal ceilings on equipment that may be with active units. Other ground equipment must be in designated permanent storage sites. The limits for equipment each side may have in active units are:

16,500 tanks
17,000 artillery pieces
27,300 armored combat vehicles (ACV's).

In connection with the CFE treaty, the six members of the Warsaw Pact signed a treaty in Budapest on November 3, 1990, which divides the Warsaw Pact allocation by country. The members of NATO have consulted through NATO mechanisms and have agreed on national entitlements. These national entitlements may be adjusted.

Country Ceilings

The treaty limits the proportion of armaments that can be held by any one country in Europe to about one third of the total for all countries in Europe — the "sufficiency" rule. This provision constrains the size of Soviet forces more than any other in the treaty. These limits are:

13,300 tanks
13,700 artillery pieces
20,000 armored combat vehicles (ACV's)
5,150 combat aircraft
1,500 attack helicopters.

Regional Arrangements

In addition to limits on the number of armaments in each category on each side, the treaty also includes regional limits to prevent destabilizing force concentrations of ground equipment.

Destruction

Equipment reduced to meet the ceilings must be destroyed or, in a limited number of cases, have its military capability destroyed, allowing the chassis to be used for nonmilitary purposes. After the treaty enters into force, there will be a 4-month baseline inspection period. After the 4-month baseline period, 25 percent of the destruction must be complete by the end of 1 year, 60 percent by the end of 2 years, and all destruction required by the treaty must be complete by the end of 3 years. Parties have 5 years to convert limited amounts of equipment.

Large amounts of equipment will be destroyed to meet the obligations of the CFE treaty. The Soviet Union alone will be obliged to destroy thousands of weapons, much more equipment than will be reduced by all the NATO countries combined. NATO will meet its destruction obligations by destroying its oldest equipment. In a process called "cascading," NATO members with newer equipment, including the U.S., have agreed to transfer some of this equipment to allies with older equipment. Cascading will not reduce NATO's destruction obligation. Under the cascading system, no U.S. equipment must be destroyed to meet CFE ceilings. Some 2,000 pieces of U.S. equipment will be transferred to our NATO allies.

Verification

The treaty includes unprecedented provisions for detailed information exchanges, on-site inspections, challenge inspections, and on-site monitoring of destruction. At the initiative of the U.S., NATO has established a system to cooperate in monitoring the treaty. Parties have an unlimited right to monitor the process of destruction. The CFE treaty is of unlimited duration and will enter into force 10 days after all parties have ratified the agreement.
(PPP Bush 1990 II: 1640-1645)

Text of the Joint Declaration of Twenty-Two States
November 19, 1990

The Heads of State or Government of Belgium, Bulgaria, Canada, the Czech and Slovak Federal Republic, Denmark, France, Germany, Greece, Hungary, Iceland, Italy, Luxembourg, the Netherlands, Norway, Poland, Portugal, Romania, Spain, Turkey, the Union of Soviet Socialist Republics, the United Kingdom and the United States of America

- greatly welcoming the historic changes in Europe,
- gratified by the growing implementation throughout Europe of a common commitment to pluralist democracy, the rule of law and human rights, which are essential to lasting security on the continent,
- affirming the end of the era of division and confrontation which has lasted for more than four decades, the improvement in relations among their countries and the contribution this makes to the security of all,
- confident that the signature of the Treaty on Conventional Armed Forces in Europe represents a major contribution to the common objective of increased security and stability in Europe, and
- convinced that these developments must form part of a continuing process of co-operation in building the structures of a more united continent,

Issue the following Declaration:

1. The signatories solemnly declare that, in the new era of European relations which is beginning, they are no longer adversaries, will build new partnerships and extend to each other the hand of friendship.

2. They recall their obligations under the Charter of the United Nations and reaffirm all of their commitments under the Helsinki Final Act. They stress that all of the ten Helsinki Principles are of primary significance and that, accordingly, they will be equally and unreservedly applied, each of them being interpreted taking into account the others. In that context, they affirm their obligation and commitment to refrain from the threat or use of force against the territorial integrity or the political independence of any State, from seeking to change existing borders by threat or use of force, and from acting in any other manner inconsistent with the principles and purposes of those documents. None of their weapons will ever be used except in self-defense or otherwise in accordance with the Charter of the United Nations.

3. They recognize that security is indivisible and that the security of each of their countries is inextricably linked to the security of all the States participating in the Conference on Security and Co-operation in Europe.

4. They undertake to maintain only such military capabilities as are necessary to prevent war and provide for effective defense. They will bear in mind the relationship between military capabilities and doctrines.

5. They reaffirm that every State has the right to be or not to be a party to a treaty of alliance.

6. They note with approval the intensification of political and military contacts among them to promote mutual understanding and confidence. They welcome in this context the positive responses made to recent proposals for new regular diplomatic liaison.

7. They declare their determination to contribute actively to conventional, nuclear and chemical arms control and disarmament agreements which enhance security and stability for all. In particular, they call for the early entry into force of the Treaty on Conventional Armed Forces in Europe and commit themselves to continue the process of strengthening peace in Europe through conventional arms control within the framework of the CSCE. They welcome the prospect of new negotiations between the United States and the Soviet Union on the reduction of their short-range nuclear forces.

8. They welcome the contribution that confidence- and security-building measures have made to lessening tensions and fully support the further development of such measures. They reaffirm the importance of the "Open Skies" initiative and their determination to bring the negotiations to a successful conclusion as soon as possible.

9. They pledge to work together with the other CSCE participating States to strengthen the CSCE process so that it can make an even greater contribution to security and stability in Europe. They recognize in particular the need to enhance political consultations among CSCE participants and to develop other CSCE mechanisms. They are convinced that the Treaty on Conventional Armed Forces in Europe and agreement on a substantial new set of CSEBMs, together with new patterns of co-operation in the framework of the CSCE, will lead to increased security and thus to enduring peace and stability in Europe.

10. They believe that the preceding points repeat the deep longing of their peoples for close co-operation and mutual understanding and declare that they will work steadily for the further development of their relations in accordance with the present Declaration as well as with the principles set forth in the Helsinki Final Act....
(PPP Bush 1990 II: 1640-1645)

Presidential Determination No. 91-37 — Memorandum to the Secretary of Defense on End Strength Level of United States Armed Forces in Europe
May 29, 1991

...Consistent with section 406(b) of the National Defense Authorization Act for Fiscal Year 1991 (Public Law 101-510; 104 Stat. 1546), I hereby authorize an end strength level of members of the Armed Forces assigned to permanent duty ashore in European member nations of the North Atlantic Treaty organization in excess of 261,855 for fiscal year 1991, and determine that the national security interests of the United States require such authorization....
(PPP Bush 1991: 579)

Declaration on Developments in the Soviet Union by the Heads of State and Government Participating in the Meeting of the North Atlantic Council in Rome

November 8, 1991

1. We, the Heads of State and Government of the North Atlantic Alliance, warmly welcome the historic events that are fundamentally transforming the Soviet Union as we have known it and the relationships among the republics. By their resolute and courageous stand against the illegal coup of 19th August, the men and women of the Soviet Union have affirmed their determination to build a new future based upon democracy, human rights, the rule of law, and economic liberty. The nations of the Atlantic Alliance pledge themselves to assist in this great endeavor. We are prepared to build our relationships with the Soviet Union and the republics on the basis of the following fundamental principles that have guided our own policies and practices for decades.

2. It is for the peoples of the Soviet Union to decide their future relationship through peaceful and democratic means. At the same time, we encourage them to progress towards a common ground of cooperation, both among themselves and with us. In this process, there is no place for threats, intimidation, coercion or violence. Authorities at all levels should respect international norms and international obligations, especially those embodied in the Helsinki Final Act, the Charter of Paris, and other CSCE documents. Consistent with these commitments, government must be based on democracy through free and fair elections, and on the rule of law. Inalienable human rights must be guaranteed, including full respect for the individual and protection of the rights of persons belonging to minorities.

3. In a period of dramatic political change, it is important also to the development of our relations that leaders of the Soviet Union and the republics implement policies that contribute to international peace and security. In this respect, it is critical that the Soviet Union and the republics take all necessary actions to ensure that international agreements signed by the USSR, especially the START Treaty, the CFE Treaty, the Non-Proliferation Treaty, and the Biological Weapons Convention are respected, ratified, and implemented. We call upon all authorities to refrain from any steps that could lead to proliferation of nuclear weapons or other means of mass destruction. We therefore welcome the intention of the Soviet leadership to ensure the safe, responsible and reliable control of these weapons under a single authority. This matter affects the security interests of the entire Atlantic Alliance, as well as those of the international community as a whole. The Soviet and republic governments should adopt firm measures to prevent the export of nuclear or other potentially destabilizing military technologies. We urge restraint in the development of conventional military forces that by their size and character could exacerbate political tensions, retard market economic

reform, and contradict efforts toward lower and more stable levels of forces as embodied in the CFE Treaty. Because it reduces the dangers of instability and enhances openness, the CFE Treaty is in everyone's interest, including those of the Soviet Union and the republics.

4. The Allies are firmly convinced that political change should be accompanied by economic liberty and the building of market economies. We support the development of economic policies that promote trade and economic cooperation among republics in the interest of growth and stability. In this context, it is essential that all the republics assume their appropriate responsibilities vis-a-vis Soviet international obligations, which would facilitate integration of the Union and the republics into the world economy. Newly established links with the international financial institutions should facilitate rapid reform towards the development of a market economy as the basis for economic recovery and prosperity for the Union and the republics. The Allies stand ready to assist in this historic undertaking, including through technical assistance in key sectors. In addition, we are providing humanitarian support to the Soviet peoples as they cope with the political and economic crises that confront them. We consider such assistance a vital contribution to the future security of Europe and of the world as a whole.

5. We hope that leaders and authorities at all levels throughout the Union and the republics will demonstrate their commitment to the values and principles we have reaffirmed in this statement.

6. The North Atlantic Council will continue to consult actively on developments in the Soviet Union, with a view to harmonizing our approach towards unfolding events.

(PPP Bush 1991 II: 1410-1416)

President Clinton's Remarks to the Departing United States Troops in Berlin
July 12, 1994

...In 1945, at the dawn of the cold war, President Truman came here to Berlin. From atop the American headquarters he raised high the Stars and Stripes and stated then his hope that one day Berlin would be part of what he called a better world, a peaceful world, a world in which all the people will have an opportunity to enjoy the good things in life. Well, today Berlin is free; Berlin is united. Berlin has taken its rightful place in that better world. The symbolic walk that the First Lady and I and Chancellor and Mrs. Kohl took through the Brandenburg Gate and the symbolic ceremony held for the first time with an American President on the eastern side of that gate, gave full evidence to the success of those efforts.

And now, with the cold war over, we gather to honor those Americans who helped to bring it to an end, who helped to unite Berlin, who helped to make it possible for us to walk through the Brandenburg Gate, the men and women of the Berlin Brigade. Few moments in the life of a nation are as proud as when we can thank our sons and daughters in uniform for a job well done. Today we share such a moment.... And I say to all of you, the members of the Berlin Brigade, America salutes you; mission accomplished.

From Checkpoint Charlie to Doughboy City to Tempelhof Airport and beyond, more than 100,000 American men and women have served in Berlin. More than anyone they showed the patience it took to win the cold war. More than anyone, they knew the dangers of a world on edge. They would have been the first casualties in the world's final war, yet they never flinched....

Now we leave, but the friendship between Germany and America and the thousands and thousands of personal friendships between Germans and Americans live on. And our commitment to the good and brave people of Berlin and Germany lives on. Together, we are building on our vision of a Europe united, pursuing a common dream of democracy, free market, security based on peace, not conquest. We stand ready to defend the interests of freedom against new threats, and I am committed to keeping some 100,000 troops in Europe to make sure that commitment is good.

Today our troops are strong. They have what they need to do the job; they deserve it and they must always have it. The lessons we have learned for 50 years tell us that we must never let the forces of tyranny rule again.

In the long struggle to free Berlin, no one ever knew for sure when the day of liberty would come, not when Harry Truman raised the flag in 1945 or when the first airlift planes landed in 1948 or when the hateful Wall went up in 1961. But in all those years, the defenders of Berlin never gave up. You stood your ground; you kept watch; you fortified an island of hope. Now we go forward to defend freedom and, strengthened by your devotion, we work for the day when we can say everywhere in the world what you made it possible for us to say here today in Berlin: Mission accomplished.
(WCPD Clinton 1994: 1472-1473)

5

Nuclear Strategy, Weaponry, and Arms Control

INTRODUCTION

Since 1945 the world has lived with the knowledge that weapons of such terrifying potential exist that the survival of civilization itself as we know it is at stake. For that reason, issues relating to nuclear weapons have assumed a high importance in U.S. national security policy. When the U.S. lost sole possession of these weapons in 1949, questions of arms control and negotiations assumed a particular importance.

1987 was an important year for arms control. In that year an entire class of nuclear weapons delivery systems was eliminated by treaty: land based intermediate range nuclear missiles. The United States and the Soviet Union did not want for means to attack one another after the signing of the INF Treaty, but the successful negotiations gave hope that future agreements were also possible. The assertion by the Reagan administration that it was necessary to be seen as manifestly willing to build the class of weapons that was being negotiated away in order to induce the other side to negotiate seriously appeared to be borne out. Similarly, the United States and the Soviet Union negotiated a treaty limiting strategic arms, those long-range weapons capable of striking one country from the other.

Another significant arms control issue was the Strategic Defense Initiative (called "Star Wars" by its critics) of the Reagan administration. The stated goal of the initiative was to counter the intercontinental ballistic missile (ICBM) force of the Soviet Union by means of a space-based system of sensors and interceptors. Whether such a system would be effective was arguable, but it certainly was not likely to be leak-proof against a massive and coordinated attack. A more limited protection against ballistic missiles, not necessarily space-based, remains under strong consideration to protect the United States from accidental launches or from the limited attack possible from Third

World states with access to modern nuclear and missile technology. Other issues besides technical feasibility included the effect on the stability of deterrence if one side had such a system in place (or even if both sides did) and the affect of the technological competition upon the Soviet Union itself. Such competition is extraordinarily expensive, and Reagan apologists are not hesitant to assert that the extra expenses of the Soviet attempt to match the SDI provided the final push that toppled the system.

Unfortunately, the problems associated with nuclear weapons did not cease with the demise of the Soviet Union. The Soviet successor states agreed to denuclearize, but proliferation concerns remain as ex-Soviet technology and skilled engineers find new markets in the Third World. Nuclear deterrence in such a decentralized milieu, with leaders of varying sophistication and motivations, will be a far more complex proposition, with results that are difficult to predict.

ARMS CONTROL AND DISARMAMENT

Treaty Between the United States of America and the Union of Soviet Socialist Republics on the Elimination of Their Intermediate-Range and Shorter-Range Missiles

December 8, 1987

...Article IV

1. Each Party shall eliminate all its intermediate-range missiles and launchers of such missiles, and all support structures and support equipment of the categories listed in the Memorandum of Understanding associated with such missiles and launchers, so that no later than three years after entry into force of this Treaty and thereafter no such missiles, launchers, support structures or support equipment shall be possessed by either Party.

2. To implement paragraph 1 of this Article, upon entry into force of this Treaty, both Parties shall begin and continue throughout the duration of each phase, the reduction of all types of their deployed and non-deployed intermediate-range missiles and deployed and non-deployed launchers of such missiles and support structures and support equipment associated with such missiles and launchers in accordance with the provisions of this Treaty. These reductions shall be implemented in two phases so that:

(a) by the end of the first phase, that is, no later than 29 months after entry into force of this Treaty:

(i) the number of deployed launchers of intermediate-range missiles for each Party shall not exceed the number of launchers that are capable of carrying or containing at one time missiles considered by the Parties to carry 171 warheads;

(ii) the number of deployed intermediate-range missiles for each Party shall not exceed the number of such missiles considered by the Parties to carry 180 warheads;

(iii) the aggregate number of deployed and non-deployed launchers of intermediate range missiles for each Party shall not exceed the number of launchers that are capable of carrying or containing at one time missiles considered by the Parties to carry 200 warheads;

(iv) the aggregate number of deployed and non-deployed intermediate range missiles for each Party shall not exceed the number of such missiles considered by the Parties to carry 200 warheads; and

(v) the ratio of the aggregate number of deployed and non-deployed intermediate range GLBMs of existing types for each Party to the aggregate number of deployed and non-deployed intermediate range missiles of existing types possessed by that Party shall not exceed the ratio of such intermediate range GLBMs to such intermediate range missiles for that Party as of November 1, 1987, as set forth in the Memorandum of Understanding; and

(b) by the end of the second phase, that is, no later than three years after entry into force of this Treaty, all intermediate range missiles of each Party, launchers of such missiles and all support structures and support equipment of the categories listed in the Memorandum of Understanding associated with such missiles and launchers, shall be eliminated.

Article V

1. Each Party shall eliminate all its shorter-range missiles and launchers of such missiles, and all support equipment of the categories listed in the Memorandum of Understanding associated with such missiles and launchers, so that no later than 18 months after entry into force of this Treaty and thereafter no such missiles, launchers or support equipment shall be possessed by either Party.

2. No later than 90 days after entry into force of this Treaty, each Party shall complete the removal of all its deployed shorter-range missiles and deployed and non deployed launchers of such missiles to elimination facilities and shall retain them at those locations until they are eliminated in accordance with the procedures set forth in the Protocol on Elimination. No later than 12 months after entry into force of this Treaty, each Party shall complete the removal of all its non-deployed shorter-range missiles to elimination facilities and shall retain them at those locations until they are eliminated in accordance with the procedures set forth in the Protocol on Elimination.

3. Shorter-range missiles and launchers of such missiles shall not be located at the same elimination facility. Such facilities shall be separated by no less than 1000 kilometers....

Article VI

1. Upon entry into force of this Treaty and thereafter, neither Party shall:

(a) produce or flight-test any intermediate-range missiles or produce any stages of Such missiles or any launchers of such missiles; or

(b) produce, flight-test or launch any shorter-range missiles or produce any stages of such missiles or any launchers of such missiles.

2. Notwithstanding paragraph 1 of this Article, each Party shall have the right to produce a type of GLBM not limited by this Treaty which uses a stage which is outwardly similar to, but not interchangeable with, a stage of an existing type of intermediate range GLBM having more than one stage, providing that that Party does not produce any other stage which is outwardly similar to, but not interchangeable with, any other stage of an existing type of intermediate range GLBM.

Article VII

For the purposes of this Treaty:

1. If a ballistic missile or a cruise missile has been flight-tested or deployed for weapon delivery, all missiles of that type shall be considered to be weapon-delivery vehicles.

2. If a GLBM or GLCM is an intermediate-range missile, all GLBMs or GLCMs of that type shall be considered to be intermediate-range missiles. If a GLBM or GLCM is a shorter-range missile, all GLBMs or GLCMs of that type shall be considered to be shorter-range missiles.

3. If a GLBM is of a type developed and tested solely to intercept and counter objects not located on the surface of the earth, it shall not be considered to be a missile to which the limitations of this Treaty apply.

4. The range capability of a GLBM not listed in Article 111 of this Treaty shall be considered to be the maximum range to which it has been tested. The range capability of a GLCM not listed in Article 111 of this Treaty shall be considered to be the maximum distance which can be covered by the missile in its standard design mode flying until fuel exhaustion, determined by projecting its flight path onto the earth's sphere from the point of launch to the point of impact. GLBMs or GLCMs that have a range capability equal to or in excess of 500 kilometers but not in excess of 100 kilometers shall be considered to be shorter-range missiles. GLBMs or GLCMs that have a range capability in excess of 1000 kilometers but not in excess of 500 kilometers shall be considered to be intermediate range missiles.

5. The maximum number of warheads an existing type of intermediate-range missile or shorter-range missile carries shall be considered to be the number listed for missiles of that type in the Memorandum of Understanding.

6. Each GLBM or GLCM shall be considered to carry the maximum number of warheads listed for a GLBM or GLCM of that type in the Memorandum of Understanding.

7. If a launcher has been tested for launching a GLBM or a GLCM, all launchers of that type shall be considered to have been tested for launching GLBMs or GLCMs.

8. If a launcher has contained or launched a particular type of GLBM or GLCM, all launchers of that type shall be considered to be launchers of that type of GLBM or GLCM.

9. The number of missiles each launcher of an existing type of intermediate-range missile or shorter-range missile shall be considered to be capable of carrying or containing at one time is the number listed for launchers of missiles of that type in the Memorandum of Understanding.

10. Except in the case of elimination in accordance with the procedures set forth in the Protocol on Elimination, the following shall apply:

(a) for GLBMs which are stored or moved in separate stages, the longest stage of an intermediate-range or shorter-range GLBM shall be counted as a complete missile;

(b) for GLBMs which are not stored or moved in separate stages, a canister of the type used in the launch of an intermediate-range GLBM, unless a Party proves to the satisfaction of the other Party that it does not contain such a missile, or an assembled intermediate range or shorter-range GLBM, shall be counted as a complete missile, and

(c) for GLCMs, the airframe of an intermediate-range or shorter-range GLCM shall be counted as a complete missile.

11. A ballistic missile which is not a missile to be used in a ground-based mode shall not be considered to be a GLBM if it is test launched at a test site from a fixed land based launcher which is used solely for test purposes and which is distinguishable from GLBM launchers. A cruise missile which is not a missile to be used in a ground-based mode shall not be considered to be a GLCM if it is test-launched at a test site from a fixed land-based launcher which is used solely for test purposes and which is distinguishable from GLCM launchers.

12. Each Party shall have the right to produce and use for booster systems, which might otherwise be considered to be intermediate-range or shorter-range missiles, only existing types of booster stages for such booster systems. Launches of such booster systems shall not be considered to be flight testing of intermediate-range or shorter range missiles provided that:

(a) stages used in such booster systems are different from stages used in those missiles listed as existing types of intermediate range or shorter range missiles in Article III of this Treaty;

(b) such booster systems are used only for research and development purposes to test objects other than the booster systems themselves;

(c) the aggregate number of launchers for such booster systems shall not exceed 35 for each Party at any one time; and

(d) the launchers for such booster systems are fixed, emplaced above ground and located only at research and development launch sites which are specified in the Memorandum of Understanding. Research and development launch sites shall not be subject to inspection pursuant to Article XI of this Treaty....

Article X

1. Each Party shall eliminate its intermediate-range and shorter-range missiles and launchers of such missiles and support structures and support equipment associated with such missiles and launchers in accordance with the procedures set forth in the Protocol on Elimination.

2. Verification by on-site inspection of the elimination of items of missile systems specified in the Protocol on Elimination shall be carried out in accordance with Article XI of this Treaty, the Protocol on Elimination and the Protocol on Inspection.

3. When a Party removes its intermediate-range missiles, launchers of such missiles and support equipment associated with such missiles and launchers from deployment areas to elimination facilities for the purpose of their elimination, it shall do so in complete deployed organizational units. For the United States of America, these units shall be Pershing II batteries and BGM-109G flights. For the Union of Soviet Socialist Republics, these units shall be SS-20 regiments composed of two or three battalions.

4. Elimination of intermediate-range and shorter-range missiles and launchers of such missiles and support equipment associated with such missiles and launchers shall be carried out at the facilities that are specified in the Memorandum of Understanding or notified in accordance with paragraph 5(b) of Article IX of this Treaty, unless eliminated in accordance with Sections IV or V of the Protocol on Elimination. Support structures, associated with the missiles and launchers subject to this Treaty, that are subject to elimination shall be eliminated in situ.

5. Each Party shall have the right, during the first six months after entry into force of this Treaty, to eliminate by means of launching no more than 100 of its intermediate-range missiles.

6. Intermediate-range and shorter-range missiles which have been tested prior to entry into force of this Treaty, but never deployed, and which are not existing types of intermediate-range or shorter-range missiles listed in Article III of this Treaty, and launchers of such missiles, shall be eliminated within six months after entry into force of this Treaty in accordance with the procedures set forth in the Protocol on Elimination. Such missiles are:

(a) for the United States of America, missiles of the type designated by the United States of America as the Pershing 1B, which is known to the Union of Soviet Socialist Republics by the grime designation; and

(b) for the Union of Soviet Socialist Republics, missiles of the type designated by the Union of Soviet Socialist Republics as the RK-55, which is known to the United States of America as the SSC-X-4....

North Atlantic Treaty Organization Communique: A Comprehensive Concept of Arms Control and Disarmament
May 30, 1989
...IV. Arms Control and Disarmament: Principles and Objectives

34. Our vision for Europe is that of an undivided continent where military forces only exist to prevent war and to ensure self-defence, as has always been the case for the Allies, not for the purpose of initiating aggression or for political or military intimidation. Arms control can contribute to the realization of that vision as an integral part of the Alliance's security policy and on our overall approach to East-West relations.

35. The goal of Alliance arms control policy is to enhance security and stability. To this end, the Allies' arms control initiatives seek a balance at a lower level of forces and armaments through negotiated agreements and, as appropriate, unilateral actions, recognizing that arms control agreements are only possible where the negotiating partners share an interest in achieving a mutually satisfactory result. The Allies' arms control policy seeks to remove destabilizing asymmetries in forces or equipment. It also pursues measures designed to build mutual confidence and to reduce the risk of conflict by promoting greater transparency and predictability in military matters.

36. In enhancing security and stability, arms control can also bring important additional benefits for the Alliance. Given the dynamic aspects of the arms control process, the principles and results embodied in one agreement may facilitate other arms control steps. In this way arms control can also make possible further reductions in the level of Alliance forces and armaments, consistent with the Alliance's strategy of war prevention. Furthermore, as noted in Chapter II, arms control can make a significant contribution to the development of more constructive East-West relations and of a framework for further cooperation within a more stable and predictable international environment. Progress in arms control can also enhance public confidence in and promote support for our overall security policy.

Guiding Principles for Arms Control

37. The members of the Alliance will be guided by the following principles:

- *Security:* Arms control should enhance the security of all Allies. Both during the implementation period and following implementation, the Allies' strategy of deterrence and their ability to defend themselves, must remain credible and effective. Arms control measures should maintain the strategic unity and political cohesion of the Alliance, and should safeguard the principle of the indivisibility of Alliance security by avoiding the creation of areas of unequal security. Arms control measures should respect the legitimate security interests of all states and should not facilitate the transfer or intensification of threats to third party states or regions.

- *Stability:* Arms control measures should yield militarily significant results that enhance stability. To promote stability, arms control measures should reduce or eliminate those capabilities which are most threatening to the Alliance. Stability can also be enhanced by steps that promote greater transparency and predictability in military matters. Military stability requires the elimination of options for surprise attack and for largescale offensive action. Crisis stability requires that no state have forces of a size and configuration which, when compared with those of others, could enable it to calculate that it might gain a decisive advantage by being the first to resort to arms. Stability also requires measures which discourage destabilizing attempts to re-establish military advantage through the transfer of resources to other types of armament. Agreements must lead to final results that are both balanced and ensure equality of rights with respect to security.
- *Verifiability:* Effective and reliable verification is a fundamental requirement for arms control agreements. If arms control is to be effective and to build confidence, the verifiability of proposed arms control measures must, therefore, be of central concern for the Alliance. Progress in arms control should be measured against the record of compliance with existing agreements. Agreed arms control measures should exclude opportunities for circumvention.

Alliance Arms Control Objectives

38. In accordance with the above principles, the Allies are pursuing an ambitious arms control agenda for the coming years in the nuclear, conventional and chemical fields.

Nuclear Forces

39. The INF Agreement represents a milestone in the Allies' efforts to achieve a more secure peace at lower levels of arms. By 1991, it will lead to the total elimination of all United States and Soviet intermediate range land-based missiles, thereby removing the threat which such Soviet systems presented to the Alliance. Implementation of the agreement, however, will affect only a small proportion of the Soviet nuclear armory, and the Alliance continues to face a substantial array of modern and effective Soviet systems of all ranges. The full realization of the Alliance agenda thus requires that further steps be taken.

Strategic Nuclear Forces

40. Soviet strategic systems continue to pose a major threat to the whole of the Alliance. Deep cuts in such systems are in the direct interests of the entire Western Alliance, and therefore their achievement constitutes a priority for the Alliance in the nuclear field.

41. The Allies thus fully support the US objectives of achieving, within the context of the Strategic Arms Reduction Talks, fifty percent reductions in US and Soviet strategic nuclear units. US proposals seek to enhance stability by placing specific restrictions on the most destabilizing elements of the threat — fast flying ballistic missiles, throw-weight and, in particular, Soviet heavy ICBMs. The proposals are based on the need to maintain the deterrent credibility of the remaining US strategic forces which would continue to provide the ultimate guarantee of security for the Alliance as a whole; and therefore on the necessity to keep such forces effective. Furthermore, the United States is holding talks with the Soviet Union on defence and space matters in order to ensure that strategic stability is enhanced.

Sub-Strategic Nuclear Forces

42. The Allies are committed to maintaining only the minimum number of nuclear weapons necessary to support their strategy of deterrence. In line with this commitment, the members of the military structure have already made major unilateral cuts in their sub-strategic nuclear armory. The number of land-based warheads in Western Europe has been reduced by over one-third since 1979 to its lowest level in over 20 years. Updating where necessary of their sub-strategic systems would result in further reductions.

43. The Allies continue to face the direct threat posed to Europe by the large numbers of shorter-range nuclear missiles deployed on Warsaw Pact territory and which have been substantially upgraded in recent years. Major reductions in Warsaw Pact systems would be of overall value to Alliance security. One of the ways to achieve this aim would be by tangible and verifiable reductions of American and Soviet land-based nuclear missile systems of shorter range leading to equal ceilings at lower levels.

44. But the sub-strategic nuclear forces deployed by member countries of the Alliance are not principally a counter to similar systems operated by members of the WTO. As is explained in chapter III, sub-strategic nuclear forces fulfill an essential role in overall Alliance deterrence strategy by ensuring that there are no circumstances in which a potential aggressor might discount nuclear retaliation in response to his military action.

45. The Alliance reaffirms its position that for the foreseeable future there is no alternative to the Alliance's strategy for the prevention of war, which is a strategy of deterrence based upon an appropriate mix of adequate and effective nuclear and conventional forces which will continue to be kept up to date where necessary. Where nuclear forces are concerned, land-, sea-, and

air-based systems, including ground-based missiles, in the present circumstances and as far as can be foreseen will be needed in Europe.

46. In view of the huge superiority of the Warsaw Pact in terms of short-range nuclear missiles, the Alliance calls upon the Soviet Union to reduce unilaterally its short range missile systems, to the current levels within the integrated military structure.

47. The Alliance reaffirms that at the negotiations on conventional stability it pursues the objectives of:

- the establishment of a secure and stable balance of conventional forces at lower levels;
- the elimination of disparities prejudicial to stability and security; and
- the elimination as a matter of high priority of the capability for launching surprise attack and for initiating large-scale offensive action.

48. In keeping with its arms control objectives formulated in Reykjavik in 1987 and reaffirmed in Brussels in 1988, the Alliance states that one of its highest priorities in negotiations with the East is reaching an arrangement on conventional force reductions which would achieve the objectives above. In this spirit, the Allies will make every effort, as evidenced by the outcome of the May 1989 Summit, to bring these conventional negotiations to an early and satisfactory conclusion. The United States has expressed the hope that this could be achieved within six to twelve months. Once implementation of such an agreement is underway, the United States in consultation with the Allies concerned, is prepared to enter into negotiations to achieve a partial reduction of American and Soviet land-based nuclear missile forces of shorter range to equal and verifiable levels. With special reference to the Western proposals on CFE tabled in Vienna, enhanced by the proposals by the United States at the May 1989 Summit, the Allies concerned proceed on the understanding that negotiated reductions leading to a level below the existing level of their SNF missiles will not be carried out until the results of these negotiations have been implemented. Reductions of Warsaw Pact SNF systems should be carried out before that date.

49. As regards the sub-strategic nuclear forces of the members of the integrated military structure, their level and characteristics must be such that they can perform their deterrent role in a credible way across the required spectrum of ranges, taking into account the threat — both conventional and nuclear — with which the Alliance is faced. The question concerning the introduction and deployment of a follow-on system for the Lance will be dealt with in 1992 in the light of overall security developments. While a decision for national authorities, the Allies concerned recognize the value of the continued funding by the United States of research and development of a

follow-on for the existing Lance short-range missile, in order to preserve their options in this respect....

Arms Control and Defense Interrelationships

60. The Alliance is committed to pursuing a comprehensive approach to security, embracing both arms control and disarmament, and defence. It is important, therefore, to ensure that interrelationships between arms control issues and defence requirements and amongst the various arms control areas are fully considered. Proposals in any one area of arms control must take account of the implications for Alliance interests in general and for other negotiations. This is a continuing process.

61. It is essential that defence and arms control objectives remain in harmony in order to ensure their complementary contribution to the goal of maintaining security at the lowest balanced level of forces consistent with the requirements of the Alliance strategy of war prevention, acknowledging that changes in the threat, new technologies, and new political opportunities affect options in both fields. Decisions on arms control matters must fully reflect the requirements of the Allies' strategy of deterrence. Equally, progress in arms control is relevant to military plans, which will have to be developed in the full knowledge of the objectives pursued in arms control negotiations and to reflect, as necessary, the results achieved therein.

62. In each area of arms control, the Alliance seeks to enhance stability and security. The current negotiations concerning strategic nuclear systems, conventional forces and chemical weapons are, however, independent of one another: the outcome of any one of these negotiations is not contingent on progress in others. However, they can influence one another: criteria established and agreements achieved in one area of arms control may be relevant in other areas and hence facilitate overall progress. These could affect both arms control possibilities and the forces needed to fulfill Alliance strategy, as well as help to contribute generally to a more predictable military environment.

63. The Allies seek to manage the interaction among different arms control elements by ensuring that the development, pursuit and realization of their arms control objectives in individual areas are fully consistent both with each other and with the Alliance's guiding principles for effective arms control. For example, the way in which START limits and sub-limits are applied in detail could affect the future flexibility of the sub-strategic nuclear forces of members of the integrated military structure. A CFE agreement would by itself make a major contribution to stability. This would be significantly further enhanced by the achievement of a global chemical weapons ban. The development of Confidence- and Security-Building Measures could influence the stabilizing measures being considered in connection with the Conventional Forces in Europe negotiations and vice versa. The removal of

the imbalance in conventional forces would provide scope for further reductions in the sub-strategic nuclear forces of members of the integrated military structure, though it would not obviate the need for such forces. Similarly, this might make possible further arms control steps in the conventional field....
(PPP Bush 1989 I: 621-637)

President Bush's Address to the Nation on United States Nuclear Weapons Reductions
September 27, 1991

...Last year, I canceled U.S. plans to modernize our ground-launched theater nuclear weapons. Later, our NATO allies joined us in announcing that the alliance would propose the mutual elimination of all nuclear artillery shells from Europe as soon as short range nuclear force negotiations began with the Soviets. But starting these talks now would only perpetuate these systems while we engage in lengthy negotiations. Last month's events not only permit but indeed demand swifter, bolder action.

I am therefore directing that the United States eliminate its entire worldwide inventory of ground-launched short-range, that is, theater nuclear weapons. We will bring home and destroy all of our nuclear artillery shells and short-range ballistic missile warheads. We will, of course, ensure that we preserve an effective air-delivered nuclear capability in Europe. That is essential to NATO's security.

In turn, I have asked the Soviets to go down this road with us, to destroy their entire inventory of ground-launched theater nuclear weapons, not only their nuclear artillery and nuclear warheads for short range ballistic missiles but also the theater systems the U.S. no longer has, systems like nuclear warheads for air-defense missiles and nuclear land mines.

Recognizing further the major changes in the international military landscape, the United States will withdraw all tactical nuclear weapons from its surface ships and attack submarines, as well as those nuclear weapons associated with our land-based naval aircraft. This means removing all nuclear Tomahawk cruise missiles from U.S. ships and submarines, as well as nuclear bombs aboard aircraft carriers. The bottom line is that under normal circumstances, our ships will not carry tactical nuclear weapons.

Many of these land and sea-based warheads will be dismantled and destroyed. Those remaining will be secured in central areas where they would be available if necessary in a future crisis.

Again, there is every reason for the Soviet Union to match our actions by removing all tactical nuclear weapons from its ships and attack submarines, by withdrawing nuclear weapons for land-based naval aircraft, and by destroying many of them and consolidating what remains at central locations. I urge them to do so.

No category of nuclear weapons has received more attention than those in our strategic arsenals. The Strategic Arms Reduction Treaty, START, which President Gorbachev and I signed last July was the culmination of almost a decade's work. It calls for substantial stabilizing reductions and effective verification. Prompt ratification by both parties is essential. But I also believe the time is right to use START as a springboard to achieve additional stabilizing changes.

First, to further reduce tensions, I am directing that all United States strategic bombers immediately stand down from their alert posture. As a comparable gesture, I call upon the Soviet Union to confine its mobile missiles to their garrisons, where they will be safer and more secure.

Second, the United States will immediately stand down from alert all intercontinental ballistic missiles scheduled for deactivation under START. Rather than waiting for the treaty's reduction plan to run its full 7 year course, we will accelerate elimination of these systems once START is ratified. I call upon the Soviet Union to do the same.

Third, I am terminating the development of the mobile Peacekeeper ICBM as well as the mobile portions of the small ICBM program. The small single-warhead ICBM will be our only remaining ICBM modernization program. And I call upon the Soviets to terminate any and all programs for future ICBM's with more than one warhead, and to limit ICBM modernization to one type of single warhead missile, just as we have done.

Fourth, I am canceling the current program to build a replacement for the nuclear short-range attack missile for our strategic bombers.

Fifth, as a result of the strategic nuclear weapons adjustments that I've just outlined, the United States will streamline its command and control procedures, allowing us to more effectively manage our strategic nuclear forces. As the system works now, the Navy commands the submarine part of our strategic deterrent, while the Air Force commands the bomber and land-based elements. But as we reduce our strategic forces, the operational command structure must be as direct as possible. And I have therefore approved the recommendation of Secretary Cheney and the Joint Chiefs to consolidate operational command of these forces into a U.S. strategic command under one commander with participation from both services.

Since the 1970's, the most vulnerable and unstable part of the U.S. and Soviet nuclear forces has been intercontinental missiles with more than one warhead. Both sides have these ICBM's in fixed silos in the ground where they are more vulnerable than missiles on submarines.

I propose that the U.S. and the Soviet Union seek early agreement to eliminate from their inventories all ICBM's with multiple warheads. After developing a timetable acceptable to both sides, we could rapidly move to modify or eliminate these systems under procedures already established in the START agreement. In short, such an action would take away the single most unstable part of our nuclear arsenals.

But there is more to do. The United States and the Soviet Union are not the only nations with ballistic missiles. Some 15 nations have them now, and in less than a decade that number could grow to 20. The recent conflict in the Persian Gulf demonstrates in no uncertain terms that the time has come for strong action on this growing threat to world peace.

Accordingly, I am calling on the Soviet leadership to join us in taking immediate concrete steps to permit the limited deployment of nonnuclear defenses to protect against limited ballistic missile strikes, whatever their source, without undermining the credibility of existing deterrent forces. And we will intensify our effort to curb nuclear and missile proliferation. These two efforts will be mutually reinforcing. To foster cooperation, the United States soon will propose additional initiatives in the area of ballistic missile early warning....

Some will say that these initiatives call for a budget windfall for domestic programs. But the peace dividend I seek is not measured in dollars but in greater security. In the near term, some of these steps may even cost money. Given the ambitious plan I have already proposed to reduce U.S. defense spending by 25 percent, we cannot afford to make any unwise or unwarranted cuts in the defense budget that I have submitted to Congress. I am counting on congressional support to ensure we have the funds necessary to restructure our forces prudently and implement the decisions that I have outlined tonight....

Tonight, as I see the drama of democracy unfolding around the globe, perhaps we are closer to that new world then every before. The future is ours to influence, to shape, to mold. While we must not gamble that future, neither can we forfeit the historic opportunity now before us....

(PPP Bush 1991 II: 1220-1224)

START

President Reagan's Statement on the United States Strategic Arms Reduction Treaty Proposal

May 8, 1987

I have directed the U.S. START negotiator in the nuclear and space talks in Geneva to present to the Soviet Union at today's meeting of the START negotiating group a draft treaty which provides for 50-percent reductions in U.S. and Soviet strategic offensive nuclear arms. The text of the U.S. draft treaty reflects the basic areas of agreement on strategic arms reductions

General Secretary Gorbachev and I reached at our meeting at Reykjavik last October.

Our draft treaty provides for both sides to reduce to 1,600 strategic nuclear delivery vehicles and 6,000 warheads, with appropriate sublimits, over a period of 7 years after such a treaty enters into force. It provides a solid basis for the creation of a fair and durable agreement. The United States proposal, in addition to the overall limits, provides for specific restrictions on the most destabilizing and dangerous nuclear systems — above all, fast-flying ballistic missiles. It includes detailed rules designed to eliminate any ambiguity as to what is agreed, and extensive verification provisions designed to ensure that each side can be confident that the other is complying fully with the agreement. The treaty is the result of intensive work by all appropriate agencies of the United States Government. I have reviewed the treaty, and it has my approval.

By tabling this text, the United States seeks to build on the significant progress made in START and to provide a vehicle for resolving the remaining differences. If the Soviets are prepared to work with us on the remaining outstanding issues, especially the need — for the purpose of ensuring strategic stability — for sublimits on ballistic missile warheads, we will be able to take a significant step toward a safer and more stable world.

While tabling this treaty is an important indication of our desire to achieve deep, equitable, and verifiable strategic arms reductions as soon as possible, I do not wish to minimize the difficult issues which remain to be resolved, particularly Soviet insistence on linking a START agreement to measures which, if accepted by the United States, would seriously constrain SDI. This is unacceptable, I cannot and I will not accept any measures which would cripple or kill our SDI program. In view of the continuing Soviet offensive buildup, combined with the long-standing Soviet activities in strategic defense, the SDI program is vital to the future security of the United States and our allies.

As we begin detailed discussion of our proposed treaty with the Soviets, we are resolved to do our part to bring about, for the first time in history, real reductions in strategic offensive arms. I hope the Soviets will demonstrate similar determination and work with us on the basis of our draft treaty to translate the areas of agreement reached at Reykjavik into concrete reductions.

(PPP Reagan 1987 I: 485-486)

Soviet-United States Joint Statement on Future Negotiations on Nuclear and Space Arms and Further Enhancing Strategic Stability
June 1, 1990

The United States of America and the Union of Soviet Socialist Republics, building on the results of the current negotiations, agree to pursue new talks on strategic offensive arms, and on the relationship between strategic offensive and defensive arms. The objectives of these negotiations will be to reduce further the risk of outbreak of war, particularly nuclear war, and to ensure strategic stability, transparency and predictability through further stabilizing reductions in the strategic arsenals of both countries. This will be achieved by seeking agreements that improve survivability, remove incentives for a nuclear first strike and implement an appropriate relationship between strategic offenses and defenses.

In order to attain these objectives, the sides have agreed as follows:

First. This year the sides will complete work on the Treaty Between the United States of America and the Union of Soviet Socialist Republics on the Reduction and Limitation of Strategic Offensive Arms. Following the signing of the Treaty, the sides will hold consultations without delay regarding future talks and these important talks will begin at the earliest practical date. Both sides in these future talks will be free to raise any issues related to any strategic offensive arms.

Within the existing negotiating framework on Nuclear and Space Arms in Geneva, the two sides will continue negotiations on ABM and space without delay. Thus, in the future talks the two sides will discuss strategic stability issues of interest to them, including the relationship between strategic offensive and defensive arms, taking into account stabilizing reductions in strategic offensive arms and development of new technologies. The sides will work toward the important goal of reaching an early outcome in these negotiations.

Second. The United States of America and the Union of Soviet Socialist Republics, as is the case in the emerging START Treaty, will, in the new negotiations, seek to reduce their strategic offensive arms in a way consistent with enhancing strategic stability. In the new negotiations, the two sides agree to place emphasis on removing incentives for a nuclear first strike, on reducing the concentration of warheads on strategic delivery vehicles, and on giving priority to highly survivable systems.

In particular, the two sides will seek measures that reduce the concentration of warheads on strategic delivery vehicles as a whole, including measures related to the question of heavy missiles and MIRVed ICBMs. Effective verification will be provided by national technical means, cooperative measures, and on-site inspection.

Third. Having agreed on the need to ensure a predictable strategic relationship between the United States of America and the Union of Soviet

Socialist Republics, the sides will, for the entire duration of the START Treaty, exchange, at the beginning of each calendar year, information on planned changes in the numbers of strategic offensive arms as of the end of the current year.

Fourth. The sides will pursue additional measures to build confidence and ensure predictability of the military activities of the United States of America and the Union of Soviet Socialist Republics that would reduce the possibility of an outbreak of nuclear war as a result of accident, miscalculation, terrorism, or unexpected technological breakthrough, and would prevent possible incidents between them....
(PPP Bush 1990 I: 742-746)

White House Fact Sheet on the Strategic Arms Reduction Treaty
July 31, 1991

Today, the United States and the Soviet Union signed the Strategic Arms Reduction Treaty. This treaty marks the first agreement between the two countries in which the number of deployed strategic nuclear weapons will actually be reduced. Reductions will take place over a period of 7 years, and will result in parity between the strategic nuclear forces of the two sides at levels approximately 30 percent below currently deployed forces. Deeper cuts are required in the most dangerous and destabilizing systems.

START provisions are designed to strengthen strategic stability at lower levels and to encourage the restructuring of strategic forces in ways that make them more stable and less threatening. The treaty includes a wide variety of very demanding verification measures designed to ensure compliance and build confidence.

Central Limits

The treaty sets equal ceilings on the number of strategic nuclear forces that can be deployed by either side. In addition, the treaty establishes an equal ceiling on ballistic missile throw-weight (a measure of overall capability for ballistic missiles). Each side is limited to no more than:

- 1,600 strategic nuclear delivery vehicles (deployed intercontinental ballistic missiles [ICBM's], submarine launched ballistic missiles [SLBM's], and heavy bombers), a limit that is 36 percent below the Soviet level declared in September 1990 and 29 percent below the U.S. level.
- 6,000 total accountable warheads, about 41 percent below the current Soviet level and 43 percent below the current U.S. level.
- 4,900 accountable warheads deployed on ICBM's or SLBM's, about 48 percent below the current Soviet level and 40 percent below the current U.S. level.

- 1,540 accountable warheads deployed on 154 heavy ICBM's, a 50 percent reduction in current Soviet forces. The U.S. has no heavy ICBM's.
- 1,100 accountable warheads deployed on mobile ICBM's.
- Aggregate throw-weight of deployed ICBM's and SLBM's equal to about 54 percent of the current Soviet aggregate throw-weight.

Ballistic Missile Warhead Accountability

The treaty uses detailed counting rules to ensure the accurate accounting of the number of warheads attributed to each type of ballistic missile.

- Each deployed ballistic missile warhead counts as 1 under the 4,900 ceiling and 1 under the 6,000 overall warhead ceiling.
- Each side is allowed 10 on-site inspections each year to verify that deployed ballistic missiles contain no more warheads than the number that is attributed to them under the treaty.

Downloading Ballistic Missile Warheads

The treaty also allows for a reduction in the number of warheads on certain ballistic missiles, which will help the sides transition their existing forces to the new regime. Such downloading is permitted in a carefully structured and limited fashion.

- The U.S. may download its three-warhead Minuteman III ICBM by either one or two warheads. The Soviet Union has already downloaded it's seven warhead SS-N-18 SLBM by four warheads.
- In addition, each side may download up to 500 warheads on two other existing types of ballistic missiles, as long as the total number of warheads removed from downloaded missiles does not exceed 1,250 at any one time.

New Types

The treaty places constraints on the characteristics of new types of ballistic missiles to ensure the accuracy of counting rules and prevent under counting of missile warheads.

- The number of warheads attributed to a new type of ballistic missile must be no less than the number determined by dividing 40 percent of the missile's total throw-weight by the weight of the lightest RV tested on that missile.
- The throw-weight attributed to a new type must be no less than the missile's throw-weight capability at specified reference ranges (11,000 km for ICBM's and 9,500 km for SLBM's).

Heavy ICBM's

START places significant restrictions on the Soviet SS-18 heavy ICBM.

- A 50 percent reduction in the number of Soviet SS-18 ICBM's; a total reduction of 154 of these Soviet missiles.
- New types of heavy ICBM's are banned.
- Downloading of heavy ICBM's is banned.
- Heavy SLBM's and heavy mobile ICBM's are banned.
- Heavy ICBM's will be reduced on a more stringent schedule than other strategic arms.

Mobile ICBM's

Because mobile missiles are more difficult to verify than other types of ballistic missiles, START incorporates a number of special restrictions and notifications with regard to these missiles. These measures will significantly improve our confidence that START will be effectively verifiable.

- Nondeployed mobile missiles and non deployed mobile launchers are numerically and geographically limited so as to limit the possibility for reload and refire.
- The verification regime includes continuous monitoring of mobile ICBM production, restrictions on movements, on-site inspections, and cooperative measures to improve the effectiveness of national technical means of intelligence collection.

Heavy Bombers

Because heavy bombers are stabilizing strategic systems (e.g., they are less capable of a short-warning attack than ballistic missiles), START counting rules for weapons on bombers are different than those for ballistic missile warheads.

- Each heavy bomber counts as one strategic nuclear delivery vehicle.
- Each heavy bomber equipped to carry only short-range missiles or gravity bombs is counted as one warhead under the 6,000 limit.
- Each U.S. heavy bomber equipped to carry long-range nuclear ALCM's (up to a maximum of 150 bombers) is counted as 10 warheads even though it may be equipped to carry up to 20 ALCM's.
- A similar discount applies to Soviet heavy bombers equipped to carry long range nuclear ALCM's. Each such Soviet heavy bomber (up to a maximum of 180) is counted as 8 warheads even though it may be equipped to carry up to 16 ALCM's.
- Any heavy bomber equipped for long range nuclear ALCM's deployed in excess of 150 for the U.S. or 180 for the Soviet Union will be accountable

by the number of ALCM's the heavy bomber is actually equipped to carry.

Verification Regime

Building on recent arms control agreements, START includes extensive and unprecedented verification provisions. This comprehensive verification regime greatly reduces the likelihood that violations would go undetected.

- START bans the encryption and encapsulation of telemetric information and other forms of information denial on night tests of ballistic missiles. However, strictly limited exemptions to this ban are granted sufficient to protect the flight-testing of sensitive research projects.
- START allows 12 different types of on site inspections and requires roughly 60 different types of notifications covering production, testing, movement, deployment, and destruction of strategic offensive arms.

Treaty Duration

START will have a duration of 15 years, unless it is superseded by a subsequent agreement. If the sides agree, the treaty may be extended for successive 5-year periods beyond the 15 years.

Noncircumvention and Third Countries

START prohibits the transfer of strategic offensive arms to third countries, except that the treaty will not interfere with existing patterns of cooperation. In addition, the treaty prohibits the permanent basing of strategic offensive arms outside the national territory of each side.

Air-Launched Cruise Missiles (ALCMs)

START does not directly count or limit ALCM's. ALCM's are limited indirectly through their association with heavy bombers.

- Only nuclear-armed ALCM's with a range in excess of 600 km are covered by START.
- Long-range, conventionally armed ALCM's that are distinguishable from nuclear-armed ALCM's are not affected.
- Long-range nuclear-armed ALCM's may not be located at air bases for heavy bombers not accountable as being equipped for such ALCM's.
- Multiple warhead long-range nuclear ALCM's are banned.

Sea Launched Cruise Missiles (SLCMs)

SLCMs are not constrained by the treaty. However, each side has made a politically binding declaration as to its plans for the deployment of nuclear-armed SLCM's. Conventionally-armed SLCM's are not subject to such a declaration.

- Each side will make an annual declaration of the maximum number of nuclear-armed SLCM's with a range greater than 600 km that it plans to deploy for each of the following 5 years.
- This number will not be greater than 880 long-range nuclear-armed SLCM's.
- In addition, as a confidence building measure, nuclear-armed SLCM's with a range of 300-600 km will be the subject of a confidential annual data exchange.

Backfire Bomber

The Soviet Backfire bomber is not constrained by the treaty. However, the Soviet side has made a politically binding declaration that it will not deploy more than 800 air force and 200 naval Backfire bombers, and that these bombers will not be given intercontinental capability.

Other Background

The START agreement consists of the treaty document itself and a number of associated documents. Together they total more than 700 pages. The treaty was signed in a public ceremony by Presidents Bush and Gorbachev in St. Vladimir's Hall in the Kremlin. The associated documents were signed in a private ceremony at Novo Ogaryevo, President Gorbachev's weekend dacha. Seven of these documents were signed by Presidents Bush and Gorbachev. Three associated agreements were signed by Secretary Baker and Foreign Minister Bessmertnykh. In addition, the START negotiators, Ambassadors Brooks and Nazarkin, exchanged seven letters related to START in a separate event at the Soviet Ministry of Foreign Affairs in Moscow.

Magnitude of START-Accountable Reductions

Following is the aggregate data from the Memorandum of Understanding, based upon agreed counting rules in START. (Because of those counting rules, the number of heavy bomber weapons actually deployed may be higher than the number shown in the aggregate.) This data is effective as of September 1990 and will be updated at entry into force:

	United States	Soviet Union
Delivery Vehicles	2,246	2,500
Warheads	10,563	10,271
Ballistic Missile Warheads	8,210	9,416
Heavy ICBM's / Warheads	None	308 / 3080
Throw-weight (metric tons)	2,361.3	6,626.3

As a result of the treaty, the above values will be reduced by the following percentages:

	United States	Soviet Union
Delivery Vehicles	29%	36%
Warheads	43%	41%
Ballistic Missile Warheads	40%	48%
Heavy ICBM's / Warheads	None	50%
Throw-weight (metric tons)	None	46%

(PPP Bush 1991 II: 988-991)

Joint Understanding on Reductions in Strategic Offensive Arms
June 17, 1992

The President of the United States of America and the President of the Russian Federation have agreed to substantial further reductions in strategic offensive arms. Specifically, the two sides have agreed upon and will promptly conclude a Treaty with the following provisions:

1. Within the seven-year period following entry into force of the START Treaty, they will reduce their strategic forces to no more than:

(a) an overall total number of warheads for each between 3800 and 4250 (as each nation shall determine) or such lower number as each nation shall decide.

(b) 1200 MIRVed ICBM warheads.

(c) 650 heavy ICBM warheads.

(d) 2160 SLBM warheads.

2. By the year 2003 (or by the end of the year 2000 if the United States can contribute to the financing of the destruction or elimination of strategic offensive arms in Russia), they will:

(a) reduce the overall total to no more than a number of warheads for each between 3000 and 3500 (as each nation shall determine) or such lower number as each nation shall decide.

(b) eliminate all MIRVed ICBMs.

(c) reduce SLBM warheads to between no more than 1100 to 1750 (as each nation shall determine).

3. For the purpose of calculating the overall totals described above:

(a) The number of warheads counted for heavy bombers with nuclear roles will be the number of nuclear weapons they are actually equipped to carry.

(b) Under agreed procedures, heavy bombers not to exceed 100 that were never equipped for long-range nuclear ALCMs and that are reoriented to conventional roles will not count against the overall total established by this agreement.

(i) Such heavy bombers will be based separately from heavy bombers with nuclear roles.

(ii) No nuclear weapons will be located at bases for heavy bombers with conventional roles.

(iii) Such aircraft and crews will not train or exercise for nuclear missions.

(iv) Current inspection procedures already agreed in the START Treaty will help affirm that these bombers have conventional roles. No new verification procedures are required.

(v) Except as otherwise agreed, these bombers will remain subject to the provisions of the START Treaty, including the inspection provisions.

4. The reductions required by this agreement will be carried out by eliminating missile launchers and heavy bombers using START procedures, and, in accordance with the plans of the two sides, by reducing the number of warheads on existing ballistic missiles other than the SS-18. Except as otherwise agreed, ballistic missile warheads will be calculated according to START counting rules....

(PPP Bush 1992 I: 961-964)

Joint United States-Russian Statement on a Global Protection System
June 17, 1992

The Presidents continued their discussion of the potential benefits of a Global Protection System (GPS) against ballistic missiles, agreeing that it is important to explore the role for defenses in protecting against limited ballistic missile attacks. The two Presidents agreed that their two nations should work together with allies and other interested states in developing a concept for such a system as part of an overall strategy regarding the proliferation of ballistic missiles and weapons of mass destruction. Such cooperation would be a tangible expression of the new relationship that exists between Russia and the United States and would involve them in an important undertaking with other nations of the world community.

The two Presidents agreed it is necessary to start work without delay to develop the concept of the GPS. For this purpose they agreed to establish a high-level group to explore on a priority basis the following practical steps:

- The potential for sharing of early warning information through the establishment of an early warning center.
- The potential for cooperation with participating states in developing ballistic missile defense capabilities and technologies.
- The development of a legal basis for cooperation, including new treaties and agreements and possible changes to existing treaties and agreements necessary to implement a Global Protection System....

(PPP Bush 1992 I: 961-964)

President Bush's Message to the Senate Transmitting the Russia-United States Treaty on Further Reduction and Limitation of Strategic Offensive Arms
January 15, 1993

...I am transmitting herewith, for the advice and consent of the Senate to ratification, the Treaty Between the United States of America and the Russian Federation on Further Reduction and Limitation of Strategic Offensive Arms (the START II Treaty) signed at Moscow on January 3, 1993. The Treaty includes the following documents, which are integral parts thereof:

- the Protocol on Procedures Governing Elimination of Heavy ICBMs and on Procedures Governing Conversion of Silo Launchers of Heavy ICBMs Relating to the Treaty Between the United States of America and the Russian Federation on Further Reduction and Limitation of Strategic Offensive Arms (the Elimination and Conversion Protocol);
- the Protocol on Exhibitions and Inspections of Heavy Bombers Relating to the Treaty Between the United States of America and the Russian Federation on Further Reduction and Limitation of Strategic Offensive Arms (the Exhibitions and Inspections Protocol); and
- the Memorandum of Understanding on Warhead Attribution and Heavy Bomber Data Relating to the Treaty Between the United States of America and the Russian Federation on Further Reduction and Limitation of Strategic Offensive Arms (the Memorandum on Attribution).

In addition, I transmit herewith, for the information of the Senate, the report of the Department of State and letters exchanged by representatives of the Parties. The letters are associated with, but not integral parts of, the START II Treaty. Although not submitted for the advice and consent of the Senate to ratification, these letters are provided because they are relevant to the consideration of the Treaty by the Senate.

The START II Treaty is a milestone in the continuing effort by the United States and the Russian Federation to address the threat posed by strategic offensive nuclear weapons, especially multiple-warhead ICBMs. It builds upon and relies on the Treaty Between the United States of America and the Union of Soviet Socialist Republics on the Reduction and Limitation of Strategic Offensive Arms (the START Treaty) signed at Moscow on July 31,1991. At the same time, the START II Treaty goes even further than the START Treaty.

The START Treaty was the first treaty actually to reduce strategic offensive arms of both countries, with overall reductions of 30-40 percent and reductions of up to 50 percent in the most threatening systems. It enhances stability in times of crisis. It not only limits strategic arms but also reduces them significantly below current levels. In addition, the START Treaty allows equality of forces and is effectively verifiable. Finally, commitments associated with the START Treaty will result in the elimination of nuclear weapons and deployed strategic offensive arms from the territories of Belarus, Kazakhstan, and Ukraine within 7 years after entry into force, and accession of these three states to the Treaty on the Non-Proliferation of Nuclear Weapons (NPT) as nonnuclear-weapon States Parties. As a result, after 7 years, only Russia and the United States will retain any deployed strategic offensive arms under the START Treaty.

The START II Treaty builds upon and surpasses the accomplishments of the START Treaty by further reducing strategic offensive arms in such a way that further increases the stability of the strategic nuclear balance. It bans deployment of the most destabilizing type of nuclear weapons system — land-based intercontinental ballistic missiles with multiple independently targetable nuclear warheads. At the same time, the START II Treaty permits the United States to maintain a stabilizing sea based force.

The central limits of the START II Treaty require reductions by January 1, 2003, to 3000-3500 warheads. Within this, there are sublimits of between 1700-1750 warheads on deployed SLBMs for each Party, or such lower number as each Party shall decide for itself; zero for warheads on deployed multiple-warhead ICBMs; and zero for warheads on deployed heavy ICBMs. Thus, the Treaty reduces the current overall deployments of strategic nuclear weapons on each side by more than two-thirds from current levels. These limits will be reached by the end of the year 2000 if both Parties reach agreement on a program of assistance to the Russian Federation with regard to dismantling strategic offensive arms within a year after entry into force of the Treaty. Acceptance of these reductions serves as a clear indication of the ending of the Cold War.

In a major accomplishment, START II will result in the complete elimination of heavy ICBMs (the SS-18s) and the elimination or conversion of their launchers. All heavy ICBMs and launch canisters will be destroyed. All but 90 heavy ICBM silos will likewise be destroyed and these 90 silos will be modified to be incapable of launching SS-18s. To address the Russians' stated concern over the cost of implementing the transition to a single-warhead ICBM force, the START II Treaty provides for the conversion of up to 90 of the 154 Russian SS-18 heavy ICBM silos that will remain after the START Treaty reductions. The Russians have unilaterally undertaken to use the converted silos only for the smaller, SS-25 type single-warhead ICBMs. When implemented, the Treaty's conversion provisions, which include extensive on-site inspection rights, will preclude the use of these silos to launch heavy ICBMs. Together with the elimination of SS-18 missiles, these provisions are intended to ensure that the strategic capability of the SS-18 system is eliminated.

START II allows some reductions to be taken by downloading, i.e., reducing the number of warheads attributed to existing missiles. This will allow the United States to achieve the reductions required by the Treaty in a cost-effective way by downloading some or all of our sea-based Trident SLBMs and land-based Minuteman III ICBMs. The Treaty also allows downloading, in Russia, of 105 of the 170 SS-19 multiple-warhead missiles in existing silos to a single-warhead missile. All other Russian launchers of multiple-warhead ICBMs — including the remaining 65 SS-19s — must be converted for single-warhead ICBMs or eliminated in accordance with START procedures.

START II can be implemented in a fashion that is fully consistent with U.S. national security. To ensure that we have the ability to respond to worldwide conventional contingencies, it allows for the reorientation, without any conversion procedures, of 100 START-accountable heavy bombers to a conventional role. These heavy bombers will not count against START II warhead limits.

The START Treaty and the START II Treaty remain in force concurrently and have the same duration. Except as explicitly modified by the START II Treaty, the provisions of the START Treaty will be used to implement START II.

The START II Treaty provides for inspections in addition to those of the START Treaty. These additional inspections will be carried out according to the provisions of the START Treaty unless otherwise specified in the Elimination and Conversion Protocol or in the Exhibitions and Inspections Protocol. As I was convinced that the START Treaty is effectively verifiable, I am equally confident that the START II Treaty is effectively verifiable.

The START Treaty was an historic achievement in our long-term effort to enhance the stability of the strategic balance through arms control. The START II Treaty represents the capstone of that effort. Elimination of heavy ICBMs and the effective elimination of all other multiple-warhead ICBMs will put an end to the most dangerous weapons of the Cold War.

In sum, the START II Treaty is clearly in the interest of the United States and represents a watershed in our efforts to stabilize the nuclear balance and further reduce strategic offensive arms. I therefore urge the Senate to give prompt and favorable consideration to the Treaty, including its Protocols and

Memorandum on Attribution, and to give its advice and consent to ratification.
(PPP Bush 1992-1993 II: 2254-2256)

SDI AND CONTINUED VIGILANCE

Public Law 102-190: Missile Defense Act of 1991
December 5, 1991
...SEC. 232. MISSILE DEFENSE GOAL OF THE UNITED STATES

(a) MISSILE DEFENSE GOAL. — It is a goal of the United States to —

(1) deploy an anti-ballistic missile system, including one or an adequate additional number of anti-ballistic missile sites and space-based sensors, that is capable of providing a highly effective defense of the United States against limited attacks of ballistic missiles;

(2) maintain strategic stability; and

(3) provide highly effective theater missile defenses (TMDs) to forward-deployed and expeditionary elements of the Armed Forces of the United States and to friends and allies of the United States.

(b) ENDORSEMENT OF ADDITIONAL MEASURES. — As an additional component of the overall goal of protecting the United States against the threat posed by ballistic missiles, Congress endorses such additional measures as —

(1) joint discussions between the United States and the Soviet Union on strengthening nuclear command and control, to include discussions concerning the use of permissive action links and post-launch destruct mechanisms on all intercontinental range ballistic missiles of the two nations;

(2) reductions that enhance stability in strategic weapons of the United States and Soviet Union to levels below the limitations of the Strategic Arms Reduction Talks (START) Treaty, to include the down-loading of multiple warhead ballistic missiles; and

(3) reinvigorated efforts to halt the proliferation of ballistic missiles and weapons of mass destruction.

SEC. 233. IMPLEMENTATION OF GOAL

(a) IN GENERAL. — To implement the goal specified in section 232(a), the Congress —

(1) directs the Secretary of Defense to take the actions specified in subsection (b); and

(2) urges the President to take the actions described in subsection (c).

(b) ACTIONS OF THE SECRETARY OF DEFENSE. —

(1) THEATER MISSILE DEFENSE OPTIONS. — The Secretary of Defense shall aggressively pursue the development of advanced theater missile

defense systems, with the objective of downselecting and deploying such systems by the mid-1990s.

(2) INITIAL DEPLOYMENT. — The Secretary shall develop for deployment by the earliest date allowed by the availability of appropriate technology or by fiscal year 1996 a cost effective, operationally effective, and ABM Treaty compliant anti ballistic missile system at a single site as the initial step toward deployment of an anti-ballistic missile system described in section 232(a)(1) designed to protect the United States against limited ballistic missile threats, including accidental or unauthorized launches or Third World attacks. The system to be developed should include —

(A) 100 ground-based interceptors, the design of which is to be determined by competition and downselection for the most capable interceptor or interceptors;

(B) fixed, ground-based, anti-ballistic missile battle management radars; and

(C) optimum utilization of space-based sensors, including sensors capable of cueing ground-based anti-ballistic missile interceptors and providing initial targeting vectors, and other sensor systems that also are not prohibited by the ABM Treaty, such as a ground-based sub-orbital surveillance and tracking system.

(3) DEPLOYMENT PLAN. — Within 180 days after the date of the enactment of this Act, the Secretary of Defense shall submit to the congressional defense committees a plan for the deployment of theater missile defense systems and an anti-ballistic missile system which meet the guidelines established in paragraphs (1) and (2).

(c) PRESIDENTIAL ACTIONS

(1) NEGOTIATIONS REGARDING THE ABM TREATY. — Congress recognizes the President's call on September 27, 1991, for "immediate concrete steps" to permit the deployment of defenses against limited ballistic missile strikes and the response of the President of the Soviet Union undertaking to consider such proposals from the United States on nonnuclear ABM systems.

(2) In this regard, Congress urges the President to pursue immediate discussions with the Soviet Union on the feasibility and mutual interests of amendments to the ABM Treaty to permit the following:

(A) Construction of anti-ballistic missile sites and deployment of ground-based anti-ballistic missile interceptors in addition to those currently permitted under the ABM Treaty.

(B) Increased use of space-based sensors for direct battle management.

(C) Clarification of what development and testing of space-based missile defenses is permissible under the ABM Treaty.

(D) Increased flexibility for technology development of advanced ballistic missile defenses.

(E) Clarification of the distinctions for the purposes of the ABM Treaty between theater missile defenses and antiballistic missile defenses, including interceptors and radars.

SEC. 234. FOLLOW-ON TECHNOLOGY RESEARCH

(a) FOLLOW-ON ANTI-BALLISTIC MISSILE TECHNOLOGIES. — To effectively develop technologies relating to achieving the goal specified in section 232(a) and to provide future options for protecting the security of the United States and the allies and friends of the United States, robust funding for research and development for promising follow-on anti-ballistic missile technologies, including Brilliant Pebbles, is required.

(b) EXCLUSION FROM INITIAL PLAN. — Deployment of Brilliant Pebbles is not included in the initial plan for the limited defense system architecture described in section 232(a).

(c) REPORT AND LIMITATION. — The Secretary of Defense shall submit to the congressional defense committees a report on conceptual and burden sharing issues associated with the option of deploying space-based interceptors (including Brilliant Pebbles) for the purpose of providing global defenses against ballistic missile attacks. Not more than 50 percent of the funds made available for the purposes described in section 237(b)(3) for the Space-Based Interceptors program element for fiscal year 1992 may be obligated for the Brilliant Pebbles program until 45 days after submission of the report.

SEC. 235. PROGRAM ELEMENTS FOR STRATEGIC DEFENSE INITIATIVE

(a) EXCLUSIVE ELEMENTS. — The following program elements shall be the exclusive program elements for the Strategic Defense Initiative:

(1) Limited Defense System.

(2) Theater Missile Defenses.

(3) Space-Based Interceptors.

(4) Other Follow-on Systems.

(5) Research and Support Activities.

(b) APPLICABILITY TO BUDGETS. — The program elements specified in subsection (a) shall be the only program elements used in the program and budget provided concerning the Strategic Defense Initiative submitted to Congress by the Secretary of Defense in support of the budget submitted to Congress by the President under section 1105 of title 31, United States Code, for any fiscal year.

SEC. 236. RESEARCH, DEVELOPMENT, TEST, AND EVALUATION OBJECTIVES FOR SDI PROGRAM ELEMENTS

(a) LIMITED DEFENSE SYSTEM PROGRAM ELEMENT. — The Limited Defense System program element shall include programs, projects, and activities (and supporting programs, projects, and activities) which have as a primary objective the development of systems, components, and architectures for a deployable anti-ballistic missile system as described in section 232(a)(1) capable of providing a highly effective defense of the United States against limited ballistic missile threats, including accidental or unauthorized launches or Third World attacks, but below a threshold that would bring into question strategic stability. Such activities shall include those activities necessary to develop and test systems, components, and architectures capable of deployment by fiscal year 1996 as part of an ABM Treaty compliant initial site defensive system. For purposes of planning, evaluation, design, and effectiveness studies, such programs, projects, and activities may take into consideration both the current limitations of the ABM Treaty and modest changes to its numerical limitations and its limitations on the use of space-based sensors.

(b) THEATER MISSILE DEFENSES PROGRAM ELEMENT. — The Theater Missile Defenses program element shall include programs, projects, and activities (including those associated before the date of the enactment of this Act with the Tactical Missile Defense Initiative) that have as primary objectives either of the following:

(1) The development of deployable and rapidly relocatable advanced theater missile defenses capable of defending forward deployed and expeditionary elements of the Armed Forces of the United States, to be carried out with the objective of selecting and deploying more capable theater missile defense systems by the mid-1990s.

(2) Cooperation with friendly and allied nations in the development of theater defenses against tactical or theater ballistic missiles.

(c) SPACE-BASED INTERCEPTORS PROGRAM ELEMENT. — The Space Based Interceptors program element shall include programs, projects, and activities (and supporting programs, projects, and activities) that have as a primary objective the conduct of research on space-based kinetic-kill interceptors and associated sensors that could provide an overlay to ground-based anti-ballistic missile interceptors.

(d) OTHER FOLLOW-ON SYSTEMS PROGRAM ELEMENT. — The other Follow-on Systems program element shall include programs, projects, and activities that have as a primary objective the development of technologies capable of supporting systems, components, and architectures that could produce highly effective defenses for the future.

(e) RESEARCH AND SUPPORT ACTIVITIES PROGRAM ELEMENT. — The Research and Support Activities program element shall include programs, projects, and activities that have as primary objectives the following:

(1) The provision of basic research and technical, engineering, and managerial support to the programs, projects, and activities within the program elements referred to in subsection (a) through (d).

(2) Innovative science and technology projects.

(3) The provision of necessary test and evaluation services other than those required for a specific program element.

(4) Program management....

(USS, 1991, Volume 105, Part 2)

6

United States Involvement in Central America

INTRODUCTION

United States relations with Latin America, in general, and Central America, in particular, have had a schizophrenic quality about them since the U.S. was powerful enough to have an impact there. On the one hand, domestic support for the Spanish American War in 1898 was based on the supposed plight of the Cuban people suffering under Spanish occupation, whatever may have been the true motives of leaders leading up to the war. Similarly, the Good Neighbor Policy of President Franklin D. Roosevelt and the Alliance for Progress of President John F. Kennedy were based on the need for the United States to be a "big brother" to its southern neighbors.

On the other hand, these well-intentioned (if patronizing) initiatives occurred in a context of frequent United States military intervention into the affairs of Latin American states. That a superpower with a strong attachment to the Monroe Doctrine should do what it could to limit the influence of outside powers in a region of key strategic importance should surprise no one, of course.

The period of these documents reflects both strains of United States policy. Economic assistance and peace initiatives were balanced by military interventions whose full scope and extent may never be known.

Nicaragua provided the most direct challenge to the Reagan administration. President Reagan was determined that Nicaragua would not become a Soviet military colony or fester as a source of insurgency for the region. Limited by Congressional resistance to direct U.S. involvement, the administration pursued a policy of supporting "private" assistance to military forces opposing the Nicaraguan government. The election of Violeta Chamorro as President of Nicaragua in relatively free elections in 1990, and the subsequent departure from office of the Sandinista government, were seen as the successful result of this policy.

The pursuit of that policy in Nicaragua in the face of very explicit Congressional limitations led to the so-called "Iran-Contra" affair. In very brief summary, arms were sold to the revolutionary Islamic government of Iran (partly to secure the return of Western hostages seized in Lebanon), and the proceeds used to supply the "Contra" guerrillas in Nicaragua. Allegations of illegality were made and the Reagan administration was put on the defensive. Speculation continues as to which members of the administration knew about this operation and who gave the orders to carry it out. Fortunately for other senior officials, the Director of Central Intelligence, William Casey, died suddenly and became a convenient scapegoat.

The Central American challenge to the Bush administration occurred in Panama, where dictator Manuel Noriega (who was apparently in the employ of the CIA at an earlier point in his career) was increasingly friendly to Fidel Castro of Cuba and was thought to be engaged in active drug smuggling operations. The Panama invasion was quick and effective, although a dispute continues as to the number of civilians who were wounded or killed by the operation. The circumstances for the invasion could hardly have been more opportune for the United States, with Army troops already stationed on Panamanian territory for defense of the Panama Canal. Casualties on both side were limited by the speed of the operation and by skilled psychological operations activities designed to eliminate pockets of resistance as peaceably as possible.

If the United States was willing to go to such lengths to assert its policy preferences in small Central American countries, one can only imagine the crisis that would emerge if similar problems developed directly on its southern border. It is not beyond imagining, although one hopes it will never come to pass, that Mexico could become seriously unstable. The results for United States policy are difficult to predict, but they would likely be significant.

REGIONAL LEVEL ACTIONS

President Reagan's Message to the Congress on Economic Assistance for Central America

March 3, 1987

...The one hundred million dollars in assistance for the Nicaraguan democratic resistance approved by the Congress in October of last year was intended as only one aspect of an integrated, comprehensive approach for United States efforts to promote economic and political development, peace, stability, and democracy in Central America and to encourage a negotiated resolution of the conflict in the region. In that law (Title II of the Act making appropriations for military construction for the fiscal year ending September 30, 1987 as contained in Public Laws 99-500 and 99-591, hereinafter "the Act"), the Congress recognized, as does the executive branch, that the Central American crisis has its roots in a long history of social injustice, extreme poverty, and political oppression. These conditions create discontent, which is often exploited by communist guerrillas in their war against democracy. The focus of United States policy in Central America goes beyond the military aspects of the problem. To help address the underlying social and economic causes of conflict in the region, the Congress directed that additional economic assistance be made available for four Central American democracies: Costa Rica, El Salvador, Guatemala, and Honduras.

Progress Toward Democracy

Democracy is making great strides in these four countries. Their progress in building societies in which their citizens enjoy freedom of choice and equal justice under law stands in marked contrast to the totalitarian subjugation suffered by the Nicaraguan people. This progress, however, cannot be sustained without concurrent economic growth. Political freedom cannot prosper in an environment of hunger and despair. Nor, as found by the National Bipartisan Commission on Central America (NBCCA), can we expect the Central American democracies to recover from a severe economic recession without significant outside assistance. The Central American democracies cannot attract adequate private investment to achieve sustainable economic growth in the current environment of violence and subversion. The four democratic nations of Central America will have little appeal for investors as long as there is an aggressive communist regime nearby — a militant regime bent on ideological expansion and already in command of the largest army in the history of Central America.

Congressional Attempt to Aid the Democracies

To help the Central American democracies preserve their hard-earned progress in making democracy work, the Congress in October 1986 approved in section 205 of the Act the transfer of three hundred million dollars in unobligated funds for economic assistance to the Central American democracies. Title III of the Act also appropriated an additional three hundred million dollars for this purpose, to be available through fiscal year 1987. Unfortunately, despite the best intentions of those in the Congress who supported the additional assistance for Central America and despite this Administration's strong support for that assistance, the Foreign Assistance Appropriations Act mandated that the three hundred million dollars be regarded as part of the specified (and very limited) FY 1987 worldwide total for economic support fund assistance, thus precluding us from considering this sum as additional assistance. As a practical result there could be no increased aid for Central

America. When this became apparent, we shared the great disappointment of bipartisan supporters in the Congress, not to mention the Central Americans who were counting on this assistance after it had been approved in both the Senate and the House of Representatives.

Report to Congress on Assistance Needs

Clearly, there is the desire in the Congress to make good on this commitment. Toward that end, there is a provision in the law that the Executive branch should develop a plan for fully funding the assistance to the Central American democracies proposed in the January 1984 report of the National Bipartisan Commission on Central America. I am transmitting that plan to the Congress with this message.

The Bipartisan Commission determined that the Central American Crisis was the result of a long history of interrelated political, security, and socio-economic conditions and recommended a greatly expanded financial assistance program for the years 1984-89. The Central American Democracy, Peace and Development Initiative (CAI), transmitted to the Congress in February 1984, was designed to accomplish most of the NBCCA's recommendations. This program concentrated on strengthening democratic institutions, arresting economic decline while promoting stabilization and recovery, and increasing the benefits of growth. Results in the political sector have been more rapid than anticipated. In the economic and social areas much also has been achieved. Nevertheless, this progress remains fragile and much remains to be done. The plan herewith transmitted to the Congress proposes a 3-year extension of the program's execution until 1992. The extension would increase the total amount of funds originally recommended in the CAI for the period FY 1984 to FY 1989 from $6.4 billion to $6.9 billion in appropriated funds for the period FY 1984 to FY 1992. As economic recovery in the region proceeds, the benefits of growth, economic, and political stabilization will be enjoyed by an ever-increasing percentage of the region's population.

After reviewing the findings of this study, I have concluded that additional assistance is required immediately in order to help meet the economic goals of the Bipartisan Commission and to keep faith with the millions of men and women who through hard work and sacrifice are making democracy a living reality in Central America.

This assistance is urgently required to help meet the great economic and social needs of the struggling democratic governments of the region. By generating conditions of violence in Central America that undermine prospects for economic growth, the communist government of Nicaragua works to discredit the democratic system as a viable alternative for development. To offset this effort, it is the responsibility of the friends of democracy to help Central America's democrats prove that even in adversity democracy offers their people a better way of life. The Soviet Union and its allies have provided the Sandinista regime military hardware and sufficient economic aid to keep Nicaragua's failed economy afloat. The United States must help those small nations in Central America that have chosen freedom.

Request for Additional Assistance

To carry out the recommendations contained in the report being forwarded to the Congress, section 215(2) of the Act further provides expedited procedures for requests from the President for additional economic assistance for the Central American democracies. I hereby request that such expedited consideration be given to my request for an additional $300,000,000 for fiscal year 1987 as economic support fund assistance for Costa Rica, El Salvador, Guatemala, and Honduras, notwithstanding section 10 of Public Law 91-672.

In order to assure that this additional assistance is fully consistent with applicable requirements of law and sound budget principles, I further request that the amounts made available for this additional economic assistance for Central America be transferred from unobligated balances in such accounts as I may designate for which appropriations were made by the Department of Defense Appropriations Act, 1985 (as contained in Public Law 98-473); the Department of Defense Appropriations Act, 1986 (as contained in Public Law 99-190); the Department of Defense Appropriations Act, 1987 (as contained in Public Laws 99-500 and 99-591); and the Department of State Appropriations Act, 1987 (as contained in Public Laws 99-500 and 99-591).

I urge the prompt enactment of a joint resolution expressing approval of this request....

(PPP Reagan 1987 I: 193-195)

Central American Peace Plan

August 5, 1987

Recognizing that the Central American Presidents are about to meet to discuss the issues involved and seek a peaceful solution to the problems in Central America, the United States desires to make known its view on certain of the basic elements that need to be included.

With respect to Nicaragua, the United States has three legitimate concerns for the well-being of the hemisphere:

1. That there be no Soviet, Cuban, or communist bloc bases established in Nicaragua that pose a threat to the United States and the other democratic governments in the hemisphere;

2. That Nicaragua pose no military threat to its neighbor countries nor provide a staging ground for subversion or destabilization of duly elected governments in the hemisphere; and

3. That the Nicaraguan Government respect the basic human rights of its people, including political rights guaranteed in the Nicaraguan Constitution and pledges made to the Organization of American States (OAS) — free speech, free press, religious liberty, and a regularly established system of free, orderly elections.

Beyond this, the United States has no right to influence or determine the identity of the political leaders of Nicaragua nor the social and economic systems of the country. These are matters wholly within the right of the Nicaraguan people. The United States affirms its support for the right of the Nicaraguan people to peaceful, democratic self-determination, free from outside intervention from any source.

In order to bring an immediate end to hostilities and begin a process of reconciliation, we propose the following:

1. An immediate cease-fire in place, on terms acceptable to the parties involved, subject to verification by the OAS or an international group of observers should be negotiated as soon as possible. When the cease-fire is in place, the United States will immediately suspend all military aid to the Contras, and simultaneously Nicaragua will stop receiving military aid from Cuba, the Soviet Union, and the communist bloc countries. Humanitarian aid can be supplied to both groups. The emergency law will be immediately suspended, and all civil rights and liberties will be restored.

An agreed, independent multiparty electoral commission will be established to assure regular elections open to free participation by all. A timetable and procedures for all elections, including those to be supervised and guaranteed by an agreed international body such as the OAS, will be established within 60 days.

2. The withdrawal of foreign military personnel and advisers from Nicaragua and its immediate neighbors that are in excess of the normal and legitimate needs of the region will be subject to negotiations among the countries of the region. The United States will suspend combat maneuvers in Honduras as a demonstration of good faith when the cease-fire is in place.

3. After the cease-fire is in place, negotiations among the Governments of the United States, Costa Rica, El Salvador, Guatemala, Honduras, and Nicaragua shall begin on reductions in standing armies in the region, withdrawal of foreign military personnel, restoration of regional military balance, security guarantees against outside support for insurgent forces, and verification and enforcement provisions. As part of this negotiating process, the United States shall enter into discussions with the governments of the region — including the Government of Nicaragua — concerning security issues. A regional agreement on security issues shall be negotiated within 60 days, unless this period is extended by mutual agreement. The OAS shall be invited to be a signatory to and guarantor of this agreement.

4. A plan of national reconciliation and dialogue among citizens of Nicaragua, including amnesty for former combatants and equal rights to participation in the political process. There shall be a plan of demobilization of both Sandinista and resistance forces. In accordance with the implementation of this plan, the United States simultaneously shall cease all resupply of resistance forces. Both the Government of Nicaragua and the Government of the United States shall encourage and support the reintegration of demobilized forces into Nicaraguan civil and political society on terms guaranteeing their safety. Nicaragua shall at this time become eligible for existing and prospective U.S. assistance programs.

5. A plan of expanded trade and long-range economic assistance for the democratic governments of Central America in which Nicaragua might participate. By the process of democratization and compliance with regional nonaggression agreements, Nicaragua would qualify for participation in the Caribbean Basin Initiative and the United States will lift its economic embargo.

6. The negotiation process shall commence immediately and be completed by September 30, 1987. If the Nicaraguan resistance, or forces under its command, should refuse to engage in this negotiating process, willfully obstruct its progress, or violate its terms, the United States shall immediately suspend all assistance to the resistance. If, because of actions taken by the Nicaraguan Government or the forces under its command, the negotiating process should not proceed, or its terms, conditions, and deadlines should not be met, the parties to these undertakings would be free to pursue such actions as they deem necessary to protect their national interest.

(DSB, October 1987: 55-59)

Statement by Assistant to the President for Press Relations Fitzwater on the Deployment of United States Armed Forces to Honduras

March 16, 1988

In light of the significant cross-border incursion by Sandinista armed forces into Honduras from Nicaragua, and at the request of the Government of Honduras, the President has ordered the immediate deployment of an infantry brigade task force consisting of two battalions of the 82d Airborne Division from Fort Bragg, North Carolina, two battalions from the 7th Infantry Division at Fort Ord, California, plus supporting units to Palmerola Air Force Base in Honduras for an emergency deployment readiness exercise.

In addition to its value as a test of the proficiency of our military units, this exercise is a measured response designed to show our staunch support to the democratic Government of Honduras at a time when its territorial integrity is being violated by the Cuban- and Soviet-supported Sandinista army. This exercise is also intended as a signal to the governments and

peoples of Central America of the seriousness with which the United States Government views the current situation in the region. The duration of this exercise has not been decided. The brigade task force will not be deployed to any area of ongoing hostilities.
(PPP Reagan 1988 I: 347)

Bipartisan Accord on Central America
March 24, 1989

The Executive and the Congress are united today in support of democracy, peace, and security in Central America. The United States supports the peace and democratization process and the goals of the Central American Presidents embodied in the Esquipulas Accord. The United States is committed to working in good faith with the democratic leaders of Central America and Latin America to translate the bright promises of Esquipulas II into concrete realities on the ground.

With regard to Nicaragua, the United States is united in its goals: democratization, an end to subversion and destabilization of its neighbors; an end to Soviet bloc military ties that threaten U.S. and regional security. Today the Executive and the Congress are united on a policy to achieve those goals.

To be successful the Central American peace process cannot be based on promises alone. It must be based on credible standards of compliance, strict timetables for enforcement, and effective on-going means to verify both the democratic and security requirements of those agreements. We support the use of incentives and disincentives to achieve U.S. policy objectives.

We also endorse an open, consultative process with bipartisanship as the watchword for the development and success of a unified policy towards Central America. The Congress recognizes the need for consistency and continuity in policy and the responsibility of the Executive to administer and carry out that policy, the programs based upon it, and to conduct American diplomacy in the region. The Executive will consult regularly and report to the Congress on progress in meeting the goals of the peace and democratization process, including the use of assistance as outlined in this Accord.

Under Esquipulas II and the El Salvador Accord, insurgent forces are supposed to voluntarily reintegrate into their homeland under safe, democratic conditions. The United States shall encourage the Government of Nicaragua and the Nicaraguan Resistance to continue the cessation of hostilities currently in effect.

To implement our purposes, the Executive will propose and the bipartisan leadership of the Congress will act promptly after the Easter Recess to extend humanitarian assistance at current levels to the Resistance through February 28, 1990, noting that the Government of Nicaragua has agreed to hold new elections under international supervision just prior to that date.

Those funds shall also be available to support voluntary reintegration or voluntary regional relocation by the Nicaraguan resistance. Such voluntary reintegration or voluntary regional relocation assistance shall be provided in a manner supportive of the goals of the Central American nations, as expressed in the Esquipulas II agreement and the El Salvador Accord, including the goal of democratization within Nicaragua, and the reintegration plan to be developed pursuant to those accords.

We believe that democratization should continue throughout Central America in those nations in which it is not yet complete with progress towards strengthening of civilian leadership, the defense of human rights, the rule of law and functioning judicial systems, and consolidation of free, open, safe, political processes in which all groups and individuals can fairly compete for political leadership. We believe that democracy and peace in Central America can create the conditions for economic integration and development that can benefit all the people of the region and pledge ourselves to examine new ideas to further those worthy goals.

While the Soviet Union and Cuba both publicly endorsed the Esquipulas Agreement, their continued aid and support of violence and subversion in Central America is in direct violation of that regional agreement. The United States believes that President Gorbachev's impending visit to Cuba represents an important opportunity for both the Soviet Union and Cuba to end all aid that supports subversion and destabilization in Central America as President Arias has requested and as the Central American peace process demands.

The United States Government retains ultimate responsibility to define its national interests and foreign policy, and nothing in this Accord shall be interpreted to infringe on that responsibility. The United States need not spell out in advance the nature or type of action that would be undertaken in response to threats to U.S. national security interests. Rather it should be sufficient to simply make clear that such threats will be met by any appropriate Constitutional means. The spirit of trust, bipartisanship, and common purpose expressed in this Accord between the Executive and the Congress shall continue to be the foundation for its full implementation and the achievement of democracy, security, and peace in Central America....

(PPP Bush 1989 I: 307-310)

Statement by Press Secretary Fitzwater on Soviet Policy in Central America

April 5, 1989

We listened carefully to what President Gorbachev had to say in Havana yesterday. While his words about not exporting revolution are welcomed, they are not matched by deeds which would give those words credence.

Today we call upon the Soviets to cut off their half-billion-dollar annual military aid to Nicaragua. The Soviets continue to pour arms into Nicaragua, a country whose army is already larger than those of all their neighbors combined. This is hard to fathom. It is a key issue in resolving the conflict in Central America. Our bipartisan plan for peace in Central America has the support of the Central American democracies. It is time for the Soviet Union to join us in Supporting that plan.

If President Gorbachev means his words, the Soviets should demonstrate through their behavior that they are adhering to this principle, and they should pressure their client states and revolutionary groups that they support to do the same. We note that the Soviets and Cuba have concluded a friendship treaty that apparently commits both parties to the peaceful resolution of conflicts in the region. We trust that the Soviets will follow these words with concrete actions.

We believe however, that to demonstrate his commitment to Esquipulas, President Gorbachev could have proposed a cutoff of military supplies to all irregular forces in the region. That is what Esquipulas calls for: an end to outside support to the guerrilla forces. This would have suggested a "new thinking" in Central America.

The United States is in compliance with Esquipulas. We are not providing military aid to the Nicaraguan resistance. The Soviet bloc, particularly Nicaragua and Cuba, continue to supply military and logistical support to the FMLN (Farabundo Marti National Liberation Front, El Salvador) and other irregular forces in Central America.

As the President and the Secretary of State have said, we reject the idea of equivalence between legitimate U.S. interests and the Soviet presence in Central America. We provide support, including military assistance, to the democratic governments of Central America. These governments are not involved in subversion of their neighbors.
(PPP Bush 1989 I: 372-373)

NICARAGUA

Presidential Determination No. 87-10 — Assistance for the Nicaraguan Democratic Resistance
March 5, 1987

...In accordance with Title II, Section 211(e) of the act making appropriations for military construction for the Department of Defense for the fiscal year ending September 30, 1987 as contained in Public Law 99-500 approved on October 18, 1986 (the act), I hereby determine that the conditions set forth in that Section with respect to provision of assistance to the Nicaraguan democratic resistance have been met, specifically:

(a) that the Central American countries have not concluded a comprehensive and effective agreement based on the Contadora Document of Objectives;

(b) that the Government of Nicaragua is not engaged in a serious dialogue with representatives of all elements of the Nicaraguan democratic opposition, accompanied by a cease-fire and an effective end to the existing constraints on freedom of speech, assembly, religion, and political activity, leading to regularly scheduled free and fair elections and the establishment of democratic institutions; and

(c) that there is no reasonable prospect of achieving such agreement, dialogue, cease-fire, and end to constraints described above through further diplomatic measures, multilateral or bilateral, without additional assistance to the Nicaraguan democratic resistance....
(PPP Reagan 1987 I: 217)

President Reagan's Address to the People of Nicaragua on the Central American Peace Plan
August 22, 1987

The four Presidents of democratic Central America sat down with the Communist ruler of Nicaragua in Guatemala to negotiate a peace plan for Central America. They emerged from this summit meeting with an agreement for regional peace based on promises of democracy. This peace plan calls for sweeping political and social change to take place in Nicaragua.

In the upcoming weeks, our hopes will be measured against reality, and promises will be measured against deeds. The signing of the Guatemalan peace plan was an important act of faith. But our faith must be tempered by realism, because faith without realism will not end in peace but in disillusionment and a permanent Communist rule that will threaten the other emerging democracies in Central America.

The Sandinistas promised to respect your rights when they signed this peace plan — rights that they have denied you for the last 8 years. They promised to respect your rights of free speech and free association. They promised political, religious, and press freedom. They promised access for all political parties and currents of opinion to the means of communication. They promised to lift the state of emergency. They promised free elections. The Sandinistas now have promised you democracy with the world as witness. Like you, I hope that they keep this promise. But like you, I also know that the civil war in Nicaragua began when the Sandinistas promised you democracy but failed to meet their commitment. This struggle will end when that promise is fulfilled.

Under the terms of the Guatemalan plan there must be democracy in Nicaragua in order for the fighting to stop. This is called simultaneity. By accepting the Guatemalan plan, it means that the Sandinistas have agreed that the repression must stop at the same time that the fighting stops. The Sandinistas have told us this before, and no one believes the Sandinistas anymore. Simultaneity must mean freedom up front, or no deal.

We will be helping the democratic leaders of Central America and your countrymen inside Nicaragua as they seek a diplomatic solution to the war that has befallen your country, but we will remain firm in our policy. Our objective remains the same: peace and democracy in Nicaragua. Your commitment to freedom and democracy has created political movement and hope for liberation. For this, the people of Nicaragua and the people of Central America owe you a list of gratitude. I know your deepest wish is to return home to a free Nicaragua. Your struggle has, and always will have, our support, because our goal is the same: democracy....
(PPP Reagan 1987 II: 975-976)

Radio Address to the Nation on the Situation in Nicaragua
September 12, 1987

...Many Americans have learned over the last few months what has really been happening in Nicaragua: how a democratic revolution was betrayed; how a tiny elite has been creating a totalitarian, Marxist-Leninist dictatorship to satisfy their own personal lust for power and to give the Soviet Union a beachhead on the mainland of this continent-only 2000 miles from the Texas border, a clear national security threat.

Yet despite all the repression and Soviet intervention, the people of Nicaragua still cling to their dream of freedom. In the best tradition of our Founding Fathers, they formed a democratic resistance against tyranny, one of the largest peasant armies in the world, with more than 17,000 freedom fighters called contras. And as the contras have grown stronger, the Communist regime has grown shakier.

So, under increasing pressure, the Communist leader Daniel Ortega recently signed, at a summit of Central American leaders, a peace plan that pledged his government to democratic reform, respect for human rights, and free elections. We welcome the Guatemala plan, but it falls short of the safeguards for democracy and our national security contained in the bipartisan plan I worked out with the congressional leadership. That is why, as Secretary Shultz said earlier this week, there should be no uncertainty about our unswerving commitment to the contras. It is their effort that has made the peace initiative possible. At the appropriate moment, I intend to put forth a $270 million request for contra aid....

As Secretary Shultz also spelled out, the Sandinista regime has a long way to go in living up to its pledge of democratic reform. Only 8 days after signing the peace agreement, Sandinista police used attack dogs, night sticks, electric cattle prods, and government-organized mobs to break up a peaceful demonstration by the Nicaraguan Democratic Coordinadora. So, too, the 6 independent Nicaraguan political parties have called efforts by the Communists to manipulate the National Reconciliation Commission set up under the plan "a Sandinista maneuver to fool the international public." They accused the Sandinistas of "violating the spirit of the Guatemala agreements." And this week we learned that Daniel Ortega will be in Moscow on November 7th, the date the Central American peace plan is to go into effect, celebrating with his Soviet allies the anniversary of the Bolshevik revolution.

What the world wants from the Sandinistas are real democratic reforms, real signs of freedom, such as reopening the newspaper La Prensa, but not censoring its copy or denying it newsprint. La Prensa and other publications must be free to report, so must the independent radio stations and TV. Freedom of religion must be respected. The Sandinistas have said they will allow three exiled priests to return, but what of the thousands of other exiles? Return is not enough; they must be free to minister, live, and organize politically without intimidation. Genuine free political competition must be permitted. The secret police, with their neighborhood block committees, must be abolished and all foreign advisers sent home. The Sandinistas should know that America and the world are watching....
(PPP Reagan 1987 II: 1024-1025)

White House Statement on the Presidential Determination on Assistance to the Nicaraguan Democratic Resistance
January 19, 1988

The President today made the determination and certification under section 111(b)(2)(A) of the fiscal year 1988 continuing resolution (P.L. 100-202) that permits resumption of transportation of military assistance to the Nicaraguan democratic resistance authorized by the Congress.

Section 111 of the continuing resolution provided for suspension of transportation of military assistance to the resistance on January 12, 1988, and for resumption of such assistance after January 18, 1988, if the President determined and certified to the Congress that:

- no cease-fire is in place that was agreed to by the Government of Nicaragua and the Nicaraguan democratic resistance;
- the failure to achieve such a cease-fire results from the lack of good faith efforts by the Government of Nicaragua to achieve such a cease-fire; and
- the Nicaraguan democratic resistance has engaged in good faith efforts to achieve such a cease-fire.

The President's determination was based on the Secretary of State's findings, set forth in his January 18, 1988, report, that the conditions for resuming assistance to the resistance have been met.

The Sandinistas have a record, beginning with promises to the organization of American States in 1979 and continuing through the Guatemala accord of August 7, 1987, of making promises of democracy and freedom that they do not keep. After the Central American Presidents summit meeting this past weekend in San José, Costa Rica, the Nicaraguan President issued yet more promises. That very weekend, the Sandinistas' internal security forces executed a wave of arrests and interrogations of leading members of the surviving democratic political elements in Nicaragua. Moreover, while the Nicaraguan President demands unilateral termination of support for the forces of freedom in Nicaragua, the massive flow to the Sandinistas of Soviet-bloc arms continues unabated.

The United States remains fully committed to the achievement of democracy in Nicaragua and security in all of Central America as the essential conditions for a just and lasting peace in the region. The events which have unfolded since the signing of the Guatemala accord on August 7, 1987, have demonstrated once again that a strong Nicaraguan democratic resistance remains essential to the achievement of those conditions.
(PPP Reagan 1988 I: 53-54)

President Reagan's Request to Congress for Assistance for the Nicaraguan Democratic Resistance
January 27, 1988

In accordance with the Constitution and laws of the United States of America, as President of the United States of America, and pursuant to section III(j)(1) of the joint resolution making further continuing appropriations for the fiscal year 1988 (Public Law 100-202), I hereby request budget and other authority to provide additional assistance for the Nicaraguan democratic resistance, as follows:

SEC. 101. POLICY

(a) General Policy. — It is the policy of the United States in implementing this request to advance democracy and security in Central America, and thereby to assist in bringing a just and lasting peace to that region in a manner compatible with the Guatemala Peace Accord of August 7, 1987 and the Declaration of the Presidents of the Central American Nations at San Jose, Costa Rica on January 16, 1988, and consistent with the national security interests of the United States.

(b) Specific Policy objective. — In pursuing the policy set forth in subsection (a), it is the objective of the United States to enhance its security as well as that of the democratic countries of Central America by assisting in the achievement of:

(1) genuine democracy in Nicaragua;

(2) an end to Soviet, Cuban, and other Communist bloc military or security assistance to, advisers in, and establishment or use of bases in, Nicaragua;

(3) an end to Nicaraguan aggression and subversion against other countries in Central America; and

(4) reduction of the military and security forces of Nicaragua to a level consistent with the security of other countries in the region.

SEC. 102. TRANSFER OF PRIOR DEFENSE APPROPRIATIONS FOR ASSISTANCE

(a) Transfer and Use. — Upon enactment of a joint resolution approving this request, there are hereby transferred to the President $36,250,000 of unobligated funds, from the appropriations accounts specified in section 106, to provide assistance for the Nicaraguan democratic resistance, to remain available until expended.

(b) Earmark for Non-Lethal Assistance Including Human Rights. — of the funds transferred by subsection (a), $32,650,000 shall be available only for non-lethal assistance, of which $450,000 shall be available only for strengthening programs and activities of the Nicaraguan democratic resistance for the observance and advancement of human rights.

(c) Prohibition on Purchase of Aircraft. — Funds transferred by subsection (a) may not be obligated or expended to purchase aircraft.

(d) Indemnification of Leased Aircraft. — (1) The President is authorized to transfer unobligated funds, from the appropriations accounts specified in section 106, solely for the indemnification of aircraft leased to transport assistance for which this request provides and assistance previously, specifically authorized by law for the Nicaraguan democratic resistance.

(2) Not more than $20,000,000 may be transferred under the authority granted by paragraph (1).

(3) The President shall transfer the balance, if any, remaining of funds transferred under paragraph (1) to the appropriations accounts from which such funds were transferred under that paragraph when the funds transferred by subsection (a) have been expended.

(e) Passive Air Defense Equipment —

(1) The Department of Defense shall make available to the department or agency administering this request passive air defense equipment (including ground-based radio detection and ranging equipment) to ensure the safety of transportation provided pursuant to this request.

(2) The Department of Defense shall not charge the department or agency receiving equipment under paragraph (1) for such equipment, and shall bear the risk of loss, damage, or deterioration of such equipment during the period of its use under the authority of paragraph (1).

(f) Initiation of Delivery of Additional Assistance. — No assistance for which this request provides shall be delivered to the Nicaraguan democratic resistance prior to March 1, 1988.

SEC. 103. RESTRICTIONS ON LETHAL ASSISTANCE

(a) Prohibition. — After February 29, 1988, no lethal assistance may be delivered to the Nicaraguan democratic resistance, except as provided in subsection (b).

(b) Resumption of Lethal Assistance. — Lethal assistance may be delivered to the Nicaraguan democratic resistance if, after March 31 1988, the President determines and certifies to the Speaker of the House of Representatives and the President of the Senate that —

(1) at the time of such certification no cease fire is in place that was agreed to by the Government of Nicaragua and the Nicaraguan democratic resistance;

(2) the failure to achieve the cease fire described in paragraph (1) results from the lack of good faith efforts by the Government of Nicaragua to comply with the requirements of the Declaration of the Presidents of the Central American Nations at San Jose, Costa Rica on January 16, 1988; and

(3) the Nicaraguan democratic resistance has engaged in good faith efforts to achieve the cease fire described in paragraph (1).

(c) Scope. — The lethal assistance to which subsections (a) and (b) refer is lethal assistance for which this request provides and lethal assistance previously authorized by law.

(d) Suspension During Ceasefire. — Delivery of lethal assistance to the Nicaraguan democratic resistance for which this request provides or which was previously authorized by law, shall be suspended during any period in which there is in place a cease fire agreed to by the Government of Nicaragua and the Nicaraguan democratic resistance, except to the extent, if any, permitted by the agreement governing such cease fire.

SEC. 104. GENERAL AUTHORITIES AND LIMITATIONS

(a) Related Statutes. — The requirements, terms and conditions of section 104 of the Intelligence Authorization Act, Fiscal Year 1988 (Public Law 100-118), section 8144 of the Department of Defense Appropriations Act, 1988 (as contained in section 101(b) of Public Law 100-202), section 10 of Public Law 91-672, section 502 of the National Security Act of 1947, section 15(a) of the State Department Basic Authorities Act of 1956, and any other provision of law shall be deemed to have been met for the transfer and use consistent with this request of the funds made available by section 102(a) and (d), and the transfer and use of equipment as provided in section 102(e).

(b) Continuation of Authority to Support, Monitor, and Manage. — The authority to support, monitor and manage activities for which funds are

provided under this request or a law which previously, specifically authorized assistance to the Nicaraguan democratic resistance shall continue until the funds transferred by section 102(a) have been expended....
(PPP Reagan 1988 I: 130-133)

President Reagan's Statement on the House of Representatives Disapproval of Aid to the Nicaraguan Democratic Resistance
March 4, 1988

By its action last night, the House of Representatives again failed to approve further assistance for the Nicaraguan freedom fighters. Without renewal of aid soon, the resistance will cease to provide the pressure necessary to ensure that the Sandinista regime honors its promises under the Guatemala accord of August 1987 and the San José Declaration of January 1988 to bring about democracy in Nicaragua.

I ask the House of Representatives and the Senate to act swiftly to renew assistance to the freedom fighters. Key elements of such a package should include:

- sufficient nonlethal assistance to sustain the resistance in the field;
- a safe and effective means for delivering; and
- procedures for expedited consideration by the Congress of a future Presidential request for additional aid if efforts to negotiate a cease-fire are unsuccessful.

In the days ahead, I will be consulting with bipartisan supporters in both Chambers to put together an effective package for aid to the resistance. Prompt renewal of assistance to the resistance remains essential to advance the national security interests of the United States.
(PPP Reagan 1988 I: 294)

President Reagan's Statement on Aid to the Nicaraguan Democratic Resistance
May 24, 1988

Two months have passed since the Congress limited U.S. assistance to the Nicaraguan democratic resistance to food, shelter, clothing, and medicine. The Congress stopped U.S. military assistance to the resistance while the Soviet bloc continued its military assistance to the Communist Sandinista regime in Nicaragua. Some thought that U.S. forbearance would bring democracy and peace to Nicaragua through negotiations between the resistance and the Sandinista regime, but it has not.

Tomorrow, as I leave on the first leg of my trip to Moscow, the resistance and the Sandinistas are scheduled to meet again. The Sandinistas will again have the opportunity to carry out the promises they have made — beginning a decade ago with promises to the Organization of American States — of establishment of freedom and democracy in Nicaragua. We do not need more pieces of paper bearing empty Sandinista promises and Sandinista signatures. We need deeds, not more words.

During the 60-day truce established under the Sapoa agreement signed March 23, the Sandinistas have continued, and indeed intensified, their repression of the Nicaraguan people. They have not carried out their commitments under the Guatemala accord of August 7, 1987, or under the Sapoa agreement. The Sandinistas have gone so far as to make it impossible to arrange through neutral parties to deliver food and medicine to resistance members inside Nicaragua.

The men and women of the Agency for International Development who have worked long and hard to ensure that the members of the resistance have the basic necessities of life deserve the thanks of our nation. The work of AID keeps the chance for democracy alive in Nicaragua.

The United States continues to support those fighting for freedom and democracy in Nicaragua. The freedom fighters of the Nicaraguan democratic resistance deserve the continued support of the United States.

If the current stalemate in the peace process persists and the Sandinistas continue their policies of repression, then we will call upon the Congress to reconsider its February 3 decision to curtail assistance to the Nicaraguan freedom fighters.

(PPP Reagan 1988 I: 638-639)

Statement by Assistant to the President for Press Relations Fitzwater on the Situation in Nicaragua

July 15, 1988

The President is pleased with the overwhelming, bipartisan votes of the Senate and the House of Representatives condemning the outrageous actions of the Sandinista Government of Nicaragua. These votes send the message to the Sandinistas that the United States is firmly committed to the achievement of freedom and democracy in Nicaragua.

Just this week, the Sandinistas have shut down the two media outlets for free expression in Nicaragua, the newspaper La Prensa and Catholic Radio. And they have brutally suppressed a peaceful demonstration for human rights, arrested leaders of the democratic opposition, and expelled the U.S. Ambassador and much of his staff.

The Sandinistas continue to snuff out any hope for democratic reform in Nicaragua, despite the solemn promises to establish democracy that they have

made and broken repeatedly in the decade since they seized power. They continue to oppress the Nicaraguan people and receive substantial Soviet-bloc military shipments. The Sandinistas' conduct makes clear that they will not institute democratic reform and cease their threats to the security of Central America unless effectively pressured and persuaded to do so. To achieve democracy in Nicaragua and security for all of Central America clearly requires a viable and effective Nicaraguan democratic resistance....
(PPP Reagan 1988-1989 II: 967)

President Bush's Statement on the Upcoming Elections in Nicaragua
July 19, 1989

Ten years ago, there was widespread satisfaction here and in Latin America that the anti-Somoza revolution in Nicaragua had triumphed and at long last democracy would be given a chance. The Sandinistas committed to the OAS [Organization of American States] in 1979 to establish a democracy and renewed that commitment when the Central American peace accord was signed nearly 2 years ago. Despite these promises, that commitment remains unfulfilled today.

The United States wanted to do its part for the success of the turn toward democracy. We had contributed to the overthrow of Somoza by cutting off military assistance. Encouraged by the Sandinistas' promise to the OAS, we provided $118 million in economic and humanitarian assistance to the new Nicaraguan government. This was substantially more than any other country gave the new regime and represented more aid than we had provided the Somoza government in the previous 4 years.

Despite our efforts to be supportive, as well as those of other democratic governments, the Sandinistas quickly embarked on a course which centralized power in their hands, brought economic ruin to their country, and forced hundreds of thousands to flee. They built up the largest army in Central America with aid from Cuba, the Soviet Union, and other Communist states. The security forces and Sandinista thugs harassed and imprisoned the opposition, including from the political parties, labor unions and businessmen, the Catholic Church, and the Miskito Indian community. Elections were postponed for 5 years, and when they were held, the Sandinista ground rules did not allow the opposition to compete freely and fairly.

Today, with the eyes of the world upon them, the Sandinistas have another opportunity to give peace and democracy a chance. But as the second anniversary of the commitments at Esquipulas approaches, what is evident is a renewed attempt to prevent a free and fair election. In strong contrast to its neighbors, who have chosen the democratic path, the Sandinista government continues to show that it fears free political competition.

The Sandinista electoral reform law, for example, was imposed upon the opposition over its objection and provides for an electoral council which is stacked in the Sandinistas' favor. Provisions for government campaign financing penalize parties that did not participate in the last election. To snuff out any chance that foreign contributions to the opposition could somehow offset official favoritism toward the Sandinista party, the law provides that 50 percent of foreign contributions be distributed to the electoral council. The Sandinista party is under no such constraints.

On paper, the electoral law permits foreign observers, but Sandinista practice to date indicates a desire to restrict them. The Sandinistas, for example, have branded National Endowment for Democracy representatives as CIA agents, expelled a Freedom House observer, and imposed visa restrictions on Americans so as to control who may report on the election. Two American diplomats were expelled for observing an opposition rally, and Sandinista restrictions on other members of the diplomatic corps provoked a protest by the EC representatives. These moves stand in sharp contrast to the Salvadoran experience, where observers from all sides were welcomed—even those critical of the Government.

The new media law also fails to meet democratic standards, as it contains vague provisions that permit prosecution for defaming the Government, and enforcement is left to the Ministry of the Interior. Unlike the other Central American countries, the Government by law owns all television broadcasting. Moreover, only government-sanctioned polling is permitted, allowing the Sandinistas to hide from the people the true extent of their unpopularity.

The Sandinistas have also shown their fear of electoral freedoms in other ways. Several opposition marches have been canceled because the Government denied permits. Labor unions have been threatened, lest their display of economic power threaten the Sandinistas. Recently, several private sector leaders were stripped of their property, not for violations of law but in a transparent attempt to silence vocal critics of Sandinista policies.

Permeating all of these Sandinista measures is a government propaganda that equates opposition with disloyalty and criticism with allegiance to a foreign power. At every point, the Sandinistas have shown that they feel they can ignore opposition demands for dialog. Last week in San José, President Ortega indicated he might be willing to change. We look for him to do so, for there will be dim prospects for national reconciliation unless the internal opposition and the Nicaraguan resistance are made full partners in this process.

We also look to the Sandinistas to make other changes to comply with their Esquipulas commitments. Recently discovered arms caches in El Salvador show that the Sandinistas continue to subvert their neighbors. Despite our having halted lethal aid to the resistance, the Sandinista military buildup continues with new deliveries from Cuba and other Communist states. And now the Sandinistas are making common cause with the Noriega regime in Panama, a dictatorship in the style of Somoza.

The bipartisan accord with Congress offers an opportunity for better relations between our two countries. We want to see democracy and national reconciliation work in Nicaragua. We remain willing to respond positively if the Sandinistas fulfill their promises— made to the OAS over 10 years ago at Esquipulas, and again last February in El Salvador — to allow Nicaraguans to exercise their democratic rights. Despite the somber prospects, we remain committed to support free elections and democracy in Nicaragua, and our sincerest hope is that next year the Nicaraguan people will truly have something to celebrate.

(PPP Bush 1989 II: 985-986)

President Bush's Statement on the Election of Violeta Chamorro as President of Nicaragua

February 26, 1990

In this remarkable year of political change, democracy won another victory yesterday. I am most pleased that there has been a free and fair election in Nicaragua and that the results are being accepted by both sides.

I am sending messages to Mrs. Chamorro congratulating her on her victory and to President Ortega congratulating him on the conduct of the election and his stated willingness to abide by the results. The United States looks forward to working with Mrs. Chamorro's new government in support of her stated goals of national reconciliation and economic reconstruction, and with President Ortega in helping ensure a peaceful transition of power. I have talked this morning with Venezuelan President Carlos Andrés Pérez, and we agree completely on the need to help all parties in Nicaragua to achieve a peaceful reconciliation and transfer of power.

We also congratulate the international observer delegations whose activities, which took place at the request of the Sandinista government, helped ensure an open and safe electoral process. There were many, but I want to mention delegations led by former President Jimmy Carter and former Governor Dan Evans, the United Nations delegation led by former Secretary Elliot Richardson, and the OAS delegation led by Secretary General Baena Soares.

We hope that all sides in this hotly fought contest will extend the hand of reconciliation and cooperate together in rebuilding their country for the good of all Nicaraguans. There is space in a democratic Nicaragua for the expression of all political points of view. We also hope that the cease-fire will be reestablished immediately and respected by all sides. Given the election's clear mandate for peace and democracy, there is no reason at all for further military activity from any quarter.

We are confident the international community will strongly support the results of yesterday's elections and will join in the effort to help all Nicaraguans to rebuild their country.
(PPP Bush 1990 I: 277)

VIOLATIONS OF JUDGEMENT AND LAW: THE IRAN-CONTRA CONTROVERSY

Statement by Principal Deputy Press Secretary Speakes on the Iran Arms and Contra Aid Controversy

January 30, 1987

The President is pleased that the first report on the Iran matter is out and that it confirms his position that he neither authorized nor was aware of the alleged transfer of funds to the contras.

The report is consistent with the President's position that, from its inception, the Iran initiative was an effort to open a dialog with top officials of a strategically important country. Numerous documents summarized in the report indicate that this was the view of Iranians, as well as those on the American side. In implementing this policy, the release of hostages was an important preliminary step intended to show that the Iranians would no longer support terrorism and the sale of arms was a gesture of good faith on the part of the United States in pursuing this strategic opening. To be sure, the linking of arms sales to the release of hostages at several points during this 15-month episode could be interpreted as a trade of arms for hostages, but this was not the policy approved by the President.

The report contains no evidence whatsoever that the President was aware of, let alone approved, any diversion of funds to the contras. The report brings to light for the first time statements by Lt. Col. Oliver North — in his initial interview with Attorney General Meese — to the effect that he did not believe that the President was aware of the alleged diversion. In addition, Admiral Poindexter's statements to Mr. Meese and Donald Regan — that he had not inquired into the matter because "he felt sorry for the contras" — substantiates the President's statements that he was never told of this plan.
(PPP Reagan 1987 I: 92)

Statement by Assistant to the President for Press Relations Fitzwater on the Iran Arms and Contra Aid Controversy

February 10, 1987

On February 4, 1987, John Tower, Chairman of the President's Special Review Board, requested that the President, acting as Commander in Chief, order Adm. John Poindexter and Lt. Col. Oliver North to appear before the

Board. In a letter dated February 6, Counsel to the President Peter Wallison advised the Board that such an order would be unlawful, because it would in effect be ordering Admiral Poindexter and Colonel North to testify against themselves. The Counsel noted that North and Poindexter have a constitutional protection against self-incrimination, as well as a similar guarantee under article 31 of the Uniform Code of Military Justice.

In giving this response, the White House Counsel relied upon a written opinion from the General Counsel of the Department of Defense, who confirmed earlier oral advice on this matter when similar issues were raised in December. Mr. Wallison also pointed out that the President has made clear his desire that both Poindexter and North cooperate fully with all ongoing inquiries, consistent with their rights. In December the President proposed a procedure for obtaining their testimony without violating their rights against self-incrimination.He asked that the Senate Select Committee on Intelligence grant limited use immunity to Poindexter and North so that the facts would be known without precluding prosecution based on other evidence.
(PPP Reagan 1987 I: 125)

Report of the President's Special Review Board
February 26, 1987
...Failure of Responsibility

The NSC system will not work unless the President makes it work. After all, this system was created to serve the President of the United States in ways of his choosing. By his actions, by his leadership, the President therefore determines the quality of its performance.

By his own account, as evidenced in his diary notes, and as conveyed to the Board by his principal advisors, President Reagan was deeply committed to securing the release of the hostages. It was this intense compassion for the hostages that appeared to motivate his steadfast support of the Iran initiative, even in the face of opposition from his Secretaries of State and Defense.

In his obvious commitment, the President appears to have proceeded with a concept of the initiative that was not accurately reflected in the reality of the operation. The President did not seem to be aware of the way in which the operation was implemented and the full consequences of U.S. participation.

The President's expressed concern for the safety of both the hostages and the Iranians who could have been at risk may have been conveyed in a manner so as to inhibit the full functioning of the system.

The President's management style is to put the principal responsibility for policy review and implementation on the shoulders of his advisors. Nevertheless, with such a complex, high risk operation and so much at stake, the President should have ensured that the NSC system did not fail him. He did not force his policy to undergo the most critical review of which the NSC participants and the process were capable. At no time did he insist upon accountability and performance review. Had the President chosen to drive the NSC system, the outcome could well have been different. As it was, the most powerful features of the NSC system — providing comprehensive analysis, alternatives and follow-up — were not utilized.

The Board found a strong consensus among NSC participants that the President's priority in the Iran initiative was the release of U.S. hostages. But setting priorities is not enough when it comes to sensitive and risky initiatives that directly affect U.S. national security. He must ensure that the content and tactics of an initiative match his priorities and objectives. He must insist upon accountability. For it is the President who must take responsibility for the NSC system and deal with the consequences.

Beyond the President, the other NSC principals and the National Security Advisor must share in the responsibility for the NSC system.

President Reagan's personal management style places an especially heavy responsibility on his key advisors. Knowing his style, they should have been particularly mindful of the need for special attention to the manner in which this arms sale initiative developed and proceeded. On this score, neither the National Security Advisor nor the other NSC principals deserve high marks.

It is their obligation as members and advisors to the Council to ensure that the President is adequately served. The principal subordinates to the President must not be deterred from urging the President not to proceed on a highly questionable course of action even in the face of his strong conviction to the contrary.

In the case of the Iran initiative, the NSC process did not fail, it simply was largely ignored. The National Security Advisor and the NSC principals all had a duty to raise this issue and insist that orderly process be imposed. None of them did so.

All had the opportunity. While the National Security Advisor had the responsibility to see that an orderly process was observed, his failure to do so does not excuse the other NSC principals. It does not appear that any of the NSC principals called for more frequent consideration of the Iran initiative by the NSC principals in the presence of the President. None of the principals called for a serious vetting of the initiative by even a restricted group of disinterested individuals. The intelligence questions do not appear to have been raised, and legal considerations, while raised, were not pressed. No one seemed to have complained about the informality of the process. No one called for a thorough reexamination once the initiative did not meet expectations or the manner of execution changed. While one or another of the NSC principals suspected that something was amiss, none vigorously pursued the issue.

Mr. Regan also shares in this responsibility. More than almost any Chief of Staff of recent memory, he asserted personal control over the White House staff and sought to extend this control to the National Security Advisor. He was personally active in national security affairs and attended almost all of the relevant meetings regarding the Iran initiative. He, as much as anyone, should have insisted that an orderly process be observed. In addition, he especially should have ensured that plans were made for handling any public disclosure of the initiative. He must bear primary responsibility for the chaos that descended upon the White House when such disclosure did occur.

Mr. McFarlane appeared caught between a President who supported the initiative and the cabinet officers who strongly opposed it. While he made efforts to keep these cabinet officers informed, the Board heard complaints from some that he was not always successful. VADM Poindexter on several occasions apparently sought to exclude NSC principals other than the President from knowledge of the initiative. Indeed, on one or more occasions Secretary Shultz may have been actively misled by VADM Poindexter.

VADM Poindexter also failed grievously on the matter of Contra diversion. Evidence indicates that VADM Poindexter knew that a diversion occurred, yet he did not take the steps that were required given the gravity of that prospect. He apparently failed to appreciate or ignored the serious legal and political risks presented. His clear obligation was either to investigate the matter or take it to the President— or both. He did neither. Director Casey shared a similar responsibility. Evidence suggests that he received information about the possible diversion of funds to the Contras almost a month before the story broke. He, too, did not move promptly to raise the matter with the President. Yet his responsibility to do so was clear.

The NSC principals other than the President may be somewhat excused by the insufficient attention on the part of the National Security Advisor to the need to keep all the principals fully informed. Given the importance of the issue and the sharp policy divergences involved, however, Secretary Shultz and Secretary Weinberger in particular distanced themselves from the march of events. Secretary Shultz specifically requested to be informed only as necessary to perform his job. Secretary Weinberger had access through intelligence to details about the operation. Their obligation was to give the President their full support and continued advice with respect to the program or, if they could not in conscience do that, to so inform the President. Instead, they simply distanced themselves from the program. They protected the record as to their own positions on this issue. They were not energetic in attempting to protect the President from the consequences of his personal commitment to freeing the hostages.

Director Casey appears to have been informed in considerable detail about the specifics of the Iranian operation. He appears to have acquiesced in and to have encouraged North's exercise of direct operational control over the operation. Because of the NSC staff's proximity to and close identification with the President, this increased the risks to the President if the initiative became public or the operation failed.

There is no evidence, however, that Director Casey explained this risk to the President or made clear to the President that LtCol North, rather than the CIA, was running the operation. The President does not recall ever being informed of this fact. Indeed, Director Casey should have gone further and pressed for operational responsibility to be transferred to the CIA.

Director Casey should have taken the lead in vetting the assumptions presented by the Israelis on which the program was based and in pressing for an early examination of the reliance upon Mr. Ghorbanifar and the second channel as intermediaries. He should also have assumed responsibility for checking out the other intermediaries involved in the operation. Finally, because Congressional restrictions on covert actions are both largely directed at and familiar to the CIA, Director Casey should have taken the lead in keeping the question of Congressional notification active.

Finally, Director Casey, and, to a lesser extent, Secretary Weinberger, should have taken it upon themselves to assess the effect of the transfer of arms and intelligence to Iran on the Iran/Iraq military balance, and to transmit that information to the President....

Specific Recommendations

In addition to its principal recommendation regarding the organization and functioning of the NSC system and roles to be played by the participants, the Board has a number of specific recommendations.

1. *The National Security Act of 1947.* The flaws of procedure and failures of responsibility revealed by our study do not suggest any inadequacies in the provisions of the National Security Act of 1947 that deal with the structure and operation of the NSC system. Forty years of experience under that Act demonstrate to the Board that it remains a fundamentally sound framework for national security decision making. It strikes a balance between formal structure and flexibility adequate to permit each President to tailor the system to fit his needs.

As a general matter, the NSC Staff should not engage in the implementation of policy or the conduct of operations. This compromises their oversight role and usurps the responsibilities of the departments and agencies. But the inflexibility of a legislative restriction should be avoided. Terms such as "operation" and "implementation" are difficult to define, and a legislative proscription might preclude some future President from making a very constructive use of the NSC Staff.

Predisposition on sizing of the staff should be toward fewer rather than more. But a legislative restriction cannot foresee the requirements of future Presidents. Size is best left to the discretion of the President, with the admonition that the role of the NSC staff is to review, not to duplicate or replace, the work of the departments and agencies.

We recommend that no substantive change be made in the provisions of the National Security Act dealing with the structure and operation of the NSC system.

2. *Senate Confirmation of the National Security Advisor.* It has been suggested that the job of the National Security Advisor has become so important that its holder should be screened by the process of confirmation, and that once confirmed he should return frequently for questioning by the Congress. It is argued that this would improve the accountability of the National Security Advisor.

We hold a different view. The National Security Advisor does, and should continue, to serve only one master, and that is the President. Further, confirmation is inconsistent with the role the National Security Advisor should play. He should not decide, only advise. He should not engage in policy implementation or operations. He should serve the President, with no collateral and potentially diverting loyalties.

Confirmation would tend to institutionalize the natural tension that exists between the Secretary of State and the National Security Advisor. Questions would increasingly arise about who really speaks for the President in national security matters. Foreign governments could be confused or would be encouraged to engage in "forum shopping."

Only one of the former government officials interviewed favored Senate confirmation of the National Security Advisor. While consultation with Congress received wide support, confirmation and formal questioning were opposed. Several suggested that if the National Security Advisor were to become a position subject to confirmation, it could induce the President to turn to other internal staff or to people outside government to play that role.

We urge the Congress not to require Senate confirmation of the National Security Advisor.

3. *The Interagency Process.* It is the National Security Advisor who has the greatest interest in making the national security process work, for it is this process by which the President obtains the information, background, and analysis he requires to make decisions and build support for his program. Most Presidents have set up interagency committees at both a staff and policy level to surface issues, develop options, and clarify choices. There has typically been a struggle for the chairmanships of these groups between the National Security Advisor and the NSC staff on the one hand, and the cabinet secretaries and department officials on the other.

Our review of the operation of the present system and that of other administrations where committee chairmen came from the departments has led us to the conclusion that the system generally operates better when the committees are chaired by the individual with the greatest stake in making the NSC system work.

We recommend that the National Security Advisor chair the senior-level committees of the NSC system.

4. *Covert Actions.* Policy formulation and implementation are usually managed by a team of experts led by policymaking generalists. Covert action requirements are no different, but there is a need to limit, sometimes severely, the number of individuals involved. The lives of many people may be at stake, as was the case in the attempt to rescue the hostages in Tehran. Premature disclosure might kill the idea in embryo, as could have been the case in the opening of relations with China. In such cases, there is a tendency to limit those involved to a small number of top officials. This practice tends to limit severely the expertise brought to bear on the problem and should be used very sparingly indeed.

The obsession with secrecy and preoccupation with leaks threaten to paralyze the government in its handling of covert operations. Unfortunately, the concern is not misplaced. The selective leak has become a principal means of waging bureaucratic warfare. Opponents of an operation kill it with a leak; supporters seek to build support through the same means.

We have witnessed over the past years a significant deterioration in the integrity of process. Rather than a means to obtain results more satisfactory than the position of any of the individual departments, it has frequently become something to be manipulated to reach a specific outcome. The leak becomes a primary instrument in that process.

This practice is destructive of orderly governance. It can only be reversed if the most senior officials take the lead. If senior decision makers set a clear example and demand compliance, subordinates are more likely to conform.

Most recent administrations have had carefully drawn procedures for the consideration of covert activities. The Reagan Administration established such procedures in January, 1985, then promptly ignored them in their consideration of the Iran initiative.

We recommend that each administration formulate precise procedures for restricted consideration of covert action and that, once formulated, those procedures be strictly adhered to.

5. *The Role of the CIA.* Some aspects of the Iran arms sales raised broader questions in the minds of members of the Board regarding the role of CIA. The first deals with intelligence.

The NSC staff was actively involved in the preparation of the May 20, 1985, update to the Special National Intelligence Estimate on Iran. It is a matter for concern if this involvement and the strong views of NSC staff members were allowed to influence the intelligence judgments contained in the update. It is also of concern that the update contained the hint that the United States should change its existing policy and encourage its allies to provide arms to Iran. It is critical that the line between intelligence and advocacy of a particular policy be preserved if intelligence is to retain its integrity and perform its proper function. In this instance, the CIA came close enough to the line to warrant concern.

We emphasize to both the intelligence community and policy makers the importance of maintaining the integrity and objectivity of the intelligence process.

6. *Legal Counsel.* From time to time issues with important legal ramifications will come before the National Security Council. The Attorney General is currently a member of the Council by invitation and should be in a position to provide legal advice to the Council and the President. It is important that the Attorney General and his department be available to interagency deliberations.

The Justice Department, however, should not replace the role of counsel in the other departments. As the principal counsel on foreign affairs, the Legal Adviser to the Secretary of State should also be available to all the NSC participants.

Of all the NSC participants, it is the Assistant for National Security Affairs who seems to have had the least access to expert counsel familiar with his activities.

The Board recommends that the position of Legal Adviser to the NSC be enhanced in stature and in its role within the NSC staff.

7. *Secrecy and Congress.* There is a natural tension between the desire for secrecy and the need to consult Congress on covert operations. Presidents seem to become increasingly concerned about leaks of classified information as their administrations progress. They blame Congress disproportionately. Various cabinet officials from prior administrations indicated to the Board that they believe Congress bears no more blame than the Executive Branch.

However, the number of Members and staff involved in reviewing covert activities is large; it provides cause for concern and a convenient excuse for Presidents to avoid Congressional consultation.

We recommend that Congress consider replacing the existing Intelligence Committees of the respective Houses with a new joint committee with a restricted staff to oversee the intelligence community, patterned after the Joint Committee on Atomic Energy that existed until the mid-1970s.

8. *Privatizing National Security Policy.* Careful and limited use of people outside the U.S. Government may be very helpful in some unique cases. But this practice raises substantial questions. It can create conflict of interest problems. Private or foreign sources may have different policy interests or personal motives and may exploit their association with a U.S. government effort. Such involvement gives private and foreign sources potentially powerful leverage in the form of demands for return favors or even blackmail.

The U.S. has enormous resources invested in agencies and departments in order to conduct the government's business. In all but a very few cases, these can perform the functions needed. If not, then inquiry is required to find out why.

We recommend against having implementation and policy oversight dominated by intermediaries. We do not recommend barring limited use of private individuals to assist in United States diplomatic initiatives or in covert activities. We caution against use of such people except in very limited ways and under close observation and supervision....

Epilogue

If but one of the major policy mistakes we examined had been avoided, the nation's history would bear one less scar, one less embarrassment, one less opportunity for opponents to reverse the principles this nation seeks to preserve and advance in the world.

As a collection, these recommendations are offered to those who will find themselves in situations similar to the ones we reviewed: under stress, with high stakes, given little time, using incomplete information, and troubled by premature disclosure. In such a state, modest improvements may yield surprising gains. This is our hope....
(Executive Office of the President, February 26, 1987)

President Reagan's Address to the Nation on the Iran Arms and Contra Aid Controversy
March 4, 1987

...I've studied the Board's report. Its findings are honest, convincing, and highly critical; and I accept them. And tonight I want to share with you my thoughts on these findings and report to you on the actions I'm taking to implement the Board's recommendations. First, let me say I take full responsibility for my own actions and for those of my administration. As angry as I may be about activities undertaken without my knowledge, I am still accountable for those activities. As disappointed as I may be in some who served me, I'm still the one who must answer to the American people for this behavior. And as personally distasteful as I find secret bank accounts and diverted funds — well, as the Navy would say, this happened on my watch.

Let's start with the part that is the most controversial. A few months ago I told the American people I did not trade arms for hostages. My heart and my best intentions still tell me that's true, but the facts and the evidence tell me it is not. As the Tower board reported, what began as a strategic opening to Iran deteriorated, in its implementation, into trading arms for hostages. This runs counter to my own beliefs, to administration policy, and to the original strategy we had in mind. There are reasons why it happened, but no excuses. It was a mistake. I undertook the original Iran initiative in order to develop relations with those who might assume leadership in a post-Khomeini government.

It's clear from the Board's report, however, that I let my personal concern for the hostages spill over into the geopolitical strategy of reaching out to Iran. I asked so many questions about the hostages welfare that I didn't ask enough about the specifics of the total Iran plan. Let me say to the hostage families: We have not given up. We never will. And I promise you we'll use every legitimate means to free your loved ones from captivity. But I must also caution that those Americans who freely remain in such dangerous areas must know that they're responsible for their own safety.

Now, another major aspect of the Board's findings regards the transfer of funds to the Nicaraguan contras. The Tower board wasn't able to find out what happened to this money, so the facts here will be left to the continuing investigations of the court-appointed Independent Counsel and the two congressional investigating committees. I'm confident the truth will come out about this matter, as well. As I told the Tower board, I didn't know about any diversion of funds to the contras. But as President, I cannot escape responsibility.

Much has been said about my management style, a style that's worked successfully for me during 8 years as Governor of California and for most of my Presidency. The way I work is to identify the problem, find the right individuals to do the job, and then let them go to it. I've found this invariably brings out the best in people. They seem to rise to their full capability, and in the long run you get more done. When it came to managing the NSC staff, let's face it, my style didn't match its previous track record. I've already begun correcting this. As a start, yesterday I met with the entire professional staff of the National Security Council. I defined for them the values I want to guide the national security policies of this country. I told them that I wanted a policy that was as justifiable and understandable in public as it was in secret. I wanted a policy that reflected the will of the Congress as well as of the White House. And I told them that there'll be no more freelancing by individuals when it comes to our national security....

For nearly a week now, I've been studying the Board's report. I want the American people to know that this wrenching ordeal of recent months has not been in vain. I endorse every one of the Tower board's recommendations. In fact, I'm going beyond its recommendations so as to put the house in even better order. I'm taking action in three basic areas: personnel, national security policy, and the process for making sure that the system works.

First, personnel — I've brought in an accomplished and highly respected new team here at the White House. They bring new blood, new energy, and new credibility and experience. Former Senator Howard Baker, my new Chief of Staff, possesses a breadth of legislative and foreign affairs skills that's impossible to match. I'm hopeful that his experience as minority and majority leader of the Senate can help us forge a new partnership with the Congress, especially on foreign and national security policies. I'm genuinely honored that he's given up his own Presidential aspirations to serve the country as my Chief of Staff. Frank Carlucci, my new national security adviser, is respected for his experience in government and trusted for his judgment and counsel. Under him, the NSC staff is being rebuilt with proper management discipline. Already, almost half the NSC professional staff is comprised of new people.

Yesterday I nominated William Webster, a man of sterling reputation, to be Director of the Central Intelligence Agency. Mr. Webster has served as Director of the FBI and as a U.S. District Court judge. He understands the meaning of "rule of law." So that his knowledge of national security matters can be available to me on a continuing basis, I will also appoint John Tower to serve as a member of my Foreign Intelligence Advisory Board. I am considering other changes in personnel, and I'll move more furniture, as I see fit, in the weeks and months ahead.

Second, in the area of national security policy, I have ordered the NSC to begin a comprehensive review of all covert operations. I have also directed that any covert activity be in support of clear policy objectives and in compliance with American values. I expect a covert policy that, if Americans saw it on the front page of their newspaper, they'd say, "That makes sense." I have issued a directive prohibiting the NSC staff itself from undertaking covert operations— no ifs, ands, or buts. I have asked Vice President Bush to reconvene his task force on terrorism to review our terrorist policy in light of the events that have occurred.

Third, in terms of the process of reaching national security decisions, I am adopting in total the Tower report's model of how the NSC process and staff should work. I am directing Mr. Carlucci to take the necessary steps to make that happen. He will report back to me on further reforms that might be needed. I've created the post of NSC legal adviser to assure a greater sensitivity to matters of law. I am also determined to make the congressional oversight process work. Proper procedures for consultation with the Congress will be followed, not only in letter but in spirit. Before the end of March, I will report to the Congress on all the steps I've taken in line with the Tower board's conclusions....

(PPP Reagan 1987 I: 208-211)

President Reagan's Letter to the Chairman and Vice Chairman of the Senate Select Committee on Intelligence on Covert Action Procedural Reforms
August 7, 1987

...In my March 31, 1987, message to Congress, I reported on those steps I had taken and intended to take to implement the recommendations of the

President's Special Review Board. These included a comprehensive review of executive branch procedures concerning presidential approval and notification to Congress of covert action programs — or so-called special activities. In my message, I noted that the reforms and changes I had made and would make "are evidence of my determination to return to proper procedures including consultation with the Congress."

In this regard, Frank Carlucci has presented to me the suggestions developed by the Senate Select Committee on Intelligence for improving these procedures. I welcome these constructive suggestions for the development of a more positive partnership between the intelligence committees and the Executive branch.

Greater cooperation in this critical area will be of substantial benefit to our country, and I pledge to work with you and the members of the two committees to achieve it. We all benefit when we have an opportunity to confer in advance about important decisions affecting our national security.

Specifically, I want to express my support for the following key concepts recommended by the Committee:

1. Except in cases of extreme emergency, all national security "Findings" should be in writing. If an oral directive is necessary, a record should be made contemporaneously and the Finding reduced to writing and signed by the President as soon as possible, but in no event more than two working days thereafter. All Findings will be made available to members of the National Security Council (NSC).

2. No Finding should retroactively authorize or sanction a special activity.

3. If the President directs any agency or persons outside of the CIA or traditional intelligence agencies to conduct a special activity, all applicable procedures for approval of a Finding and notification to Congress shall apply to such agency or persons.

4. The intelligence committees should be appropriately informed of participation of any government agencies, private parties, or other countries involved in assisting with special activities.

5. There should be a regular and periodic review of all ongoing special activities both by the intelligence committees and by the NSC. This review should be made to determine whether each such activity is continuing to serve the purpose for which it was instituted. Findings should terminate or "sunset" at periodic intervals unless the President, by appropriate action, continues them in force.

6. I believe we cannot conduct an effective program of special activities without the cooperation and support of Congress. Effective consultation with the intelligence committees is essential, and I am determined to ensure that these committees can discharge their statutory responsibilities in this area. In all but the most exceptional circumstances, timely notification to Congress under Section 501(b) of the National Security Act of 1947, as amended, will

not be delayed beyond two working days of the initiation of a special activity. While I believe that the current statutory framework is adequate, new Executive branch procedures nevertheless are desirable to ensure that the spirit of that framework is fully implemented. Accordingly, I have directed my staff to draft for my signature executive documents to implement appropriately the principles set forth in this letter.

While the President must retain the flexibility as Commander in Chief and Chief Executive to exercise those constitutional authorities necessary to safeguard the nation and its citizens, maximum consultation and notification is and will be the firm policy of this Administration....
(PPP Reagan 1987 II: 926-927)

President Reagan's Address to the Nation on the Iran Arms and Contra Aid Controversy and Administration Goals
August 12, 1987

...[A] major issue of the hearings, of course, was the diversion of funds to the Nicaraguan Contras. Colonel North and Admiral Poindexter believed they were doing what I would have wanted done — keeping the democratic resistance alive in Nicaragua. I believed then and I believe now in preventing the Soviets from establishing a beachhead in Central America. Since I have been so closely associated with the cause of the Contras, the big question during the hearings was whether I knew of the diversion. I was aware the resistance was receiving funds directly from third countries and from private efforts, and I endorsed those endeavors wholeheartedly; but — let me put this in capital letters — I did not know about the diversion of funds. Indeed, I didn't know there were excess funds.

Yet the buck does not stop with Admiral Poindexter, as he stated in his testimony; it stops with me. I am the one who is ultimately accountable to the American people. The admiral testified that he wanted to protect me; yet no President should ever be protected from the truth. No operation is so secret that it must be kept from the Commander in Chief. I had the right, the obligation, to make my own decision. I heard someone the other day ask why I wasn't outraged. Well, at times, I've been mad as a hornet. Anyone would be — just look at the damage that's been done and the time that's been lost. But I've always found that the best therapy for outrage and anger is action.

I've tried to take steps so that what we've been through can't happen again, either in this administration or future ones. But I remember very well what the Tower board said last February when it issued this report. It said the failure was more in people than in process. We can build in every precaution known to the world. We can design that best system ever devised by man. But in the end, people are going to have to run it. And we will never be free of human hopes, weaknesses, and enthusiasms.

Let me tell you what I've done to change both the system and the people who operate it. First of all, I've brought in a new and knowledgeable team. I have a new National Security Adviser, a new Director of the CIA, a new Chief of Staff here at the White House. And I've told them that I must be informed and informed fully. In addition, I adopted the Tower board's model of how the NSC process and staff should work, and I prohibited any operational role by the NSC staff in covert activities.

The report I ordered reviewing our nation's covert operations has been completed. There were no surprises. Some operations were continued, and some were eliminated because they'd outlived their usefulness. I am also adopting new, tighter procedures on consulting with and notifying the Congress on future covert action findings. We will still pursue covert operations when appropriate, but each operation must be legal, and it must meet a specific policy objective.

The problem goes deeper, however, than policies and personnel. Probably the biggest lesson we can draw from the hearings is that the executive and legislative branches of government need to regain trust in each other. We've seen the results of that mistrust in the form of lies, leaks, divisions, and mistakes. We need to find a way to cooperate while realizing foreign policy can't be run by committee. And I believe there's now the growing sense that we can accomplish more by cooperating. And in the end, this may be the eventual blessing in disguise to come out of the Iran-contra mess....
(PPP Reagan 1987 II: 942-945)

PANAMA

Statement by Assistant to the President for Press Relations Fitzwater on the Situation in Panama

February 26, 1988

We condemn all efforts to perpetuate military rule in Panama, including efforts to remove President Delvalle from office. We want to reiterate our unqualified support for civilian constitutional rule in Panama. There is but one legitimate sovereign authority in Panama, and that is the Panamanian people exercising their democratic right to vote and elect their leadership in a free society. We have also initiated a series of consultations to learn the views of other countries in the hemisphere with regard to this situation.
(PPP Reagan 1988 I: 264)

Statement by Assistant to the President for Press Relations Fitzwater on the Situation in Panama
March 8, 1988

The United States welcomes the statements issued by President Delvalle, Vice President Esquivel, and the political parties and Civilian Crusade of Panama favoring a government of national reconciliation. This is a blueprint for progress toward democracy in Panama. We support their goal of restoring democratic government and civilian constitutional order. Once this goal has been achieved, we will work cooperatively with the Government of Panama toward the recovery of Panama's financial and economic health. The United States remains committed to fulfilling its Panama Canal treaty obligations, and we are prepared to resume working with the Panamanian Defense Forces under the treaty once civilian rule and constitutional democracy are established.
(PPP Reagan 1988 I: 304)

President Reagan's Statement on Economic Sanctions Against Panama
March 11, 1988

The United States has had a long and mutually productive relationship with Panama. The people of the United States consider the people of Panama to be near neighbors and friends. The historic Panama Canal treaties exemplify the close cooperation that has traditionally characterized the friendship between the two countries, which created one of the great engineering works of the human race.

Out of concern for our friendship, we have been saddened and increasingly worried in recent years as Panama's political crisis deepened. Our policy with respect to the situation in Panama is clear: We strongly favor a rapid restoration of democracy and the resumption by the Panamanian Defense Forces of a role consistent with constitutional democracy. In the present circumstances, I believe that General Noriega would best serve his country by complying with the instruction of President Delvalle to relinquish his post. In so doing, General Noriega would contribute very substantially to reducing political tensions and set the stage for a prompt transition to democracy in Panama. Until such a time as democratic government is restored in Panama, the United States cannot proceed on a business as usual basis.

Today, therefore, I have taken a number of steps against the illegitimate Noriega regime that will contribute significantly to the goal of a democratic, stable, and prosperous Panama. I have directed that actions be taken to suspend trade preferences available to Panama under the Generalized System of Preferences (GSP) and the Caribbean Basin Initiative.

Further, in keeping with the spirit of our war against drugs, I have ordered that Panama be subject to intensified scrutiny by our Immigration and

Customs Services in order to apprehend drug traffickers and money launderers. Moreover, because we recognize President Delvalle as the lawful head of government in Panama, I have directed that all departments and agencies inventory all sources of funds due or payable to the Republic of Panama from the U.S. Government, for purposes of determining those that should be placed in escrow for the Delvalle government on behalf of the Panamanian people.

In that light, I have directed that certain payments due to Panama from the Panama Canal Commission be placed in escrow immediately. This step is in complete compliance with our obligations under the terms of the Panama Canal treaties. I am prepared to take additional steps, if necessary, to deny the transfer of funds to the Noriega regime from other sources in the United States.

We have welcomed the recent statements issued by President Delvalle, the political parties, and the Civilian Crusade of Panama calling for a government of national reconciliation. We support their goal of restoring democratic government and constitutional order. Once Panamanians achieve this goal the United States is fully prepared to work with the Government of Panama to help quickly restore Panama's economic health. The United States has been, and remains, committed to fulfilling faithfully its obligations under the Panama Canal treaties. We are also prepared to resume our close working relationships with the Panamanian Defense Forces once civilian government and constitutional democracy are reestablished.

(PPP Reagan 1988 I: 321-322)

Statement by Assistant to the President for Press Relations Fitzwater on the Transfer of United States Funds to Panama

March 31, 1988

We commend those persons who are resisting General Noriega's threats and intimidations to provide him with financial resources. We urge all U.S. companies and persons to comply with the lawful requests of President Delvalle concerning payment of financial obligations to the Government of Panama. Meanwhile, the U.S. Government is taking the following steps in support of the legitimate Government of Panama:

1. United States Government payments due the Government of Panama are to be deposited in an account of the Government of Panama at the Federal Reserve Bank of New York. This account will be set up at President Delvalle's request.

2. The Department of Justice will participate in actions by private parties who have debts to the Government of Panama to declare that President Delvalle is the leader of the recognized Government of Panama. Pursuant to

court orders, the Secretary of the Treasury will assist in the establishment of an account to be available for the deposit of funds.

3. The Internal Revenue Service will issue guidance to U.S. taxpayers explaining how tax credit may be claimed for Panamanian income taxes paid into an account to be specified at the Federal Reserve Bank of New York.

Through these measures, we are giving U.S. companies and persons an incentive and opportunity not to provide financial support to the Noriega regime. Should these measures prove insufficient, we will review additional legal steps that may be necessary to deny transfer of funds to the Noriega regime from U.S. companies and persons.

These measures are in addition to the following actions that were announced on March 11:

1. Withdrawal of trade preferences available to Panama under the Generalized System of Preferences and the Caribbean Basin Initiative.

2. Increased scrutiny of Panama by the Immigration and Customs Services in order to apprehend drug traffickers and money launderers.

3. Placing in escrow certain payments by the Panama Canal Commission to the Government of Panama.

The United States remains committed to the goal of restoring democratic government and constitutional order in Panama. When that goal is achieved, the United States is fully prepared to work with the Government of Panama to help restore quickly Panama's economic health. In addition, the U.S. Government is providing one quarter million dollars to support the Caritas emergency feeding program in Panama. We will continue to examine the food needs of the poor in Panama.
(PPP Reagan 1988 I: 415-416)

President Bush's Statement on the Presidential Elections in Panama
April 27, 1989

The people of Panama clearly yearn for a free and fair election on May 7th so that their country can again take its rightful place in this hemisphere's community of democratic nations. Only the threat of violence and massive fraud by the Noriega regime will keep the Panamanian people from realizing that aspiration for democracy.

Free and fair elections on May 7th and respect for the results can produce a legitimate government in Panama which will end that nation's political and economic crisis and international isolation. That is clearly what the people of Panama deserve and desire.

The Noriega regime promised that free and fair elections would in fact take place May 7th and that international observers would be permitted to observe them. In recent weeks the Noriega regime has taken steps to commit systematic fraud. Through violence and coercion, it threatens and intimidates

Panamanian citizens who believe in democracy. It is attempting to limit and obstruct the presence of observers from around the world and the ability of journalists to report freely on the election.

Nevertheless many observers intend to travel to Panama to shine the spotlight of world opinion on the Panamanian elections just us they did previously in nations like the Philippines and El Salvador. We admire their commitment to democracy and their courage and will fully support their efforts

The days of rule by dictatorship in Latin America are over. They must end in Panama as well. There is still time for Panama to resolve its current crisis through free and fair elections. The people and Government of the United States will not recognize fraudulent election results engineered by Noriega. The aspirations of the people of Panama for democracy must not be denied. *(PPP Bush 1989 I: 491)*

President Bush's Remarks on the Situation in Panama
May 11, 1989

...The people of Latin America and the Caribbean have sacrificed, fought, and died to establish democracy. Today elected constitutional government is the clear choice of the vast majority of the people in the Americas, and the days of the dictator are over. Still, in many parts of our hemisphere, the enemies of democracy lie in wait to overturn elected governments through force or to steal elections through fraud. All nations in the democratic community have a responsibility to make it clear, through our actions and our words that efforts to overturn constitutional regimes or steal elections are unacceptable. If we fail to send a clear signal when democracy is imperiled, the enemies of constitutional government will become more dangerous. And that's why events in Panama place an enormous responsibility on all nations in the democratic community.

This past week, the people of Panama, in record numbers, voted to elect a new democratic leadership of their country; and they voted to replace the dictatorship of General Manuel Noriega. The whole world was watching. Every credible observer — the Catholic Church, Latin and European observers, leaders of our Congress, and two former Presidents of the United States — tell the same story: The opposition won. It was not even a close election. The opposition won by a margin of nearly 3 to 1.

The Noriega regime first tried to steal this election through massive fraud and intimidation and now has nullified the election and resorted to violence and bloodshed. In recent days, a host of Latin American leaders have condemned this election fraud. They've called on General Noriega to heed the will of the people of Panama. We support and second those demands. The United States will not recognize nor accommodate with a regime that holds power through force and violence at the expense of the Panamanian people's right to be free. I've exchanged these views over the last several days with democratic leaders in Latin America and in Europe. These consultations will continue.

The crisis in Panama is a conflict between Noriega and the people of Panama. The United States stands with the Panamanian people. We share their hope that the Panamanian defense forces will stand with them and fulfill their constitutional obligation to defend democracy. A professional Panamanian defense force can have an important role to play in Panama's democratic future.

The United States is committed to democracy in Panama. We respect the sovereignty of Panama, and of course, we have great affection for the Panamanian people. We are also committed to protect the lives of our citizens, and we're committed to the integrity of the Panama Canal treaties, which guarantee safe passage for all nations through the Canal. The Panama Canal treaties are a proud symbol of respect and partnership between the people of the United States and the people of Panama.

In support of these objectives and after consulting this morning with the bipartisan leadership of the Congress, I am taking the following steps: First, the United States strongly supports and will cooperate with initiatives taken by governments in this hemisphere to address this crisis through regional diplomacy and action in the organization of American States and through other means. Second, our Ambassador in Panama, Arthur Davis, has been recalled, and our Embassy staff will be reduced to essential personnel only. Third, U.S. Government employees and their dependents living outside of U.S. military bases or Panama Canal commissioned housing areas will be relocated out of Panama or to secure U.S. housing areas within Panama. This action will begin immediately. It will be completed as quickly and in an orderly a manner as possible. Fourth, the State Department, through its travel advisory, will encourage U.S. business representatives resident in Panama to arrange for the extended absences of their dependents wherever possible. Fifth, economic sanctions will continue in force. Sixth, the United States will carry out its obligations and will assert and enforce its treaty rights in Panama under the Panama Canal treaties. And finally, we are sending a brigade-size force to Panama to augment our military forces already assigned there. If required, I do not rule out further steps in the future....
(PPP Bush 1989 I: 536-538)

Statement by Press Secretary Fitzwater on the Banning of Panamanian-Flag Vessels from United States Ports

November 30, 1989

President Bush has directed that Panamanian-flag vessels not be permitted to enter U.S. ports after January 31, 1990. This measure will deny Noriega and his puppet regime tens of millions of dollars of revenue. Noriega's cronies will also be deprived of millions of dollars of illegal income in the form of bribes and kickbacks.

This ban is consistent with international efforts to further isolate the Noriega regime, which is currently shunned by the democratic nations of Latin America and around the world. The resolution of the recently concluded General Assembly of the Organization of American States was sharply critical of the Noriega regime and is only one example of the international condemnation of Noriega. The President has made it very clear that there will be no accommodation with the illegal Panamanian regime.

The United States will continue various efforts designed to assist the Panamanian people in their endeavor to bring about Noriega's departure and the establishment of democratic institutions responsive to the will of the people.

The United States regrets the hardship which Noriega has brought to the people of Panama, who deserve to be led by a government of their choice. The United States will continue to exercise its rights and comply with its obligations under the Panama Canal treaties and looks forward to a time when it can work closely with a democratically elected, constitutional government in Panama dedicated to serving the interests and welfare of the Panamanian people.

(PPP Bush 1989 II: 1614)

President Bush's Address to the Nation Announcing United States Military Action in Panama

December 20, 1989

...Last Friday, Noriega declared his military dictatorship to be in a state of war with the United States and publicly threatened the lives of Americans in Panama. The very next day, forces under his command shot and killed an unarmed American serviceman; wounded another; arrested and brutally beat a third American serviceman; and then brutally interrogated his wife, threatening her with sexual abuse. That was enough.

General Noriega's reckless threats and attacks upon Americans in Panama created an imminent danger to the 35,000 American citizens in Panama. As President, I have no higher obligation than to safeguard the lives of American citizens. And that is why I directed our armed forces to protect the lives of American citizens in Panama and to bring General Noriega to justice in the

United States. I contacted the bipartisan leadership of Congress last night and informed them of this decision, and after taking this action I also talked with leaders in Latin America, the Caribbean, and those of other U.S. allies.

At this moment, U.S. forces, including forces deployed from the United States last night, are engaged in action in Panama. The United States intends to withdraw the forces newly deployed to Panama as quickly as possible. Our forces have conducted themselves courageously and selflessly. And as Commander in Chief, I salute every one of them and thank them on behalf of our country.

Tragically, some Americans have lost their lives in defense of their fellow citizens, in defense of democracy. And my heart goes out to their families. We also regret and mourn the loss of innocent Panamanians.

The brave Panamanians elected by the people of Panama in the elections last May, President Guillermo Endara and Vice Presidents Calderon and Ford, have assumed the rightful leadership of their country. You remember those horrible pictures of newly elected Vice President Ford, covered head to toe with blood, beaten mercilessly by so-called "dignity battalions." Well, the United States today recognizes the democratically elected government of President Endara. I will send our Ambassador back to Panama immediately.

Key military objectives have been achieved. Most organized resistance has been eliminated, but the operation is not over yet: General Noriega is in hiding. And nevertheless, yesterday a dictator ruled Panama, and today constitutionally elected leaders govern.

I have today directed the Secretary of the Treasury and the Secretary of State to lift the economic sanctions with respect to the democratically elected government of Panama and, in cooperation with that government, to take steps to effect an orderly unblocking of Panamanian Government assets in the United States. I'm fully committed to implement the Panama Canal treaties and turn over the Canal to Panama in the year 2000. The actions we have taken and the cooperation of a new, democratic government in Panama will permit us to honor these commitments. As soon as the new government recommends a qualified candidate — Panamanian — to be administrator of the Canal, as called for in the treaties, I will submit this nominee to the Senate for expedited consideration....

(Unless otherwise noted, presidential statements and documents that follow encompassing December 20 through December 26, 1989, are quoted from PPP Bush 1989 II: 1722-1727, 1734, 1738-1739.)

Statement by Press Secretary Fitzwater on United States Military Action in Panama
December 20, 1989

...The President is pleased with the military progress so far. Major military objectives have been met. The operations have been smooth. Communications at all levels of the command structure have been very effective. The operation is moving according to plan. The Endara government is beginning to take shape. All aspects of the operation are ongoing....

President Bush's Memorandum to the Secretary of Defense on the Arrest of General Manuel Noriega in Panama
December 20, 1989

...In the course of carrying out the military operation in Panama which I have directed, I hereby direct and authorize the units and members of the Armed Forces of the United States to apprehend General Manuel Noriega and any other persons in Panama currently under indictment in the United States for drug-related offenses. I further direct that any persons apprehended pursuant to this directive are to be turned over to civil law enforcement officials of the United States as soon as practicable. I also authorize and direct members of the Armed Forces of the United States to detain and arrest any persons apprehended pursuant to this directive if, in their judgment, such action is necessary.

President Bush's Memorandum to the Secretaries of State and Treasury Terminating Economic Sanctions Against Panama
December 20, 1989

...The democratically elected government is now in place in Panama. With respect to that government, I hereby direct you to lift the economic sanctions imposed by Executive Order No. 12635. Therefore payments from the United States and payments by U.S. persons in Panama to that government are not prohibited. You are directed to take steps to ensure that the prohibitions will not be applied to that government of Panama and in cooperation with that government to effect an orderly unblocking of Panamanian government assets in the United States.

Statement by Press Secretary Fitzwater on United States Military Action in Panama
December 21, 1989

Good progress continues to be made on the ground in Panama. Three major objectives were achieved last night by U.S. forces: the Marriott was secured with minimal resistance, Radio Nacional was taken off the air, and the legislative building was secured. General Noriega remains at large and U.S. military operations are targeted at locating him.

Latest casualty figures show 18 U.S. military killed in action, 117 wounded, and 1 missing. One U.S. civilian dependent was also killed. Over 100 of the U.S. servicemen who were wounded have been returned to the United States for treatment at Kelly Air Force Base in San Antonio, TX.

Ambassador Davis, the U.S. Ambassador, has returned to Panama last night. There are reports of scattered weapons firing around the vicinity of the U.S. Embassy, but the Embassy has sustained no new damages beyond that which was reported yesterday. All U.S. Embassy personnel are reported safe.

As we said yesterday, organized resistance to U.S. forces appears to have ended.

There continue to be roving bands of individuals conducting looting. We are endeavoring to help bring the situation under control. General Powell announced yesterday that 2,500 military police are arriving in Panama to help with police activities. We have received reports of a number of Americans held against their will, but those reports are unclear. Needless to say, we are following up with our military on all such reports.

The freely elected government of Panama, under President Endara and Vice Presidents Calderon and Ford, is moving to establish itself. They have named their Ambassadors to the U.N. and the OAS. They are Lawrence Chewning Fabrega to the OAS and Eduardo Vallarino to the United Nations....

The Endara government is in the process of setting up operations which will enable them to utilize the $400 million in funds available under the lifting of the sanctions. President Bush is pleased by the effective conduct of the military operation and, most significantly, by the efforts of the new democratically elected government to begin taking charge of the country.

President Bush spoke with President Endara yesterday to encourage his efforts and to offer our support. President Endara had called the President to thank him for prompt recognition of his government. He reported that the former opposition parties were united behind his Presidency. President Endara discussed some preliminary plans to return to full freedoms, such as restoration of a free press. President Endara spoke of the need for medical supplies, and President Bush agreed to provide supplies just as soon as specific needs can be identified....

President Bush's Letter to the Speaker of the House of Representatives and the President Pro Tempore of the Senate on United States Military Action in Panama

December 21, 1989

...On December 15, 1989, at the instigation of Manuel Noriega, the illegitimate Panamanian National Assembly declared that a state of war existed between the Republic of Panama and the United States. At the same time, Noriega gave a highly inflammatory anti-American speech. A series of vicious and brutal acts directed at U.S. personnel and dependents followed these events.

On December 16, 1989, a U.S. Marine officer was killed without justification by Panama Defense Forces (PDF) personnel. Other elements of the PDF beat a U.S. Naval officer and unlawfully detained, physically abused, and threatened the officer's wife. These acts of violence are directly attributable to Noriega's dictatorship, which created a climate of aggression that places American lives and interests in peril.

These and other events over the past two years have made it clear that the lives and welfare of American citizens in Panama were increasingly at risk, and that the continued safe operation of the Panama Canal and the integrity of the Canal Treaties would be in serious jeopardy if such lawlessness were allowed to continue.

Under these circumstances, I ordered the deployment of approximately 11,000 additional U.S. Forces to Panama. In conjunction with the 13,000 U.S. Forces already present, military operations were initiated on December 20, 1989, to protect American lives, to defend democracy in Panama, to apprehend Noriega and bring him to trial on the drug-related charges for which he was indicted in 1988, and to ensure the integrity of the Panama Canal Treaties.

In the early morning of December 20, 1989, the democratically elected Panamanian leadership announced formation of a government, assumed power in a formal swearing-in ceremony, and welcomed the assistance of U.S. Armed Forces in removing the illegitimate Noriega regime.

The deployment of U.S. Forces is an exercise of the right of self-defense recognized in Article 51 of the United Nations Charter and was necessary to protect American lives in imminent danger and to fulfill our responsibilities under the Panama Canal Treaties. It was welcomed by the democratically elected government of Panama. The military operations were ordered pursuant to my constitutional authority with respect to the conduct of foreign relations and as Commander in Chief....

Statement by Press Secretary Fitzwater on the Situation in Panama
December 26, 1989

...Secretary Cheney reports from his trip to Panama yesterday that morale among U.S. soldiers is high, a degree of normalcy is returning to Panama City and the PDF [Panamanian Defence Forces] continues to surrender or otherwise report themselves to U.S. forces.

The American military continues to find tens of thousands of weapons in warehouses at various locations. These include grenade launchers, rocket-propelled grenades, heavy machine guns and other military weapons. We continue to see encouraging signs of support for the Endara Government including the widespread showing of white flags, the traditional symbol of the opposition parties.

The Endara Government is making significant steps in the process of reconstruction. Their cabinet has met. Plans are being made to meet food and housing needs. A special economic group from the Endara Government will meet with the administration's Economic Reconstruction Task Force this afternoon. This task force includes State and Treasury Department representatives who are assessing the needs of the Panamanian people....

The United States continues to operate refugee centers, help with restoring law and order in the streets of the city and the providing of medical assistance. The military is airlifting some 1,200 tons of food and medical supplies into Panama this week. Our training of the security forces is going well with nearly 1,000 former PDF members now joining the U.S. military on street patrols. More than 5,000 U.S. troops are on patrol.

The United States continues its efforts to bring General Noriega to the United States for justice. We are having discussions through established diplomatic channels with all parties involved including the Endara Government and the Papal Nuncio. We will not comment on the nature of those discussions or any specific reactions. The only other member of the PDF indicted by U.S. courts besides Noriega, Col. Luis del Cid has been apprehended and returned to the United States. He is currently in the custody of U.S. marshals and will be arraigned today in the Federal court in Miami.

The Panama Canal is now open 24 hours per day. The two major airports in Panama City, Torrijos and Tocumen, are now open for operation during limited hours. The Treasury Department has expedited the return of escrow funds to Panama. That money is now going to the Endara Government to help with the reconstruction process. There is roughly $371 million in total progress that has been made in helping the Panamanian Government assets blocked in the United States. Our Ambassador has allocated $25,000 in emergency/disaster relief funds immediately for food and medicine for refugees....

President Bush's Remarks Announcing the Surrender of General Manuel Noriega in Panama
January 3, 1990

...At about 8:50 p.m. this evening, General Noriega turned himself in to U.S. authorities in Panama with the full knowledge of the Panamanian Government. He was taken to Howard Air Force Base in Panama, where he was arrested by DEA. A U.S. Air Force C-130 is now transporting General Noriega to Homestead Air Force Base, Florida. He will be arraigned in the U.S. District Court in Miami on charges stemming from his previous indictment for drug trafficking.

I want to thank the Vatican and the Papal Nuncio in Panama for their evenhanded, statesmanlike assistance in recent days. The United States is committed to providing General Noriega a fair trial. Nevertheless, his apprehension and return to the United States should send a clear signal that the United States is serious in its determination that those charged with promoting the distribution of drugs cannot escape the scrutiny of justice.

The return of General Noriega marks a significant milestone in operation Just Cause. The U.S. used its resources in a manner consistent with political, diplomatic, and moral principles.

The first U.S. combat troops have already been withdrawn from Panama; others will follow as quickly as the local situation will permit. We are now engaged in the final stages of a process that includes the economic and political revitalization of this important friend and neighbor, Panama.

An economic team under the direction of Deputy Secretary of State Eagleburger and Deputy Secretary of Treasury Robson is just returning from Panama. A team of experts has remained on hand there to assess the full range of needs. We will continue to extend to the Panamanian people our support and assistance in the days ahead....
(PPP Bush 1990 I: 8-9)

President Bush's Letter to Congressional Leaders Transmitting Certification of Panama's Cooperation in the Control of Illegal Narcotics
January 26, 1990

...I am transmitting to you my certification that Panama is fully cooperating with us on the war on drugs. In addressing the urgent issues connected with rebuilding virtually every aspect of Panamanian society since coming into office, the Government of President Guillermo Endara has made the war against drugs a centerpiece of its program. Panamanian leaders have demonstrated their commitment by cooperating in returning Manuel Noriega to face trial in the United States, by freezing hundreds of bank accounts at U.S. request, and by concluding a comprehensive narcotics control agreement with us.

I am convinced that the Panamanian people and their government recognize that it is in their direct national interest to end their association with the scourge of drugs. I have firmly concluded that the vital national interests of the United States require that assistance and benefits be provided to Panama, and that the United States support multilateral development bank assistance to that country.

I therefore urge you to enact a joint resolution approving my determination immediately.

(PPP Bush 1990 I: 120)

President Bush's Statement on Signing the Urgent Assistance for Democracy in Panama Act of 1990 [Public Law 101-243]

February 14, 1990

...I would like to express my appreciation to the Congress in passing this legislation, which will allow us to proceed expeditiously on Phase I of our plan to foster economic recovery in Panama. We plan now to proceed with the broad range of activities that officials of my Administration have been discussing with interested members of Congress in consultations that have taken place over the last several weeks. This program contains a range of AID, OPIC, Eximbank, and other assistance, as well as restoration of Caribbean Basin Initiative and Generalized System of Preferences trade benefits for Panama.

I am further appreciative of the provisions that will permit us to provide certain assistance for Panamanian law enforcement agencies on an expedited basis. This will facilitate our efforts to have the Panamanians assume the law enforcement responsibilities now being shouldered by our military forces....

(PPP Bush 1990 I: 221)

President Bush's Statement on the Sentencing of Manuel Noriega

July 10, 1992

The sentence imposed today on Manuel Noriega is a fitting punishment for drug crimes that have harmed all Americans. It demonstrates that international drug felons are not above the law, no matter how great their wealth, their status, or their armed might.

Illegal drugs inflict great suffering throughout our Nation and the world. Anyone who trafficks in them should be brought to justice. Operation Just Cause freed the people of Panama from a brutal tyranny; the sentence handed down today demonstrates that it also led to the conviction and just punishment of an unrepentant drug criminal. For that, Americans and our allies abroad have reason to be proud.

(PPP Bush 1992 I: 1109)

7

The Persian Gulf

INTRODUCTION

While United States policies in many places of the world emphasize values such as human rights, U.S. national security policy in the Persian Gulf has been more clearly dominated by geopolitical and domestic economic considerations than these more humane interests. The growing U.S. dependence on imported energy has heightened security concerns with respect to the region, but our intervention there is not new. Note the successful effort by the CIA in 1953 to keep the Shah of Iran on the throne. The effort could not be repeated in 1978, when he was finally overthrown and replaced by religious fundamentalists.

As the period of these documents begins, a U.S. Navy guided missile frigate, *USS Stark*, was attacked — apparently mistakenly — by an Iraqi aircraft firing Exocet missiles. Since the primary U.S. opponent in the region at that time was Iran, the incident was not used as a pretext for action against Iraq.

Action was taken against Iran, however, in response to Iranian attacks on shipping in the Persian Gulf. Airstrikes were made against Iranian oil platforms there. Unfortunately, in an almost incredible sequence of human errors, a U.S. guided missile cruiser, *USS Vincennes*, mistook an Iranian jetliner for an incoming attack on the battle group. Despite the fact that the aircraft was traveling in an internationally recognized air corridor on a published schedule, and was climbing, not descending for an attack, the ship destroyed the airliner with a surface to air missile.

The severest test of U.S. policy in the region came in response to the August, 1990 attack on neighboring Kuwait by Iraq, which claimed Kuwait as its "19th province." Historians and policy-makers will debate whether a firmer show of U.S. resolve earlier would have headed off this attack, but the U.S. response was immediate: put forces ashore as quickly as possible to defend Saudi Arabia. Supported by United Nations resolutions and bolstered by troops from U.S. allies, the American military presence grew rapidly during Operation Desert Shield.

With the invasion of Kuwait to expel the Iraqis, Operation Desert Shield became Operation Desert Storm. Again with the support of United Nations resolutions and with significant assistance from NATO and other allies, U.S. forces led the attack. Casualties were much fewer than expected on the U.S. side, although it may never be known how many Iraqis perished. Humanitarian concerns and a wish not to upset the balance of power in the region caused the coalition forces to call off the war as soon as Iraqi forces were driven from Kuwait. The failure to alter the political structure in Iraq led to continuing problems, and President Clinton felt compelled to order a missile attack on the headquarters of the Iraqi intelligence service.

Given the strategic importance of the region and its continued volatility, future U.S. intervention cannot be ruled out. Of continuing concern will be the development of weapons of mass destruction (nuclear, biological, and chemical) by both Iraq and Iran.

THE SEEDS OF TENSION

U.S. Interests in the Persian Gulf

Secretary of State George Shultz's statement before the Senate Foreign Relations Committee
January 27, 1987

I appreciate this opportunity to testify on American interests in the Persian Gulf and the importance of some recent developments there. Chief among these is the Iran-Iraq war, whose continuation threatens the stability of neighboring states and the pursuit of our interests in the region. The outcome of this war will affect the strategic shape of the Persian Gulf and Middle East for years to come. It is, therefore, important to focus on U.S. policy toward the war and the region at large. Stability in the Persian Gulf matters to us for three reasons.

First, it is critical to the economic health of the West. An interruption in the flow of oil or control of these energy resources by an unfriendly power could have devastating effects on the pattern of world trade and on our economy.

Second, our interests would suffer greatly if Iranian expansionism were to subvert friendly states or otherwise boost anti-American forces within the region.

Third, as part of the strategic crossroads of the Middle East, this area must not come under the domination of a power hostile to the United States and its allies. Therefore, America's near-term priority is to reassure the gulf

Arab states of our support and to stand fast on our antiterrorism and arms embargo policies.

U.S. Policy Toward the War

Since the beginning of the Iran-Iraq war in September 1980, the United States has sought the earliest possible end to the conflict — one which would secure the independence and territorial integrity of both countries, as well as security for third parties in the region who now are directly threatened by the conflict. We have pursued these goals through the following policies.

- We have been denying Munitions List equipment to both Iran and Iraq. There was a limited exception to this policy, as you know. There will be no further exceptions — no more transfers of U.S.-military equipment to Iran, either directly or through any third party.
- We are supporting all reasonable diplomatic efforts to encourage Iran to abandon its unwillingness to negotiate an end to the war. These efforts have included U.S. encouragement of the UN Secretary General, the Nonaligned Movement, and the Organization of the Islamic Conference — which is holding its summit in Kuwait this week. The problem has been lack of Iranian interest in any peace proposal — except on Iranian terms.
- Therefore, we are also energetically pursuing efforts to inhibit the resupply to Iran from third countries of significant weapons systems and spare parts which might enable Iran to carry the war further into Iraqi territory. This is our Operation Staunch, which we will continue to pursue in an energetic and determined manner.

Because of our concern over the possible spread of the Iran-Iraq conflict to third countries in the gulf, we have publicly and privately reiterated our firm commitments to the security of nonbelligerent gulf states. We have repeatedly warned Iran that any extension of the conflict would be regarded as a major threat to U.S. interests.

Our relations with these countries — including the members of the Gulf Cooperation Council (Kuwait, Saudi Arabia, Bahrain, Qatar, the United Arab Emirates, and Oman) — are important to our long-term security interests. The war directly threatens their security as well as their economic survival. We have publicly stated our fundamental interest in helping the gulf states defend themselves against attack or subversion.

The war has also highlighted overlapping interests with Iraq, as it defends itself against Iranian attack. The news of our limited arms shipments to Iran was a shock to Baghdad, and it has put some strain in our relationship. Nevertheless, I think both sides understand that we share an overriding common interest in finding an early end to the war. For our part, the United

States will continue to pursue this objective; and we will do all we can to reaffirm the strength of our policies toward the gulf.

Long-Term American Interests

Our current policies, of course, reflect longstanding interests in this region. Hence I want to review our goals and objectives in the region as a whole.

American interests in the Persian Gulf have long been readily defined. We have an overriding strategic interest in denying the Soviet Union either direct control or increased influence over the region or any of its states. We have major political interests in the nonbelligerent gulf states, both in their own right and because of their influence within the gulf and beyond. And we have a vital economic stake in seeing that the region's supply of oil to the West continues unimpeded.

Our multiple interests in the gulf give us common ground with its various states. As I have mentioned, they share our overriding concern with economic and political stability. Their economic life depends on the flow of oil to the industrialized world. Anything that might disrupt their commerce — war, political instability, terrorism, or subversion — is against their interests as well as ours.

Iran is an important element of our considerations as we pursue these multiple interests. That country has been, and remains, a major factor in the region, both because of its size and strength and because of its strategic location alongside the Soviet Union and Soviet occupied Afghanistan. Iranian policy has a direct impact on our strategic, political, and economic stakes in the gulf. And the current Iranian Government directly affects us in another way: through terrorism, which it continues to support and export as an instrument of state policy.

Historically, we have also shared a strategic interest with Iran, whose geography makes it a natural buffer between the Soviet land mass and the Persian Gulf. Soviet designs in the region can be seen in the Soviet occupation of Iran in 1946 and in its invasion and subsequent occupation of Afghanistan. The Government of Iran has, of course, been highly critical of the Soviet occupation of Afghanistan — a political fact that underlines a certain commonality of interests between us.

Our various interests in the region give the United States an obvious stake in better relations with Iran. As you know, we sent a signal of our intentions in the form of an authorized transfer of arms to that country. That signal did not elicit an acceptable Iranian response; and it will not be repeated. While we have an interest in improving our relations with Iran, the Iranians have an interest in normal dealings with us as well. And until they recognize their own interests, and act upon them, our relations are unlikely to improve. We have said, and we reiterate, that several issues stand in the way of better relations between us: the Iran-Iraq war and Iranian support for terrorism and subversion in the neighboring states.

Let me conclude with a note about the future of our relations with Iran. The President has said that the United States recognizes the Iranian revolution as "a fact of history." We bear no malice toward the Iranian people. But American interests are directly threatened by the Iranian Government's pursuit of its war with Iraq, by its sponsorship of terrorism, and by its collusion with terrorist forces elsewhere in the region. We cannot hope for progress without fundamental changes in Iranian policy and practice. Nor can we pursue better relations with Iran to the detriment of or many other interests and commitments in the region.

We look to an eventual improvement in U.S.-Iranian relations. But American good will cannot wish that future into existence. Iran's rejection of its bellicose and terrorist policies will be a necessary first step to any progress that might follow.
(DSB March 1987: 19-20)

U.S.S. Stark Hit by Iraqi Missiles
Secretary Shultz's Statement, May 17, 1987

At approximately 2:10 p.m., Washington time, the U.S. Navy frigate, the U.S.S. *Stark*, was hit by two missiles fired from an Iraqi F-1 Mirage aircraft. At the time of the attack, the *Stark* was located about 70 miles northeast of Bahrain. The ship, at last report, was dead in the water, and the entire crew was being taken off. There have been serious casualties.

The United States regards this attack with grave seriousness. The President was informed at once, of course, and is following the situation closely. I've been in touch with Secretary [of Defense] Weinberger, White House Chief of Staff Baker, and national security adviser Carlucci.

We have called in the Iraqi Ambassador here in Washington and issued the strongest protest and demanded a full accounting. Our Ambassador in Baghdad has been instructed to deliver our protest there, and we are in continuous contact with our Embassies in Baghdad and Bahrain.

This event underscores once more the seriousness of the Iran-Iraq war, not only to the countries directly involved but to others. It shows how easily it escalates, and it underlines once more the seriousness of the tensions that exist in the Middle East and the importance of trying to do something about them.

But I want to assure you that we take this event with the utmost seriousness. We know the source of this missile that hit our ship, and we demand a full accounting, and as we have more information, of course, we will be meeting on it and seeing what further action may be necessary.

President Reagan's Statement, May 18, 1987

I know and I share the sense of concern and anger that Americans feel over the yesterday's tragedy in the Persian Gulf. We have protested this attack in the strongest terms and are investigating the circumstances of the incident. When our investigation of the facts is completed, I will report to the American people about this matter and any further steps that are warranted. For that reason, I have convened a meeting of the national security planning group to review the entire situation in the Persian Gulf.

In the meanwhile, I want to express my deepest sympathies to the families of the brave men killed and injured yesterday aboard the U.S.S. *Stark*. Their loss and suffering will not be in vain. The mission of the men of the U.S.S. *Stark* — safeguarding the interests of the United States and the free world in the gulf — remains crucial to our national security and to the security of our friends throughout the world.

The hazards to our men and women in uniform in the defense of freedom can never be understated. The officers and crew of the U.S.S. *Stark* deserve our highest admiration and appreciation. And I would also like to express my sincere gratitude to Saudi Arabia and Bahrain for their prompt assistance in responding to the stricken U.S.S. *Stark*.

This tragic incident underscores the need to bring the Iran-Iraq war to the promptest possible end. We and the rest of the international community must redouble our diplomatic efforts to hasten the settlement that will preserve the sovereignty and territorial integrity for both Iran and Iraq. At the same time, we remain deeply committed to supporting the self-defense of our friends in the gulf and to ensuring the free flow of oil through the Strait of Hormuz.

White House Statement, May 18, 1987

President Reagan met with the national security planning group in the Situation Room from 2:30 until 3:45 this afternoon to discuss the status of the attack on the *U.S.S. Stark* in the Persian Gulf. The President has ordered a higher state of alert for U.S. vessels in the area. The belligerents in the war, Iran and Iraq, will be formally notified today of this change in status. Under this status, aircraft of either country flying in a pattern which indicates hostile intent will be fired upon, unless they provide adequate notification of their intentions.

The Administration will consult with Congress on these changes and related issues.

We have issued a vigorous protest to the Government of Iraq. We have noted the profound regrets issued by the Iraqi Ambassador in the name of his Foreign Minister and Iraqi President Saddam Hussein. However, we are awaiting official notification of this statement. We expect an apology and compensation for the men who died in this tragic incident. We also seek compensation for the ship. The President shares the sense of concern and anger that Americans feel at this time. We will monitor the situation on a continuing basis.

Assistant Secretary of State Murphy's Statement, May 19, 1987

...This Administration, like its predecessors, regards the gulf as an area of major interest to the United States and is committed to maintaining the free flow of oil through the Strait of Hormuz. Consistent with our national heritage, it attaches great importance to the principle of freedom of navigation. The Administration is also firmly committed as a matter of national policy to support the individual and collective self-defense of the Arab gulf states. These longstanding U.S. undertakings flow from the strategic, economic, and political importance of the region to us.

U.S. Policies Toward the Gulf War

Over the past 3 months, the President has reaffirmed the direction of our long term policy. Given the increasing dangers in the war, with its accompanying violence in the gulf, we have taken a series of specific decisions designed to ensure our strategic position in the gulf and reassert the fundamental U.S. stabilizing role. Frankly, in the light of the Iran-*contra* revelations, we had found that the leaders of the gulf states were questioning the coherence and seriousness of U.S. policy in the gulf along with our reliability and staying power. We wanted to be sure the countries with which we have friendly relations — Iraq and GCC [Gulf Cooperation Council] states — as well as the Soviet Union and Iran understood the firmness of our commitments. On January 23 and again on February 25, President Reagan issued statements reiterating our commitment to the flow of oil through the strait and U.S. support for the self-defense effort of the gulf states. He also endorsed Operation Staunch, our effort to reduce the flow of weapons from others to Iran.

While neutral toward the Iran-Iraq war, the U.S. Government views the continuation of this conflict, as well as its potential expansion, as a direct threat to our interests. We are working intensively for the earliest possible end to the conflict, with the territorial integrity and independence of both sides intact. As the President asserted in his February 25 statement on the war, we believe that "the time to act on this dangerous and destructive war is now." He urged an intensified international effort to seek an end to the war, and we have taken a lead in UN Security Council (UNSC) consultations to achieve this aim. As we announced May 7, the United States is "ready in principle to support the application of appropriate enforcement measures against either party which refuses to cooperate with formal UNSC efforts to end the war."

While there remains much work to be done in New York, I believe that an international consensus is growing that this war has gone on too long — the suffering of the Iraqi and Iranian peoples has been too great — and the threat to international interests is so direct that more active measures are required. As you know, Iraq has long shown its willingness to end the fighting; Iran remains recalcitrant.

Operation Staunch has been pursued in recent months with new vigor. I believe its effectiveness has not been seriously impaired, as many expected, by the Iran revelations.

Shipping Problems in the Persian Gulf

In addition to the inherent tragedy and suffering in Iraq and Iran, as the fighting drags on, with mounting casualties and drains on the economies of these two nations, so grows the threat of the war spilling over to nearby friendly states in the gulf. The fresh threats to international shipping are one example of such spill over effect.

In the past 18 months, attacks on neutral shipping passing through the Strait of Hormuz have increased in intensity. A total of nearly 100 vessels were hit by Iran and Iraq in 1986; in the first 3 months of this year, some 30 ships were attacked, including a Soviet merchant ship. Since the first of May, Iran has attacked 5 ships of nonbelligerent countries, virtually all in commerce with Kuwait. Attacks now occur at night as well as day, by sea as well as air, by small boats armed with light weapons as well as by helicopters launched from Iranian warships. While Iran has yet to sink a ship, most of those attacked have suffered damage, some seriously, and innocent lives have been lost.

The May 17 attack on the U.S.S. *Stark* was the first attack on a U.S. warship in the war. This tragic accident gives emphasis to our caution to both belligerents that the war in the gulf could lead to mistakes and miscalculations; it must be ended. We have increased the state of alert of U.S. Navy ships in the gulf and warned belligerent states (i.e., Iran and Iraq) that our ships will fire if one of their aircraft should approach in a manner indicating possible hostile intent — as did the Iraqi F-1 which attacked the U.S.S. *Stark*.

The recent Chinese delivery to and testing by Iran of Chinese Silkworm antiship missiles at the Strait of Hormuz present a potentially serious threat to U.S. and other shipping. With their 85-kilometer range and 1,100-pound warhead, these missiles can span the strait at its narrowest point and represent, for the first time, a realistic Iranian capability to sink large oil tankers. Whatever Iran's motivation for procuring such threatening missiles their presence gives Iran the ability both to intimidate the gulf states and gulf shippers and to cause a real or *de facto* closure of the strait. The Chinese decision to sell such weaponry to Iran is most unwelcome and disturbing. We have made clear to both Iran and China the seriousness with which we consider the Silkworm threat. Other concerned governments have done the same. It is our hope that a sustained international diplomatic campaign will convince Iran not to use the Silkworms.

For the past year, Iran has been using a combination of military action, attacks on gulf shipping, and terrorism, as well as shrewd diplomacy to intimidate the gulf states not involved in the war. It has tried to impress upon gulf states the hopelessness of their looking to the United States for help and to divide the gulf states one from the other.

Since last summer, Kuwait has been a particular target of Iranian threats. While not a belligerent, Kuwait's size and location make it highly vulnerable to intimidation. The Iranian regime has inspired terrorist and sabotage incidents within Kuwait, fired missiles on Kuwaiti territory on the eve of the January Islamic summit, and attacked over 24 vessels serving Kuwaiti ports since last September. The most recent example of the active intimidation efforts was the explosion at the TWA office in Kuwait city, May 11, which killed one employee. Over the last 3 years, Iranian-influenced groups have attempted a series of bombings and attacks including on the ruler of Kuwait himself, in an attempt to liberate terrorists being held in Kuwait who were convicted of bombing the U.S. and French Embassies.

Several months ago, Kuwait and other GCC states expressed to us their concern about the continuing attacks by Iran on tankers. Kuwait asked for our assistance, fearing potential damage to its economic lifeline. Consistent with longstanding U.S. commitment to the flow of oil through the gulf and the importance we attach to the freedom of navigation in international waters, as well as our determination to assist our friends in the gulf, the President decided that the United States would help in the protection of Kuwaiti tankers. In the context of these developments, Kuwait asked to register a number of ships in its tanker fleet under U.S. flag. We informed Kuwait that if the vessels in question met ownership and other technical requirements under U.S. laws and regulations, they could be registered under the U.S. flag. This is in accordance with our established position on qualifications for U.S. flag registration of commercial vessels in general. We also informed the Kuwaitis that by virtue of the fact that these vessels would fly the American flag, they would receive the U.S. Navy protection given any U.S. flag vessel transiting the gulf. The U.S. Navy has always had the mission to provide appropriate protection for U.S. commercial shipping worldwide within the limits of available resources and consistent with international law.

Kuwait welcomed our response, and we have together proceeded with the registry process. The Coast Guard has begun inspection of the vessels in order to determine their conformity with U.S. safety and other technical standards.

We view the reflagging of Kuwaiti tankers in the United States as an unusual measure to meet an extraordinary situation. It would not, however, set a precedent for the normal conduct of commercial shipping or affect the broad interests of the U.S. maritime industry. U.S. flagging procedures minimally require that only the captain of each vessel be a U.S. citizen. Because these vessels will not be calling at U.S. ports, there is no requirement that they carry U.S. seamen or other U.S. crew members. These new U.S. flag vessels will be sailing in areas where other U.S. flag vessels have generally not frequented since the war began.

To date, Iran has been careful to avoid confrontations with U.S. flag vessels when U.S. Navy vessels have been in the vicinity. U.S. Military Sealift Command and other commercial U.S. flag vessels have transited the gulf each month under U.S. Navy escort without incident. We believe that our naval presence will continue to have this deterrent effect. Iran lacks the sophisticated aircraft and weaponry used by Iraq in the mistaken attack on the U.S.S. *Stark*. Moreover, we will make sure in advance that Iran knows which ships have been reflagged and are under U.S. protection.

Our response to Kuwait demonstrates our resolve to protect our interests and those of our friends in the region, and it has been warmly welcomed by those governments with which we have had traditionally close ties. Our goal is to deter, not provoke; we believe this is understood by the parties in the region — including Iran. We will pursue our program steadily and with determination.

In providing this protection, our actions will be fully consistent with the applicable rules of international law, which clearly recognize the right of a neutral state to escort and protect ships flying its flag which are not carrying contraband. In this case, this includes the fact that U.S. ships will not be carrying oil from Iraq. Neither party to the conflict will have any basis for taking hostile action against U.S. naval ships or the vessels they will protect.

Our judgment is that, in light of all the surrounding circumstances, the protection accorded by U.S. naval vessels to these U.S. flag tankers transiting international waters or straits does not constitute introduction of our armed forces into a situation where "imminent involvement in hostilities is clearly indicated." The War Powers Resolution accordingly, is not implicated by our actions. On the contrary, our actions are such as to make it clear that any prospect of hostilities is neither imminent or clearly indicated. I repeat that our intention is to deter, not provoke, further military action. We will, however, keep the situation under careful review — particularly in light of the May 17 attack on the U.S.S. *Stark* — and keep Congress closely informed.

Kuwait has also discussed with other maritime powers commercial charter arrangements in the interest of deterring further Iranian attacks on its vessels. We understand that Kuwait broached this issue with all permanent members of the UN Security Council and has entered into an agreement with the Soviet Union to charter three long-haul, Soviet flag vessels to transport some of its oil out of the gulf.

A constant of U.S. policy for decades has been U.S. determination to prevent enhanced Soviet influence and presence in the gulf. We do not want the Soviet Union to obtain a strategic position from which it could threaten vital free-world interests in the region. We believe our arrangement with

Kuwait will limit Soviet advances in the region; they would have welcomed the opportunity to replace us and used this position to try to expand further their role in the gulf. We understand that their commercial charter arrangement for long-haul charters out of the gulf does not necessitate an increase in the Soviet naval presence or establishment of facilities in the gulf. This we would not welcome and have made our position clear.

I want to be frank to acknowledge, however, that the disturbing trend in the war — its spread in geographic terms and its increasing impact on third parties like Kuwait — creates the circumstances in which the Soviets may find more opportunities to insert themselves. The U.S.S.R. plays a fundamentally different role in the gulf and is viewed by Iran as directly threatening to Tehran. Aside from the long northern border, Soviets occupy Afghanistan to Iran's east and are Iraq's primary source of arms. The unescorted Soviet ship recently attacked had, in the past, carried arms to Iraq. The Soviets sent warships into the gulf for the first time last fall after Iran boarded and searched a Soviet arms carrying vessel. Iran should ponder this development as it maintains its intransigent war policy. We certainly believe the Soviet actions in the gulf and their attempts to enhance their presence there further emphasize the need to bring this war to an end.

Conclusion

In conclusion, the Administration is following a clear and consistent set of policies in support of our national interests in the gulf. Our policies are carefully conceived — and they focus on steps needed to end the war. They are calm and steady in purpose, not provocative in intent. they should help deter Iranian miscalculations and actions that would require a strong response. By supporting the defensive efforts of the moderate gulf states, including the sale of appropriate defensive arms, we help to enable them to defend the interests we share in the gulf and to reduce the prospects for closer ties with the Soviet Union as well as any inclination to accommodate Iranian hegemony....

Department of State Statement, May 20, 1987

Just prior to the Iraqi Mirage F-1 attack on U.S.S. *Stark* on Sunday, two Royal Air Force F-15s were scrambled from their base at Dhahran and ordered by Saudi authorities to fly a combat air patrol (CAP) mission over the Saudi coastline. This is a routine action based on prior agreement to defend our AWACS [airborne warning and control system] and Saudi facilities.

Once it was clear that the *Stark* had been attacked, the U.S. Air Force AWACS and the Saudi controller aboard the E-3A asked the Saudi sector command center at Dhahran for authority to commit the Saudi F-15s to intercept the Iraqi F-1 with the intention of forcing it down in Saudi territory. The Saudi chief controller on the ground advised that he did not have the authority to authorize such action and immediately sought approval from higher authority. Before such approval could be obtained, the Iraqi aircraft was well on its way back to its base. In addition, the Saudi F-15s were low on fuel and had to return to base.

It should be noted there is no prearranged plan for the Royal Saudi Air Force to come to the aid of U.S. vessels in the gulf. There was no official U.S. Government request for the Saudi Air Force to intercept the Iraqi aircraft.

Throughout the incident, the Saudi personnel aboard the AWACS and the F-15 crews were eager to run the intercept; the initiative originated with them and the U.S. personnel aboard the AWACS. However desirable an intercept of the attacking aircraft might have been, the incident does illustrate the discipline of the Saudi Air Force's command and control system.

Finally, it should also be noted that Saudi officials immediately launched helicopters to assist in the search-and-rescue effort and dispatched a Saudi naval vessel to close on *Stark* to lend assistance. The Saudi military hospital at Dhahran also was placed on disaster alert to assist with casualties if needed.

Secretary Shultz's Letter to Congress, May 20, 1987

For nearly forty years, the United States has maintained a limited naval presence in the Persian Gulf for the purpose of providing for the safety of U.S. flag vessels in the area and for other reasons essential to our national security. This has been done pursuant to the authority of the President under the Constitution as Commander-in-Chief, and the duty to provide protection for U.S. forces and U.S. vessels that are engaging in peaceful activities on the high seas. Congress has been fully and repeatedly advised of our policy.

Our naval presence in the Gulf has been fully within our rights under international law, and we have respected all the relevant international rules of conduct. We have remained neutral in the Iran-Iraq war, and our vessels have taken no action that could provide any basis for hostile action against them by either country. Until this past Sunday, no U.S. warship or other U.S. flag vessel in the Gulf had been the object of any attack from any source.

Shortly after 2 pm (EDT) on May 17, an Iraqi Air Force F-1 Mirage launched an Exocet missile, which struck the USS *Stark*, causing heavy damage. Within the hour, the USS *Stark* was stopped and listing, but damage control parties were able to stabilize its condition, and the vessel has now returned to port. At this time, a total of 37 members of the crew are reported dead or missing, and two more are seriously injured.

The United States immediately contacted the Iraqi Government through diplomatic channels, to protest in the strongest terms and demand an explanation of the incident and appropriate compensation. President Saddam Hussein sent a letter expressing deepest regret over this tragic accident and his condolences and sympathy to the families of the victims, explaining that Iraqi forces had in no way intended to attack U.S. vessels but rather had been authorized only to attack Iranian targets. A joint U.S.-Iraq review has been agreed upon to determine more precisely the circumstances surrounding the Iraqi attack, and to ensure that there is no recurrence.

Our naval forces in the area have been instructed to assume a higher state of alert readiness in carrying out the standing Rules of Engagement. Ship commanders continue to have the authority to take such steps as may be necessary to protect their vessels from attack. However, we have no reason at this time to believe that Iraqi forces have deliberately targeted U.S. vessels, and no reason to believe that further hostile action will occur.

Our forces are not in a situation of actual hostilities, nor does their continued presence in the area place them in a situation in which imminent involvement in hostilities is indicated, although we are mindful of recent Iranian statements threatening U.S. and other ships under protection. In accordance with his desire to keep the Congress fully informed, the President nonetheless has asked that I provide this account to the Congress of what has transpired, and has directed that the relevant Committees and leadership of Congress be fully briefed on these events.

Quite apart from the Iraqi attack on the USS *Stark*, Iran continues publicly and privately to threaten shipping in the Gulf. It is this basic Iranian threat to the free flow of oil and to the principle of freedom of navigation which is unacceptable. The frequent and accelerating Iranian attacks on shipping have spread the war geographically to the lower Gulf and have heightened the risk to all littoral states. The *Stark* incident provides no reason for altering the policy which we have adopted in the Gulf area of being prepared to defend U.S. vessels and U.S. interests when necessary. We intend to proceed with plans to provide protection for ships flying the U.S. flag in the Gulf, including certain Kuwaiti tankers which have applied for U.S. registry. It is not our intention to provoke military action, but to deter it. Sunday's incident, although regrettable and tragic for our courageous seamen aboard the USS *Stark*, does not suggest that either of the countries involved in the war have decided to attack U.S. vessels in the Gulf.

At the same time that we are taking these steps, we want to assure you that the Administration is actively pressing for comprehensive and effective international action, including at the United Nations, to bring this bloody, wasteful and dangerous war to an end....
(DSB July 1987: 58-63)

President Reagan's Letter to the Speaker of the House of Representatives and the President Pro Tempore of the Senate on the United States Air Strike in the Persian Gulf

September 24, 1987

...At approximately 4:00 p.m. (EDT) on September 21, 1987, Armed Forces of the United States assigned to the Middle East Joint Task Force observed an Iranian landing craft, the "IRAN AJR", engaging in nighttime minelaying near U.S. forces in international waters of the Persian Gulf. This hostile action posed a direct threat to the safety of U.S. warships and other U.S. flag vessels. Accordingly, acting in self-defense and pursuant to standing Peacetime Rules of Engagement for the region, two U.S. helicopters operating off the USS JARRETT engaged the Iranian vessel, which subsequently resumed its mine laying activities. Thereupon, the helicopters re-engaged the AJR, disabling it with rocket and machine gun fire, and curtailed the further release of mines.

Subsequently, at first light in the Persian Gulf on September 22, U.S. forces boarded the disabled craft, which proved to have been manned by regular elements of the Iranian navy. Three crewmen were found dead on the vessel and nine mines were found on deck. Twenty-six survivors were recovered from the water and from lifeboats and taken to U.S. naval ships for examination and medical treatment. Arrangements are being made to turn the survivors over to an appropriate humanitarian organization. Two members of the crew of the IRAN AJR are believed missing. Search and rescue operations for them have been undertaken, as well as operations to find and clear a number of mines that, according to discussion with surviving crewmen of the IRAN AJR, were laid prior to action against the vessel by U.S. forces.

The actions taken by U.S. forces were conducted in the exercise of our right of self-defense under Article 51 of the United Nations Charter. Mining of the high seas, without notice and in an area of restricted navigation, is unlawful and a serious threat to world public order and the safety of international maritime commerce. These Iranian actions were taken despite warnings given to the Government of Iran, subsequent to the recent mine damage done to the U.S.-flag vessel BRIDGETON, that the U.S. Government would take the action necessary to defend U.S. vessels from attacks of this nature.

U.S. forces in the area have returned to their prior state of alert readiness. They will remain prepared to take any further defensive action necessary to protect U.S. vessels and U.S. lives from unlawful attack....

(PPP Reagan 1987 II: 1074-1076)

President Reagan's Letter to the Speaker of the House of Representatives and the President Pro Tempore of the Senate on the United States Air Strike in the Persian Gulf

October 10, 1987

...At approximately 2:50 p.m. (EDT) on October 8, 1987, three helicopters of the U.S. Middle East Joint Task Force, while on routine nighttime patrol over international waters of the Persian Gulf, were fired upon without warning by three (possibly four) small Iranian naval vessels. This unprovoked attack posed an immediate and direct threat to the safety of the helicopters and their crewmen. Accordingly, acting in self-defense and pursuant to standing Peacetime Rules of Engagement for the region, the helicopters returned fire with rockets and machine guns. Three Iranian vessels were hit, and one of them subsequently sank. No U.S. personnel were injured in this brief exchange of fire.

U.S. patrol boats were dispatched to the scene and recovered six Iranian crewmen from the water. Although all available medical care was provided, two of the crewmen subsequently died. The four surviving crewmen currently are aboard the USS RALEIGH. Two of them are seriously injured, and all are receiving complete medical evaluation and treatment. When the survivors are capable of being moved, efforts will be made to repatriate them through a third country with the assistance of an appropriate humanitarian organization.

At approximately 3:30 p.m. (EDT), another helicopter belonging to the U.S. Middle East Joint Task Force was performing surveillance operations over international waters of the Persian Gulf in the vicinity of an oil platform under Iranian control. Although the helicopter observed fire from an unidentified source, it is not clear that the fire was directed at the U.S. aircraft and U.S. forces did not return fire.

U.S. forces, which sustained no damage or casualties, have returned to their prior state of alert readiness in carrying out the standing Peacetime Rules of Engagement for the Persian Gulf region. Although they will remain prepared to take any additional defensive action necessary to protect U.S. forces and U.S. lives, there has been no further hostile action by Iranian forces and we regard this incident as closed.

The limited defensive action described above was taken in accordance with our right of self-defense under Article 51 of the United Nations Charter, and pursuant to my constitutional authority with respect to the conduct of foreign relations and as Commander-in-Chief.

(PPP Reagan 1987 II: 1164-1165)

President Reagan's Statement on the United States Reprisal Against Iran
October 19, 1987

Acting pursuant to my authority as Commander in Chief, United States naval vessels at 7 a.m. e.d.t. today struck an Iranian military platform in international waters in the central Persian Gulf. This platform has been used to assist in a number of Iranian attacks against nonbelligerent shipping. Iran's unprovoked attacks upon U.S. and other nonbelligerent shipping, and particularly deliberate laying of mines and firing of Silkworm missiles, which have hit U.S.-flag vessels, have come in spite of numerous messages from the Government of the United States to the Government of Iran warning of the consequences.

The action against the Iranian military platform came after consultations with congressional leadership and friendly governments. It is a prudent yet restrained response to this unlawful use of force against the United States and to numerous violations of the rights of other nonbelligerents. It is a lawful exercise of the right of self defense enshrined in article 51 of the United Nations Charter and is being so notified to the President of the United Nations Security Council.

The United States has no desire for a military confrontation with Iran, but the Government of Iran should be under no illusion about our determination and ability to protect our ships and our interests against unprovoked attacks. We have informed the Government of Iran of our desire for an urgent end to tensions in the region and an end to the Iran-Iraq war through urgent implementation of Security Council Resolution 598.
(PPP Reagan 1987 II: 1201-1202)

President Reagan's Statement on Trade Sanctions Against Iran
October 26, 1987

I have directed the Secretaries of Treasury and State to take action to place an embargo on all U.S. imports from Iran. At the same time, we are instituting a ban on the export to Iran of 14 broad categories of U.S. products with potential military application. As required by law, we have consulted with Congress on these actions and are presently engaged in formally notifying Congress with regard to them. The ban on imports of Iranian goods will take effect as soon as possible. The additional controls on exports to Iran will go into effect in a week to 10 days.

The Congress itself has moved quickly and decisively in this important area, and the administration looks forward to cooperating closely with the Congress to ensure that any future legislation serves our broader goals of implementing United Nations Security Council Resolution 598 and restoring peace and stability to the Persian Gulf region.

The measures I am initiating are a direct result of the Iranian Government's own actions, including its unprovoked attacks on U.S. forces and U.S. merchant vessels, its refusal to implement U.N. Security Council Resolution 598, its continued aggression against nonbelligerent nations of the Persian Gulf, and its sponsorship of terrorism there and elsewhere in the world. These measures will remain in place so long as Iran persists in its aggressive disregard for the most fundamental norms of international conduct.

Let me emphasize that we are taking these economic measures only after repeated but unsuccessful attempts to reduce tensions with Iran and in response to the continued and increasingly bellicose behavior of the Iranian Government. They do not reflect any quarrel with the Iranian people. Indeed, as I have said a number of times, the United States accepts the Iranian revolution as a fact and respects the right of the Iranian people to choose any government that they wish.

The United States hopes that more normal relations with Iran will evolve as Iranian belligerence and tensions in the area diminish. We have made these points known repeatedly to Iran, through diplomatic channels as well as public statements. Unfortunately, the Iranian Government's response to date, in deeds as well as in words, has been entirely unconstructive.
(PPP Reagan 1987 II: 1232)

Statement by Assistant to the President for Press Relations Fitzwater on the United States Military Strike in the Persian Gulf
April 18, 1988

Acting under his authority as Commander in Chief, the President has directed United States forces at 1 a.m. eastern daylight time today to strike Iranian military targets in the southern Persian Gulf. Our forces attacked oil platforms at Sirri and Sassan in the southern Gulf. These platforms are used as command and control radar stations for the Iranian military. The attacks are underway at this time. These actions were taken in response to Iran's recent resumption of mine-laying in international waters and its mine attack on the U.S.S. *Samuel B. Roberts*. The Government of Iran has been repeatedly warned about the consequences of such hostile acts.

Our actions were taken following consultations with congressional leadership and after informing friendly governments. They are designed and intended to deter further Iranian mining. They represent a measured response to Iran's unlawful use of force against the United States and to Iran's numerous violations of the rights of other nonbelligerents. And they constitute a lawful exercise of the United States inherent right of self-defense under article 51 of the United Nations Charter. Appropriate notification of such actions is being provided to the President of the United Nations Security Council.

We have repeatedly told Iran that we do not desire military confrontation, but the Government of Iran should understand that we will protect our ships and our interests against unprovoked attacks. We urgently seek an end to tensions in the region and to the Iran-Iraq war. This would benefit the people of both nations who have suffered so much from the brutal conflict. We urge Iran to accept Security Council Resolution 598 and to agree to its rapid and comprehensive implementation. Iran has nothing to gain from continuation of the war.
(PPP Reagan 1988 I: 463)

President Reagan's Letter to the Speaker of the House of Representatives and the President Pro Tempore of the Senate on the United States Military Strike in the Persian Gulf
April 19, 1988

...On April 14, 1988, the USS SAMUEL B. ROBERTS struck a mine in international waters of the Persian Gulf. Lookouts on the Roberts had spotted three mines lying perpendicular to the ship's course and about 700 yards away. The Roberts struck a mine set deeper than the others and not visible from the ship. Ten servicemen were injured. The detonation caused a nine-foot hole in the ship's hull near the main engine room, below the water line; a split in the ship's bulkhead between the main engine room and an auxiliary machinery room; and a fire. The Roberts is now safely in a repair facility.

An examination of the mines remaining in the water established that they were M-08 mines, the same type Iran was caught placing in the water from the IRAN AJR on September 21, 1987. They had been freshly laid in an area transited by U.S. convoys. No barnacles or marine growth were on the mines. Most important, the mines bore markings of the same type and series as on those laid by the IRAN AJR. No doubt exists that Iran laid these mines for the specific purpose of damaging or sinking U.S. or other non-belligerent ships. We have warned Iran repeatedly against such hostile acts.

In response to this attack on the ROBERTS and commencing at approximately 1:00 a.m. (EDT), April 18, 1988, Armed Forces of the United States assigned to the Joint Task Force Middle East, after warning Iranian personnel and providing an opportunity to escape, attacked and effectively neutralized the Sassan and Sirri Platforms, which have been used to support unlawful Iranian attacks on non-belligerent shipping. While these events were taking place, an Iranian helicopter and small boats attacked an oil rig and the U.S.-flag vessel WILLI TIDE in the Mubarak oil field. In response, U.S. A-6 aircraft attacked three Iranian Boghammar small boats, sinking at least one.

Subsequently, U.S. Forces were attacked by the Iranian PTG JOSHAN, FFG SAHAND, and FFG SABALAN. In response to these attacks, U.S. Forces severely damaged or sank the Iranian vessels. Iranian F-4 fighters also approached the USS SIMPSON and the USS WAINWRIGHT in a threatening manner; the SIMPSON and WAINWRIGHT fired at the aircraft, causing their retreat.

Search and rescue efforts were undertaken to locate a missing AH-l Cobra helicopter from the WAINWRIGHT. The helicopter had two men on board. As of 7:00 a.m. (EDT) today, the search and rescue efforts were continuing.... *(PPP Reagan 1988 I: 477-478)*

President Reagan's Letter to the Speaker of the House of Representatives and the President Pro Tempore of the Senate on the Destruction of an Iranian Jetliner by the United States Navy over the Persian Gulf
July 4, 1988

...On July 3, 1988, the USS VINCENNES and USS ELMER MONTGOMERY were operating in international waters of the Persian Gulf near the Strait of Hormuz. (On July 2, the Montgomery had responded to a distress signal from a Danish tanker that was under attack by Iranian small boats and had fired a warning shot, which caused the breaking off of the attack.) Having indications that approximately a dozen Iranian small boats were congregating to attack merchant shipping, the VINCENNES sent a Mark III LAMPS Helicopter on investigative patrol in international airspace to assess the situation. At about 1010 local Gulf time (2:10 a.m. EDT), when the helicopter had approached to within only four nautical miles, it was fired on by Iranian small boats (the VINCENNES was ten nautical miles from the scene at this time). The LAMPS helicopter was not damaged and returned immediately to the VINCENNES.

As the VINCENNES and MONTGOMERY were approaching the group of Iranian small boats at approximately 1042 local time, at least four of the small boats turned toward and began closing in on the American warships. At this time, both American ships opened fire on the small craft, sinking two and damaging a third. Regrettably, in the course of the U.S. response to the Iranian attack, an Iranian civilian airliner was shot down by the VINCENNES, which was firing in self defense at what it believed to be a hostile Iranian military aircraft. We deeply regret the tragic loss of life that occurred. The Defense Department will conduct a full investigation.

The actions of U.S. forces in response to being attacked by Iranian small boats were taken in accordance with our inherent right of self-defense, as recognized in Article 51 of the United Nations Charter, and pursuant to my constitutional authority with respect to the conduct of foreign relations and as Commander in Chief. There has been no further hostile action by Iranian forces, and, although U.S. forces will remain prepared to take additional

defensive action to protect our units and military personnel, we regard this incident as closed. U.S. forces suffered no casualties or damage....
(PPP Reagan 1988-1989 II: 920-921)

Statement by Assistant to the President for Press Relations Fitzwater on United States Policy Regarding the Accidental Attack on an Iranian Jetliner over the Persian Gulf
July 11, 1988

The President has reviewed U.S. policy in the Persian Gulf, where our military forces are protecting vital interests of the free world. He has expressed his complete satisfaction with the policy and reiterated his belief that the actions of the U.S.S. *Vincennes* on July 3 in the case of the Iranian airliner were justifiable defensive actions. At the same time, he remains personally saddened at the tragic death of the innocent victims of this accident and has already expressed his deep regret to their families. Prompted by the humanitarian traditions of our nation, the President has decided that the United States will offer compensation on an *ex gratia* basis to the families of the victims who died in the Iranian airliner incident. Details concerning amounts, timing, and other matters remain to be worked out. It should be clearly understood that payment will go to the families, not governments, and will be subject to the normal U.S. legal requirements, including, if necessary, appropriate action by Congress. In the case of Iran, arrangements will be made through appropriate third parties. This offer of *ex gratia* compensation is consistent with international practice and is a humanitarian effort to ease the hardship of the families. It is offered on a voluntary basis, not on the basis of any legal liability or obligation.

The responsibility for this tragic incident, and for the deaths of hundreds of thousands of other innocent victims as a result of the Iran-Iraq war, lies with those who refuse to end the conflict. A particularly heavy burden of responsibility rests with the Government of Iran, which has refused for almost a year to accept and implement Security Council Resolution 598 while it continues unprovoked attacks on innocent neutral shipping and crews in the international waters of the Gulf.

In fact, at the time of the Iran Air incident, U.S. forces were militarily engaged with Iranian forces as a result of the latter's unprovoked attacks upon neutral ships and a U.S. Navy helicopter. The urgent necessity to end this conflict is reinforced by the dangers it poses to neighboring countries and the deplorable precedent of the increasingly frequent use of chemical weapons by both sides, causing still more casualties.

Only an end to the war, an objective we desire, can halt the immense suffering in the region and put an end to innocent loss of life. Our goal is peace in the Gulf and on land. We urge Iran and Iraq to work with the

Security Council for an urgent comprehensive settlement of the war pursuant to Resolution 598. Meanwhile, United States forces will continue their mission in the area, keenly aware of the risks involved and ready to face them. *(PPP Reagan 1988-1989 II: 934-935)*

President Reagan's Letter to the Speaker of the House of Representatives and the President Pro Tempore of the Senate on United States Military Action in the Persian Gulf

July 14, 1988

...At approximately 11:30 a.m. (EDT), July 12, 1988, a Panamanian tanker (Japanese owned) sent out a distress call reporting it was under attack by two small boats and in need of assistance. Units of the U.S. Middle East Joint Task Force, responding to the ship's distress call, dispatched five U.S. helicopters to an area approximately 23 nautical miles west north west of Farsi Island in the Northern Persian Gulf. Two of the helicopters, while on their way to provide assistance, observed two small boats heading towards Farsi Island. As they closed to identify visually the boats, the boats fired at the U.S. helicopters. This hostile action posed an immediate and direct threat to the safety of the helicopters. Accordingly, acting in self-defense, the helicopters returned fire, firing rockets and machine gun rounds at the small boats, which then left the scene. At this time it is believed that one of the boats may have been hit with a rocket. The extent of damage to the boat is unknown. There were no casualties or damage to U.S. forces; the tanker caught fire as a result of the attack....

(PPP Reagan 1988-1989 II: 963)

OPERATION DESERT SHIELD

Statement by Deputy Press Secretary Popadiuk on the Iraqi Invasion of Kuwait

August 2, 1990

National Security Adviser Brent Scowcroft has been chairing an interagency task force in the Situation Room monitoring the Iraqi invasion of Kuwait. The President was informed of the initial signs of the Iraqi action at approximately 9 p.m. yesterday by National Security Adviser Scowcroft and has been receiving periodic updates since.

The United States is deeply concerned about this blatant act of aggression and demands the immediate and unconditional withdrawal of all Iraqi forces. We do not have exact details at this time concerning the extent of the Iraqi action, although it is clearly extensive. We have no reports of any harm to

American citizens. The State Department is in constant contact with our Embassy in Kuwait concerning the status of U.S. citizens.

At the urging of Kuwait and the United States, the United Nations Security Council will be meeting early this morning to consider this matter. In addition, we have been informed that the Arab League and the organization of the Islamic Conference will be convening to review the situation. We are urging the entire international community to condemn this outrageous act of aggression.

The United States is reviewing all options in its response to the Iraqi aggression.

(Unless otherwise noted, presidential statements and documents that follow encompassing August 2-December 31, 1990, are quoted from PPP Bush 1990 II: 1082-1085, 1088-1089, 1095-1096, 1107-1109, 1116-1118, 1123-1124, 1128-1129, 1143, 1156-1157, 1164-1165, 1172-1175, 1596, 1617-1618)

President Bush's Remarks and an Exchange with Reporters on the Iraqi Invasion of Kuwait

August 2, 1990

...The United States strongly condemns the Iraqi military invasion of Kuwait. We call for the immediate and unconditional withdrawal of all the Iraqi forces. There is no place for this sort of naked aggression in today's world, and I've taken a number of steps to indicate the deep concern that I feel over the events that have taken place.

Last night I instructed our Ambassador at the United Nations, Tom Pickering, to work with Kuwait in convening an emergency meeting of the Security Council. It was convened, and I am grateful for that quick, overwhelming vote condemning the Iraqi action and calling for immediate and unconditional withdrawal. Tom Pickering will be here in a bit, and we are contemplating with him further United Nations action.

Second, consistent with my authority under the International Emergency Economic Powers Act, I've signed an Executive order early this morning freezing Iraqi assets in this country and prohibiting transactions with Iraq. I've also signed an Executive order freezing Kuwaiti assets. That's to ensure that those assets are not interfered with by the illegitimate authority that is now occupying Kuwait. We call upon other governments to take similar action.

Third, the Department of State has been in touch with governments around the world urging that they, too, condemn the Iraqi aggression and consult to determine what measures should be taken to bring an end to this totally unjustified act. It is important that the international community act together to ensure that Iraqi forces depart Kuwait immediately....

President Bush's Memorandum to Heads of All Departments and Agencies on the Withholding of Assistance to Iraq
August 2, 1990

...Effective immediately, you are instructed not to provide any form of assistance to Iraq, including, but not limited to, financial assistance, loan guarantees, and export licenses.

President Bush's Message to the Congress on the Declaration of a National Emergency with Respect to Iraq
August 3, 1990

...Pursuant to section 204(b) of the International Emergency Economic Powers Act, 50 U.S.C. section 1703(b), and section 201 of the National Emergencies Act, 50 U.S.C. section 1621, I hereby report that I have exercised my statutory authority to declare a national emergency and to issue two Executive orders that:

- prohibit exports and imports of goods and services between the United States and Iraq and the purchase of Iraqi goods by U.S. persons for sale in third countries;
- prohibit transactions related to travel to or from Iraq, except for transactions necessary for journalistic travel or prompt departure from Iraq;
- prohibit transactions related to transportation to or from Iraq, or the use of vessels or aircraft registered in Iraq by U.S. persons;
- prohibit the performance of any contract in support of Government of Iraq projects;
- ban all extensions of credit and loans by U.S. persons to the Government of Iraq;
- block all property of the Government of Iraq now or hereafter located in the United States or in the possession or control of U.S. persons, including their foreign branches; and
- prohibit all transfers or other transactions involving assets belonging to the Government of Kuwait now or hereafter located in the United States or in the possession or control of U.S. persons, including their foreign branches.

The Secretary of the Treasury is authorized to issue regulations implementing these prohibitions....

I have authorized these measures in response to the Iraqi invasion of Kuwait, which clearly constitutes an act of aggression and a flagrant violation of international law. This action is in clear violation of the national sovereignty and independence of Kuwait and the Charter of the United Nations. It threatens the entire structure of peaceful relations among nations in this critical region. It constitutes an unusual and extraordinary threat to the national security, foreign policy, and economy of the United States.

The measures we are taking to block Iraqi assets will have the effect of expressing our outrage at Iraq's actions, and will prevent that government from drawing on monies and properties within U.S. control to support its campaign of military aggression against a neighboring state. Our ban on exports to Iraq will prevent the Iraqi government from profiting from the receipt of U.S. goods and technology. Our ban on imports, while not preventing sales of Iraqi oil to third countries, denies Iraq access to the lucrative U.S. market for its most important product.

At the same time, in order to protect the property of the legitimate Government of Kuwait from possible seizure, diversion or misuse by Iraq, and with the approval of the Kuwaiti government, we are blocking Kuwaiti assets within the jurisdiction of the United States or in the possession or control of U.S. persons....

President Bush's Address to the Nation Announcing the Deployment of United States Armed Forces to Saudi Arabia

August 8, 1990

In the life of a nation, we're called upon to define who we are and what we believe. Sometimes these choices are not easy. But today as President, I ask for your support in a decision I've made to stand up for what's right and condemn what's wrong, all in the cause of peace.

At my direction, elements of the 82d Airborne Division as well as key units of the United States Air Force are arriving today to take up defensive positions in Saudi Arabia. I took this action to assist the Saudi Arabian Government in the defense of its homeland. No one commits America's Armed Forces to a dangerous mission lightly, but after perhaps unparalleled international consultation and exhausting every alternative, it became necessary to take this action. Let me tell you why.

Less than a week ago, in the early morning hours of August 2d, Iraqi Armed Forces, without provocation or warning, invaded a peaceful Kuwait. Facing negligible resistance from its much smaller neighbor, Iraq's tanks stormed in blitzkrieg fashion through Kuwait in a few short hours. With more than 100,000 troops, along with tanks, artillery, and surface-to-air missiles, Iraq now occupies Kuwait. This aggression came just hours after Saddam Hussein specifically assured numerous countries in the area that there would be no invasion. There is no justification whatsoever for this outrageous and brutal act of aggression.

A puppet regime imposed from the outside is unacceptable. The acquisition of territory by force is unacceptable. No one, friend or foe, should doubt our desire for peace; and no one should underestimate our determination to confront aggression.

Four simple principles guide our policy. First, we seek the immediate, unconditional, and complete withdrawal of all Iraqi forces from Kuwait. Second, Kuwait's legitimate government must be restored to replace the puppet regime. And third, my administration, as has been the case with every President from President Roosevelt to President Reagan, is committed to the security and stability of the Persian Gulf. And fourth, I am determined to protect the lives of American citizens abroad.

Immediately after the Iraqi invasion, I ordered an embargo of all trade with Iraq and, together with many other nations, announced sanctions that both freeze all Iraqi assets in this country and protected Kuwait's assets. The stakes are high. Iraq is already a rich and powerful country that possesses the world's second largest reserves of oil and over a million men under arms. It's the fourth largest military in the world. Our country now imports nearly half the oil it consumes and could face a major threat to its economic independence. Much of the world is even more dependent upon imported oil and is even more vulnerable to Iraqi threats.

We succeeded in the struggle for freedom in Europe because we and our allies remain stalwart. Keeping the peace in the Middle East will require no less. We're beginning a new era. This new era can be full of promise, an age of freedom, a time of peace for all peoples. But if history teaches us anything, it is that we must resist aggression or it will destroy our freedoms. Appeasement does not work. As was the case in the 1930's, we see in Saddam Hussein an aggressive dictator threatening his neighbors. Only 14 days ago, Saddam Hussein promised his friends he would not invade Kuwait. And 4 days ago, he promised the world he would withdraw. And twice we have seen what his promises mean: His promises mean nothing.

In the last few days, I've spoken with political leaders from the Middle East, Europe, Asia, and the Americas; and I've met with Prime Minister Thatcher, Prime Minister Mulroney, and NATO Secretary General Woerner. And all agree that Iraq cannot be allowed to benefit from its invasion of Kuwait.

We agree that this is not an American problem or a European problem or a Middle East problem: It is the world's problem. And that's why, soon after the Iraqi invasion, the United Nations Security Council, without dissent, condemned Iraq, calling for the immediate and unconditional withdrawal of its troops from Kuwait. The Arab world, through both the Arab League and the Gulf Cooperation Council, courageously announced its opposition to Iraqi aggression. Japan, the United Kingdom, and France, and other governments around the world have imposed severe sanctions. The Soviet Union and China ended all arms sales to Iraq.

And this past Monday, the United Nations Security Council approved for the first time in 23 years mandatory sanctions under chapter VII of the United Nations Charter. These sanctions, now enshrined in international law, have the potential to deny Iraq the fruits of aggression while sharply limiting its ability to either import or export anything of value, especially oil.

I pledge here today that the United States will do its part to see that these sanctions are effective and to induce Iraq to withdraw without delay from Kuwait.

But we must recognize that Iraq may not stop using force to advance its ambitions. Iraq has massed an enormous war machine on the Saudi border capable of initiating hostilities with little or no additional preparation. Given the Iraqi government's history of aggression against its own citizens as well as its neighbors, to assume Iraq will not attack again would be unwise and unrealistic.

And therefore, after consulting with King Fahd, I sent Secretary of Defense Dick Cheney to discuss cooperative measures we could take. Following those meetings, the Saudi Government requested our help, and I responded to that request by ordering U.S. air and ground forces to deploy to the Kingdom of Saudi Arabia.

Let me be clear: The sovereign independence of Saudi Arabia is of vital interest to the United States. This decision, which I shared with the congressional leadership, grows out of the longstanding friendship and security relationship between the United States and Saudi Arabia. U.S. forces will work together with those of Saudi Arabia and other nations to preserve the integrity of Saudi Arabia and to deter further Iraqi aggression. Through their presence, as well as through training and exercises, these multinational forces will enhance the overall capability of Saudi Armed Forces to defend the Kingdom.

I want to be clear about what we are doing and why. America does not seek conflict, nor do we seek to chart the destiny of other nations. But America will stand by her friends. The mission of our troops is wholly defensive. Hopefully, they will not be needed long. They will not initiate hostilities, but they will defend themselves, the Kingdom of Saudi Arabia, and other friends in the Persian Gulf.

We are working around the clock to deter Iraqi aggression and to enforce U.N. sanctions. I'm continuing my conversations with world leaders. Secretary of Defense Cheney has just returned from valuable consultations with President Mubarak of Egypt and King Hassan of Morocco. Secretary of State Baker has consulted with his counterparts in many nations, including the Soviet Union, and today he heads for Europe to consult with President Özal of Turkey, a staunch friend of the United States. And he'll then consult with the NATO Foreign Ministers.

I will ask oil-producing nations to do what they can to increase production in order to minimize any impact that oil flow reductions will have on the world economy. And I will explore whether we and our allies should draw down our strategic petroleum reserves. Conservation measures can also help; Americans everywhere must do their part. And one more thing: I'm asking the oil companies to do their fair share. They should show restraint and not abuse today's uncertainties to raise prices....

President Bush's Letter to Congressional Leaders on the Deployment of United States Armed Forces to Saudi Arabia and the Middle East
August 9, 1990

...On August 2, 1990, Iraq invaded and occupied the sovereign state of Kuwait in flagrant violation of the Charter of the United Nations. In the period since August 2, Iraq has massed an enormous and sophisticated war machine on the Kuwaiti-Saudi Arabian border and in southern Iraq, capable of initiating further hostilities with little or no additional preparation. Iraq's actions pose a direct theat to neighboring countries and to vital U.S. interests in the Persian Gulf region.

In response to this threat and after receiving the request of the Government of Saudi Arabia, I ordered the forward deployment of substantial elements of the United States Armed Forces into the region. I am providing this report on the deployment and mission of our Armed Forces in accordance with my desire that Congress be fully informed and consistent with the War Powers Resolution.

Two squadrons of F-15 aircraft, one brigade of the 82nd Airborne Division, and other elements of the Armed Forces began arriving in Saudi Arabia at approximately 9:00 a.m. (EDT) on August 8, 1990. Additional U.S. air, naval, and ground Forces also will be deployed. The Forces are equipped for combat, and their mission is defensive. They are prepared to take action in concert with Saudi forces, friendly regional forces, and others to deter Iraqi aggression and to preserve the integrity of Saudi Arabia.

I do not believe involvement in hostilities is imminent; to the contrary, it is my belief that this deployment will facilitate a peaceful resolution of the crisis. If necessary, however, the Forces are fully prepared to defend themselves. Although it is not possible to predict the precise scope and duration of this deployment, our Armed Forces will remain so long as their presence is required to contribute to the security of the region and desired by the Saudi government to enhance the capability of Saudi armed forces to defend the Kingdom.

President Bush's Letter to Congressional Leaders on Additional Economic Measures Taken with Respect to Iraq and Kuwait
August 9, 1990

...On August 2, 1990, I reported to the Congress that pursuant to section 204(b) of the International Emergency Economic Powers Act, 50 U.S.C. section 1703(b), and section 201 of the National Emergencies Act, 50 U.S.C. section 1621, I exercised my statutory authority to declare a national emergency and to issue two Executive orders that imposed a comprehensive economic embargo against Iraq and blocked both Iraqi and Kuwaiti government property within the jurisdiction of the United States or under the control of U.S. persons.

In the days after the imposition of U.S. economic sanctions, the Iraqi government has tightened its unlawful grip over the territory of Kuwait and has installed a puppet regime that in no way represents the people or legitimate Government of Kuwait. On August 6, the United Nations Security Council, to bring the invasion and occupation of Kuwait to an end and to restore the sovereignty, independence, and territorial integrity of Kuwait, decided that all nations shall impose sweeping economic sanctions against both Iraq and Kuwait.

Today, I have taken additional steps to respond to these developments and to ensure that the economic measures we are taking with respect to Iraq and Kuwait conform to United Nations Security Council Resolution 661 of August 6, 1990. Specifically, pursuant to section 204(b) of the International Emergency Economic Powers Act, 50 U.S.C. section 1703(b), section 201 of the National Emergencies Act, 50 U.S.C. section 1621, and the United Nations Participation Act, 22 U.S.C. section 287(c), I have issued two new Executive orders.

The order I have issued with respect to Iraq:

- prohibits exports and imports of goods and services between the United States and Iraq, and any activity that promotes or is intended to promote such exportation and importation;
- prohibits any dealing by a U.S. person in connection with property of Iraqi origin exported from Iraq after August 6, 1990, or intended for exportation to or from Iraq to any country, and related activities;
- prohibits transactions related to travel to or from Iraq or to activities by any such person within Iraq, except for transactions necessary for prompt departure from Iraq, the conduct of official business of the United States Government or of the United Nations, or journalistic travel;
- prohibits transactions related to transportation to or from Iraq, or the use of vessels or aircraft registered in Iraq by U.S. persons;
- prohibits the performance by any U.S. person of any contract in support of certain categories of project in Iraq;

- prohibits the commitment or transfer of funds or other financial or economic resources by any U.S. person to the Government of Iraq, or any other person in Iraq;
- blocks all property of the Government of Iraq now or hereafter located in the United States or in the possession or control of U.S. persons, including their foreign branches; and
- clarifies that the definition of U.S. persons includes vessels of U.S. registry.

In a separate order, I have extended to Kuwait all economic sanctions currently in effect against Iraq. Specifically, that order:

- prohibits exports and imports of goods and services between the United States and Kuwait, and any activity that promotes or is intended to promote such exportation or importation;
- prohibits any dealing by a U.S. person in connection with property of Kuwaiti origin exported from Kuwait after August 6, 1990, or intended for exportation to or from Kuwait to any country, and related activities;
- prohibits transactions related to travel to or from Kuwait or to activities by any such person within Kuwait, except for transactions necessary for prompt departure from Kuwait, the conduct of official business of the United States Government or of the United Nations, or journalistic travel;
- prohibits transactions related to transportation to or from Kuwait, or the use of vessels or aircraft registered in Kuwait by U.S. persons;
- prohibits the performance by any U.S. person of any contract in support of certain categories of projects in Kuwait;
- prohibits the commitment or transfer of funds or other financial or economic resources by any U.S. person to the Government of Kuwait, or any other person in Kuwait;
- blocks all property of the Government of Kuwait now or hereafter located in the United States or in the possession or control of U.S. persons, including their foreign branches; and
- clarifies that definition of U.S. persons includes vessels of U.S. registry.

Today's orders provide that the Secretary of the Treasury, in consultation with the Secretary of State, is authorized to take such actions, including the promulgation of rules and regulations, as may be necessary to carry out the purposes of those orders. The orders were effective at 8:55 pm e.d.t., August 9, 1990.

The declarations of national emergency made by Executive orders 12722 and 12723, and any other provision of those orders not inconsistent with today's orders, remain in force and are unaffected by today's orders....

Statement by Press Secretary Fitzwater on the Arab League's Statement on the Persian Gulf Crisis

August 10, 1990

We welcome the Arab League statement as a positive and significant statement.

We are pleased with the very strong condemnation of Iraqi behavior and the equally strong support for Kuwaiti sovereignty and the return of the legitimate government. We are gratified to see the explicit statement of support for the measures taken by Saudi Arabia as regards its right to self-defense. We see as positive the fact that the Arab summit resolution provides a basis for individual governments to send forces to support Saudi Arabia and other Arab States of the Gulf.

Excerpts of a Statement by Press Secretary Fitzwater on the Persian Gulf Crisis

August 11, 1990

President Bush called President Mubarak of Egypt at 5:45 a.m. this morning to congratulate him on the successful outcome of the Arab League meeting. President Bush praised President Mubarak's constructive role in securing passage of the resolution to send Arab troops to participate in a multinational force. The President said the Arab League action was very favorable and gives us significant optimism for the future of the mission.

President Bush this morning also telephoned Amir 'Isa bin Salman Al Khalifa of Bahrain to thank him for his efforts on behalf of the resolution and to discuss the situation generally. President Bush plans to call Amir Khalifa bin Hamad Al Thani of Qatar.

The United States welcomes the participation of forces from so many countries in our joint efforts to fight the aggression of Saddam Hussein. Military participation by Canada, Australia, West Germany, France, Belgium, and the United Kingdom signal a high degree of unity. We expect others to join this group as well. The NATO pledge of support was also important with so many individual countries bringing their resources to bear on the situation.

We are pleased to confirm that 11 Americans, including Penelope Nabokov, have been able to leave Iraq and cross the border into Jordan. We do not have details on their departure, but it is encouraging that this group has been able to join other Americans in leaving Iraq and Kuwait. Our Embassy is in contact almost hourly with Iraqi officials concerning the safety of U.S. citizens.

There are news reports this morning in three different publications showing three different levels of eventual troop strength in Saudi Arabia. We will not comment on these stories nor provide any numbers on troop strength for obvious national security reasons. Similarly, we will have no comment on the stories today about a possible blockade. We have said in the past that planning for a blockade is underway, should it be necessary.

Right now the United Nations sanctions are being widely implemented, and there is no Iraqi oil leaving Turkey or Saudi Arabia. The embargo appears to be having a considerable effect. We are pleased that Venezuela, Iran, and other countries have indicated ability to make up for oil shortfalls. Fortunately, oil stocks in the United States are quite high, and the surge capacity around the world is also high. America is in a very positive situation in terms of its ability to withstand existing oil disruptions.

Statement by Press Secretary Fitzwater on the Persian Gulf Crisis
August 12, 1990

This morning the President received a letter from His Highness, Sheik Jabir al-Ahmad al-Jabir Al Sabah, the Amir of Kuwait, requesting on behalf of the Government of Kuwait and in accordance with article 51 of the U.N. Charter and the right of individual and collective self-defense that the United States Government take appropriate steps as necessary to ensure that the U.N.-mandated economic sanctions against Iraq and Kuwait are immediately and effectively implemented.

In view of the Amir's request, the President has decided that the United States will do whatever is necessary to see that relevant U.N. sanctions are enforced. The President stressed that these efforts will complement, not substitute, for individual and collective compliance that has been highly successful thus far. The United States will coordinate its efforts with the Governments of other nations to whom the Kuwaiti Government has made similar requests.

Regarding Saddam Hussein's proposals announced today, the United States categorically rejects them. We join the rest of the U.N. Security Council in unanimously calling for the immediate, complete, and unconditional withdrawal of Iraqi forces from Kuwait and the restoration of Kuwait's legitimate government. These latest conditions and threats are another attempt at distracting from Iraq's isolation and at imposing a new status quo. Iraq continues to act in defiance of U.N. Resolutions 660, 661, and 662, the basis for resolving Iraq's occupation. The United States will continue to pursue the application of those resolutions in all their parts.

Statement by Press Secretary Fitzwater on the Treatment of Foreign Nationals in Iraq and Kuwait
August 18, 1990

On several occasions since the Iraqi invasion and subsequent occupation of Kuwait, the President has stated publicly his interest in the well-being of

American citizens and all foreign nationals in both Iraq and Kuwait. The President thus views yesterday's statement by the Speaker of Iraq's National Assembly [Sadi Mahdi], that Iraq will "play host to the citizens of these aggressive nations as long as Iraq remains threatened with an aggressive war," to be totally unacceptable. He is deeply troubled by the indication that Iraqi authorities intend to relocate these individuals within Iraq against their will. The President is also deeply concerned about today's announcement by the Government of Iraq that foreign nationals may not have access to adequate quantities of food.

The use of innocent civilians as pawns to promote what Iraq sees to be its self-interest is contrary to international law and, indeed, to all accepted norms of international conduct. We urge that Iraq immediately reconsider its refusal to allow any foreign national desiring to leave to do so without delay or condition. We would also hope that Iraq would take note of yesterday's statement by the U.N. Security Council President expressing the Council's concern and anxiety over the situation of foreign nationals in Iraq and Kuwait and calling upon the Secretary-General to take all appropriate steps. The United States intends to consult with other governments with citizens being held in Iraq and Kuwait to determine what additional measures ought to be taken.

Statement by Press Secretary Fitzwater on the Mobilization of United States Reserves

August 22, 1990

The President today authorized the Secretary of Defense to call Reserve units of the Armed Forces to active duty. The order permits the Secretary of Defense to call to duty selected members and units of the Reserve components of the Army, Navy, Air Force, and Marine Corps as needed to support United States and multinational operations now underway. The President signed the order after the Secretary of Defense advised him that the effective conduct of military operations in and around the Arabian Peninsula may require augmentation of Active components of the Armed Forces. The actual number of Reserve personnel to be called to active duty will depend upon the operational needs of the Armed Forces, but at this time, we do not anticipate approaching the full 200,000 authority provided by law.

The Total Force Policy, which was established in 1973, allocates various military capabilities among the Active Reserve and National Guard components that together make up the Armed Forces of the United States. Under this policy, the capability to perform certain critical military activities has been concentrated in the Reserve component. Activating reservists to support operations such as those now underway has been a central feature of this approach.

The skills concentrated in the Reserve component include airlift, food and water handling, surface transportation, cargo handling, medical services, construction, and intelligence. By making judicious use of the President's authorization, the Secretary of Defense will be able to ensure that essential capabilities such as these and others are available to support our operational requirements.

The President issued the order authorizing the Secretary of Defense to call reserve units to active duty in accordance with section 673b of title 10 of the United States Code. The order also authorizes the Secretary of Transportation to call to active duty elements of the Coast Guard Reserve. Another order signed by the President permits the Secretary of Defense greater flexibility in military personnel management actions.

Executive Order 12727 — Ordering the Selected Reserve of the Armed Forces to Active Duty

August 22, 1990

By the authority vested in me as President by the Constitution and the laws of the United States of America, including sections 121 and 673b of title 10 of the United States Code, I hereby determine that it is necessary to augment the active armed forces of the United States for the effective conduct of operational missions in and around the Arabian Peninsula. Further, under the stated authority, I hereby authorize the Secretary of Defense, and the Secretary of Transportation with respect to the Coast Guard when the latter is not operating as a service in the Department of the Navy, to order to active duty units and individual members not assigned to units, of the Selected Reserve....

Statement by Press Secretary Fitzwater on United Nations Authorization of Enforcement of Economic Sanctions Against Iraq

August 25, 1990

The United Nations Security Council passed Resolution 665 calling for enforcement measures to maintain the comprehensive sanctions against Iraq. The unanimous vote further underlines the deep concern of the world community regarding the blatant aggression by Iraq against Kuwait. The resolve of the international community is strong. The vote exhibits the commitment of the world to act effectively to achieve the complete, immediate, and unconditional withdrawal of Iraq from Kuwait. The United States pledges its complete support of the United Nations action.

Excerpt of a Statement by Press Secretary Fitzwater on Soviet President Mikhail Gorbachev's Endorsement of United Nations Economic Sanctions Against Iraq

August 25, 1990

President Gorbachev's statement yesterday supporting the United Nations sanctions was a very important development. We welcome his voice to the world condemnation of the aggression by Saddam Hussein. The United Nations resolution passed last night further strengthens the world resolve to force Iraq out of Kuwait. We are encouraged by the progress of events at the United Nations and by President Gorbachev's strong support.

President Bush's Remarks at a White House Briefing for Members of Congress on the Persian Gulf Crisis

August 28, 1990

...When this administration began, we sought to strengthen the cease-fire between Iran and Iraq and to improve relations with Iraq. We held no illusions about that. We hoped, along with many in the Congress, that Iraqi behavior might be moderated. But even before the current crisis, though, Iraq was moving at odds to our interests and to the interests of many around the world. So, we suspended the provisions of the CCC [Commodity Credit Corporation] agricultural credits, stopped the export of furnaces that had the potential to contribute to Iraq's nuclear capabilities.

You all know the events of the last several weeks. Iraq threatened Kuwait, lied about its intentions, and finally invaded. In 3 days, Iraq had 120,000 troops and 850 tanks in Kuwait, moving south toward the Saudi border. And it was this clear and rapidly escalating threat that led King Fahd of Saudi Arabia to ask for our assistance. We knew that an Iraq that had the most powerful military machine in the Gulf and controlled 20 percent of the world's proven reserves of oil would pose a threat to the Persian Gulf, to the Middle East, and to the entire world. We responded to this quickly, without hesitation. Our objectives were obvious from the start: the immediate, complete, and unconditional withdrawal of all Iraqi forces from Kuwait; the restoration of Kuwait's legitimate government; security and stability of Saudi Arabia and the Persian Gulf; and the protection of American citizens abroad.

Our actions to achieve these objectives have been equally clear. Within hours of the assault the United States moved to freeze Iraq's assets in this country and to protect those of Kuwait. I asked Dick Cheney, Secretary Cheney, to go to Saudi Arabia, Egypt, and Morocco to arrange for military cooperation between us and key Arab States. And I asked Jim Baker, Secretary Baker, to go to Turkey and to Brussels to rally the support of our NATO allies. Both of these missions were extraordinarily successful. The world response to Iraq was a near-unanimous chorus of condemnation.

With great speed, the United Nations Security Council passed five resolutions. These resolutions condemned Iraq's invasion of Kuwait, demanded Iraq's immediate and unconditional withdrawal, and rejected Iraq's annexation of Kuwait. The U.N. has also mandated sanctions against Iraq, those chapter VII sanctions, and endorsed all measures that may be necessary to enforce these sanctions. And the United Nations has demanded that Iraq release all foreign nationals being held against their will without delay.

The United Nations sanctions are in effect and have been working remarkably well, even on a voluntary basis. Iraqi oil no longer flows through pipelines to ports in Turkey and Saudi Arabia. And again, I want to thank both the Saudis and the Turks for their lead role in all of this. And today reports indicate that traffic through Aqaba has come virtually to a halt.

U.S. military forces stand shoulder to shoulder with forces of many Arab and European States to deter and, if need be, defend Saudi Arabia against attack. And U.S. naval forces sail with the navies of many other states to make the sanctions as watertight as possible. This is not, as Saddam Hussein claims, the United States against Iraq. It is truly Iraq against the majority in the Arab world, Iraq against the rest of the world.

And so, the basic elements of our strategy are now in place. And where do we want to go? Well, our intention, and indeed the intention of almost every country in the world, is to persuade Iraq to withdraw, that it cannot benefit from this illegal occupation, that it will pay a stiff price by trying to hold on and an even stiffer price by widening the conflict. And of course, we seek to achieve these goals without further violence. The United States supports the U.N. Secretary-General and other leaders working to promote a peaceful resolution of this crisis on the basis of Security Council Resolution 660.

I also remain deeply concerned about the American and other foreign nationals held hostage by Iraq. As I've said before, when it comes to the safety and well-being of American citizens held against their will, I will hold Baghdad responsible....

President Bush's Letter to Congressional Leaders on the Extension of Active Duty of the Selected Reserve of the Armed Forces

November 13, 1990

...I have today, pursuant to section 673b(I) of title 10, United States Code, authorized the Secretary of Defense, and the Secretary of Transportation with respect to the Coast Guard when it is not operating as a service within the Department of the Navy, to extend for an additional 90 days the period of active duty of units and individual members not assigned to units organized to serve as units of the Selected Reserve ordered to active duty pursuant to section 673b(a) or title 10, United States Code and Executive

Order No. 12727 of August 22, 1990. The continued need for units and members of the Selected Reserve to augment the active Armed Forces of the United States for the effective support and conduct of operational missions in and around the Arabian Peninsula necessitates this action....

President Bush's Letter to Congressional Leaders on the Deployment of Additional United States Armed Forces to the Persian Gulf
November 16, 1990

...There have been a number of important developments in the Persian Gulf region since my letter of August 9, 1990, informing you of the deployment of U.S. Armed Forces in response to Iraq's invasion of Kuwait. In the spirit of consultation and cooperation between our two branches of Government and in the firm belief that working together as we have we can best protect and advance the Nation's interests, I wanted to update you on these developments.

As you are aware, the United States and Allied and other friendly governments have introduced elements of their Armed Forces into the region in response to Iraq's unprovoked and unlawful aggression and at the request of regional governments. In view of Iraq's continued occupation of Kuwait, defiance of 10 U.N. Security Council resolutions demanding unconditional withdrawal, and sustained threat to other friendly countries in the region, I determined that the U.S. deployments begun in August should continue. Accordingly, on November 8, after consultations with our Allies and coalition partners, I announced the continued deployment of U.S. Armed Forces to the Persian Gulf region. These Forces include a heavy U.S. Army Corps and a Marine expeditionary force with an additional brigade. In addition, three aircraft carriers, a battleship, appropriate escort ships, a naval amphibious landing group, and a squadron of maritime prepositioning ships will join other naval units in the area.

I want to emphasize that this deployment is in line with the steady buildup of U.S. Armed Forces in the region over the last 3 months and is a continuation of the deployment described in my letter of August 9. I also want to emphasize that the mission of our Armed Forces has not changed. Our Forces are in the Gulf region in the exercise of our inherent right of individual and collective self-defense against Iraq's aggression and consistent with U.N. Security Council resolutions related to Iraq's ongoing occupation of Kuwait. The United States and other nations continue to seek a peaceful resolution of the crisis. We and our coalition partners share the common goals of achieving the immediate, complete, and unconditional withdrawal of Iraqi forces from Kuwait, the restoration of Kuwait's legitimate government, the protection of the lives of citizens held hostage by Iraq both in Kuwait and Iraq, and the restoration of security and stability in the region. The deployment will ensure that the coalition has an adequate offensive military option should that be necessary to achieve our common goals.

In my letter August 9, I indicated that I did not believe that involvement in hostilities was imminent. Indeed, it was my belief that the deployment would facilitate a peaceful resolution of the crisis. I also stated that our Armed Forces would remain in the Persian Gulf region so long as required to contribute to the security of the region and desired by host governments. My view on these matters has not changed....

OPERATION DESERT STORM

President Bush's Message to Allied Nations on the Persian Gulf Crisis
January 8, 1991

More than 5 months ago, in the early morning hours of August 2d, Iraqi forces rolled south and the rape of Kuwait began. That unprovoked invasion was more than an attack on Kuwait, more than the brutal occupation of a tiny nation that posed no threat to its large and powerful neighbor. It was an assault on the very notion of international order.

My purpose in speaking to you, the people of countries united against this assault, is to share with you my view of the aims and objectives that must guide us in the challenging days ahead. From the center of the crisis in the Middle East, to people and countries on every continent, to the families with loved ones held hostage, to the many millions sure to suffer at the hands of one man with a stranglehold on the world's economic lifeline, Iraq's aggression has caused untold suffering, hardship, and uncertainty.

In the more than 5 months since August 2d, Iraqi troops have carried out a systematic campaign of terror on the people of Kuwait — unspeakable atrocities against men and women and, among the maimed and murdered, even innocent children. In the more than 5 months since August 2d, Iraq's action has imposed economic strains on nations large and small — among them some of the world's newest democracies at the very moment they are most vulnerable. And yet, Iraq's aggression did not go unchallenged.

In the 5 months since August 2d, the world has witnessed the emergence of an unprecedented coalition against aggression. In the United Nations, Iraq's outlaw act has met a chorus of condemnation in 12 resolutions with the overwhelming support of the Security Council. At this moment, forces from 27 nations — rich and poor, Arab and Muslim, European, Asian, African, and American — stand side by side in the Gulf, determined that Saddam's aggression will not stand.

We're now entering the most critical period of this crisis. For the past 5 months, Saddam has held the world and the norms of civilized conduct in contempt. In the next few days, Iraq arrives at a deadline that spells the limit of the civilized world's patience.

Let me be clear about the upcoming deadline. January 15 is not a "date certain" for the onset of armed conflict; it is a deadline for Saddam Hussein to choose, to choose peace over war. The purpose of declaring this deadline was to give Saddam fair warning: Withdraw from Kuwait, without condition and without delay, or — at any time on or after that date — face a coalition ready and willing to employ "all means necessary" to enforce the will of the United Nations.

Every one of us, each day of this crisis, has held out hope for a peaceful solution. Even now, as the deadline draws near, we continue to seek a way to end this crisis without further conflict. And that is why, back on November 30, I offered to have Secretary Baker travel to Baghdad to meet with Saddam Hussein. And that is why, even after Saddam failed to respond, failed to find time to meet on any of the 15 days we put forward, I invited Iraq's Foreign Minister to meet with Secretary Baker in Geneva on January 9th.

In Geneva, we will be guided by the will of the world community — expressed in those 12 U.N. resolutions I mentioned a moment ago. I didn't send Secretary Baker to Geneva to compromise or to offer concessions. This meeting offers Saddam Hussein a chance — possibly the final chance — before the U.N. deadline to resolve by peaceful means the crisis that he has created.

Saddam may seek to split the coalition, to exploit our sincere desire for peace, to secure for himself the spoils of war. He will fail — just as he has failed for more than 5 months. I know that pressures are now building to provide Saddam some means of saving face, or to accept a withdrawal that is less than unconditional. The danger in this course should be clear to all. The price of peace now on Saddam's terms will be paid many times over in greater sacrifice and suffering. Saddam's power will only grow, along with his appetite for more conquest. The next conflict will find him stronger still — perhaps in possession even of nuclear weapons — and far more difficult to defeat. And that is why we simply cannot accept anything less than full compliance with the United Nations dictates: Iraq's complete and unconditional withdrawal from Kuwait.

I began by saying that Iraq's action was more than an attack on one nation — it is an assault on us all, on the international order we all share. We who have witnessed in this past year an end to the long years of cold war and conflict, we who have seen so much positive change, stand now at a critical moment, one that will shape the world we live in for years, even decades, to come.

The key now in meeting this challenge is for this remarkable coalition to remain steadfast and strong. If we remain in the days ahead nations united

against aggression, we will turn back not only the actions of an ambitious dictator; we will, as partners, step forward toward a world of peace....
(Unless otherwise noted, presidential statements and documents that follow encompassing January 1 through May 31, 1991, are quoted from PPP Bush 1991 I: 12-14, 42-44, 47, 52-53, 142-143, 165-166, 168-171, 176, 187-188, 265, 521-522)

President Bush's Letter to Congressional Leaders on the Persian Gulf Crisis
January 8, 1991

...The current situation in the Persian Gulf, brought about by Iraq's unprovoked invasion and subsequent brutal occupation of Kuwait, threatens vital U.S. interests. The situation also threatens the peace. It would, however, greatly enhance the chances for peace if Congress were now to go on record supporting the position adopted by the UN Security Council on twelve separate occasions. Such an action would underline that the United States stands with the international community and on the side of law and decency; it also would help dispel any belief that may exist in the minds of Iraq's leaders that the United States lacks the necessary unity to act decisively in response to Iraq's continued aggression against Kuwait. Secretary of State Baker is meeting with Iraq's Foreign Minister on January 9. It would have been most constructive if he could have presented the Iraqi government a Resolution passed by both houses of Congress supporting the UN position and in particular Security Council Resolution 618. As you know, I have frequently stated my desire for such a Resolution. Nevertheless, there is still opportunity for Congress to act to strengthen the prospects for peace and safeguard this country's vital interests.

I therefore request that the House of Representatives and the Senate adopt a Resolution stating that Congress supports the use of all necessary means to implement UN Security Council Resolution 678. Such action would send the clearest possible message to Saddam Hussein that he must withdraw without condition or delay from Kuwait. Anything less would only encourage Iraqi intransigence; anything else would risk detracting from the international coalition arrayed against Iraq's aggression....

Public Law 102-1: Joint Resolution to authorize the use of United States Armed Forces pursuant to United Nations Security Council Resolution 678
January 14, 1991

...Whereas the Government of Iraq without provocation invaded and occupied the territory of Kuwait on August 2, 1990;

Whereas both the House of Representatives (in H.J. Res. 658 of the 101st Congress) and the Senate (in S. Con. Res. 147 of the 101st. Congress) have condemned Iraq's invasion of Kuwait and declared their support for international action to reverse Iraq's aggression;

Whereas, Iraq's conventional, chemical, biological, and nuclear weapons and ballistic missile programs and its demonstrated willingness to use weapons of mass destruction pose a grave threat to world peace;

Whereas the international community has demanded that Iraq withdraw unconditionally and immediately from Kuwait and that Kuwait's independence and legitimate government be restored;

Whereas the United Nations Security Council repeatedly affirmed the inherent right of individual or collective self-defense in response to the armed attack by Iraq against Kuwait in accordance with Article 51 of the United Nations Charter;

Whereas, in the absence of full compliance by Iraq with its resolutions, the United Nations Security Council in Resolution 678 has authorized member states of the United Nations to use all necessary means, after January 15, 1991, to uphold and implement all relevant Security Council resolutions and to restore international peace and security in the area; and

Whereas Iraq has persisted in its illegal occupation of, and brutal aggression against Kuwait: Now, therefore, be it

Resolved by the Senate and House of Representatives of the United States of America in Congress assembled....

SEC. 2. AUTHORIZATION FOR USE OF UNITED STATES ARMED FORCES

(a) AUTHORIZATION. — The President is authorized, subject to subsection (b), to use United States Armed Forces pursuant to United Nations Security Council Resolution 678 (1990) in order to achieve implementation of Security Council Resolutions 660, 661 662, 664, 665, 666, 667, 669, 670, 674, and 677.

(b) REQUIREMENT FOR DETERMINATION THAT USE OF MILITARY FORCE IS NECESSARY. — Before exercising the authority granted in subsection (a), the President shall make available to the Speaker of the House of Representatives and the President pro tempore of the Senate his determination that —

(1) the United States has used all appropriate diplomatic and other peaceful means to obtain compliance by Iraq with the United Nations Security Council resolutions cited in subsection (a); and

(2) that those efforts have not been and would not be successful in obtaining such compliance.

(C) WAR POWERS RESOLUTION REQUIREMENTS. —

(1) SPECIFIC STATUTORY AUTHORIZATION. — Consistent with section 8(a)(1) of the War Powers Resolution, the Congress declares that this

section is intended to constitute specific statutory authorization within the meaning of section 5(b) of the War Powers Resolution.

(2) APPLICABILITY OF OTHER REQUIREMENTS. — Nothing in this resolution supersedes any requirement of the War Powers Resolution.

SEC. 3. REPORTS TO CONGRESS

At least once every 60 days, the President shall submit to the Congress a summary on the status of efforts to obtain compliance by Iraq with the resolutions adopted by the United Nations Security Council in response to Iraq's aggression....

(USS, 1991, Volume 105, Part 1)

Statement by Press Secretary Fitzwater Confirming Iraqi Missile Attacks on Israel and Saudi Arabia

January 17, 1991

The Department of Defense has confirmed the firing of missiles from Iraq into Israel and Saudi Arabia. Damage assessments are being made.

President Bush was informed of this action by NSC [National Security Council] adviser Brent Scowcroft earlier this evening. The President has also discussed this matter with Secretary of State Baker and Secretary of Defense Cheney. The President is outraged at, and condemns, this further aggression by Iraq.

Coalition forces in the Gulf are attacking missile sites and other targets in Iraq.

Statement by Press Secretary Fitzwater on United States Response to Iraqi Missile Attacks on Israel

January 17, 1991

The United States has been in touch with the Government of Israel to express its outrage over the missile attacks by Iraq. Secretary Baker discussed the matter with Prime Minister Shamir by telephone from the White House tonight. The Secretary assured the Prime Minister that the United States is continuing its efforts to eliminate this threat.

The United States expects to remain in close consultation with Israel on this issue. The U.S. has also been in contact with its coalition partners....

President Bush's Letter to Congressional Leaders on the Persian Gulf Conflict

January 18, 1991

...On January 16, 1991, I made available to you, consistent with section 2(b) of the Authorization for Use of Military Force Against Iraq Resolution

(H.J. Res. 77, Public Law 102-1), my determination that appropriate diplomatic and other peaceful means had not and would not compel Iraq to withdraw unconditionally from Kuwait and meet the other requirements of the U.N. Security Council and the world community. With great reluctance, I concluded, as did the other coalition leaders, that only the use of armed force would achieve an Iraqi withdrawal together with the other U.N. goals of restoring Kuwait's legitimate government, protecting the lives of our citizens, and reestablishing security and stability in the Persian Gulf region. Consistent with the War Powers Resolution, I now inform you that pursuant to my authority as Commander in Chief, I directed U.S. Armed Forces to commence combat operations on January 16, 1991, against Iraqi forces and military targets in Iraq and Kuwait. The Armed Forces of Saudi Arabia, Kuwait, the United Kingdom, France, Italy, and Canada are participating as well.

Military actions are being conducted with great intensity. They have been carefully planned to accomplish our goals with the minimum loss of life among coalition military forces and the civilian inhabitants of the area. Initial reports indicate that our forces have performed magnificently. Nevertheless, it is impossible to know at this time either the duration of active combat operations or the scope or duration of the deployment of U.S. Armed Forces necessary fully to accomplish our goals.

The operations of U.S. and other coalition forces are contemplated by the resolutions of the U.N. Security Council, as well as H.J. Res. 77, adopted by Congress on January 12, 1991. They are designed to ensure that the mandates of the United Nations and the common goals of our coalition partners are achieved and the safety of our citizens and forces is ensured....

President Bush's Letter to Congressional Leaders on the Activation of the Ready Reserve

January 18, 1991

...I have today, pursuant to section 673 of title 10, United States Code, authorized the Secretaries of the Army, Navy, and Air Force, and the Secretary of Transportation with respect to the Coast Guard when it is not operating as a service within the Department of the Navy, to order to active duty units and individual members not assigned to units of the Ready Reserve. The continued deployment of United States forces in and around the Arabian Peninsula necessitates this action....

Statement by Press Secretary Fitzwater on Allied Bombing in Baghdad
January 18, 1991

Last night, coalition forces bombed a military command and control center in Baghdad that, according to press reports, resulted in a number of civilian casualties.

The loss of civilian lives in time of war is a truly tragic consequence. It saddens everyone to know that innocent people may have died in the course of military conflict. America treats human life as our most precious value. That is why even during this military conflict in which the lives of our service men and women are at risk, we will not target civilian facilities. We will continue to hit only military targets. The bunker that was attacked last night was a military target, a command and control center that fed instructions directly to the Iraqi war machine, painted and camouflaged to avoid detection and well documented as a military target. We have been systematically attacking these targets since the war began.

We don't know why civilians were at this location, but we do know that Saddam Hussein does not share our value in the sanctity of life. Indeed, he time and again has shown a willingness to sacrifice civilian lives and property that further his war aims. Civilian hostages were moved in November and December to military sites for use as human shields. POW's reportedly have been placed at military sites. Roving bands of execution squads search out deserters among his own ranks of servicemen. Command and control centers in Iraq have been placed on top of schools and public buildings. Tanks and other artillery have been placed beside private homes and small villages. And only this morning we have documentation that two MIG 21's have been parked near the front door of a treasured archaeologic site which dates back to the 27th century B.C.

His environmental terrorism spreads throughout the Persian Gulf, killing wildlife and threatening human water supplies. And finally, Saddam Hussein aims his Scud missiles at innocent civilians in Israel and Saudi Arabia. He kills civilians intentionally and with purpose.

Saddam Hussein created this war. He created the military bunkers. And he can bring the war to an end. We urge him once again to save his people and to comply with the U.N. resolutions....

President Bush's Remarks on the Persian Gulf Conflict
February 22, 1991

...The United States and its coalition allies are committed to enforcing the United Nations resolutions that call for Saddam Hussein to immediately and unconditionally leave Kuwait. In view of the Soviet initiative which, very frankly, we appreciate, we want to set forth this morning the specific criteria that will ensure Saddam Hussein complies with the United Nations mandate.

Within the last 24 hours alone we have heard a defiant, uncompromising address by Saddam Hussein, followed less than 10 hours later by a statement in Moscow that, on the face of it, appears more reasonable. I say "on the face of it" because the statement promised unconditional Iraqi withdrawal from Kuwait, only to set forth a number of conditions. And needless to say, any conditions would be unacceptable to the international coalition and would not be in compliance with the United Nations Security Council Resolution 660's demand for immediate and unconditional withdrawal.

More importantly, and more urgently, we learned this morning that Saddam has now launched a scorched-earth policy against Kuwait, anticipating perhaps that he will now be forced to leave. He is wantonly setting fires to and destroying the oil wells, the oil tanks, the export terminals, and other installations of that small country. Indeed, they're destroying the entire oil production system of Kuwait. At the same time that that Moscow press conference was going on and Iraq's Foreign Minister was talking peace, Saddam Hussein was launching Scud missiles.

After examining the Moscow statement and discussing it with my senior advisers here late last evening and this morning, and after extensive consultation with our coalition partners, I have decided that the time has come to make public with specificity just exactly what is required of Iraq if a ground war is to be avoided.

Most important, the coalition will give Saddam Hussein until noon Saturday to do what he must do: begin his immediate and unconditional withdrawal from Kuwait. We must hear publicly and authoritatively his acceptance of these terms. The statement to be released, as you will see, does just this and informs Saddam Hussein that he risks subjecting the Iraqi people to further hardship unless the Iraqi Government complies fully with the terms of the statement....

Statement by Press Secretary Fitzwater on the Persian Gulf Conflict
February 22, 1991

...Full compliance with the Security Council resolutions has been a consistent and necessary demand of the international community. The world must make sure that Iraq has, in fact, renounced its claim to Kuwait and accepted all relevant U.N. Security Council resolutions.

Indeed, only the Security Council can agree to lift sanctions against Iraq, and the world needs to be assured in concrete terms of Iraq's peaceful intentions before such action can be taken. In a situation where sanctions have been lifted, Saddam Hussein could simply revert to using his oil resources once again, not to provide for the well-being of his people but instead to rearm.

So, in a final effort to obtain Iraqi compliance with the will of the international community, the United States, after consulting with the Government of Kuwait and her other coalition partners, declares that a ground campaign will not be initiated against Iraqi forces if, prior to noon Saturday, February 23, New York time, Iraq publicly accepts the following terms and authoritatively communicates that acceptance to the United Nations:

First, Iraq must begin large-scale withdrawal from Kuwait by noon New York time, Saturday, February 23. Iraq must complete military withdrawal from Kuwait in 1 week. Given the fact that Iraq invaded and occupied Kuwait in a matter of hours, anything longer than this from the initiation of the withdrawal would not meet Resolution 660's requirement of immediacy.

Within the first 48 hours, Iraq must remove all its forces from Kuwait City and allow for the prompt return of the legitimate government of Kuwait. It must withdraw from all prepared defenses along the Saudi-Kuwait and Saudi-Iraq borders, from Bubiyan and Warbah Islands, and from Kuwait's Rumaylah oilfield within the 1 week specified above. Iraq must return all its forces to their positions of August 1st, in accordance with Resolution 660.

In cooperation with the International Red Cross, Iraq must release all prisoners of war and third country civilians being held against their will and return the remains of killed and deceased servicemen. This action must commence immediately with the initiation of the withdrawal and must be completed within 48 hours.

Iraq must remove all explosives or booby traps, including those on Kuwaiti oil installations, and designate Iraqi military liaison officers to work with Kuwaiti and other coalition forces on the operational details related to Iraq's withdrawal, to include the provision of all data on the location and nature of any land or sea mines.

Iraq must cease combat aircraft flights over Iraq and Kuwait except for transport aircraft carrying troops out of Kuwait, and allow coalition aircraft exclusive control over and use of all Kuwaiti airspace.

It must cease all destructive actions against Kuwaiti citizens and property and release all Kuwaiti detainees.

The United States and its coalition partners reiterate that their forces will not attack retreating Iraqi forces and, further, will exercise restraint so long as withdrawal proceeds in accordance with the above guidelines and there are no attacks on other countries.

Any breach of these terms will bring an instant and sharp response from coalition forces in accordance with United Nations Security Council Resolution 678....

Statement by Press Secretary Fitzwater on the Persian Gulf Conflict
February 23, 1991

CENTCOM reports that they have detected no military activity which would indicate any withdrawal of Saddam Hussein from Kuwait. Similarly, there has been no communication between Iraq and the United Nations that would suggest a willingness to withdraw under the conditions of the coalition plan. Iraq continues its scorched earth policy in Kuwait, setting fire to oil facilities. It's a continuing outrage that Saddam Hussein is still intent upon destroying the environment of the Gulf, and still intent upon inflicting the most brutal kind of rule on his own population, yet appears to have no intention of complying with the U.N. resolutions. Indeed, his only response at noon was to launch another Scud missile attack on Israel.

The coalition forces have no alternative but to continue to prosecute the war.

As we indicated last night, the withdrawal proposal the Soviets discussed with Tariq 'Aziz in Moscow was unacceptable because it did not constitute an unequivocal commitment to an immediate and unconditional withdrawal. Thus, the Iraqi approval of the Soviet proposal is without effect....

Statement by Press Secretary Fitzwater on the Persian Gulf Conflict
February 23, 1991

We regret that Saddam Hussein took no action before the noon deadline to comply with the United Nations resolutions. We remain determined to fulfill the U.N. resolutions. Military action continues on schedule and according to plan.

President Bush's Address to the Nation Announcing Allied Military Ground Action in the Persian Gulf
February 23, 1991

...Yesterday, after conferring with my senior national security advisers, and following extensive consultations with our coalition partners, Saddam Hussein was given one last chance — set forth in very explicit terms — to do what he should have done more than 6 months ago: withdraw from Kuwait without condition or further delay, and comply fully with the resolutions passed by the United Nations Security Council.

Regrettably, the noon deadline passed without the agreement of the Government of Iraq to meet demands of United Nations Security Council Resolution 660, as set forth in the specific terms spelled out by the coalition to withdraw unconditionally from Kuwait. To the contrary, what we have seen is a redoubling of Saddam Hussein's efforts to destroy completely Kuwait and its people.

I have therefore directed General Norman Schwarzkopf, in conjunction with coalition forces, to use all forces available including ground forces to eject the Iraqi army from Kuwait. Once again, this was a decision made only after extensive consultations within our coalition partnership.

The liberation of Kuwait has now entered a final phase. I have complete confidence in the ability of the coalition forces swiftly and decisively to accomplish their mission....

President Bush's Address to the Nation on the Suspension of Allied Offensive Combat Operations in the Persian Gulf
February 27, 1991

Kuwait is liberated. Iraq's army is defeated. Our military objectives are met. Kuwait is once more in the hands of Kuwaitis, in control of their own destiny. We share in their joy, a joy tempered only by our compassion for their ordeal.

Tonight the Kuwaiti flag once again flies above the capital of a free and sovereign nation. And the American flag flies above our Embassy.

Seven months ago, America and the world drew a line in the sand. We declared that the aggression against Kuwait would not stand. And tonight, America and the world have kept their word.

This is not a time of euphoria, certainly not a time to gloat. But it is a time of pride: pride in our troops; pride in the friends who stood with us in the crisis; pride in our nation and the people whose strength and resolve made victory quick, decisive, and just. And soon we will open wide our arms to welcome back home to America our magnificent fighting forces.

No one country can claim this victory as its own. It was not only a victory for Kuwait but a victory for all the coalition partners. This is a victory for the United Nations, for all mankind, for the rule of law, and for what is right.

After consulting with Secretary of Defense Cheney, the Chairman of the Joint Chiefs of Staff, General Powell, and our coalition partners, I am pleased to announce that at midnight tonight eastern standard time, exactly 100 hours since ground operations commenced and 6 weeks since the start of Desert Storm, all United States and coalition forces will suspend offensive combat operations. It is up to Iraq whether this suspension on the part of the coalition becomes a permanent cease-fire.

Coalition political and military terms for a formal cease-fire include the following requirements:

Iraq must release immediately all coalition prisoners of war, third country nationals, and the remains of all who have fallen. Iraq must release all Kuwaiti detainees. Iraq also must inform Kuwaiti authorities of the location and nature of all land and sea mines. Iraq must comply fully with all relevant United Nations Security Council resolutions. This includes a rescinding of

Iraq's August decision to annex Kuwait and acceptance in principle of Iraq's responsibility to pay compensation for the loss, damage, and injury its aggression has caused.

The coalition calls upon the Iraqi Government to designate military commanders to meet within 48 hours with their coalition counterparts at a place in the theater of operations to be specified to arrange for military aspects of the cease-fire. Further, I have asked Secretary of State Baker to request that the United Nations Security Council meet to formulate the necessary arrangements for this war to be ended.

This suspension of offensive combat operations is contingent upon Iraq's not firing upon any coalition forces and not launching Scud missiles against any other country. If Iraq violates these terms, coalition forces will be free to resume military operations.

At every opportunity, I have said to the people of Iraq that our quarrel was not with them but instead with their leadership and, above all, with Saddam Hussein. This remains the case. You, the people of Iraq, are not our enemy. We do not seek your destruction. We have treated your POW's with kindness. Coalition forces fought this war only as a last resort and look forward to the day when Iraq is led by people prepared to live in peace with their neighbors.

We must now begin to look beyond victory and war. We must meet the challenge of securing the peace. In the future, as before, we will consult with our coalition partners. We've already done a good deal of thinking and planning for the postwar period, and Secretary Baker has already begun to consult with our coalition partners on the region's challenges. There can be, and will be, no solely American answer to all these challenges. But we can assist and support the countries of the region and be a catalyst for peace. In this spirit, Secretary Baker will go to the region next week to begin a new round of consultations....

Statement by Press Secretary Fitzwater on Iraqi President Saddam Hussein's Use of Force Against the Iraqi People

March 13, 1991

Saddam Hussein has a track record of using his military against his own population. We have received information over the past week that he has been using helicopters in an effort to quell civil disturbances against his regime. We are obviously very concerned about this. President Bush expressed his concern at the news conference. This behavior is clearly inconsistent with the type of behavior the international community would like to see Iraq exhibiting. Iraq has to convince the world that its designs, both against the international community and its own population, are not military and aggressive.

State Department Fact Sheet: UN Security Council Resolution 687 — Cease-fire in the Gulf
April 8, 1991

On April 3, 1991, the UN Security Council passed Resolution 687, which established a formal cease-fire between Iraq and the UN coalition. The vote was 12 for, 1 against (Cuba; with Yemen and Ecuador abstaining). Following is a summary of the resolution.

Resolution 687

- Affirms the 13 previous resolutions on the Gulf conflict.

International Boundary

- Declares the boundary between Iraq and Kuwait and the allocation of islands as that agreed by Iraq and Kuwait in 1963.
- Guarantees the inviolability of that boundary and asks Kuwait and Iraq, with the assistance of the Secretary General, to demarcate the 1963 boundary and report back within 1 month.

Observer Force

- Requests the Secretary General to submit a plan within 3 days for an observer force to monitor a demilitarized zone extending 10 km into Iraq and 5 km into Kuwait and to deploy it immediately after council approval.

Missile Systems and Weapons of Mass Destruction

- Requires Iraq to agree to the destruction or removal of all chemical and biological weapons and all ballistic missiles with a range of greater than 150 kilometers and to identify their locations within 15 days.
- Requests the Secretary General, in coordination with the coalition and the World Health Organization, to submit a plan to the council within 45 days designating a special commission which will inventory chemical and biological items and ballistic missile sites.
- Provides for a special commission, within 46 days following approval of the plan, to oversee destruction of missile systems and launchers and take possession of all chemical and biological weapons-related items/sites.
- Requires Iraq to submit a list of its nuclear weapons or nuclear weapons-usable material or related facilities to the Secretary General within 15 days and place all nuclear weapons usable material under the exclusive control of the International Atomic Energy Agency for custody and removal.

- Requests the Secretary General to carry out immediate on-site inspection of Iraq's nuclear capabilities and develop a plan for their destruction within 45 days.
- Requires Iraq to declare that it will not acquire or develop chemical, biological, and nuclear weapons or ballistic missiles in the future. The special commission will develop a plan for on-going monitoring and verification of Iraqi compliance.

Compensation

- Reaffirms Iraqi liability for direct losses, including environmental damage, and creates a commission and fund to handle compensation.
- Directs the Secretary General to present a plan to the council within 30 days for administering the fund.
- Decides that a percentage of Iraqi oil revenues will go to the fund.
- Immediately lifts sanctions on food (With notification to the Sanctions Committee) and supplies for essential civilian needs (with Sanctions Committee approval) and provides for council review of remaining import sanctions every 60 days, taking account of Iraqi policies and practices.
- Indicates all sanctions on Iraqi exports will be lifted when Iraq agrees to the destruction of its weapons of mass destruction and missiles, provides their locations to the Special Commission, and agrees not to acquire or develop them in the future, and when the Security Council approves the Secretary General's plan for the compensation fund.
- Institutes an embargo on conventional armaments; weapons of mass destruction; missiles; licensing and technology transfer, personnel or materials for training, technical support, or maintenance. The council will review the embargo on conventional weapons periodically.
- Calls on states to institute controls to ensure compliance with the embargo.

Kuwaiti Property and Detainees

- Provides for return of Kuwaiti property and confirms Iraqi responsibility to repatriate and account for all Kuwaiti and third country nationals in coordination with the International Committee of the Red Cross.

Terrorism

- Requires a commitment from Iraq that it will not commit or support acts of terrorism or terrorist organizations.

Cease-fire

- Declares a cease-fire will go into effect upon formal Iraqi acceptance of the provisions of the resolution.

(DSD, April 8, 1991: 236-239)

President Bush's Letter to Congressional Leaders on the Situation in the Persian Gulf

May 17, 1991

...On March 19, 1991, I reported to you consistent with the Authorization for Use of Military Force Against Iraq Resolution (Public Law 102-1), on the successful conduct of military operations aimed at the liberation of Kuwait. Since that time, the United Nations Security Council has adopted Resolution 687, which set forth the preconditions for a formal cease-fire. Iraq has accepted those terms, and the cease-fire and withdrawal of coalition forces from southern Iraq have been concluded. The Iraqi repression of the Kurdish people has, however, necessitated a limited introduction of U.S. forces into northern Iraq for emergency relief purposes. I am reporting these matters to you as part of our continuing effort to keep the Congress fully informed on these developments.

Resolution 687 required, as a precondition for a formal cease-fire, that Iraq officially notify the United Nations of its acceptance of the provisions of the resolution. These provisions included: (1) respect for the international boundary as agreed between Iraq and Kuwait in 1963, which the Security Council guaranteed; (2) the creation of a demilitarized zone along the Iraq Kuwait border and the deployment of a U.N. observer unit into that zone; (3) the destruction, removal, or rendering harmless of all chemical and biological weapons, ballistic missiles with a range greater than 150 kilometers, and nuclear-weapons-usable material, together with facilities related to them, and international supervision and inspection to verify compliance; (4) the creation of a fund, drawn from future Iraqi oil revenues, to pay compensation for losses caused by the Iraqi invasion and occupation of Kuwait; (5) the continuation of the embargo of all exports of arms to Iraq; (6) the phased relaxation of certain other aspects of the U.N. sanctions against Iraq as Iraq complies with its obligations under the resolution; and (7) the renunciation by Iraq of support for international terrorism.

Iraq offcially accepted those terms on April 6, and a formal cease-fire has gone into effect. Accordingly, United States Armed Forces deployed in southern Iraq began withdrawing as U.N. peacekeeping personnel deployed into the zone, and this withdrawal was completed on May 9. The United States has been assisting the U.N. Secretary General in his efforts to implement the other provisions of Resolution 687, particularly with respect to boundary demarcation, compensation, and weapons of mass destruction.

During this same period, however, Iraqi forces engaged in a campaign of brutal repression of internal opposition, with the result that many hundreds of thousands of civilians left their homes in search of safety in the regions along the Turkish and Iranian borders. In response to this situation, on April 5 the Security Council adopted Resolution 688, which insisted that Iraq cease its repression and allow immediate access by international humanitarian organizations, and appealed to all Member States to assist in these humanitarian relief efforts.

I immediately ordered United States Armed Forces to begin air-dropping large amounts of food and other essential items to these refugees. However, it soon became clear that even this massive effort would not be enough to deal with the desperate plight of the hundreds of thousands of men, women, and children stranded and suffering in these mountainous areas. Accordingly, on April 16 I directed United States Armed Forces to begin to establish immediately several temporary encampments in northern Iraq where geographical conditions would be more suitable for relief efforts. United States, British, and French forces are providing security for these encampments.

This effort is not intended as a permanent solution to the plight of the Iraqi Kurds. It is a humanitarian measure designed to save lives, consistent with Resolution 688. It is also not an attempt to intervene militarily into the internal affairs of Iraq or to impair its territorial integrity. We intend to turn over the administration and security for these temporary sites as soon as possible to the United Nations (a process that has already begun), and to complete our total withdrawal from Iraq. Our long term objective remains the same: for Iraqi Kurds, and indeed for all Iraqi refugees and displaced persons, to return home and to live in peace, free from repression....

SADDAM HUSSEIN LINGERS

Statement by Press Secretary Fitzwater on Iraq
September 18, 1991

Under U.N. Security Council Resolutions 687 and 707, Iraq is obligated to eliminate its weapons of mass destruction and its ballistic missile capabilities. Iraq is also required to permit U.N. Special Commission and International Atomic Energy Agency inspection teams to verify Iraqi compliance.

In order to fulfill its inspection responsibilities, the U.N. Special Commission needs to be able to use its helicopters and other aircraft over Iraq. Iraq has refused to allow U.N. helicopters to operate unimpeded in Iraq. This is a clear violation of U.N. Security Council Resolution 707, which permits the use of helicopters without condition. The United States and other members of the U.N. Security Council have therefore been discussing the most appropriate means to continue inspections in Iraq.

Consistent with those discussions, military planners have examined options to provide helicopters and support necessary to continue U.N. inspections. But there has been no decision to deploy these U.S. forces, nor will such a decision be required if Iraq complies with the provisions of U.N. Resolutions 687 and 707.

In the meantime, the Government of Saudi Arabia has requested deployment of U.S. Patriot units to the Kingdom as a deterrent against the continuing Iraqi missile threat. The United States has granted the request for this purely defensive system in light of the current Iraqi threat and continued Iraqi noncompliance with U.N. Security Council resolutions.

Iraq continues to employ concealment and deception to evade U.N. Special Commission inspection teams and thus to preserve a residual capability to produce and deploy these weapons illegally. We believe Iraq still possesses several hundred Scud missiles of the type used against Saudi Arabia during the Gulf war.
(PPP Bush 1991 II: 1178)

Statement by Press Secretary Fitzwater on Free Elections in Kuwait
October 7, 1992

The President is pleased to note that this week Kuwait held free parliamentary elections. The United States has been a strong supporter of this process since the Amir's decision to hold elections was announced during the Iraqi occupation. We have also been encouraged by the statement by the Crown Prince that the Kuwaiti Government will soon propose legislation to amend the constitution to broaden the electorate and specifically to give women the right to vote in future elections. The Amir and the Kuwaiti people are to be congratulated on this latest stage in Kuwait's progress toward full recovery and reconstruction.

These elections reaffirm Kuwait's hard won independence and the freedoms enjoyed by the Kuwaiti people, in sharp contrast to the agony the Iraqi people still endure from Saddam. The gulf between Kuwait's determination to begin a democratic process and Saddam's brutalities against the Iraqi people is a vivid reminder of why the coalition had no choice but to use force to liberate Kuwait. The United States remains committed both to supporting Kuwait in its physical and political reconstruction and to support the efforts of the Iraqi opposition toward building a democratic future for the people of Iraq.
(PPP Bush 1992-1993 II: 1772)

President Clinton's Letter to Congressional Leaders on the Strike on Iraqi Intelligence Headquarters

June 28, 1993

...Commencing at approximately 4:22 p.m. (EST) on June 26, 1993, at my direction, U.S. naval forces launched a Tomahawk cruise missile strike on the Iraqi Intelligence Service's (IIS) principal command and control complex in Baghdad. This facility is the headquarters for the IIS, which planned the failed attempt to assassinate former President Bush during his visit to Kuwait in April of this year. This U.S. military action was completed upon impact of the missiles on target at approximately 6 p.m. (EST).

Operating under the United States Central Command, two U.S. Navy surface ships launched a total of 23 precision-guided Tomahawk missiles in this coordinated strike upon the key facilities in the IIS compound. The USS PETERSON (DD 969) launched 14 missiles from its position in the Red Sea, while the USS CHANCELLORSVILLE (CG 62) in the Arabian Gulf launched nine missiles. The timing of this operation, with missiles striking at approximately 2:00 a.m. local Iraqi time, was chosen carefully so as to minimize risks to innocent civilians. Initial reports indicate that heavy damage was inflicted on the complex. Regrettably, there were some collateral civilian casualties.

I ordered this military response only after I considered the results of a thorough and independent investigation by U.S. intelligence and law enforcement agencies. The reports by Attorney General Reno and Director of Central Intelligence Woolsey provided compelling evidence that the operation that threatened the life of President Bush in Kuwait City in April was directed and pursued by the Iraqi Intelligence Service and that the Government of Iraq bore direct responsibility for this effort.

The Government of Iraq acted unlawfully in attempting to carry out Saddam Hussein's threats against former President Bush because of actions he took as President. The evidence of the Government of Iraq's violence and terrorism demonstrates that Iraq poses a continuing threat to United States nationals and shows utter disregard for the will of the international community as expressed in Security Council Resolutions and the United Nations Charter. Based on the Government of Iraq's pattern of disregard for international law, I concluded that there was no reasonable prospect that new diplomatic initiatives or economic measures could influence the current Government of Iraq to cease planning future attacks against the United States.

Consequently, in the exercise of our inherent right of self-defense as recognized in Article 51 of the United Nations Charter and pursuant to my constitutional authority with respect to the conduct of foreign relations and as Commander in Chief, I ordered a military strike that directly targeted a facility Iraqi intelligence implicated in the plot against the former Chief Executive. In accordance with Article 51 of the United Nations Charter, this action was reported immediately to the Security Council on June 26. On June

27, Ambassador Albright provided evidence of Iraq's assassination attempts to the United Nations Security Council, which had been convened in emergency session at our request.

I am certain that you share my sincere hope that the limited and proportionate action taken by the United States Government will frustrate and help deter and preempt future unlawful actions on the part of the Government of Iraq. Nonetheless, in the event that Iraqi violence, aggression, or state-sponsored terrorism against the United States continues, I will direct such additional measures in our exercise of the right of self-defense as may he necessary and appropriate to protect United States citizens....
(WCPD Clinton 1993: 1183)

President Clinton's Letter to Congressional Leaders on Iraq
August 5, 1994

...The International Atomic Energy Agency (IAEA) has effectively disbanded the Iraqi nuclear weapons program at least for the near term. The United Nations has destroyed Iraqi missile launchers, support facilities, and a good deal of Iraq's indigenous capability to manufacture prohibited missiles. U.N. Special Commission on Iraq (UNSCOM) teams have reduced Iraq's ability to produce chemical weapons.

Notably, UNSCOM's Chemical Destruction Group (CDG) concluded its activities on June 14 after establishing an excellent record of destroying Iraq's stocks of chemical munitions, agents, precursor chemicals, and equipment procured for chemical weapons production. With as many as 12 nations participating at any one time, the CDG destroyed over 480,000 liters of chemical warfare agents, over 28,000 chemical munitions, and over 1,040,000 kilograms and 648 barrels of some 45 different precursor chemicals for the production of chemical warfare agents.

Significant gaps in accounting for Iraq's weapons of mass destruction (WMD) programs remain, however. This is particularly true in the biological weapons area. Due to Iraq's insistence that the relevant documentation on its past programs has been destroyed, UNSCOM has had to resort to other, more time-consuming procedures to fill in the gaps.

The United Nations is now preparing a long-term monitoring regime for Iraq as required by U.N. Security Council Resolution (UNSCR) 715. This program must be carefully designed if it is to be so thorough that Iraq cannot rebuild a covert program, as it did before the Gulf War, when it claimed to be in compliance with the Nonproliferation Treaty. Continued vigilance is necessary because we believe that Saddam Hussein is committed to rebuilding his WMD capability once sanctions are lifted.

It is, therefore, extremely important that this monitoring regime be effective, comprehensive, and sustainable. A program of this magnitude is unprecedented and will require continued, substantial assistance for UNSCOM from supporting nations. Rigorous and extensive trial and field testing will be required before UNSCOM can judge the program's effectiveness. The Secretary General's report of June 24 has detailed those areas where work remains to be done.

Rolf Ekeus, the Chairman of UNSCOM, has told Iraq that it must establish a clear track record of compliance before he can report favorably to the Security Council. Chairman Ekeus has said he expects to be able to report by September on the start-up of the long-term monitoring program. We strongly endorse Chairman Ekeus' approach and reject any attempt to limit UNSCOM's flexibility by the establishment of a timetable for determining whether Iraq has complied with UNSCR 715. We insist on a sustained period of complete and unquestionable compliance with the monitoring and verification plans.

The "no-fly zones" over northern and southern Iraq permit the monitoring of Iraq's compliance with UNSCRs 687 and 688. Over the last 3 years, the northern no-fly zone has deterred Iraq from a major military offensive in the region. Tragically, on April 14, 1994, two American helicopters in the no-fly zone were shot down by U.S. fighter aircraft causing 26 casualties. The Department of Defense has completed and made public the unclassified portions of the investigation into the circumstances surrounding this incident.

In southern Iraq, the no-fly zone has stopped Iraq's use of aircraft against its population. However, Iraqi forces still wage a land-based campaign in the marshes, and the shelling of marsh villages continues.

In the spring of 1994, the Iraqi military intensified its campaign to destroy the southern marshes, launching a large search-and-destroy operation. The operation has included the razing of villages concentrated in the triangle bounded by An Nasiriya, Al Qurnah, and Basrah. Iraqi government engineers are draining the marshes of the region while the Iraqi Army is systematically burning thousands of dwellings to ensure that the marsh inhabitants are unable to return to their ancestral homes. The population of the region, whose marsh culture has remained essentially unchanged since 3500 B.C., has in the last few years been reduced by an estimated three-quarters.

As a result of the "browning" of the marshes, civilian inhabitants continue to flee toward Iran, as well as deeper into the remaining marshes. This campaign is a clear violation of UNSCR 688. In northern Iraq, in the vicinity of Mosul, we continue to watch Iraqi troop movements carefully. Iraq's intentions remain unclear.

Iraq still refuses to recognize Kuwait's sovereignty and the inviolability of the U.N. demarcated border, which was reaffirmed by the Security Council in UNSCRs 773 and 833. Iraq has not met its obligations concerning Kuwaitis and third-country nationals it detained during the war and has taken no substantive steps to cooperate fully with the International Committee of the

Red Cross (ICRC), as required by UNSCR 687. Indeed, Iraq refused even to attend the ICRC meetings held in July and November 1993 to discuss these issues. While Iraq did attend such a meeting in July 1994, it provided no substantive information on missing individuals. Iraq also has not responded to more than 600 files on missing individuals. We continue to press for Iraqi compliance and regard Iraq's actions on these issues as essential to the resolution of conflict in the region.

The Special Rapporteur of the U.N. Commission on Human Rights (UNHRC), Max van der Stoel, continues to report on the human rights situation in Iraq, particularly the Iraqi military's repression against its civilian populations in the marshes. The Special Rapporteur asserted in this February 1994 report that the Government of Iraq has engaged in war crimes and crimes against humanity, and may have committed violations of the 1948 Genocide Convention. Regarding the Kurds, the Special Rapporteur has judged that the extent and gravity of reported violations place the survival of the Kurds in jeopardy.

The Special Rapporteur has noted that there are essentially no freedoms of opinion, expression, or association in Iraq. Torture is widespread in Iraq and results from a system of state-terror successfully directed at subduing the population. The Special Rapporteur repeated his recommendation for the establishment of human rights monitors strategically located to improve the flow of information and to provide independent verification of reports.

...Examples of Iraqi noncooperation and noncompliance continue in other areas. For instance, reliable reports have indicated that the Government of Iraq is offering reward money for terrorist acts against U.N. and humanitarian relief workers in Iraq. And for 3 years there has been a clear pattern of criminal acts linking the Government of Iraq to a series of assassinations and attacks in northern Iraq on relief workers, U.N. guards, and foreign journalists. Ten persons have been injured and two have been killed in such attacks this year. The offering of bounty for such acts, as well as the commission of such acts, in our view constitute violations of UNSCRs 687 and 688.

...The Iraqi government has refused to sell $1.6 billion in oil, as previously authorized by the Security Council in UNSCRs 706 and 712, to pay for humanitarian goods. Talks between Iraq and the United Nations on implementing these resolutions ended unsuccessfully in October 1993. Iraq could use proceeds from such sales to purchase foodstuffs, medicines, and materials and supplies for essential civilian needs of its population, subject to U.N. monitoring of sales and the equitable distribution of humanitarian supplies (including to its northern provinces). Iraq's refusal to implement UNSCRs 706 and 712 continues to cause needless suffering.

Proceeds from oil sales also would be used to compensate persons injured by Iraq's unlawful invasion and occupation of Kuwait. Of note regarding oil sales, discussions are underway with Turkish officials concerning the possible flushing of Iraqi oil now in the Turkish pipeline that extends from Iraq through Turkey. The flushing is necessary to preserve the pipeline that would then be resealed. The proceeds would be deposited in a U.N. escrow account and used by Turkey to purchase humanitarian goods for Iraq.

The U.N. Compensation Commission (UNCC) has received about 2.4 million claims so far, with another 100,000 expected. The United States Government has now filed a total of 8 sets of individual claims with the Commission, bringing U.S. claims filed to about 3,200 with a total asserted value of over $205 million. One panel of UNCC Commissioners recently submitted its report on the first installment of individual claims for serious personal injury or death. The UNCC Commissioners' report recommended awards for a group of about 670 claimants, of which 11 were U.S. claimants. The Governing Council of the UNCC approved the Panel's recommendations at its session in later May. This summer the first U.S. claimants are expected to receive compensation for their losses. The UNCC Commissioners are expected to finish reviewing by the end of the year all claims filed involving death and serious personal injury.

...With respect to corporate claims, the United States filed two more groups of claims with the UNCC in June. Along with our initial filing in early May, the United States Government has filed a total of approximately $1.4 billion in corporate claims against the Government of Iraq, representing almost 140 business entities. Those claims represented a multitude of enterprises ranging from small family-owned businesses to large multinational corporations.

The United States Government also expects to file five Government claims with the UNCC this August. The five claims are for non-military losses, such as damage to Government property (e.g., the U.S. Embassy compound in Kuwait) and the costs of evacuating U.S. nationals and their families from Kuwait and Iraq. These Government claims have an asserted value of about $17 million. In the future, the United States Government also intends to file one or more additional Government claim(s) involving the costs of monitoring health risks associated with oil well fires and other environmental damage in the Persian Gulf region.
(WCPD Clinton 1994: 1637-1640)

President Clinton's Address to the Nation on Iraq
October 10, 1994

...Three and a half years ago, the men and women of our Armed Forces, under the strong leadership of President Bush, General Powell, and General Schwarzkopf, fought to expel Iraq from Kuwait and to protect our interests in that vital region. Today we remain committed to defending the integrity of that nation and to protecting the stability of the Gulf Region. Saddam Hussein has shown the world before, with his acts of aggression and his weapons of mass destruction, that he cannot be trusted. Iraq's troop movements and threatening statements in recent days are more proof of this. In 1990, Saddam Hussein assembled a force on the border of Kuwait and then invaded. Last week, he moved another force toward the same border. Because of what happened in 1990, this provocation requires a strong response from the United States and the international community.

Over the weekend I ordered the George Washington Carrier Battle Group, cruise missile ships, a Marine expeditionary brigade, and an Army mechanized task force to the Gulf. And today I have ordered the additional deployment of more than 350 Air Force aircraft to the region. We will not allow Saddam Hussein to defy the will of the United States and the international community.

Iraq announced today that it will pull back its troops from the Kuwait border. But we're interested in facts, not promises, in deeds, not words. And we have not yet seen evidence that Iraq's troops are in fact pulling back. We'll be watching very closely to see that they do so.

Our policy is clear: we will not allow Iraq to threaten its neighbors or to intimidate the United Nations as it ensures that Iraq never again possesses weapons of mass destruction. Moreover, the sanctions will be maintained until Iraq complies with all relevant U.N. resolutions. That is the answer to Iraq's sanctions problems: full compliance, not reckless provocation....
(WCPD Clinton 1994: 1986-1988)

8

Nagging Conflicts

INTRODUCTION

The conflict in Bosnia and U.S. actions in Somalia and Haiti mark the future strategic environment for U.S. national security policy. Seldom will conflicts present themselves as clear choices between good and evil, with unambiguous moral choices and U.S. interests clearly defined. Future conflicts will more likely be choices between the lesser of two evils, with U.S. interests ambiguous and no vital interest threatened directly. Such involvements are contrary to the dictates of the "American way of war," which prefers neat categories of right and wrong, and clear indications of national interest.

In Bosnia, there is certainly enough blame to go around. An early, even precipitous, elevation of the Yugoslavian regional boundaries of Slovenia, Croatia, and especially Bosnia-Herzegovina into international borders, despite the fierce opposition of a high percentage of the population, helped plunge the ex-Yugoslavian region into chaos. The U.S. was unwilling to intervene early in the conflict, when it might have made a strategic difference, and the European allies had no united policy themselves.

The conflict itself often assumes the character of a blood feud, and the level of the devastation and personal violence directed against both military personnel and civilian populations on all sides is reminiscent of the Thirty Years' War of 1618-1648. This violence includes artillery barrages, snipers taking deliberate aim at children, mortar attacks on market areas, mass deportations, concentration camps, and destruction of cultural edifices. It is practiced to varying degrees by each side in the conflict. How U.S. forces could operate in such a setting, what their role would be, what a successful outcome might look like, and how U.S. domestic support could be sustained are very difficult to imagine.

The humanitarian intervention in Somalia is an excellent example of the insufficiency of good intentions for sound national security policy. The original objective of averting an early mass starvation was achieved, but U.S.

and United Nations forces became embroiled in political actions and had to be withdrawn without achieving their objective of neutralizing the most powerful warlord in Somalia. Worse, from an American point of view, inadequate Army coordination and planning caused the death of a number of U.S. special operations personnel, and Somalis loyal to the warlord made a public spectacle out of a downed U.S. helicopter containing American dead. As a result, public support for missions mandated by the United Nations is quite low, and it is uncertain if the U.S. public would support U.S. military participation in future missions — especially if control is in UN hands.

The Republic of Haiti is much closer to the U.S., and the U.S. ability to intervene there militarily is high. U.S. interests there are more cultural and philosophical than strategic, although it was felt important to improve the political climate there to stem a growing tide of "boat people" seeking asylum in the United States. A last-minute diplomatic effort by former President Jimmy Carter, former Chairman of the Joint Chiefs of Staff General Colin Powell, and then-Chairman of the Senate Armed Services Committee Senator Sam Nunn paved the way for an unopposed entry of U.S. forces, so an invasion was not necessary. The operation is now under the auspices of the United Nations, and the final resolution is still unclear. The short term gains of a military occupation are easier to achieve than the long term success of nation building, however, and one may safely predict that the difficult part of the mission is just beginning.

These operations will be continuing objects of study by scholars and policy makers seeking to understand the new and highly ambiguous strategic realities.

THE BOSNIAN CONFLICT: U.S. AND WESTERN INACTION

President Bush's Statement on Humanitarian Assistance to Bosnia

October 2, 1992

All Americans, and people of compassion everywhere, remain deeply troubled by the cruel war in Bosnia, and the broader turmoil in what was Yugoslavia. We took several important initiatives in August, and today I am announcing further steps to help ease this conflict.

The United States has been working intensively with other concerned nations to contain the conflict, alleviate the human misery it is causing, and exact a heavy price for aggression. This international effort has produced some results. The recent London conference set up an international mechanism for addressing all aspects of the Yugoslav problem and put in motion all active negotiation. The tenuous truce in Croatia is holding. International observers are on their way to neighboring countries and other parts of the former Yugoslavia to prevent the violence from spreading. The United

Nations trade embargo has idled roughly half the industry of Serbia, whose leader bears heavy responsibility for the aggression in Bosnia. Our demand that the Red Cross be given access to detention camps has begun to yield results, and the release of detainees has now begun. The U.N. resolution we obtained to authorize "all necessary measures" to get relief supplies into Bosnia has led to the creation of a new U.N. force to be deployed for that purpose.

We will continue to honor our pledge to get humanitarian relief to the people of Sarajevo and elsewhere in Bosnia. To this end, I have directed the Secretary of Defense to resume American participation in the Sarajevo airlift tomorrow morning. I wish I could say that there is no risk of attack against these flights, but I cannot, although we are taking precautions. We can be proud of the Americans who, along with courageous personnel from other countries, will go in harm's way to save innocent lives.

Still, the savage violence persists in Bosnia. Despite agreements reached at the London conference, Bosnian cities remain under siege, the movement of humanitarian relief convoys is still hazardous, and innocent civilians continue to be slaughtered. At London, the parties agreed to a ban on all military flights over Bosnia. Yet the bombing of defenseless population centers has actually increased. This flagrant disregard for human life and for a clear agreement requires a response from the international community, and we will take steps to see that the ban is respected.

Now, a new enemy is about to enter the battlefield: winter. Some weeks ago, I asked for an assessment of the effects that the combination of war and winter could inflict on the suffering people of Bosnia. The answer was profoundly disturbing: thousands of innocent people, some uprooted, others trapped, could perish from cold, hunger, and disease. Anticipating this danger, the United States has been working with other nations and with the United Nations to mount a major expansion of the international relief effort and to support the tireless negotiations of U.N. and EC envoys, Cyrus Vance and David Owen, to get the fighting stopped.

I want the American people to know what the United States intends to do to help prevent this dreadful forecast from becoming a tragic reality. I have decided to take a number of further steps:

First, having authorized a resumption of U.S. relief nights into Sarajevo, I am prepared to increase the U.S. share of the airlift.

Second, we will make available air and sea lift to speed the deployment of the new U.N. force needed immediately in Bosnia to protect relief convoys. The United States will also provide a hospital and other critical support for this force.

Third, the United States will furnish $12 million in urgently needed cash to the U.N. High Commissioner for Refugees for the purpose of accelerating preparations for the winter. This is in addition to the $85 million in financial and material support we have already committed.

Fourth, we will offer to the United Nations and the Red Cross help in transporting and caring for those who are being freed from detention camps. We have already provided $6 million for this purpose

Fifth, in cooperation with our friends and allies, we will seek a new U.N. Security Council resolution, with a provision for enforcement, banning all flights in Bosnian airspace except those authorized by the United Nations. If asked by the United Nations, the United States will participate in enforcement measures.

Sixth, we are taking steps in concert with other nations to increase the impact of sanctions on Serbia. I call on the Serbian authorities to cooperate fully with the United Nations and to comply with its resolutions.

Seventh, we have been working with the United Nations, European Community, and our other allies to introduce an international presence into Kosovo. The United States and the international community will continue to monitor the situation closely.

There is no easy solution to the Bosnian conflict, let alone the larger Balkan crisis. So we will persist in our strategy of containing and reducing the violence, making the aggressors pay, and relieving the suffering of victims, all the while lending our full support to the quest for a settlement. History shows that what this troubled region needs is not more violence but peaceful change, and I am confident that the steps I am announcing today will help the innocent victims, strengthen the hand of the negotiators and reinforce the pressures for peace.
(PPP Bush 1992-1993 II: 1738-1739)

President Clinton's Statement Announcing Airdrops Providing Humanitarian Aid to Bosnia-Herzegovina
February 25, 1993

The war that has raged in Bosnia Herzegovina over the past year has taken a staggering toll: Thousands have been killed or imprisoned, thousands more are at risk due to hunger and exposure, and over a million people have been forced from their homes. The humanitarian need is particularly great in eastern Bosnia, where areas have been denied basic food and medicines.

In view of the emergency humanitarian need, I am announcing today that in coordination with the United Nations and UNHCR, the United States will conduct humanitarian airdrops over Bosnia. The airdrops are an extension of the airlift currently underway into Sarajevo. Their purpose is to supplement land convoys. This is a temporary measure designed to address the immediate needs of isolated areas that cannot be reached at this time by ground. Regular overland deliveries are the best means to ensure that the long-term needs of the Bosnian population are met, and the United States calls on the parties to guarantee the safe passage of the humanitarian convoys throughout Bosnia.

The priority for air deliveries will be determined without regard to ethnic or religious affiliation. These airdrops are being carried out strictly for humanitarian purposes; no combat aircraft will be used in this operation. The Department of Defense will be working with the UNHCR to determine the timing and locations for the airdrops.

I am grateful for the considerable international support given to this initiative.

(WCPD Clinton 1993: 318)

President Clinton's Letter to Congressional Leaders Reporting on the No-Fly Zone over Bosnia

April 13, 1993

...Beginning with U.N. Security Council Resolution 713 of September 25, 1991, the United Nations has been actively addressing the crisis in the former Yugoslavia. The Security Council acted in Resolution 781 to establish a ban on all unauthorized military flights over Bosnia-Herzegovina. There have, however, been blatant violations of the ban, and villages in Bosnia have been bombed.

In response to these violations, the Security Council decided, in Resolution 816 of March 31, 1993, to extend the ban to all unauthorized flights over Bosnia-Herzegovina and to authorize Member States, acting nationally or through regional organizations, to take all necessary measures to ensure compliance. NATO's North Atlantic Council (NAC) agreed to provide NATO air enforcement for the no-fly zone. The U.N. Secretary General was notified of NATO's decision to proceed with operation DENY FLIGHT, and an activation order was delivered to participating allies.

The United States actively supported these decisions. At my direction, the Joint Chiefs of Staff sent an execute order to all U.S. forces participating in the NATO force, for the conduct of phased air operations to prevent flights not authorized by the United Nations over Bosnia-Herzegovina. The U.S. forces initially assigned to this operation consist of 13 F-15 and 12 F-18A fighter aircraft and supporting tanker aircraft. These aircraft commenced enforcement operations at 8:00 a.m. e.d.t. on April 12, 1993. The fighter aircraft are equipped for combat to accomplish their mission and for self-defense.

NATO has positioned forces and has established combat air patrol (CAP) stations within the control of Airborne Early Warning (AEW) aircraft. The U.S. CAP aircraft will normally operate from bases in Italy and from an aircraft carrier in the Adriatic Sea. Unauthorized aircraft entering or approaching the no-fly zone will be identified, interrogated, intercepted,

escorted/monitored, and turned away (in that order). If these steps do not result in compliance with the no-fly zone, such aircraft may be engaged on the basis of proper authorization by NATO military authorities and in accordance with the approved rules of engagement, although we do not expect such action will be necessary. The Commander of UNPROFOR (the United Nations Protection Force currently operating in Bosnia-Herzegovina) was consulted to ensure that his concerns for his force were fully considered before the rules of engagement were approved....
(WCPD Clinton 1993: 586)

Executive Order 12846-Additional Measures with Respect to the Federal Republic of Yugoslavia (Serbia and Montenegro)
April 25, 1993

By the authority vested in me as President by the Constitution and the laws of the United States of America, including the International Emergency Economic Powers Act (50 U.S.C. 1701 *et seq.*), the National Emergencies Act (50 U.S.C. 1601 *et seq.*), section 5 of the United Nations Participation Act of 1945, as amended (22 U.S.C. 287c), and section 301 of title 3, United States Code, in view of United Nations Security Council Resolution No. 757 of May 30, 1992, No. 787 of November 16, 1992, and No. 820 of April 17, 1993, and in order to take additional steps with respect to the actions and policies of the Federal Republic of Yugoslavia (Serbia and Montenegro) and the national emergency described and declared in Executive Order No. 12808 and expanded in Executive Order No. 12810 and No. 12831,

I, William J. Clinton, President of the United States of America, hereby order:

Section 1. Notwithstanding the existence of any rights or obligations conferred or imposed by any international agreement or any contract entered into or any license or permit granted before the effective date of this order, except to the extent provided in regulations, orders, directives, or licenses which may hereafter be issued pursuant to this order;

(a) All property and interests in property of all commercial, industrial, or public utility undertakings or entities organized or located in the Federal Republic of Yugoslavia (Serbia and Montenegro), including, without limitation, the property and interests in property of entities (wherever organized or located) owned or controlled by such undertakings or entities, that are in the United States, that hereafter come within the United States, or that are or hereafter come within the possession or control of United States persons, including their overseas branches, are hereby blocked;

(b) All expenses incident to the blocking and maintenance of property blocked under Executive Order Nos. 12808, 12810, 12831 or this order shall be charged to the owners or operators of such property, which expenses shall not be met from blocked funds. Such property may also be sold or liquidated and the proceeds placed in a blocked interest-bearing account in the name of the owner.

(c) All vessels, freight vehicles, rolling stock, aircraft and cargo that are within or hereafter come within the United States and are not subject to blocking under Executive Order Nos. 12808, 12810, 12831 or this order, but which are suspected of a violation of United Nations Security Council Resolution Nos. 713, 757, 787 or 820, shall be detained pending investigation and, upon a determination by the Secretary of the Treasury that they have been in violation of any of these resolutions, shall he blocked. Such blocked conveyances and cargo may also he sold or liquidated and the proceeds placed in a blocked interest-bearing account in the name of the owner;

(d) No vessel registered in the United States or owned or controlled by United States persons, other than a United States naval vessel, may enter the territorial waters of the Federal Republic of Yugoslavia (Serbia and Montenegro); and

(e) Any dealing by a United States person relating to the importation from, exportation to, or transshipment through the United Nations Protected Areas in the Republic of Croatia and those areas of the Republic of Bosnia-Herzegovina under the control of Bosnian Serb forces, or activity of any kind that promotes or is intended to promote such dealing, is prohibited.

Sec. 2. The Secretary of the Treasury, in consultation with the Secretary of State, is hereby authorized to take such actions, including the promulgation of rules and regulations, and to employ all powers granted to the President by the International Emergency Economic Powers Act and the United Nations Participation Act as may be necessary to carry out the purposes of this order. The Secretary of the Treasury may redelegate the authority set forth in this order to other officers and agencies of the Federal Government, all agencies of which are hereby directed to take all appropriate measures within their authority to carry out the provisions of this order, including suspension or termination of licenses or other authorizations in effect as of the date of this order.

Sec. 3. Nothing in this order shall apply to activities related to the United Nations Protection Force, the International Conference on the Former Yugoslavia, and the European Community Monitor Mission.

Sec. 4. The definitions contained in section 5 of Executive Order No. 12810 apply to the terms used in this order.

Sec. 5. Nothing contained in this order shall create any right or benefit, substantive or procedural, enforceable by any party against the United States, its agencies or instrumentalities, its officers or employees, or any other person.

Sec. 6. This order shall not affect the provisions of licenses and authorizations issued pursuant to Executive Order Nos. 12808, 12810, 12831 and in

force on the effective date of this order, except as such licenses or authorization may hereafter be terminated, modified or suspended by the issuing federal agency....
(WCPD Clinton 1993: 685-687)

Presidential Determination 93-20
May 3, 1993

...Pursuant to the authority vested in me by section 610(a) of the Foreign Assistance Act of 1961, as amended (the "Act"), I hereby determine that it is necessary for the purposes of the Act that $5 million of funds made available for section 23 of the Arms Export Control Act for fiscal year 1993 for the cost of direct loans be transferred to, and consolidated with, funds made available for section 551 of the Act.

Pursuant to the authority vested in me by section 614(a)(1) of the Act, I hereby determine that it is important to the security interests of the United States to furnish $5 million for assistance for sanctions enforcement against Serbia and Montenegro without regard to any provision of law within the scope of section 614(a)(1), including section 660 of the Act. I hereby authorize the furnishing of such assistance....
(WCPD Clinton 1993: 743-744)

Presidential Determination 93-22
May 19, 1993

...Pursuant to section 2(c)(1) of the Migration and Refugee Assistance Act of 1962, as amended, 22 U.S.C. 2601(c)(1), I hereby determine that it is important to the national interest that up to $30,000,000 be made available from the U.S. Emergency Refugee and Migration Assistance Fund to meet the urgent and unexpected needs of refugees and conflict victims in Bosnia and Croatia. These funds may be contributed on a multilateral or bilateral basis, as appropriate, to international and nongovernmental organizations....
(WCPD Clinton 1993: 913)

President Clinton's Letter to Senate Leaders on the Conflict in Bosnia
October 20, 1993

...The violent conflict in the former Yugoslavia continues to be a source of deep concern. As you know, my Administration is committed to help stop the bloodshed and implement a fair and enforceable peace agreement, if the parties to the conflict can reach one. I have stated that such enforcement potentially could include American military personnel as part of a NATO operation. I have also specified a number of conditions that would need to be met before our troops would participate in such an operation.

I also have made clear that it would be helpful to have a strong expression of support from the United States Congress prior to the participation of U.S. forces in implementation of a Bosnian peace accord. For that reason, I would welcome and encourage congressional authorization of any military involvement in Bosnia.

The conflict in Bosnia ultimately is a matter for the parties to resolve, but the nations of Europe and the United States have significant interests at stake. For that reason, I am committed to keep our nation engaged in the search for a fair and workable resolution to this tragic conflict....
(WCPD Clinton 1993: 2123)

Remarks at the Bosnian Federation Signing Ceremony
March 18, 1994

...We have come to bear witness to a moment of hope. For 33 months the flames of war have raged through the nations of the former Yugoslavia. By signing these agreements today, Bosnian and Croatian leaders have acted to turn back those flames and to begin the difficult process of reconciliation.

Around the globe the tension between ethnic identity and statehood presents one of the great problems of our time. But nowhere have the consequences been more tragic than in the former Yugoslavia. There nationalists and religious factions aggravated by Serbian aggression, have erupted in a fury of ethnic cleansing and brutal atrocity.

The agreements signed today offer one of the first clear signals that parties to this conflict are willing to end the violence and begin a process of reconstruction. The accords call for a federation between Muslims and Croats of Bosnia. This Muslim-Croat entity has agreed on the principles of a confederation with Croatia. Together these steps can help support the ideal of a multiethnic Bosnia and provide a basis for Muslims and Croats to live again in peace as neighbors and compatriots. The agreements are as important for Croatia's future as they are for Bosnia's. And it is the hope of all present today that the Serbs will join in this process toward peace as well.

These agreements are a testament to the perseverance and to the resolve of many people: the Croatian and Bosnian diplomats who kept probing for openings toward peace; the U.N. soldiers from many nations, here represented today, who have worked to bring both stability and humanitarian supplies; the NATO pilots who have helped put our power in the service of diplomacy....

For while documents like these can define the parameters of peace, the people of the region themselves must create that peace. Economic, political, and security arrangements for the new federation must be given a chance to work. The cease fire between Croats and Bosnian Government forces must hold. Croats and Muslims who have fought with such intensity must now apply that same intensity to restoring habits of tolerance and coexistence.

The issue of the Petrinja region of Croatia must be resolved. Serbia and the Serbs of Bosnia cannot sidestep their own responsibility to achieve an enduring peace.

The new progress toward peace will likely come under attack by demagogues, by rogue riflemen, by all those who believe they can profit most from continued violence, aggression, and human suffering. Such attacks must be met with the same steadiness and leadership that have produced these agreements today. Neither the United States nor the international community can guarantee the success of this initiative. But the U.S. has stood by the parties as they have taken risks for peace, and we will continue to do so. I have told Presidents Izetbegovic and Tudjman that the U.S. is prepared to contribute to the economic reconstruction that will bolster these agreements. And as I have said before, if an acceptable, enforceable settlement can be reached, the U.S. is prepared through NATO to help implement it....
(WCPD Clinton 1994: 558-559)

President Clinton's Letter to the Chairman of the Senate Committee on Armed Services on the Arms Embargo on Bosnia-Herzegovina
August 11, 1994

...I am writing to reaffirm my Administration's support for lifting the international arms embargo on Bosnia and Herzegovina imposed by United Nations Security Council Resolution 713 of September 25, 1991. It has been my long-held view that the arms embargo has unfairly and unintentionally penalized the victim in this conflict and that the Security Council should act to remedy this injustice.

At the same time, I believe lifting the embargo unilaterally would have serious implications going well beyond the conflict in Bosnia itself. It could end the current negotiating process, which is bringing new pressure to bear on the Bosnian Serbs. Our relations with our Western European allies would be seriously strained and the cohesiveness of NATO threatened. Our efforts to build a mature and cooperative relationship with Russia would be damaged. It would also greatly increase American responsibility for the outcome of the conflict. The likelihood of greater U.S. military involvement in Bosnia would be increased, not decreased.

The July 30 Contact Group ministerial was an important step in our strategy of giving negotiations a chance and, at the same time, building an international consensus in support of multilateral action on the arms embargo, should the Bosnian Serbs continue to reject the Contact Group's proposal.

Contact Group unity has been key to the effectiveness of our approach to date, which has brought new pressure to bear on the Bosnian Serbs. This unity will be especially critical as we approach the Contact Group's final option of lifting the arms embargo. As Secretary Christopher made clear in Geneva, we will not allow the process leading to a Security Council decision on the arms embargo to be delayed indefinitely.

In this regard, if by October 15 the Bosnian Serbs have not accepted the Contact Group's proposal, of July 6, 1994, it would be my intention within two weeks to introduce formally and support a resolution at the United Nations Security Council to terminate the arms embargo on Bosnia and Herzegovina. Further, as my Administration has indicated previously, if the Security Council for some reason fails to pass such a resolution within a reasonable period of time, it would be my intention to consult with the Congress thereafter regarding unilateral termination of the arms embargo.... *(WCPD Clinton 1994: 1663-1664)*

President Clinton's Letter to Congressional Leaders on Bosnia-Herzegovina
August 22, 1994

...Since the adoption of United Nations Security Council Resolution 713 on September 25, 1991, the United Nations has actively sought solutions to the humanitarian and ethnic crisis in the former Yugoslavia. Under United Nations Security Council Resolution 824 (May 6, 1993), certain parts of Bosnia-Herzegovina have been established as safe areas. Sarajevo is specifically designated a safe area that should be "free from armed attacks and from any other hostile act."

A mortar attack on Sarajevo on February 4, 1994, caused numerous civilian casualties, including some 68 deaths. The United Nations Secretary General thereafter requested NATO to authorize, at his request, air operations against artillery or mortar positions determined by the United Nations Protection Forces (UNPROFOR) to have been involved in attacks on civilians.

On February 9, 1994, NATO responded to the Secretary General's request by authorizing air operations if needed, using agreed coordination procedures with UNPROFOR. The North Atlantic Treaty Organization's decision set a deadline for the withdrawal of heavy weapons within 20 kilometers of the center of Sarajevo or for the regrouping and placement of such weapons under United Nations control. As of February 21, 1994 all heavy weapons found within the Sarajevo exclusion zone, unless controlled by UNPROFOR, would be subject to NATO air strikes. In response to the NATO ultimatum, heavy weapons were removed from the exclusion zone or placed in collection sites under UNPROFOR control.

On August 5, 1994, Bosnian Serb forces entered an UNPROFOR heavy weapons collection site near the town of Ilidza and removed several heavy

weapons— a tank, two armored personnel carriers, and a 30mm anti-aircraft system. An UNPROFOR helicopter dispatched to monitor the situation was fired upon and was forced to make an emergency landing. UNPROFOR troops were unsuccessful in attempting to regain custody of the weapons. As a result, UNPROFOR requested assistance from NATO forces in finding the weapons so they could be retrieved or destroyed. NATO responded by making various French, Dutch, British, and U.S. aircraft available for air strikes, if necessary. Unable to locate the specific weapons removed from the collection site, UNPROFOR and NATO decided to proceed against other targets in the Sarajevo exclusion zone. Accordingly, on August 5, a U.S. A-10 aircraft strafed a Bosnian Serb M-18 76mm self-propelled antitank gun located inside the exclusion zone. No U.S. personnel were injured or killed nor was U.S. equipment damaged in connection with this action. Later on August 5, the Bosnian Serbs called the UNPROFOR Commander, General Rose, and asked him to call off the attacks. They offered to return the heavy weapons that they had taken from the storage site. General Rose agreed and the weapons were returned to UNPROFOR's control....
(WCPD Clinton 1994: 1699-1700)

Executive Order 12934 — Blocking Property and Additional Measures with Respect to the Bosnian Serb-Controlled Areas of the Republic of Bosnia and Herzegovina
October 25, 1994

...I, William J. Clinton, President of the United States of America, hereby order:

Section 1. Notwithstanding the existence of any rights or obligations conferred or imposed by any international agreement or any contract entered into or any license or permit granted before the effective date of this order, except to the extent provided in regulations, orders, directives, or licenses, which may hereafter be issued pursuant to this order, all property and interests in property of:

(a) the Bosnian Serb military and paramilitary forces and the authorities in those areas of the Republic of Bosnia and Herzegovina under the control of those forces;

(b) any entity, including any commercial, industrial, or public utility undertaking, organized or located in those areas of the Republic of Bosnia and Herzegovina under the control of Bosnian Serb forces;

(c) any entity, wherever organized or located, which is owned or controlled directly or indirectly by any person in, or resident in, those areas of the Republic of Bosnia and Herzegovina under the control of Bosnian Serb forces;

(d) any person acting for or on behalf of any person included within the scope of paragraph (a), (b), or (c) of this section; that are in the United States, that hereafter come within the United States, or that are or hereafter come within the possession or control of United States persons, including their overseas branches, are blocked.

Sec.2. Notwithstanding the existence of any rights or obligations conferred or imposed by any international agreement or any contract entered into or any license or permit granted before the effective date of this order, except to the extent provided in regulations, orders, directives, or licenses, which may hereafter be issued pursuant to this order:

(a) the provision or exportation of services to those areas of the Republic of Bosnia and Herzegovina under the control of Bosnian Serb forces, or to any person for the purpose of any business carried on in those areas, either from the United States or by a United States person, is prohibited; and

(b) No vessel registered in the United States or owned or controlled by a United States person, other than a United States naval vessel, may enter the riverine ports of those areas of the Republic of Bosnia and Herzegovina under the control of Bosnian Serb forces.

Sec. 3. Any transaction by any United States person that evades or avoids, or has the purpose of evading or avoiding, or attempts to violate, any of the prohibitions set forth in this order is prohibited....
(WCPD Clinton 1994: 2155-2156)

SOMALIA: AN UNCERTAIN HOPE RESTORED

Statement by Press Secretary Fitzwater on the Military Airlift for Humanitarian Aid to Somalia

August 13, 1992

The President has ordered the Department of Defense to offer a U.S. military airlift to transport a U.N. guard force and its associated equipment to Somalia. Authorized by U.N. Security Council Resolution 751, the force of 500 guards will help provide the security needed to deliver food and other relief supplies so desperately needed in Somalia. Now that the relevant Somali factions have agreed with the United Nations, the guards should be transported to Mogadishu as soon as possible.

This order to the United Nations of airlift assistance is part of a broader U.S. effort to prevent suffering and starvation in Somalia. The total U.S. contribution to Somali relief to date has exceeded $76 million, and we will be intensifying our efforts in the days and weeks to come.
(PPP Bush 1992-1993 II: 1354)

Statement by Press Secretary Fitzwater on Additional Humanitarian Aid for Somalia

August 14, 1992

The growing suffering and mass death by starvation in Somalia is a major human tragedy. The United States Government and other international donors have already made significant contributions to alleviate this manmade famine. Because armed bands are stealing and hoarding food as well as attacking international relief workers, the primary challenge that the international community faces is the delivery of relief supplies.

The United States will take a leading role with other nations and international organizations to overcome the obstacles and ensure that food reaches those who so desperately need it.

On Thursday, we announced our offer to transport U.N. troops to enhance security for food deliveries in Mogadishu. Today, the President is announcing the following additional measures:

1. The Defense Department will begin as soon as possible emergency airlift operations to deliver food. We are asking the Kenyan Government to join us in supporting airlifts to northern Kenya for Somali refugees and drought-stricken Kenyans and to locations inside Somalia where there is sufficient security to support these relief operations. We are also examining other means of delivering food to Somalia.

2. Ambassador Perkins at the United Nations will begin immediate consultations to seek a Security Council resolution that would authorize the use of additional measures to ensure that humanitarian relief can be delivered.

3. We are also proposing that the United Nations convene a donors conference to include representatives of the major Somali factions so that their cooperation can be gained. Such cooperation would be the most important step to accelerate delivery of relief supplies and minimize security problems.

4. The President has also directed that an additional 145,000 tons of American food be made available for Somalia.

5. Finally, to ensure that all U.S. relief activities are properly coordinated, Andrew Natsios, Assistant Administrator of AID for Food and Humanitarian Assistance, has been appointed as Special Coordinator for Somali Relief.

The President calls upon other nations to join us in this urgent and important effort to alleviate starvation in Somalia.

(PPP Bush 1992-1993 II: 1360)

Statement by Press Secretary Fitzwater on the United Nations Vote to Authorize Use of Military Forces in Somalia

December 3, 1992

We are pleased by the U.N. vote to authorize military forces to ensure the delivery of humanitarian aid to alleviate the starvation and human suffering in Somalia. President Bush will meet tomorrow morning with congressional leaders to discuss U.S. participation in a U.N. military action. Since August 14, the United States has airlifted 21,000 tons of food and medicine to Somalia. But the crisis remains urgent.

(PPP Bush 1992-1993 II: 2174)

President Bush's Address to the Nation on the Situation in Somalia

December 4, 1992

I want to talk to you today about the tragedy in Somalia and about a mission that can ease suffering and save lives. Every American has seen the shocking images from Somalia. The scope of suffering there is hard to imagine. Already, over a quarter million people, as many people as live in Buffalo, New York, have died in the Somali famine. In the months ahead 5 times that number, 1 ½ million people, could starve to death.

For many months now, the United States has been actively engaged in the massive international relief effort to ease Somalia's suffering. All told, America has sent Somalia 200,000 tons of food, more than half the world total. This summer, the distribution system broke down. Truck convoys from Somalia's ports were blocked. Sufficient food failed to reach the starving in the interior of Somalia.

So in August, we took additional action. In concert with the United Nations, we sent in the U.S. Air Force to help fly food to the towns. To date, American pilots have flown over 1,400 flights, delivering over 17,000 tons of food aid. And when the U.N. authorized 3,500 U.N. guards to protect the relief operation, we flew in the first of them, 500 soldiers from Pakistan.

But in the months since then, the security situation has grown worse. The U.N. has been prevented from deploying its initial commitment of troops. In many cases, food from relief flights is being looted upon landing; food convoys have been hijacked; aid workers assaulted; ships with food have been subject to artillery attacks that prevented them from docking. There is no government in Somalia. Law and order have broken down. Anarchy prevails.

One image tells the story. Imagine 7,000 tons of food aid literally bursting out of a warehouse on a dock in Mogadishu, while Somalis starve less than a kilometer away because relief workers cannot run the gauntlet of armed gangs roving the city. Confronted with these conditions, relief groups called for outside troops to provide security so they could feed people. It's now clear that military support is necessary to ensure the safe delivery of the food Somalis need to survive.

It was this situation which led us to tell the United Nations that the United States would be willing to provide more help to enable relief to be delivered. Last night the United Nations Security Council, by unanimous vote and after the tireless efforts of Secretary-General Boutros-Ghali, welcomed the United States offer to lead a coalition to get the food through.

After consulting with my advisers, with world leaders, and the congressional leadership, I have today told Secretary-General Boutros-Ghali that America will answer the call. I have given the order to Secretary Cheney to move a substantial American force into Somalia. As I speak, a Marine amphibious ready group, which we maintain at sea, is offshore Mogadishu. These troops will be joined by elements of the 1st Marine Expeditionary Force, based out of Camp Pendleton, California, and by the Army's 10th Mountain Division out of Fort Drum, New York. These and other American forces will assist in Operation Restore Hope. They are America's finest. They will perform this mission with courage and compassion, and they will succeed.

The people of Somalia, especially the children of Somalia, need our help. We're able to ease their suffering. We must help them live. We must give them hope. America must act.

In taking this action, I want to emphasize that I understand the United States alone cannot right the world's wrongs. But we also know that some crises in the world cannot be resolved without American involvement, that American action is often necessary as a catalyst for broader involvement of the community of nations. Only the United States has the global reach to place a large security force on the ground in such a distant place quickly and efficiently and thus save thousands of innocents from death.

We will not, however, be acting alone. I expect forces from about a dozen countries to join us in this mission. When we see Somalia's children starving, all of America hurts. We've tried to help in many ways. And make no mistake about it, now we and our allies will ensure that aid gets through. Here is what we and our coalition partners will do:

First, we will create a secure environment in the hardest hit parts of Somalia, so that food can move from ships over land to the people in the countryside now devastated by starvation.

Second, once we have created that secure environment, we will withdraw our troops, handing the security mission back to a regular U.N. peacekeeping force. Our mission has a limited objective: To open the supply routes, to get the food moving, and to prepare the way for a U.N. peacekeeping force to keep it moving. This operation is not open-ended. We will not stay one day longer than is absolutely necessary.

Let me be very clear: our mission is humanitarian, but we will not tolerate armed gangs ripping off their own people, condemning them to death by starvation. General Hoar and his troops have the authority to take whatever military action is necessary to safeguard the lives of our troops and the lives of Somalia's people. The outlaw elements in Somalia must understand this is serious business. We will accomplish our mission. We have no intent to remain in Somalia with fighting forces, but we are determined to do it right, to secure an environment that will allow food to get to the starving people of Somalia.

To the people of Somalia I promise this: We do not plan to dictate political outcomes. We respect your sovereignty and independence. Based on my conversations with other coalition leaders, I can state with confidence: We come to your country for one reason only, to enable the starving to be fed....
(PPP Bush 1992-1993 II: 1274-1276)

Statement by Press Secretary Fitzwater on Operation Restore Hope
December 8, 1992

President Bush is pleased by the success of the initial landing phase of Operation Restore Hope in Somalia. United States forces went ashore at approximately 8:30 p.m. e.s.t., this evening (4:30 a.m. Somali time). This initial phase will focus on establishing secure airport and port facilities. President Bush will be advised of developments in Somalia on a regular basis by his national security staff in the White House Situation Room.

Earlier today the President spoke by telephone with Ambassador Robert Oakley, our special envoy in Somalia. Ambassador Oakley briefed the President on his meetings with relief agency representatives and Somali factional leaders. Ambassador Oakley indicated that the discussions were encouraging. The President also spoke by phone with United Nations Secretary-General Boutros-Ghali and discussed with him the latest developments and plans for the humanitarian effort.

The President met with his national security advisers around 5 p.m. this afternoon for a final update on the status of the coalition preparations. General Colin Powell, Chairman of the Joint Chiefs of Staff, said Operation Restore Hope was on schedule and proceeding well. The response from other nations to join the coalition has been quite positive. Forces from several countries are being integrated into the overall operation.
(PPP Bush 1992-1993 II: 2178)

President Bush's Letter to Congressional Leaders on the Situation in Somalia
December 10, 1992

...Beginning in January of this year with the adoption of U.N. Security Council Resolution 733, the United Nations has been actively addressing the humanitarian crisis in Somalia. The United States has been assisting the U.N.

effort to deal with a human catastrophe. Over 300,000 Somalis have died of starvation. Five times that number remain at risk, beyond the reach of international relief efforts in large part because of the security situation. As a result, voluntary relief organizations from the United States and other countries have appealed for assistance from outside security forces.

On November 29, 1992, the Secretary General of the United Nations reported to the Security Council that the deteriorating security conditions in Somalia had severely disrupted international relief efforts and that an immediate military operation under U.N. authority was urgently required. On December 3, the Security Council adopted Resolution 794, which determined that the situation in Somalia constituted a threat to international peace and security, and, invoking Chapter VII of the U.N. Charter, authorized Member States to use all necessary means to establish a secure environment for humanitarian relief operations in Somalia. In my judgment, the deployment of U.S. Armed Forces under U.S. command to Somalia as part of this multilateral response to the Resolution is necessary to address a major humanitarian calamity, avert related threats to international peace and security, and protect the safety of Americans and others engaged in relief operations.

In the evening, Eastern Standard Time, on December 8, 1992, U.S. Armed Forces entered Somalia to secure the airfield and port facility of Mogadishu. Other elements of the U.S. Armed Forces and the Armed Forces of other members of the United Nations are being introduced into Somalia to achieve the objectives of U.N. Security Council Resolution 794. No organized resistance has been encountered to date.

U.S. Armed Forces will remain in Somalia only as long as necessary to establish a secure environment for humanitarian relief operations and will then turn over the responsibility of maintaining this environment to a U.N. peacekeeping force assigned to Somalia. Over 15 nations have already offered to deploy troops. While it is not possible to estimate precisely how long the transfer or responsibility may take, we believe that prolonged operations will not be necessary.

We do not intend that U.S. Armed Forces deployed to Somalia become involved in hostilities. Nonetheless, these forces are equipped and ready to take such measures as may be needed to accomplish their humanitarian mission and defend themselves if necessary. They also will have the support of any additional U.S. Armed Forces necessary to ensure their safety and the accomplishment of their mission.

I have taken these actions pursuant to my constitutional authority to conduct our foreign relations and as Commander in Chief and Chief Executive, and in accordance with applicable treaties and laws. In doing so, I have taken into account the views expressed in H. Con. Res. 370, S. Con.

Res. 132, and the Horn of Africa Recovery and Food Security Act, Public Law 102-274, on the urgent need for action in Somalia....
(PPP Bush 1992-1993 II: 2179-2180)

President Clinton's Remarks Welcoming Home Military Personnel from Somalia
May 5, 1993

...General Johnston has just reported to me: Mission accomplished. And so, on behalf of all the American people, I say to you, General, and to all whom you brought with you: Welcome home, and thank you for a job very, very well done.

You represent the thousands who served in this crucial operation, in the First Marine Expeditionary Force, in the Army 10th Mountain Division, aboard the Navy's Tripoli Amphibious Ready Group, in the Air Force and Air National Guard airlift squadrons, and in other units in each of our services. Over 30,000 American military personnel served at sometime in these last 5 months in Somalia. And serving alongside you were thousands of others from 20 nations.

Although your mission was humanitarian and not combat, you nonetheless faced difficult and dangerous conditions. You sometimes were subjected to abuse and forced to dodge rocks and even bullets. You saw first hand the horror of hunger, disease, and death. But you pressed on with what you set out to do, and you were successful. You have served in the best tradition of the Armed Forces of the United States, and you have made the American people very, very proud....

To understand the magnitude of what our forces in Somalia accomplished, the world need only look back at Somalia's condition just 6 months ago. Hundreds of thousands of people were starving; armed anarchy ruled the land and the streets of every city and town. Today, food is flowing; crops are growing; schools and hospitals are reopening. Although there is still much to be done if enduring peace is to prevail, one can now envision a day when Somalia will be reconstructed as a functioning civil society.

If all of you who served had not gone, it is absolutely certain that tens of thousands would have died by now. You saved their lives. You gave the people of Somalia the opportunity to look beyond starvation and focus on their future and the future of their children. Although you went on a mission of peace, eight Americans did not return. We salute each of them. We thank them and their families. America will never forget what they did or what they gave. To their loved ones we extend our hearts and our prayers.

As we honor the service of those who have returned and those who did not, it is fitting that we reflect on what the successful mission signifies for the future. This, the largest humanitarian relief operation in history, has written an important new chapter in the international annals of peacekeeping and humanitarian assistance.

You have shown that the work of the just can prevail over the arms of the warlords. You have demonstrated that the world is ready to mobilize its resources in new ways to face the challenges of a new age. And you have proved yet again that American leadership can help to mobilize international action to create a better world.

You also leave behind a U.N. peacekeeping force with a significant American component. This force is a reflection of the new era we have entered, for it has Americans participating in new ways. Just hours ago, General Johnston turned over command to General Bir of Turkey as UNITAF became UNOSOM 11. You set the stage and made it possible for that force to do its mission and for the Somalis to complete the work of rebuilding and creating a peaceful, self sustaining, and democratic civil society.

Your successful return reminds us that other missions lie ahead for our Nation. Some we can foresee, and others we cannot. As always we stand ready to defend our interests, working with others where possible and by ourselves where necessary. But increasingly in this new era, we will need to work with an array of multinational partners, often in new arrangements. You have proved again that that is possible. You have proved again that our involvement in multilateral efforts need not be open-ended or ill-defined, that we can go abroad and accomplish some distinct objectives, and then come home again when the mission is accomplished.

Some will ask why, if the cold war ended, we must still support the world's greatest military forces, the kind that General Johnston and his comrades represent. I say it is because we still have interests; we still face threats; we still have responsibilities. The world has not seen the end of evil, and America can lead other countries to share more of the responsibilities that they ought to be shouldering.

Some will ask why we must so often be the one to lead. Well, of course we cannot be the world's policeman, but we are, and we must continue to be, the world's leader. That is the job of the United States of America. And so today, America opens its arms in a hearty welcome home....
(WCPD Clinton 1993: 754-755)

President Clinton's Letter to Congressional Leaders on the Situation in Somalia
June 10, 1993

...On December 10, 1992, President Bush reported to the Congress that U.S. Armed Forces had been deployed to Somalia to assist the United Nations effort to deal with the human catastrophe in that country, to avert related threats to international peace and security, and to protect the safety of

Americans and others engaged in relief operations. This action was part of a multilateral response to U.N. Security Council Resolution 794, which authorized Member States, under Chapter VII of the U.N. Charter, to use all necessary means to establish a secure environment for humanitarian relief operations in Somalia. Since that time, my Administration and its predecessor have endeavored, through briefings and other means, to keep you informed about the progress of U.S. efforts in Somalia. I am providing this further report, consistent with the War Powers Resolution, in light of the passage of 6 months since President Bush's initial report on the deployment of U.S. Armed Forces to Somalia.

As you are aware, the U.S.-led operation, known as Operation Restore Hope, was responsible for stemming the tragic situation and saving many lives by ensuring that desperately needed relief efforts in behalf of the civilian population could proceed. Owing in large measure to the success of the U.S.-led Unified Task Force in Somalia (UNITAF), the responsibility for the continuing operation was transferred in an orderly fashion to the operational control of the U.N. operation in Somalia (UNOSOM II) on May 4, 1993, pursuant to U.N. Security Council Resolution 814. This Resolution similarly invoked Chapter VII of the U.N. Charter and endowed UNOSOM II with the right to use force to ensure that the mandate is implemented.

The United States continues to support U.N. efforts in Somalia by providing approximately 3,000 U.S. logistics and other support personnel under the operational control of UNOSOM II. In addition, approximately 1,100 U.S. troops remain in the area as a Quick Reaction Force (QRF), under the operational control of the Commander in Chief, U.S. Central Command, for use in emergency situations. The UNOSOM II deputy commander, a U.S. Army general who is the U.S. contingent commander, is authorized to send the QRF into action as may be necessary.

On June 5, 1993, UNOSOM II forces operating in Mogadishu encountered attacks instigated by one of Somalia's factional leaders, resulting in the deaths of 23 Pakistani military personnel. Three U.S. military personnel assigned to UNOSOM II sustained minor injuries. As envisioned in response to such situations, the QRF was called upon to assist in quelling the violence against the lawful activities of UNOSOM II in implementing the U.N. mandate. On June 6, 1993, the U.N. Security Council adopted Resolution 837, reaffirming the authority of UNOSOM II to take all necessary measures against those responsible for these armed attacks.

Our forces will remain equipped and prepared to accomplish their humanitarian mission and defend themselves, if necessary; they also will be provided such additional U.S. support as may be necessary to ensure their safety and the accomplishment of their mission.

I have continued the deployment of U.S. Armed Forces to Somalia pursuant to my constitutional authority to conduct U.S. foreign relations and

as Commander in Chief and Chief Executive and in accordance with applicable treaties and laws. This deployment is consistent with S.J. Res. 45, as adopted by the Senate on February 4, 1993, and as modified and adopted by the House on May 25, 1993....
(WCPD Clinton 1993: 1060-1061)

President Clinton's Address to the Nation on Somalia
October 7, 1993

Today I want to talk with you about our Nation's military involvement in Somalia. A year ago, we all watched with horror as Somali children and their families lay dying by the tens of thousands, dying the slow, agonizing death of starvation, a starvation brought on not only by drought, but also by the anarchy that then prevailed in that country.

This past weekend we all reacted with anger and horror as an armed Somali gang desecrated the bodies of our American soldiers and displayed a captured American pilot, all of them soldiers who were taking part in an international effort to end the starvation of the Somali people themselves. These tragic events raise hard questions about our effort in Somalia. Why are we still there? What are we trying to accomplish? How did a humanitarian mission turn violent? And when will our people come home?

These questions deserve straight answers. Let's start lay remembering why our troops went into Somalia in the first place. We went because only the United States could help stop one of the great human tragedies of this time. A third of a million people had died of starvation and disease. Twice that many more were at risk of dying. Meanwhile, tons of relief supplies piled up in the capital of Mogadishu because a small number of Somalis stopped food from reaching their own countrymen.

Our consciences said, enough. In our Nation's best tradition, we took action with bipartisan support. President Bush sent in 28,000 American troops as part of a United Nations humanitarian mission. Our troops created a secure environment so that food and medicine could get through. We saved close to one million lives. And throughout most of Somalia, everywhere but in Mogadishu, life began returning to normal. Crops are growing. Markets are reopening. So are schools and hospitals.

Nearly a million Somalis still depend completely on relief supplies, but at least the starvation is gone. And none of this would have happened without American leadership and America's troops.

Until June, things went well, with little violence. The United States reduced our troop presence from 28,000 down to less than 5,000, with other nations picking up where we left off. But then in June, the people who caused much of the problem in the beginning started attacking American, Pakistani, and other troops who were there just to keep the peace.

Rather than participate in building the peace with others, these people sought to fight and to disrupt, even if it means returning Somalia to anarchy and mass famine. And make no mistake about it, if we were to leave Somalia tomorrow, other nations would leave, too. Chaos would resume. The relief effort would stop, and starvation soon would return.

That knowledge has led us to continue our mission. It is not our job to rebuild Somalia's society or even to create a political process that can allow Somalia's clans to live and work in peace. The Somalis must do that for themselves. The United Nations and many African states are more than willing to help. But we, we in the United States must decide whether we will give them enough time to have a reasonable chance to succeed.

We started this mission for the right reasons, and we're going to finish it in the right way. In a sense, we came to Somalia to rescue innocent people in a burning house. We've nearly put the fire out, but some smoldering embers remain. If we leave them now, those embers will reignite into flames, and people will die again. If we stay a short while longer and do the right things, we've got a reasonable chance of cooling off the embers and getting other firefighters to take our place.

We also have to recognize that we cannot leave now and still have all our troops present and accounted for. And I want you to know that I am determined to work for the security of those Americans missing or held captive. Anyone holding an American right now should understand, above all else, that we will hold them strictly responsible for our soldiers' well-being. We expected them to be well-treated, and we expect them to be released.

So now we face a choice. Do we leave when the job gets tough, or when the job is well done? Do we invite a return of mass suffering, or do we leave in a way that gives the Somalis a decent chance to survive?

Recently, General Colin Powell said this about our choices in Somalia. "Because things get difficult, you don't cut and run. You work the problem and try to find a correct solution." I want to bring our troops home from Somalia. Before the events of this week, as I said, we had already reduced the number of our troops there from 28,000 to less than 5,000. We must complete that withdrawal soon, and I will. But we must also leave on our terms. We must do it right. And here is what I intend to do.

This past week's events make it clear that even as we prepare to withdraw from Somalia, we need more strength there. We need more armor, more air power, to ensure that our people are safe and that we can do our job. Today, I have ordered 1,700 additional Army troops and 104 additional armored vehicles to Somalia to protect our troops and to complete our mission. I've also ordered an aircraft carrier and two amphibious groups with 3,600 combat Marines to be stationed offshore. These forces will be under American command.

Their mission, what I am asking these young Americans to do, is the following:

First, they are there to protect our troops and our bases. We did not go to Somalia with a military purpose. We never wanted to kill anyone. But those who attack our soldiers must know they will pay a very heavy price.

Second, they are there to keep open and secure the roads, the port, and the lines of communication that are essential for the United Nations and the relief workers to keep the flow of food and supplies and people moving freely throughout the country so that starvation and anarchy do not return.

Third, they are there to keep the pressure on those who cut off relief supplies and attacked our people, not to personalize the conflict but to prevent a return to anarchy.

Fourth, through their pressure and their presence, our troops will help to make it possible for the Somali people, working with others, to reach agreements among themselves so that they can solve their problems and survive when we leave. That is our mission.

I am proposing this plan because it will let us finish leaving Somalia on our own terms and without destroying all that two administrations have accomplished there. For, if we were to leave today, we know what would happen. Within months, Somali children again would be dying in the streets. Our own credibility with friends and allies would be severely damaged. Our leadership in world affairs would be undermined at the very time when people are looking to America to help promote peace and freedom in the post-cold-war world. And all around the world, aggressors, thugs, and terrorists will conclude that the best way to get us to change our policies is to kill our people. It would be open season on Americans.

That is why I am committed to getting this job done in Somalia, not only quickly but also effectively. To do that, I am taking steps to ensure troops from other nations are ready to take the place of our own soldiers. We've already withdrawn some 20,000 troops, and more than that number have replaced them from over two dozen other nations. Now we will intensify efforts to have other countries deploy more troops to Somalia to assure that security will remain when we're gone.

And we'll complete the replacement of U.S. military logistics personnel with civilian contractors who can provide the same support to the United Nations. While we're taking military steps to protect our own people and to help the U.N. maintain a secure environment, we must pursue new diplomatic efforts to help the Somalis find a political solution to their problems. That is the only kind of outcome that can endure.

For fundamentally, the solution to Somalia's problems is not a military one, it is political. Leaders of the neighboring African states, such as Ethiopia and Eritrea, have offered to take the lead in efforts to build a settlement among the Somali people that can preserve order and security. I have directed my representatives to pursue such efforts vigorously. And I've asked Ambassador Bob Oakley, who served effectively in two administrations as our representative in Somalia, to travel again to the region immediately to advance this process.

Obviously, even then there is no guarantee that Somalia will rid itself of violence and suffering. But at least we will have given Somalia a reasonable chance. This week some 15,000 Somalis took to the streets to express sympathy for our losses, to thank us for our effort. Most Somalis are not hostile to us but grateful. And they want to use this opportunity to rebuild their country.

It is my judgment and that of my military advisers that we may need up to 6 months to complete these steps and to conduct an orderly withdrawal. We'll do what we can to complete the mission before then. All American troops will be out of Somalia no later than March the 31st, except for a few hundred support personnel in noncombat roles.

If we take these steps, if we take the time to do the job right, I am convinced we will have lived up to the responsibilities of American leadership in the world. And we will have proved that we are committed to addressing the new problems of a new era.

When our troops in Somalia came under fire this last weekend, we witnessed a dramatic example of the heroic ethic of our American military. When the first Black Hawk helicopter was downed this weekend, the other American troops didn't retreat although they could have. Some 90 of them formed a perimeter around the helicopter, and they held that ground under intensely heavy fire. They stayed with their comrades. That's the kind of soldiers they are. That's the kind of people we are.

So let us finish the work we set out to do. Let us demonstrate to the world, as generations of Americans have done before us, that when Americans take on a challenge, they do the job right.

Let me express my thanks and my gratitude and my profound sympathy to the families of the young Americans who were killed in Somalia. My message to you is, your country is grateful, and so is the rest of the world, and so are the vast majority of the Somali people. Our mission from this day forward is to increase our strength, do our job, bring our soldiers out, and bring them home....

(WCPD Clinton 1993: 2022-2025)

President Clinton's Message to the Congress Transmitting a Report on Somalia

October 13, 1993

...In transmitting this report, I want to reiterate the points that I made on October 6 and to the American people in remarks on October 7. We went to

Somalia on a humanitarian mission. We saved approximately a million lives that were at risk of starvation brought on by civil war that had degenerated into anarchy. We acted after 350,000 already had died.

Ours was a gesture of a great nation, carried out by thousands of American citizens, both military and civilian. We did not then, nor do we now plan to stay in that country. The United Nations agreed to assume our military mission and take on the additional political and rehabilitation activities required so that the famine and anarchy do not resume when the international presence departs.

For our part, we agreed with the United Nations to participate militarily with a much smaller U.S. force for a period of time, to help the United Nations create a secure environment in which it could ensure the free flow of humanitarian relief. At the request of the United Nations and the United States, approximately 30 nations deployed over 20,000 troops as we reduced our military presence.

With the recent tragic casualties to American forces in Somalia, the American people want to know why we are there, what we are doing, why we cannot come home immediately, and when we will come home. Although the report answers those questions in detail, I want to repeat concisely my answers:

- We went to Somalia because without us a million people would have died. We, uniquely, were in a position to save them, and other nations were ready to share the burden after our initial action.
- What the United States is doing there is providing, for a limited period of time, logistics support and security so that the humanitarian and political efforts of the United Nations, relief organizations, and others can have a reasonable chance of success. The United Nations, in turn, has a longer term political, security, and relief mission designed to minimize the likelihood that famine and anarchy will return when the United Nations leaves. The U.S. military mission is not now nor was it ever one of "nation building."
- We cannot leave immediately because the United Nations has not had an adequate chance to replace us, nor have the Somalis had a reasonable opportunity to end their strife. We want other nations to assume more of the burden of international peace. To have them do so, they must think that they can rely on our commitments when we make them. Moreover, having been brutally attacked, were American forces to leave now we would send a message to terrorists and other potential adversaries around the world that they can change our policies by killing our people. It would be open season on Americans.
- We will, however, leave no later than March 31, 1994, except for a few hundred support troops. That amount of time will permit the Somali

> people to make progress toward political reconciliation and allow the United States to fulfill our obligations properly, including the return of any Americans being detained. We went there for the right reasons and we will finish the job in the right way.

While U.S. forces are there, they will be fully protected with appropriate American military capability.

Any Americans detained will be the subject of the most complete and thorough efforts of which this Government is capable, with the unrelenting goal of returning them home and returning them to health....
(WCPD Clinton 1993: 2065-2066)

HAITI: SUCCESSFUL STANDOFF

President Bush's Statement on Denying Use of United States Ports to Vessels Trading with Haiti

May 28, 1992

I have today directed the Secretary of the Treasury and the Secretary of Transportation to deny the use of American ports to ships that violate the trade embargo against Haiti. This action is being taken in support of the resolution adopted by the Organization of American States on May 17, which calls on OAS member states to deny port facilities to vessels trading with Haiti in disregard of the OAS embargo.

The United States remains committed unequivocally to the restoration of democratic government in Haiti. We will continue working in close concert with our OAS allies toward a negotiated settlement of the political crisis that began with the overthrow of President Jean-Bertrand Aristide last September 30. In addition to today's action, and in accordance with the recent OAS resolution, we are examining other steps to tighten sanctions against the illegal regime in Port-au-Prince.

Our actions are directed at those in Haiti who are opposing a return to democracy, not at the Haitian poor. We are continuing to provide substantial, direct humanitarian assistance to the people of Haiti and are working to intensify those efforts. Our current programs total $47 million and provide food for over 600,000 Haitians and health care services that reach nearly 2 million. While tightening the embargo, we will continue to encourage others to ship food staples and other humanitarian items to those in need. The action that I have directed will not affect vessels carrying permitted items.

We are expanding opportunities for Haitians who fear persecution in their homeland to apply for admission to the United States as refugees with our Embassy in Port-au-Prince. The Embassy has been receiving such applications since early February, and all persons who believe they may be

qualified are urged to avail themselves of our expanded refugee operation in Haiti. I have asked the Department of State to ensure that Embassy personnel will also be available outside Port-au-Prince to assist applicants in other parts of the country in pursuing their claims.
(PPP Bush 1992 I: 838-839)

President Bush's Message to the Congress Reporting on the National Emergency with Respect to Haiti
September 30, 1992

...1. On October 4, 1991, in Executive order No. 12775, I declared a national emergency to deal with the threat to the national security, foreign policy, and economy of the United States caused by events that had occurred in Haiti to disrupt the legitimate exercise of power by the democratically elected government of that country (56 FR 50641). In that order, I ordered the immediate blocking of all property and interests in property of the Government of Haiti (including the Banque de la Republique d'Haiti) then or thereafter located in the United States or within the possession or control of a U.S. person, including its overseas branches. I also prohibited any direct or indirect payments or transfers to the de facto regime in Haiti of funds or other financial or investment assets or credits by any U.S. person or any entity organized under the laws of Haiti and owned or controlled by a U.S. person.

Subsequently, on October 28, 1991, I issued Executive order No. 12779 adding trade sanctions against Haiti to the sanctions imposed on October 4, 1991 (56 FR 55975). Under this order, I prohibited exportation from the United States of goods, technology, and services, and importation into the United States of Haitian-origin goods and services, after November 5, 1991, with certain limited exceptions. The order exempts trade in publications and other informational materials from the import, export, and payment prohibitions, and permits the exportation to Haiti of donations to relieve human suffering as well as commercial sales of five food commodities: rice, beans, sugar, wheat flour, and cooking oil. In order to permit the return to the United States of goods being prepared for U.S. customers by Haiti's substantial "assembly sector," the order also permitted, through December 5, 1991, the importation into the United States of goods assembled or processed in Haiti that contained parts or materials previously exported to Haiti from the United States. On February 5, 1992, it was announced that this exception could be applied for on a case-by-case basis by U.S. persons wishing to resume a pre-embargo import/export relationship with the assembly sector in Haiti.

2. The declaration of the national emergency on October 4, 1991, was made pursuant to the authority vested in me as President by the Constitution and laws of the United States, including the International Emergency Economic Powers Act (50 U.S.C. 1701 *et seq.*), the National Emergencies Act

(50 U.S.C. 1601 *et seq.*), and section 301 of title 3 of the United States Code. I reported the emergency declaration to the Congress on October 4, 1991, pursuant to section 204(b) of the International Emergency Economic Powers Act (50 U.S.C. 1703(b)). The additional sanctions set forth in my order of October 28, 1991, were imposed pursuant to the authority vested in me by the Constitution and laws of the United States, including the statutes cited above, and implemented in the United States Resolution MRE/RES. 2/91, adopted by the Ad Hoc Meeting of Ministers of Foreign Affairs of the Organization of American States ("OAS") on October 8, 1991, which called on Member States to impose a trade embargo on Haiti and to freeze Government of Haiti assets. The present report is submitted pursuant to 50 U.S.C. 1641(c) and 1703(c), and discusses Administration actions and expenses directly related to the national emergency with respect to Haiti declared in Executive Order No. 12775, as implemented pursuant to that order and Executive Order No. 12779.

3. On March 31, 1992, the Office of Foreign Assets Control of the Department of the Treasury ("FAC"), after consultation with the Department of State and other federal agencies, issued the Haitian Transactions Regulations ("HTR"), 31 C.F.R. Part 580 (57 FR 10820, March 31, 1992), to implement the prohibitions set forth in Executive Orders No. 12775 and No. 12779. Since my last report, there have been two amendments to the HTR.

On June 5, 1992, new section 580.211 was added (57 FR 23954, June 5, 1992) prohibiting vessels calling in Haiti on or after that date from entering the United States without authorization by FAC. This amendment is explained more fully in section 6 of this report. In addition, effective August 27, 1992, new section 580.516 (57 FR 39603, September 1, 1992) authorizes the exportation to Haiti of certain additional food items (corn and corn flour, milk (including powdered milk), and edible tallow), as well as the issuance of specific licenses permitting, on a case-by-case basis, exports of propane for noncommercial use. Copies of these amendments are attached to this report.

4. The ouster of Jean-Bertrand Aristide, the democratically elected President of Haiti, in an illegal coup by elements of the Haitian military on September 30, 1991, was immediately repudiated and vigorously condemned by the OAS. The convening on September 30, 1991, of an emergency meeting of the OAS Permanent Council to address this crisis reflected an important first use of a mechanism approved at the 1991 OAS General Assembly in Santiago, Chile, requiring the OAS to respond to a sudden or irregular interruption of the functioning of a democratic government anywhere in the Western Hemisphere. As an OAS Member State, the United States has participated actively in OAS diplomatic efforts to restore democracy in Haiti and has supported fully the OAS resolutions adopted in response to the crisis, including Resolution MRE/RES. 2/91 and MRE/RES. 3/92.

5. In the first year of the Haitian sanctions program, FAC has made extensive use of its authority to specifically license transactions with respect to Haiti in an effort to mitigate the effects of the sanctions on the legitimate Government of Haiti and on the livelihood of Haitian workers employed by Haiti's export assembly sector having established relationships with U.S. firms, and to ensure the availability of necessary medicines and medical supplies and the undisrupted flow of humanitarian donations to Haiti's poor. For example, specific licenses have been issued (1) permitting expenditures from blocked assets for the operations of the legitimate Government of Haiti, (2) permitting U.S. firms with pre-embargo relationships with product assembly operations in Haiti to resume those relationships in order to continue employment for their workers or, if they choose to withdraw from Haiti, to return to the United States assembly equipment, machinery, and parts and materials previously exported to Haiti, (3) permitting U.S. companies operating in Haiti to establish, under specified circumstances, interest-bearing blocked reserve accounts in commercial or investment banking institutions in the United States for deposit of amounts owed the *de facto* regime, (4) permitting the continued material support of U.S. and international religious, charitable, public health, and other humanitarian organizations and projects operating in Haiti, and (5) authorizing commercial sales of agricultural inputs such as fertilizer and food crop seeds.

6. The widespread supply of embargoed goods, particularly petroleum products, to Haiti by foreign-flag vessels led to the adoption on May 17, 1992, by the Ad hoc Meeting of Ministers of Foreign Affairs of the OAS of Resolution MRE/RES. 3/92 urging, among other things, a port ban on vessels engaged in trade with Haiti in violation of the OAS embargo. There was broad consensus among OAS member representatives, as well as European permanent observer missions, on the importance of preventing oil shipments to Haiti. Vessels from some non-OAS Caribbean ports and European countries have been involved in trade, particularly oil supplies, that undermines the embargo.

In response to Resolution MRE/RES. 3/92, section 580.211 was added to the HTR on June 5, 1992, prohibiting vessels calling in Haiti on or after that date from entering the United States without FAC authorization. Vessels seeking such authorization must demonstrate that all calls in Haiti on or after June 5 were (1) for transactions exempted or excepted from the applicable prohibitions of the HTR, (2) specifically licensed by FAC, or authorized by an OAS Member State pursuant to Resolution MRE/RES. 3/92, or (3) made under a contract of voyage that was fully completed prior to the vessel's proposed entry into a U.S. port.

Strict enforcement of the new regulation has benefitted from the close coordination between FAC, the U.S. Embassy at Port-au-Prince, the U.S.

Customs Service, the U.S. Navy, and the U.S. Coast Guard in monitoring vessel traffic to and from Haiti.

7. Since the issuance of Executive Order No. 12779, FAC has worked closely with the U.S. Customs Service to ensure both that prohibited imports and exports (including those in which the Government of Haiti has an interest) are identified and interdicted and that permitted imports and exports move to their intended destinations without undue delay. Violations and suspected violations of the embargo are being investigated, and appropriate enforcement actions have been initiated.

Since my last report, penalties totalling more than $30,000 have been collected for U.S. banks for violations involving unlicensed transfers from blocked Government of Haiti accounts or the failure to block payments to the *de facto* regime. Additional penalties totalling nearly $175,000 have been proposed for other violations of the HTR, including penalties against the masters of vessels violating the new regulation effective June 5, 1992, applicable to vessels calling in Haiti on or after that date.

8. The expenses incurred by the Federal Government in the 6-month period from April 4, 1992, through October 3, 1992, that are directly attributable to the authorities conferred by the declaration of a national emergency with respect to Haiti are estimated at $2.3 million, most of which represent wage and salary costs for Federal personnel. Personnel costs were largely centered in the Department of the Treasury (particularly in FAC, the U.S. Customs Service, and the Office of the General Counsel), the Department of State, the U.S. Coast Guard, and the Department of Commerce.

9. The assault on Haiti's democracy represented by the military's forced exile of President Aristide continues to pose an unusual and extraordinary threat to the national security, foreign policy, and economy of the United States. The United States remains committed to a multilateral resolution of this crisis through its actions implementing the resolutions of the OAS with respect to Haiti. I shall continue to exercise the powers at my disposal to apply economic sanctions against Haiti as long as these measures are appropriate, and will continue to report periodically to the Congress on significant developments pursuant to 50 U.S.C. 1703(c)....
(PPP Bush 1992-1993 II: 1724-1727)

President Bush's Notice on Continuation of Haiti Emergency
September 30, 1992

On October 4, 1991, by Executive Order No. 12775, I declared a national emergency to deal with the unusual and extraordinary threat to the national security and foreign policy of the United States constituted by the grave events that had occurred in the Republic of Haiti to disrupt the legitimate exercise of power by the democratically elected government of that

country. On October 28, 1991, by Executive Order No. 12779, I took additional measures by prohibiting, with certain exceptions, trade between the United States and Haiti. Because the assault on Haiti's democracy represented by the military's forced exile of President Aristide continues to pose an unusual and extraordinary threat to the national security, foreign policy, and economy or the United States, I am continuing the national emergency with respect to Haiti in accordance with section 202(d) of the National Emergencies Act (50 U.S.C. 1622(d)).
(PPP Bush 1992-1993 II: 1724-1727)

Statement by the Director of Communications on the Situation in Haiti
March 2, 1993

Today the Supreme Court heard arguments concerning the current repatriation policy regarding Haitian asylum-seekers. At that time, the Justice Department supported the President's legal authority to carry out the practice of direct return. The President believes it is essential that he retain the ability to implement such measures when exceptional circumstances demand.

The current practice of direct returns is based on the President's conviction that it is necessary to avert a humanitarian tragedy that could result from a large boat exodus. Hundreds, if not thousands, could lose their lives in overloaded, unseaworthy vessels if the United States reversed the practice of direct return precipitously.

At the same time, the President regards the current practice of direct return as a policy for exceptional circumstances. It is continually under review and will adjusted when conditions permit.

In addition, the President is taking a series of initiatives to promote human rights and democratization in Haiti and to enhance the safety and well-being of those who have reason to fear persecution.

First, the Clinton administration strongly has supported the negotiating process undertaken by the United Nations and the Organization of American States (U.N./OAS) and has urged other nations, both within and outside the hemisphere, to provide diplomatic and financial support to the U.N./OAS effort. A U.N./OAS civilian monitoring team now is being deployed in Haiti. We hope and expect that their presence will create an atmosphere conducive to respect for human rights and political dialog, including progress on a settlement to this crisis.

The President will continue efforts to move the negotiating process forward as expediously as possible, leading to the restoration of constitutional government and the return of President Aristide. President Clinton will meet with President Aristide on March 16 to review the progress that has been achieved and the challenges that lie ahead.

Second, the President is committed to enhancing the safety and well-being of those in Haiti who have reason to fear reprisal for their political activities and affiliation, and has taken a number of actions to improve in-country processing of Haitian refugees, the procedures by which Haitians may apply in Haiti for refugee status and resettlement in the United States.

Shortly after January 20, the President directed that U.S. officials double our capacity for the interviewing of refugee applicants in Haiti by officials of the Immigration and Naturalization Service. The President also directed the State Department to send a technical mission to Haiti to develop detailed proposals for:

- more rapid refugee processing;
- making it easier for Haitians outside Port-Au-Prince to apply for refugee status and U.S. resettlement; and
- enhancing the safety of the repatriation process for returnees.

Since return of the technical team, we streamlined procedures and added staff in Port-au-Prince and have reduced considerably the processing time for refugee applications in Haiti. We have already developed the capacity to reduce processing time and high priority cases from 2 months or more to about 7 working days.

The technical team, which also included congressional staff and representatives from the INS, made a series of additional recommendations for improvements in procedures, including the addition of personnel at the U.S. Refugee Processing Center in Haiti to serve as liaison with human rights groups and as a resource for INS adjudicators; procedures for identifying those who may be especially at risk; and the establishment of processing centers outside of the Port-au-Prince to enhance access to the program for Haitians throughout Haiti.

Based on these and other recommendations made by the team, the president has directed that U.S. officials implement further improvements in the process. To accomplish these goals, the President is authorizing expenditure of up to $5 million from the Emergency Refugee and Migration Assistance Fund (ERMA).

The United States has been in the forefront of refugee protection around the world. We will continue to play this important role in the years to come. *(WCPD Clinton 1993: 348-349)*

President Clinton's Statement on Sanctions Against Haiti

June 4, 1993

One of the cornerstones of our foreign policy is to support the global march toward democracy and to stand by the world's new democracies. The promotion of democracy, which not only reflects our values but also increases our security, is especially important in our own hemisphere. As part of that goal, I consider it a high priority to return democracy to Haiti and to return its democratically elected President, Jean-Bertrand Aristide, to his office.

We should recall Haiti's strides toward democracy just a few years back. Seven years ago, tired of the exploitative rule that had left them the poorest nation in our hemisphere, the Haitian people rose up and forced the dictator Jean-Claude Duvalier to flee. In December 1990, in a remarkable exercise of democracy, the Haitian people held a free and fair election, and two-thirds of them voted for President Aristide.

Nineteen months ago, however, that progress toward democracy was thwarted when the Haitian military illegally and violently ousted President Aristide from office. Since taking office in January, the United States Government has worked steadily with the international community in an effort to restore President Aristide and democracy to Haiti. The OAS and United Nations Special Envoy, Dante Caputo, has demonstrated great dedication and tenacity. To support Mr. Caputo's effort, Secretary of State Christopher in March named U.S. Ambassador Lawrence Pezzullo as our Special Adviser for Haiti.

We and the international community have made progress. The presence of the International Civilian Mission has made a concrete contribution to human rights in Haiti. Mr. Caputo's consultations with all the parties indicated that a negotiated solution is possible.

Unfortunately, the parties in Haiti have not been willing to make the decisions or take the steps necessary to begin democracy's restoration. And while they seek to shift responsibility, Haiti's people continue to suffer.

In light of their own failure to act constructively, I have determined that the time has come to increase the pressure on the Haitian military, the de facto regime in Haiti and their supporters.

The United States has been at the forefront of the international community's efforts to back up the U.N./OAS negotiations with sanctions and other measures. Beginning in October 1991, we froze all Haitian Government assets in the United States and prohibited unlicensed financial transactions with Haitian persons. Today, I am acting to strengthen those existing provisions in several ways.

First, I have signed a proclamation pursuant to Section 212(f) of the Immigration and Nationality Act prohibiting the entry into the U.S. of Haitian nationals who impede the progress of negotiations designed to restore constitutional government to Haiti and of the immediate relatives of such persons. The Secretary of State will determine the persons whose actions are impeding a solution to the Haitian crisis. These people will be barred from entering the United States.

Second, pursuant to the authority of the International Emergency Economic Powers Act and the Executive orders on the Haiti emergency, I have directed the Secretary of the Treasury to designate as "specially designated nationals" those Haitians who act for or on behalf of the junta, or who make material, financial, or commercial contributions to the de facto regime or the Haitian armed forces. In effect, this measure will freeze the personal assets of such persons subject to U.S. jurisdiction and bar them from conducting any transactions whatsoever with the individuals and entities named.

Third, I have directed Secretary Christopher to consult with the OAS and its member states on ways to enhance enforcement of the existing OAS sanctions program. And I have directed Secretary Christopher and Ambassador Albright to consult with the U.N. and member states on the possibility of creating a worldwide sanctions program against Haiti.

Sanctions alone do not constitute a solution. The surest path toward the restoration of democracy in Haiti is a negotiated solution that assures the safety of all parties. We will therefore strongly support a continuation and intensification of the negotiating effort. We will impress on all parties the need to take seriously their own responsibilities for a successful resolution to this impasse.

Our policy on Haiti is not a policy for Haiti alone. It is a policy in favor of democracy everywhere. Those who seek to derail a return to constitutional government, whether in Haiti or Guatemala, must recognize that we will not be swayed from our purpose.

At the same time, individuals should not have to fear that supporting democracy's restoration will ultimately put their own safety at risk. Those who have opposed President Aristide in the past should recognize that, once President Aristide has returned, we and the rest of the international community will defend assiduously their legitimate political rights.

It is my hope that the measures we have announced today will encourage greater effort and flexibility in the negotiations to restore democracy and President Aristide to Haiti.

(WCPD Clinton 1993: 1029-1030)

Executive Order 12853 — Blocking Government of Haiti Property and Prohibiting Transactions with Haiti

June 30, 1993

By the authority vested in me as President by the Constitution and the laws of the United States of America, including the International Emergency Economic Powers Act (50 U.S.C. 1701 *et seq.*), the National Emergencies Act (50 U.S.C. 1601 *et seq.*), section 5 of the United Nations Participation Act of 1945, as amended (22 U.S.C. 287c), and section 301 of title 3 of the United

States Code, in view of United Nations Security Council Resolution No. 841 of June 16, 1993, and in order to take additional steps with respect to the actions and policies of the *de facto* regime in Haiti and the national emergency described and declared in Executive Order No. 12775,

I, William J. Clinton, President of the United States of America, hereby order:

Section 1. Except to the extent provided in regulations, orders, directives, or license which may hereafter be issued pursuant to this order, and notwithstanding the existence of any rights or obligations conferred or imposed by any international agreement or any contract entered into or any license or permit granted before the effective date of the order, all property and interests in property of the Government of Haiti and the *de facto* regime in Haiti, or controlled directly or indirectly by the Government of Haiti or the *de facto* regime in Haiti, or by entities, wherever located or organized, owned or controlled by the Government of Haiti or the *de facto* regime in Haiti, that are in the United States that hereafter come within the United States or that are or hereafter come within the possession or control of United States persons, including their overseas branches, are blocked.

Sec. 2. Except to the extent provided in regulations, orders, directives, or licenses which may hereafter be issued pursuant to this order, all property and interests in property of any Haitian national providing substantial financial or material contributions to the de facto regime in Haiti, or doing substantial business with the *de facto* regime in Haiti, as identified by the Secretary of the Treasury, that are in the United States, that hereafter come within the United States, or that are or hereafter come within the possession or control of United States persons, including their overseas branches, are blocked.

Sec. 3. The following are prohibited, notwithstanding the existence of any rights or obligations conferred or imposed by any international agreement or any contract entered into or any license or permit granted before the effective date of this order, except to the extent provided in regulations, orders, directives, or licenses which may hereafter be issued pursuant to this order:

(a) The sale or supply, by United States persons, or from the United States, or using U.S.-registered vessels or aircraft, of petroleum or petroleum products or arms and related materiel of all types, including weapons and ammunition, military vehicles and equipment, police equipment and spare parts for the aforementioned, regardless of origin, to any person or entity in Haiti or to any person or entity for the purpose of any business carried on in or operated from Haiti, and any activities by United States persons or in the United States which promote or are calculated to promote such sale or supply;

(b) The carriage on U.S.-registered vessels of petroleum or petroleum products, or arms and related materiel of all types, including weapons and ammunition, military vehicles and equipment, police equipment and spare parts for the aforementioned, regardless of origin, with entry into, or with the intent to enter, the territory or territorial sea of Haiti;

(c) Any transaction by any United States person that evades or avoids, or has the purpose of evading or avoiding, or attempts to violate, any of the prohibitions set forth in this order.

Sec. 4. The exemption for exportation from the United States to Haiti of rice, beans, sugar, wheat flour, and cooking oil in Section 2(c)(iii) of Executive Order No. 12779 shall not apply to exportations in which either the *de facto* regime in Haiti or any person identified by the Secretary of the Treasury pursuant to section 2 of this order is a direct or indirect party.

Sec. 5. For the purposes of this order:

(a) The term "Haitian national" means a citizen of Haiti, wherever located; an entity or body organized under the laws of Haiti; and any other person, entity, or body located in Haiti and engaging in the importation, storage, or distribution of products or commodities controlled by sanctions imposed on Haiti pursuant to resolutions adopted either by the United Nations Security Council or the Organization of American States, or otherwise facilitating transactions inconsistent with those sanctions.

(b) The definitions contained in section 3 of Executive Order No. 12779 apply to the terms used in this order.

Sec. 6. The Secretary of the Treasury, in consultation with the Secretary of State, is hereby authorized to take such actions, including the promulgation of rules and regulations, and to employ all powers granted to me by the International Emergency Economic Powers Act and the United Nations Participation Act, as may be necessary to carry out the purpose of this order. Such actions may include the prohibition or regulation of entry into the United States of any vessel or aircraft which is determined to have been in violation of United Nations Security Council Resolution No. 841. The Secretary of the Treasury may redelegate any of these functions to other officers and agencies of the United States Government, all agencies of which are hereby directed to take all appropriate measures within their authority to carry out the provisions of this order, including suspension or termination of licenses or other authorizations in effect as of the date of this order.

Sec. 7. Section 4 of Executive Order No. 12775 and sections 2(c) and 4 of Executive Order No. 12779 are hereby revoked to the extent inconsistent with this order. Otherwise, the provisions of this order supplement the provisions of Executive Order No. 12779....

(WCPD Clinton 1993: 1206-1207)

Executive Order 12872 — Blocking Property of Persons Obstructing Democratization in Haiti

October 18, 1993

By the authority vested in me as President by the Constitution and the laws of the United States of America, including the International Emergency Economic Powers Act (50 U.S.C. 1701 *et seq.*), the National Emergencies Act (50 U.S.C. 1601 *et seq.*), and section 301 of title 3, United States Code, and in order to take additional steps with respect to the grave events that have occurred in the Republic of Haiti to disrupt the legitimate exercise of power by the democratically elected government of that country and with respect to the national emergency described and declared in Executive Order No. 12775,

I, William J. Clinton, President of the United States of America, hereby order:

Section 1. Except to the extent provided in regulations, orders, directives, or licenses, which may hereafter be issued pursuant to this order, and notwithstanding the existence of any rights or obligations conferred or imposed by any international agreement or any contract entered into or any license or permit granted before the effective date of this order, all property and interests in property of persons:

(a) Who have contributed to the obstruction of the implementation of the United Nations Security Council Resolutions 841 and 873, the Governors Island Agreement of July 3, 1993, or the activities of the United Nations Mission in Haiti;

(b) Who have perpetuated or contributed to the violence in Haiti; or

(c) Who have materially or financially supported any of the foregoing, that are in the United States, that hereafter come within the United States, or that are or hereafter come within the possession or control of United States persons, including their overseas branches, are blocked.

Sec. 2. Any transaction subject to U.S. jurisdiction that evades or avoids, or has the purpose of evading or avoiding, or attempts to violate, any of the prohibitions set forth in this order, or in Executive Orders Nos. 12775, 12779 or 12853, is prohibited, notwithstanding the existence of any rights or obligations conferred or imposed by any international agreement or any contract entered into or any license or permit granted before the effective date of this order, except to the extent provided in regulations, orders, directives, or licenses issued pursuant to the relevant Executive order and in effect on the effective date of this order.

Sec. 3. The Secretary of the Treasury, in consultation with the Secretary of State, is hereby authorized to take such actions, including the promulgation of rules and regulations, and to employ all powers granted to me by the International Emergency Economic Powers Act, as may be necessary to carry out the purpose of this order. The Secretary of the Treasury may redelegate

any of these functions to other officers and agencies of the United States Government, all agencies of which are hereby directed to take all appropriate measures within their authority to carry out the provisions of this order, including suspension or termination of licenses or other authorizations in effect as of the date of this order....
(WCPD Clinton 1993: 2103)

President Clinton's Letter to Congressional Leaders on Haiti
October 20, 1993

...I have directed the deployment of U.S. Naval Forces to participate in the implementation of the petroleum and arms embargo of Haiti. At 11:59 p.m. E.S.T., October 18, units under the command of the Commander in Chief, U.S. Atlantic Command, began enforcement operations in the waters around Haiti, including the territorial sea of that country, pursuant to my direction and consistent with United Nations Security Council Resolutions 841,873, and 875. I am providing this report, consistent with the War Powers Resolution, to ensure that the Congress is kept fully informed about this important U.S. action to support multilateral efforts to restore democracy in Haiti and thereby promote democracy throughout the hemisphere.

During the past week, the world has witnessed lawless, brutal actions by Haiti's military and police authorities to thwart the Haitian people's manifest desire for democracy to be returned to their country. With our full support, the United Nations Security Council has responded resolutely to these events. On October 16, the Security Council, acting under Chapters VII and VIII of the United Nations Charter, adopted Resolution 875. This resolution calls upon Member States, "acting nationally or through regional agencies or arrangements, cooperating with the legitimate Government of Haiti, to use such measures commensurate with the specific circumstances as may be necessary" to ensure strict implementation of sanctions imposed by Resolutions 841 and 873. The maritime interception operations I have directed are conducted under U.S. command and control. In concert with allied navies, U.S. Naval Forces will ensure that merchant vessels proceeding to Haiti are in compliance with the embargo provisions set forth in the Security Council resolutions.

The initial deployment includes six U.S. Navy ships and supporting elements under the command of the U.S. Atlantic Command. These U.S. forces and others as may be necessary, combined with those forces that other Member States have committed to this operation, will conduct intercept operations to ensure that merchant ships proceeding to Haiti are in compliance with United Nations Security Council sanctions. On the first day of the operation, one of our ships, with U.S. Navy and Coast Guard personnel aboard, carried out an interception of a Belize-flag vessel and allowed it to proceed to its destination after determining that it was in compliance with the embargo. In addition, the forces of the U.S. Atlantic Command will remain prepared to protect U.S. citizens in Haiti and, acting in cooperation with U.S. Coast Guard, to support the Haitian Alien Migrant Interdiction Operations (AMIO) of the United States, as may be necessary.

The United States strongly supports the Governor's Island Agreement and restoration of democracy in Haiti. The measures I have taken to deploy U.S. Armed Forces in "Operation Restore Democracy" are consistent with United States goals and interests and constitute crucial support for the world community's strategy to overcome the persistent refusal of Haitian military and police authorities to fulfill their commitments under the Governor's Island Agreement. I have ordered the deployment of U.S. Armed Forces for these purposes pursuant to my constitutional authority to conduct foreign relations and as Commander in Chief and Chief Executive....
(WCPD Clinton 1993: 2125-2126)

Executive Order 12927 — Ordering the Selected Reserve of the Armed Forces to Active Duty
September 15, 1994

By the authority vested in me as President by the Constitution and the laws of the United States of America, including sections 121 and 673b of title 10 of the United States Code, I hereby determine that it is necessary to augment the active armed forces of the United States for the effective conduct of operational missions to restore the civilian government in Haiti. Further, under the stated authority, I hereby authorize the Secretary of Defense, and the Secretary of Transportation with respect to the Coast Guard when it is not operating as a service in the Department of the Navy, to order to active duty any units, and any individual members not assigned to a unit organized to serve as a unit, of the Selected Reserve....
(WCPD Clinton 1994: 1778)

President Clinton's Address to the Nation on Haiti
September 15, 1994

...Earlier today, I ordered Secretary of Defense Perry to call up the military reserve personnel necessary to support United States troops in any action we might undertake in Haiti. I have also ordered two aircraft carriers, U.S.S. *Eisenhower* and the U.S.S. *America* into the region. I issued these orders after giving full consideration to what is at stake. The message of the United States to the Haitian dictators is clear. Your time is up. Leave now, or we will force you from power....

The Haitian people should know that we come in peace. And you, the American people, should know that our soldiers will not be involved in rebuilding Haiti or its economy. The international community, working together, must provide that economic, humanitarian, and technical assistance necessary to help the Haitians rebuild.

When this first phase is completed, the vast majority of our troops will come home, in months, not years. I want our troops and their families to know that we'll bring them home just as soon as we possibly can.

Then, in the second phase, a much smaller U.S. force will join forces from other members of the United Nations. And their mission will leave Haiti after elections are held next year and a new Haitian takes office in early 1996.

Tonight, I can announce that President Aristide has pledged to step down when his term ends, in accordance with the constitution he has sworn to uphold. He has committed himself to promote reconciliation among all Haitians and to set an historic example by peacefully transferring power to a duly elected successor. He knows, as we know, that when you start a democracy, the most important election is the second election.

President Aristide has told me that he will consider his mission fulfilled not when he regains office but when he leaves office to the next democratically elected President of Haiti. He has pledged to honor the Haitian voters who put their faith in the ballot box....
(WCPD Clinton 1994: 1779-1982)

President Clinton's Address to the Nation on Haiti
September 18, 1994

My fellow Americans, I want to announce that the military leaders of Haiti have agreed to step down from power. The dictators have recognized that it is in their best interest and in the best interest of the Haitian people to relinquish power peacefully, rather than to face imminent action by the forces of the multinational coalition we are leading....

As all of you know, at my request, President Carter, General Colin Powell, and Senator Sam Nunn went to Haiti to facilitate the dictators' departure just yesterday. I have been in constant contact with them for the last 2 days. They have worked tirelessly, almost around the clock. And I want to thank them for undertaking this crucial mission on behalf of all Americans. Just as important, I want also to thank the men and women of the United States Armed Forces. It was their presence and their preparations that played a pivotal part in this agreement.

Under the agreement, the dictators have agreed to leave power as soon as the Haitian Parliament passes an amnesty law, as called for by the Governors Island Agreement, but in any event, no later than October 15th. They've agreed to immediate introduction of troops from the international coalition, beginning, as I said, as early as tomorrow. They have also pledged to cooperate fully with the coalition troops during the peaceful transition of power, something we have wanted very much.

I have directed United States forces to begin deployment into Haiti as a part of the U.N. coalition. And General Shelton, our commander, will be there tomorrow. The presence of the 15,000 member multinational force will guarantee that the dictators carry out the terms of the agreement. It is clear from our discussions with the delegation that this agreement only came because of the credible and imminent threat of the multinational force. In fact, it was signed after Haiti received evidence that paratroopers from our 82d Airborne Division, based at Fort Bragg, North Carolina, had begun to load up to begin the invasion, which I had ordered to start this evening. Indeed, at the time the agreement was reached, 61 American planes were already in the air....
(WCPD Clinton 1994: 1799)

Letter to Congressional Leaders on Haiti
September 18, 1994

...I am providing this report, consistent with the sense of Congress in section 8147(c) of the Department of Defense Appropriations Act, 1994 (Public Law 103-139), to advise you of the objectives and character of the planned deployment of U.S. Armed Forces into Haiti.

(1) The deployment of U.S. Armed Forces into Haiti is justified by United States national security interests: to restore democratic government to Haiti; to stop the brutal atrocities that threaten tens of thousands of Haitians; to secure our borders; to preserve stability and promote democracy in our hemisphere; and to uphold the reliability of the commitments we make and the commitments others make to us.

From the very beginning of the coup against the democratic government of Haiti, the United States and the rest of the international community saw the regime as a threat to our interests in this hemisphere. Indeed President Bush declared that the coup "constitute[d] an unusual and extraordinary threat to the national security, foreign policy, and economy of the United States."

The United States' interest in Haiti is rooted in a consistent U.S. policy, since the 1991 coup, to help restore democratic government to that nation. The United States has a particular interest in responding to gross abuses of human rights when they occur so close to our shores.

The departure of the coup leaders from power is also the best way to stem another mass outflow of Haitians, with consequences for the stability of our region and control of our borders. Continuing unconstitutional rule in Haiti would threaten the stability of other countries in this hemisphere by emboldening elements opposed to democracy and freedom.

The agreement regarding the transition between the de facto government and the elected government, negotiated by former President Jimmy Carter, Senator Sam Nunn, and General Colin Powell, will achieve the objective of facilitating the departure of the coup leaders. Their departure will substantially decrease the likelihood of armed resistance.

(2) Despite this agreement, this military operation is not without risk. Necessary steps have been taken to ensure the safety and security of U.S. Armed Forces. Our intention is to deploy a force of sufficient size to serve as a deterrent to armed resistance. The force will have a highly visible and robust presence with firepower ample to overwhelm any localized threat. This will minimize casualties and maximize our capability to ensure that essential civil order is maintained and the agreement arrived at is implemented. The force's rules of engagement allow for the use of necessary and proportionate force to protect friendly personnel and units and to provide for individual self-defense, thereby ensuring that our forces can respond effectively to threats and are not made targets by reason of their rules of engagement.

(3) The proposed mission and objectives are most appropriate for U.S. Armed Forces, and the forces proposed for deployment are necessary and sufficient to accomplish the objectives of the proposed mission. Pursuant to U.N. Security Council Resolution 940, a multinational coalition has been assembled to use "all necessary means" to restore the democratic government to Haiti and to provide a stable and secure environment for the implementation of the Governors Island Accords. The deployment of U.S. Armed Forces is required to ensure that United States national security interests with respect to Haiti remain unchallenged and to underscore the reliability of U.S. and UN commitments....

(4) Clear objectives for the deployment have been established. These limited objectives are: to facilitate the departure of the military leadership, the prompt return of the legitimately elected President and the restoration of the legitimate authorities of the Government of Haiti. We will assist the Haitian government in creating a civilian-controlled security force. We will also ensure the protection of U.S. citizens and U.S. facilities.

(5) An exit strategy for ending the deployment has been identified. Our presence in Haiti will not be open-ended. After a period of months, the coalition will be replaced by a UN peacekeeping force (UNMIH). By that time, the bulk of U.S. forces will have departed. Some U.S. forces will make up a portion of the UNMIH and will be present in Haiti for the duration of the U.N. mission. The entire U.N. mission will withdraw from Haiti after elections are held next year and a new Haitian Government takes office in early 1996, consistent with U.N. Security Council Resolution 940....

(WCPD Clinton 1994: 1799-1802)

President Clinton's Letter to Congressional Leaders on Haiti
September 21, 1994

...On September 19, at approximately 9:25 a.m. e.d.t., units under the command of the Commander in Chief, U.S. Atlantic Command, were introduced into Haitian territory, including its territorial waters and airspace. United States Armed Forces participating in the deployment include forces from the U.S. Army's 18th Airborne Corps, including the 10th Mountain Division; U.S. Naval Forces from the U.S. Atlantic Fleet, including the U.S. Second Fleet and U.S. Marine Forces and amphibious ships. U.S. Air Forces, including the 12th Air Force; and various units from U.S. Special Forces.

Air-landed and seaborne U.S. forces successfully secured initial entry points at Port au Prince International Airport and the Port au Prince port facilities. Approximately 1,500 troops were involved in these initial efforts. No resistance was encountered and there were no U.S. casualties. Over the next several days, it is anticipated that U.S. troop strength in Haiti will increase by several thousand in order to ensure the establishment and maintenance of a secure and stable environment.

As to the duration of the mission, our presence in Haiti will not be open-ended. As I indicated on September 18, the coalition will be replaced after a period of months by a U.N. peacekeeping force, the U.N. Mission in Haiti (UNMIH). By that time, the bulk of U.S. forces will have departed. Some U.S. forces will make up a portion of the UNMIH and will be present in Haiti for the duration of the U.N. mission. The entire U.N. mission will withdraw from Haiti after elections are held next year and a new Haitian government takes office in early 1996, consistent with U.N. Security Council Resolution 940....
(WCPD Clinton 1994: 1823-1824)

9

Notes on Primary Sources

Robert A. Vitas

The Select Bibliography which follows this chapter encompasses secondary sources on U.S. national security policy from 1988 to 1995. For earlier citations, please refer to the references and select bibliography in the earlier book on this topic, which list sources from 1948 to 1988.

This chapter deals with primary research sources. The earlier book had the advantage of covering four decades of developments in the U.S. national security community. That period produced reams of documentation with obvious advantages for the researcher. The present volume had to rely on fewer primary sources, which are sketched below.

The president finds his greatest power in the roles of Chief Diplomat and Commander-in-Chief. The key to presidential activity in this and other spheres of policy is *Public Papers of the Presidents of the United States*, issued twice annually. The volume contains speeches, reports to Congress, news releases, and other presidential documentation. Each volume possesses an index, but with the advent of the Carter administration, the indices switched from citing document numbers to citing pages. In addition, they are poorer in quality and, in fact, an error was detected in the first volume published for 1979.

More recent presidential documents may be found in *Weekly Compilation of Presidential Documents*. As of the Carter administration, *Public Papers* is simply a compendium of the *Weekly Compilations*. Earlier versions of *Public Papers* contained indices only for proclamations and executive orders. The actual documents for these years are in the *Code of Federal Regulations*, Title 3, The President, which is issued every several years. More recent such material is in the *Federal Register*. The U.S. Office of the Federal Register can provide information on these publications.

Through 1989, the U.S. State Department's Bureau of Public Affairs published the monthly *Department of State Bulletin*. As of January 1990, this was converted to the weekly *Department of State Dispatch*, containing statements by the secretary and other officials, analyses, and texts of foreign agreements. Some presidential statements are reprinted here. These materials, along with other State Department information, are also found online and on CD-ROM. Recent foreign agreements are more easily found in the *Dispatch*, for *United States Treaties and Other International Agreements*, also published by the State Department, possesses a long lead time due to ratification and adherence delays, which can take several years. Several volumes of *United States Treaties* are published annually. They certainly give one an appreciation of the complexity of international negotiation and transactions.

The State Department's Office of the Historian publishes the annual *American Foreign Policy: Current Documents*, which consolidates much of the material in the *Dispatch*.

Congressional Quarterly Weekly Report and *Congressional Digest*, while not government publications, can guide the researcher to when and how issues were, or are being, resolved. They also guide one to Public Laws, that is, the legislation which is the foundation for almost all government national security activity. The *U.S. Code Congressional and Administrative News* serves the same function.

Legislation may be found in *United States Statutes at Large*. It is a better reference tool than the *United States Code* for *United States Statutes* gives the legislation as actually passed, for example, the Goldwater-Nichols Department of Defense Reorganization Act of 1986 (PL 99-433), whereas the *United States Code*, updated every several years, is a compilation of legislation still in force dissected into the various federal legislative titles and regrouped into the relevant legal order. Thus *United States Statutes* is geared toward the scholar, while the *United State Code* is published for the convenience of the practicing attorney. *United States Statutes* is published by the Office of the Federal Register. The *United States Code* is published by the Office of Law Revision, Counsel of the House of Representatives, with the assistance of West Publishing Company.

Another legal publication is the *Cumulative Digest of United States Practice in International Law*, published by the State Department's Office of the Legal Adviser. Different themes are organized around historical background, relevant statements by officials, links to U.S. municipal law, and U.S. interpretation of international law. One can get an overview of the deterioration of ANZUS during the 1980s, for example, from this reference.

More recent legislation may be found in the *Congressional Record* along with debates, reports, and related material. The *Congressional Record Index* appears many times annually and is a guide to the often complex issues and debates. The U.S. Office of the Congressional Record located at the Capitol can offer specific information on these publications.

The Office of the Assistant to the Secretary of Defense for Public Affairs is the best initial point of contact for current national security information.

For the scholar wishing to find his way around the Pentagon, a useful publication is the *DoD Organization and Functions Guidebook*, prepared periodically by the Directorate for Organizational Management Planning for the Office of the Secretary of Defense (OSD), Defense Agencies, and DoD Field Activities.

The OSD's Public Affairs Office began publishing *Fact File* in July 1993. It was designed and edited for the media, and to assist military public affairs offices in providing maximum access and information. Updates are made on a regular basis. Its almost six hundred pages give comprehensive and comprehensible breakdowns on DoD organizations, weapons large and small, ships, aircraft, and vehicles.

The Organization of the Joint Chiefs of Staff has issued several publications of interest to national security historians. The arm for this activity is the JCS Joint History Office. The following are available from it: *Organizational Development of the Joint Chiefs of Staff, 1942-1989, Role and Functions of the Joint Chiefs of Staff: A Chronology, The Evolution of the Joint Strategic Planning System, 1947-1989, The Joint Chiefs of Staff and the Joint Education System, 1943-1986*, and the *History of the Unified Command Plan, 1946-1975*. The following are available from the Superintendent of Documents: Several volumes in the series *The Joint Chiefs of Staff and National Policy, The Chairmen of the Joint Chiefs of Staff*, and *The Development of the Base Force, 1989-1992*. In 1993, the U.S. Army Military History Institute, Carlisle Barracks, Pennsylvania, published *A Bibliography on U.S. Joint and Combined Warfare in Historical Perspective*, which can be requested directly from the Institute.

For annual policy, the Secretary of Defense publishes his *Annual Report to the President and the Congress*. This extensive volume contains broad political-military discussions, as well as the budgetary needs and implications of defense programs. The Chairman of the JCS issues his *Posture Statement* to the Secretary of Defense and the Congress every year. This is a shorter publication dealing with more purely military innovations, highlights, priorities and — especially since the passage of the Goldwater-Nichols Act — joint activities.

There are other recurring publications. *Defense* is a bi-monthly magazine distributed to official personnel but available to the public. Developments over time can be chronicled in *Defense's* annual *Almanac* issue. *Joint Force Quarterly* is published for the CJCS by the Institute for National Strategic Studies, National Defense University, located at Fort McNair in Washington, D.C. NDU produces many books and special studies annually.

The National Security Council issues the president's annual *National Security Strategy of the United States* report. It is also useful to contact the public affairs offices of the individual military departments. Federal depository libraries are located in every congressional district and contain the latest Public Laws, committee prints, and hearing reports.

Sources prior to the scope of the current volume, but of use to the national security researcher, are discussed in the remainder of this chapter.

Several indices are particularly useful. Two are the *Codification of Presidential Proclamations and Executive Orders* and the set of indices for *Foreign Relations of the United States*, published for the years 1939-1945 by Kraus. Two especially useful indices are *The Cumulated Indexes to the Public Papers of the Presidents of the United States*, published by Oceana, and the indices to *United States Treaties and Other International Agreements*, published for the years 1776-1975, and also numerically, chronologically, by country and subject, by Heinz.

Foreign Relations of the United States is the most extensive reference tool produced by the State Department's Office of the Historian. It contains internal government memoranda, which often take the scholar away from public rationales given for certain actions. For example, discussions leading up to the adoption of NSC 68, President Truman's containment policy, as well as the text itself, may be found here. Each year can have several volumes, and there are some special series, such as those dealing with the Geneva Conferences and Vietnam. However, the confidentiality and classification of many of its documents require a long lead time, approximately thirty years. *Foreign Relations* gives one an appreciation for the complexity of the issues involved. It also shows conscientious public servants grappling with, and debating, them.

Although the Joint Chiefs of Staff have issued their own historical studies, cited above, these have been specially written. As opposed to the State Department's documentation, Defense Department historical documents, such as directives or statements from the secretary, are generally unpublished by, and unavailable through, DoD publications. This includes material pertaining to the Civil War through the Vietnam conflict. For example, Secretary Melvin Laird's statement of January 27, 1973 announcing the end of conscription would be unavailable from DoD. Historical files of DoD and the military departments are under the jurisdiction of the National Archives and Records Administration. Ultimately, of course, all records will fall under NARA's jurisdiction.

Primary sources are the foundation and, hopefully, strength of the present volume. They assist the researcher in viewing public displays - and material never intended for public display. They show what political-military actors said and what they meant, for the two do not always correspond. Primary sources provide the researcher with new insights and a fresh perspective, perhaps discovering what was unknown at the time of a particular event or, thanks to the passage of time, discerning ironies of policy and history.

Select Bibliography

Allison, Graham, and Gregory F. Treverton, eds. *Rethinking America's Security: Beyond Cold War to New World Order*. New York: Norton, 1992.

Andrianopoulos, Gerry Argyris. *Kissinger and Brzezinski: The NSC and the Struggle for Control of US National Security Policy*. New York: St. Martin's Press, 1991.

Avent, Deborah D. *Political Institutions and Military Change: Lessons From Peripheral Wars*. Ithaca, NY: Cornell University Press, 1994.

Banks, William C., and Peter Raven-Hansen. *National Security Law and the Power of the Purse*. New York: Oxford University Press, 1994.

Beede, Benjamin R. *Military and Strategic Policy: An Annotated Bibliography*. New York: Greenwood, 1990.

Berkowitz, Bruce D., and Allan E. Goodman. *Strategic Intelligence for American National Security*. Princeton, NJ: Princeton University Press, 1989.

Blechman, Barry M. *The Politics of National Security: Congress and U.S. Defense Policy*. New York: Oxford University Press, 1990.

Boll, Michael M. *National Security Planning: Roosevelt Through Reagan*. Lexington: University Press of Kentucky, 1988.

Brzezinski, Zbigniew K. *In Quest of National Security*. Boulder, CO: Westview, 1988.

Carey, Roger, and Trevor C. Salmon, eds. *International Security in the Modern World*. New York: St. Martin's, 1992.

Carpenter, Ted Galen, ed. *Collective Defense or Strategic Independence? Alternative Strategies for the Future*. Washington, DC: Cato Institute, 1989.

Carter, Ashton B, William J. Perry, and John D. Steinbruner. *A New Concept of Cooperative Security*. Washington, DC: Brookings Institute, 1992.

Clarke, Duncan L. *American Defense and Foreign Policy Institutions: Toward a Sound Foundation*. New York: Harper & Row, 1989.

Deitchman, Seymour J. *Beyond the Thaw: A New National Strategy*. Boulder, CO: Westview, 1991.

Edwards, George C., III, and Wallace Earl Walker, eds. *National Security and the U.S. Constitution: The Impact of the Political System*. Baltimore: Johns Hopkins University Press, 1988.

Ford, Harold P. *Estimative Intelligence: The Purposes and Problems of National Intelligence Estimating*. Lanham, MD: University Press of America, 1992.

Franck, Thomas M. *Political Questions/Judicial Answers: Does the Rule of Law Apply to Foreign Affairs?* Princeton, NJ: Princeton University Press, 1992.

Franck, Thomas M., and Michael J. Glennon. *Foreign Relations and National Security Law*. St. Paul, MN: West, 1993.

Friedman, Norman. *The US Maritime Strategy*. London and New York: Jane's Publishing, 1988.

Godson, Roy, ed. *Intelligence Requirements for the 1990s: Collection, Analysis, Counterintelligence, and Covert Action*. Lexington, MA: Lexington Books, 1989.

Haglund, David G., ed. *Can America Remain Committed? U.S. Security Horizons in the 1990s*. Boulder, CO: Westview, 1992.

Hartmann, Frederick, H. *Defending America's Security*, 2nd rev. ed. Washington, DC: Brassey's, 1990.

Heisenberg, Wolfgang. *Strategic Stability and Nuclear Deterrence in East-West Relations*. New York: Institute for East-West Security Studies, 1989.

Holt, Pat M. *Secret Intelligence and Public Policy: A Dilemma of Democracy*. Washington, DC: Congressional Quarterly Press, 1995.

Jensen, Lloyd. *Bargaining for National Security: The Postwar Disarmament Negotiations*. Columbia: University of South Carolina Press, 1988.

Jordan, Amos A., William J. Taylor, Jr., and Lawrence J. Korb. *American National Security: Policy and Process*. Baltimore: Johns Hopkins University Press, 1993.

Kaufman, Daniel J., David S. Clark, and Kevin P. Sheehan, eds. *U.S. National Security Strategy for the 1990s*. Baltimore: Johns Hopkins University Press, 1991.

Koh, Harold Hongju. *The National Security Constitution: Sharing Power After the Iran-Contra Affair*. New Haven, CT: Yale University Press, 1990.

Kolodziej, Edward A., and Patrick M. Morgan, eds. *Security and Arms Control*. New York: Greenwood, 1989.

Kozak, David L., and James L. Keagle, eds. *Bureaucratic Politics and National Security: Theory and Practice*. Boulder, CO: Rienner, 1988.

Krepon, Michael, and Amy E. Smithson, eds. *Open Skies, Arms Control, and Cooperative Security*. New York: St. Martin's Press, 1992.

Kupchan, Charles. *The Vulnerability of Empire*. Ithaca, NY: Cornell University Press, 1994.

Livingstone, Neil C., and Terrell E. Arnold, eds. *Beyond the Iran-Contra Crisis: The Shape of U.S. Antiterrorism Policy in the Post-Reagan Era.* Lexington, MA: Lexington Books, 1988.

Lord, Carnes. *The Presidency and the Management of National Security.* New York: Free Press, 1988.

Mandel, Robert. *The Changing Face of National Security: A Conceptual Analysis.* Westport, CT: Greenwood, 1994.

Mangold, Peter. *National Security and International Relations.* New York: Routledge, 1990.

Manwaring, Max G., ed. *Gray Area Phenomena: Confronting the New World Disorder.* Boulder, CO: Westview, 1993.

Meinhold, Richard J. *Beyond the Sound of Cannon: Military Strategy in the 1990s.* Jefferson, NC: McFarland, 1992.

Menges, Constantine Christopher. *Inside the National Security Council: The True Story of the Making and Unmaking of Reagan's Foreign Policy.* New York: Simon and Schuster, 1988.

Moore, John Norton, Frederick S. Tipson, and Robert F. Turner, eds. *National Security Law.* Durham, NC: Carolina Academic Press, 1990.

Moore, John Norton, Guy B. Roberts, and Robert F. Turner, eds. *National Security Law Documents.* Durham, NC: Carolina Academic Press, 1995.

Moskos, Charles C., and Frank R. Wood, eds. *The Military: More Than Just a Job?* Washington, DC: Pergamon-Brassey's, 1988.

Nitze, Paul H. *Paul H. Nitze on National Security and Arms Control.* Eds. Kenneth W. Thompson and Steven L. Rearden. Lanham, MD: University Press of America, 1990.

Pfaltzgraff, Robert L., and Jacquelyn K. Davis. *National Security Decisions: The Participants Speak.* Lexington, MA: Lexington Books, 1990.

Pitsvada, Bernard T. *The Senate, Treaties, and National Security, 1945-1974.* Lanham, MD: University Press of America, 1991.

Prados, John. *Keepers of the Keys: A History of the National Security Council From Truman to Bush.* New York: Morrow, 1991.

Quinn, Dennis J., ed. *Peace Support Operations and the U.S. Military.* Washington, D.C. National Defense University Press, 1994.

Sarkesian, Sam C. *U.S. National Security: Policymakers, Processes, and Politics*, 2nd ed. Boulder, CO: Rienner, 1995.

Sarkesian, Sam C., and John Mead Flanagin, eds. *U.S. Domestic and National Security Agendas: Into the Twenty-First Century.* Westport, CT: Greenwood, 1994.

Sarkesian, Sam C., and Robert A. Vitas, eds. *U.S. National Security Policy and Strategy: Documents and Policy Proposals.* New York: Greenwood, 1988.

Sarkesian, Sam C., and John Allen Williams, eds. *The U.S. Army in a New Security Era.* Boulder, CO: Rienner, 1990.

Sarkesian, Sam C., John Allen Williams, and Fred B. Bryant. *Soldiers, Society, and National Security*. Boulder, CO: Rienner, 1995.

Scott, Wilbur J., and Sandra Carson Stanley, eds. *Gays and Lesbians in the Military: Issues, Concerns, and Contrasts*. New York: Aldine de Gruyter, 1994.

Scowcroft, Brent, ed. *Defending Peace and Freedom: Toward Strategic Stability in the Year 2000*. Lanham, MD: University Press of America, 1988.

Segal, David R. *Recruiting for Uncle Sam: Citizenship and Military Manpower Policy*. Lawrence: University Press of Kansas, 1989.

Shoemaker, Christopher C. *The NSC Staff: Counseling the Council*. Boulder, CO: Westview, 1991.

Shultz, Richard, Roy Godson, and Ted Greenwood. *Security Studies for the 1990s*. Washington, DC: Brassey's, 1993.

Shuman, Howard E., and Walter R. Thomas, eds. *The Constitution and National Security: A Bicentennial View*. Washington, DC: National Defense University Press, 1990.

Snow, Donald M. *National Security: Defense Policy for a New International Order*. New York: St. Martin's Press, 1995.

Tritten, James John. *Our New National Security Strategy: America Promises to Come Back*. Westport, CT: Praeger, 1992.

Tritten, James John, and Paul N. Stockton, eds. *Reconstituting America's Defense: The New U.S. National Security Strategy*. Westport, CT: Praeger, 1992.

Turner, Robert F. *Repealing the War Powers Resolution: Restoring the Rule of Law in U.S. Foreign Policy*. Washington, DC: Brassey's, 1991.

Watson, Cynthia Ann, ed. *U.S. National Security Policy Groups: Institutional Profiles*. New York: Greenwood, 1990.

Zimmerman, William, ed. *Beyond the Soviet Threat: Rethinking American Security Policy in a New Era*. Ann Arbor: University of Michigan Press, 1992.

Index

About the Editors

ROBERT A. VITAS is Assistant Executive Director and Treasurer of the Inter-University Seminar on Armed Forces and Society at Northwestern University. He is the author of *The United States and Lithuania: The Stimson Doctrine of Nonrecognition* (Praeger, 1990). With Sam C. Sarkesian, he prepared an earlier volume of documents, *U.S. National Security Policy and Strategy,* covering the years 1947–1986 (Greenwood, 1988).

JOHN ALLEN WILLIAMS is Associate Professor and Chairman of the Department of Political Science at Loyola University Chicago. He is also Vice Chairman and Executive Director of the Inter-University Seminar on Armed Forces and Society, and is a Captain in the U.S. Naval Reserve. With Sam C. Sarkesian and Fred B. Bryant, he co-authored *Soldiers, Society, and National Security* (1995), and co-edited and contributed to *The U.S. Army in a New Security Era* (1990) with Sam C. Sarkesian.

ISBN 0-313-29635-9
90000>
EAN
9 780313 296352
HARDCOVER BAR CODE